"In today's higher education climate, it's to focus on learning solely for learning's sake. Students and their families expect more, and employers demand more. Having a strong career center is important, but institutions that don't want to be left behind need to make student career readiness a campus-wide priority. Readers of *Mapping the Future of Undergraduate Career Education* will find new strategies for placing a deliberate, impactful focus on ensuring that students can connect what they are learning in college to their first job and their long-term career."

Paul Timmins, *Executive Director, University of Oregon Career Center, Former President, National Career Development Association, USA*

"This text is timely and provocative: a much-needed resource for institutions that strive to be *student ready* and forward thinking in their approach to undergraduate career preparation."

La'Tonya Rease Miles, *PhD, Partner and Director of Scale and Support, Career Launch Co-editor,* Campus Service Workers Supporting First-Generation Students (*Routledge, 2021*)

Mapping the Future of Undergraduate Career Education

This timely book explores current trends and future possibilities for undergraduate career education, the nature of the changing workplace, and its impact on students in colleges and universities.

Built on decades of experience in career development and professional learning, the editors raise and investigate multiple critical issues facing career educators in higher education today: preparing students for the future of work; exploring the increasing centrality of experiential learning in career education; examining innovative paradigm shifts in career education; and developing strategies for equity-focused and inclusive programming for all students.

Reckoning with the effects of Covid-19 on the world of career development, this book draws on contributions from leading scholars, entrepreneurs, and practitioners from across the fields of education, business, STEM, and the humanities to offer an inclusive and innovation-focused approach to supporting scholars, practitioners, and students involved with career education, development, and counseling for a new generation – and a new world of work.

Melanie V. Buford is an instructor of leadership education at the University of Minnesota, Twin Cities, USA, and has worked for over ten years in career development across the US and abroad.

Michael J. Sharp is an Associate Professor of Experiential Learning at the University of Cincinnati, USA.

Michael J. Stebleton is Professor of Higher Education at the University of Minnesota, Twin Cities, USA.

Mapping the Future of Undergraduate Career Education

Equitable Career Learning, Development, and Preparation in the New World of Work

Edited by
Melanie V. Buford,
Michael J. Sharp, and
Michael J. Stebleton

Routledge
Taylor & Francis Group

NEW YORK AND LONDON

Cover image: © Getty images

First published 2023
by Routledge
605 Third Avenue, New York, NY 10158

and by Routledge
4 Park Square, Milton Park, Abingdon, Oxon, OX14 4RN

Routledge is an imprint of the Taylor & Francis Group, an informa business

Library of Congress Cataloging-in-Publication Data
A catalog record for this title has been requested

ISBN: 978-1-032-08114-4 (hbk)
ISBN: 978-1-032-08113-7 (pbk)
ISBN: 978-1-003-21300-0 (ebk)

DOI: 10.4324/9781003213000

Typeset in Goudy
by Newgen Publishing UK

To our wonderful writing team, without whom
this volume would still be merely an idea.

To our families and friends,
consistent sources of support, humor, wisdom, and learning.

And to:
Shreya
Rashné, Riya, Rohan (RJ3)
Jennifer, Ethan, Riley

Contents

Figures and Tables

Figures

Tables

About the Editors

Melanie V. Buford is a writer, career coach, and leadership instructor who has worked for more than ten years in career development across the United States and abroad. She brings a sharp equity-driven lens to her writing, and has published numerous articles on identity, generational differences, and the pursuit of meaningful work. She has been featured on the *Happen to Your Career Podcast* series, a national top five podcast on career satisfaction. In 2019, she received the Ralph W. Tyler Award for Distinguished Research and Publication for her work examining the efficacy of career courses on Millennial and Gen-Z students, and in 2021 received the Kenneth B. Hoyt Career Practitioner Award for excellence in career education and practice from the National Career Development Association. The YWCA named her a Rising Star in 2016 for her social impact work in the community.

Michael J. Sharp has a deep footprint in the field of experiential learning – focused on service-learning innovation and the hybridization of experiential learning programs. He has pioneered several novel programs at the University of Cincinnati, including the Service-Learning Collaboratory, a class that was recognized via the Dean's Award for Innovative Instruction. Sharp is senior editor of *Experience Magazine: Practice + Theory + Podcast*, and co-creator and co-host of the Tapioca Radio Show. His doctoral dissertation was awarded dissertation of the year by the National Society for Experiential Education, and was contracted for publication by UC Press. He sits on the boards of two experiential learning associations: Cooperative Education and Internship Association and Campus Compact.

Michael J. Stebleton is Professor and Coordinator of the Higher Education program at the University of Minnesota-Twin Cities. His research and teaching interests focus on college student development, career development, student mental health issues, and success factors that contribute to college student persistence, with a focus on marginalized student populations. Stebleton teaches both at the undergraduate and graduate levels. He has been actively involved with career development and first-year student experience initiatives in the College of Education and Human Development. He also engages in teaching and research issues on college student mental health, sense of belonging, and wellbeing. In 2017, he received the Merit Award for significant contributions to the field of career development from the National Career Development Association. Currently, he serves as contributing editor to the *Journal of College and Character*.

About the Contributors

Erik Alanson serves as an Associate Professor and Director of the University of Cincinnati's Division of Experience-Based Learning and Career Education. He oversees work-integrated learning experiences for students in computing and information technology disciplines. He also serves on the editorial board for the *International Journal of Work-Integrated Learning*. Erik has experience as a subject matter expert for the US Department of Labor, Routledge Publishing, and Microsoft.

Ingrid Bårdsdatter Bakke is a postdoctoral fellow and Assistant Professor in the Guidance section at the Inland Norway University of Applied Sciences (INN). Her research interests are conceptualizations of career and how they relate to cultural context, in addition to career guidance in the welfare system. She teaches the masters' program in career guidance at the university, focusing on career theory, thesis supervision, and integrated career guidance.

Elif Balin is an Assistant Professor in the Department of Counseling at San Francisco State University in the Career Counseling and College Counseling specializations. Dr. Balin's career priority is to train professional counselors who understand and apply career counseling and college counseling through systemic and culturally competent practices in various service and advocacy areas in higher education, community mental health settings, and beyond.

Tierney Bates is the Assistant Vice Chancellor of Special Projects and Executive Director of University of Career Services at the University of North Carolina at Chapel Hill. Dr. Bates' research interests focus on diversity, equity, and inclusion in career development and fundraising, along with student engagement and innovative design thinking. He has given over 120 talks, keynote speeches, and workshops on strategic initiatives and solutions on historically underrepresented students, faculty, and staff.

Sharon Belden Castonguay Castonguay is an adult developmental psychologist and career counselor with over 20 years of experience working with professionals

xvi   About the Contributors

at all levels of their careers. She is the Executive Director of Wesleyan University's Gordon Career Center and the instructor for Career Decisions: From Insight to Impact on Coursera. Her TEDx talk, *The Psychology of Career Decisions*, considers themes of identity, culture, and decision making.

Joseph M. Catrino is an Executive Director of Career & Life Design, works to expand career development services while creating an ecosystem of design-thinking and innovation across the college for Trinity students and for the college's partners. Through his teaching and knowledge of the "design-thinking" framework, Joe has been instrumental in transforming the way students think and problem-solve their career goals.

Andrea DePetris is a clinical psychologist. Her research has focused on mental health disparities, marginalized populations, the impact of experiencing racial discrimination, and racial/ethnic identity formation.

Lisa Y. Flores is a Professor in the Department of Psychological Sciences at the University of Missouri. She has over 100 publications and over 200 conference presentations on Latinxs' and women's career development. She has been PI and co-PI on grants totaling $5.1 million from NSF, USDA, and US Department of Education. Dr. Flores' research aims to understand the impact of psychosocial, cultural, and contextual variables on the educational and vocational decisions of Latinx in engineering.

Mark Franklin is the award-winning practice leader of CareerCycles, a career management social enterprise based in Toronto, co-founder of OneLifeTools, instructor at University of Toronto, and producer of the Career Buzz radio show and podcast.

Tristram Hooley is a Professor of Career Education at the Inland Norway University of Applied Sciences (INN) and the University of Derby, UK. His work focuses on career and career guidance and examines how these phenomena interact with politics and technology. He writes the Adventures in Career Development blog at https://adventuresincareerdevelopment.wordpress.com/

Rashné R. Jehangir, PhD. is an Associate Professor of Higher Education and the Beck Chair of Ideas in the College of Education and Human Development at the University of Minnesota-Twin Cities. Her research raises questions about the (in) equities of structure, policy, and practice in higher education with specific attention to the experience of poor and working class, first-generation college students, students of color, and refugee and immigrant students.

Nasitta Keita is a graduate student studying Counseling Psychology at the University of Missouri. Her research aims to investigate how Black women and girls resist and heal from gendered racism occurring in educational and career spaces. She has experience providing counseling services in community mental health and higher education settings.

Arame Mbodj has dedicated the past few years of her work to the underrepresented student experience, bringing identity to the forefront within the career space. Her unique role allows her to work with marginalized students at the intersection of career and identity. Dedicated to supporting the underrepresented community, she enjoys helping students to feel empowered to integrate their backgrounds, experience, and skills to deeply explore and reflect on their experiences and impact their future paths.

J.P. Michel is the creator of the Challenge mindset and the founder of SparkPath. J.P. holds a master's degree in industrial-organizational psychology from the University of Manchester and a degree in psychology from the University of Ottawa. He is a TEDx speaker and the recipient of the 2017 Outstanding Career Professional award from the Career Professionals of Canada.

Kimberlie Moock has dedicated her professional work to creating campus ecologies that support student success. Her recent research focuses on the effect of social class identity on college student career readiness and transition to work. She has developed undergraduate curriculum and teaches courses centering career planning and applied experiences. Kimberlie has held national leadership roles with NASPA and NODA, frequently presenting on student success topics.

Heather Nester is an Assistant Professor of Career Education with a focus on multidisciplinary initiatives at the University of Cincinnati. She teaches and coaches students across industries, in arts and sciences disciplines, and those students who have not yet chosen a major to promote self-reflection, discovery, and the pursuit of finding a job worth having as they individually define it. Her research focuses on career exploration and the development of professional identity and has presented at the local, regional, and international level.

James R. Stellar is a Professor of Behavioral Neuroscience at the University at Albany SUNY, with a history in senior university administration. His lab analyzes literature on the impact of learning from experience that is combined with classical academic study as a strategy that fits with how our brains are built. He writes a blog, co-hosts a podcast, and has published two books on neuroscience and experiential learning. He started his career in basic neuroscience dopamine research.

Mei Tang is a Professor and the Doctoral Program Coordinator of the Counseling Program in the School of Human Services, University of Cincinnati. Dr. Tang's research focus includes career development and assessment, cultural identity and acculturation, counselor education and supervision, and application of ecological counseling.

Emilie Wapnick is an award-winning author and community builder. Her TED talk has been viewed 8 million times. Her book, *How to Be Everything*, was published by HarperCollins in 2017. It has been translated into 13 languages and won a Nautilus Book Award. She is the founder and creative director at Puttylike.com, where she helps people integrate all of their interests to create dynamic, fulfilling, and fruitful careers and lives.

Maya Williams is currently a graduate student studying Counseling Psychology at the University of Missouri. Her interests include culturally informed mental health services for racial/ethnic minority emerging adults and college students. She has experience providing counseling services in alternative education, higher education, and community mental health settings. She is a recipient of the APA Minority Fellowship.

Todd B. Williams is Executive Director of the Center for Sales Leadership and Education at the University of Minnesota. Todd helps better prepare students for a variety of sales and marketing careers in Fortune 500 companies, entrepreneurial startups, and international organizations. Todd also has experience leading Diversity and Inclusion and Diverse Market Segmentation initiatives in corporate America.

Foreword

Rich Feller

Rarely does an edited volume go beyond each individual author's intentions, especially from a group of international writers interested in transformative innovation. *Mapping the Future* delivers a unified clarity about significant themes and elements useful to practitioners and scholars.

Within the context of higher education reform, previous authors have often poked at most every corner of campus without a clear or rich synthesis. What does "reform" intend to reform about undergraduate education? How can career education be re-positioned as a change strategy as *The Next Rules of Work* (Bolles, 2021) are being written? This group of authors presents a convincing argument that it is possible.

As a student of Ken Hoyt, the father of career education, I respect the authors' struggle. As a professor of 30 plus years myself, I have translated my learnings from career education's golden years. Each semester I try to integrate academic and professional training, infuse career development principles into curriculum, and work to help evolve career services fast enough to meet marketplace needs. Efforts to build inclusive programming based on dignity, belonging, and justice are well received. As a result, I turn to my author-colleagues for additional answers to the difficult questions they now confront.

After engaging in this text, I gained hope from the authors about exploring the connection among experiential education, reflective practice, and career development. *Mapping* provides collective insights to those who witness student disconnect between educational experience and professional aspirations. The text promotes equity-focused programming for all as a given. Its strategies to prepare students for success within life roles while navigating a lifetime of transitions are music to my ears. To suggest this volume is timely, necessary, and instructive is an understatement.

While writing this preface, I'm reading *American Made: What Happens to People When Work Disappears* (Stockman, 2021), as it shares the story of a community struggling to invent itself. It's a story about race, class, and American values, and how jobs serve as the foundation of people's lives and drive powerful social movements. Studs

Terkel's classic *Working* (1974) offered an earlier translation of a community's pulse amidst a transformative time.

Similarly, *Mapping*'s authors' examination of higher education offers hope to re-inventing the power of the career education movement, a movement which drew from the many themes Terkel's and Stockman's books exposed. Exploring the influence of community and engagement and issues of the less advantaged and marginalized people adds fuel for changing higher education's assumptions and practice. *Mapping*'s insights to counter the students' cost of experiencing a disconnect between educational experience and professional aspirations move me. The book's underlying theme of promoting equity-focused programming for all is imperative for higher education's future.

Post-secondary education faces considerable structural, curriculum, personnel, and political resistance to change. It inherently has a bias to maintain the status quo and lags workplace needs. As the rate of work, learning, and development change accelerates, it is easy to ask, "are we learning as fast as the world is changing?" Add the digital exhaustion of the virtual experience to the pandemic funk, and one welcomes *Mapping*'s concrete suggestions to increase student engagement, interdisciplinary and self-directed learning, new mindsets, and meaning making from lived experiences.

To take this volume as seriously as it deserves means to forever look at career education differently. We need to see how technology has shifted the traditional career trajectory, embrace more inclusive programming, and better address well-being. To consider cross-cultural needs in hiring is critical to employers. Examining the differing needs of first-generation and low-income students is more than a great investment. Delivering career education by applying design thinking, addressing the rise of social media, and respecting how multipotentials may choose multiple careers are important initiatives. As is moving from focusing on "job lists" to adapting a challenge mindset to explore opportunities.

Embracing the power of storytelling and gamification in life-career planning, supporting the growth of infusing career preparation within credit-bearing courses, and promoting internships are key recommendations. Advocating for experiential learning and undergraduate STEM research is prerequisite to becoming a career education champion. Currency in the neuroscience of learning and the changing nature of attention, technology, and learning is a professional development necessity. To value these lessons from *Mapping* means taking our work and roles even more seriously.

As readers take their place in helping students develop and prepare for a new world of work, I sense a hunger for signs of hope. As career educators we are ready for direction to gain a sense of efficacy and searching for resiliency in our progress. We yearn to be optimistic about the future and need to intentionally welcome change. Remaining curious and wanting clarity about expectations with a "growth mindset" is essential for success. These traits, which I describe as a HEROIC mindset, are what I find evident within this volume's chapters (Feller & Chapman, 2018). It is what I sense each career education leader wants for all learners. It has become a "future-ready" requirement for each undergraduate student. I'm inspired by and take seriously how the delivery of such a graduate is enhanced by the wisdom within this volume.

Rich Feller, Professor of Counseling and Career Development and University Distinguished Teaching Scholar at Colorado State University, is a former National Career Development Association President.

References

Bolles, G. A. (2021). *The next rules of work: The mindset, skillset and toolset to lead your organization through uncertainty.* Kogan Page.

Feller, R., & Chapman, V. (2018). The HEROIC mindset: Navigating a lifetime of career transitions. *Asia Pacific Career Development Journal, 1*(1), 61–74.

Stockman, F. (2021). *American made: What happens to people when work disappears.* Random House.

Terkel, S. (1974). *Working: People talk about what they do all day and how they feel about what they do.* Pantheon Books.

Introduction

Melanie V. Buford, Michael J. Sharp, and Michael J. Stebleton

Our world continues to shift dramatically. The Covid-19 pandemic, global calls for social justice, and climate shifts have only contributed to the rapid evolution of higher education, the world of work – and of students themselves. Yet, as we know, many of these changes have brought with them tremendous loss and ongoing challenges. In the face of these challenges, we, as international educators, are presented with a unique opportunity to adapt and evolve to meet them (Bhargava & Gupta, 2020; McGowan & Shipley, 2020; McKinsey & Company, 2020; Weir, 2020; Willcocks, 2021).

Higher education administrators, student affairs practitioners, and scholars alike have recognized the need for transformative innovation in higher education. More specifically, many writers have raised the need to rethink our efforts to prepare this and future generations of students for the fourth industrial revolution and a new world of work, given the sweeping impact of the Covid-19 pandemic that started in early 2020 (Abe, 2021; Avis, 2020; Blass & Hayward, 2014; McGowan & Shipley, 2020; McKinsey & Company, 2021; Ruyter et al., 2019; Staley, 2019; Willcocks, 2021).

Students represent an essential voice in this call for reform and have expressed concerns about the financial strain of higher education and their preparedness for work and career. One survey of Generation Z students, released in 2021, stated that only 54% believed that the education system is preparing them for the future. It also cited students' lack of confidence in their professional skills and knowledge (EY, 2021). Employers echoed these concerns, describing similar and widening gaps in new employees' career preparation, and requesting stronger attention to career education in colleges and universities. The need for responses to these concerns remains significant and timely (Anderson, 2020; Broadbent et al., 2017; Hamilton et al., 2021; Klebs et al., 2021; McKinney, 2020; Wiley Education Services & Future Workplace, 2019).

The 2019 edited volume *Handbook of Innovative Career Counseling* sounded a global call for more research and writing on career innovation:

DOI: 10.4324/9781003213000-1

> That there is need for knowledge production and publications on career counselling is evident in the vast gaps worldwide...This is especially so in the application of this field of practice in less advantaged communities, marginalized groups and poorer countries generally....This need emanates from the challenges facing most nations in the contexts of employment, schooling, vocational guidance, career guidance and education, career pathing and development, career counselling, life designing and the multitude of other career-related assessment and intervention needs...It is no longer adequate to continue pushing techniques of old.
>
> (Pillay, 2019, p. v)

In its current form, the field of career education represents the culmination of years of research, practice, innovation, collaboration, and reform (Dey & Cruzvergara, 2014; Hoyt, 2001; Kretovics et al., 1999; Pope, 2000). Yet, now, we are primed for a new kind of rebirth.

This edited volume evolved out of a shared sense of the potential of undergraduate career education. We believe that it can provide current and future generations of students with the means to navigate the daunting challenges we foresee in the world of work and to take advantage of the opportunities before us as a global community. Our goal was to bring together a truly diverse, international writing team of scholars, leaders, entrepreneurs, and practitioners who represented different disciplines and brought varied lenses to reimagining the future of career education. Our premise was the belief that complex, evolving problems require transdisciplinary, collaborative thinkers and innovative solutions. The writers of this work have brought different identities and values, different preparation and training, and different roles and positionality in the field to this collaboration. Though this is primarily an academic volume, it is unique in that it includes voices along the spectrum from scholar to practitioner, and from both inside and outside of the field of higher education. The book is intended to put scholarly ideas into application.

Our hope was that this writing team would not only contribute transdisciplinary perspectives, but that we would all engage in conversation and evolve our own ideas and perspectives through the creation and development of this volume, in order to provide a comprehensive resource for career educators across sectors. The venues for this edited text include graduate-level and upper-division courses in career development, career counseling, human resource development/human resources–industrial relations, career management and planning, and related courses. The book could be used as a stand-alone text for these courses, or as a supplemental resource for these areas.

Additionally, the text aims to reach a wider audience of readers, including career development educators, career coaches, human resource professionals, academic administrators, and other professionals in higher education who wish to learn more about ways in which to support undergraduate career education and students. Although the majority of examples and recommendations are aimed at undergraduate students attending four-year universities and colleges, the content and concepts can be applied to students attending community colleges and other short-term training programs.

The work is structured to include multifaceted narratives of how career education has evolved to this point, and to speculate about where we might go from here. Each chapter integrates historical narratives, current research, and future directions. At the end of each topical chapter, authors have included a section of recommendations for practice, so that this volume can serve as both a work of academic context and research, and as a practical resource to grapple with pressing challenges in the field.

Finally, and most importantly, we address issues of equity and inclusion throughout the text. As a writing team, we stand firmly behind the idea that educational innovation is incomplete if it does not serve all students. Each chapter of this work was written with equity in mind, and we offer strategies for supporting all students in the many educational contexts in which career learning occurs.

Part I of this volume describes the current landscape of career education, changes to the world of work, and what we now know about the characteristics, learning styles, and career aspirations of Generation Z. These chapters provide a foundational context for this exploration of the future of career education.

Part II assesses the field of career education holistically, describing critical consideration for inclusion and equity, and exploring global trends in the field. This section includes considerations for serving students of color, first-generation students, LGBTQPIA+ students, working-class students, international students, and those with other marginalized and intersectional identities. It also brings in the lens of mental health, and discusses the mental health impacts of work, economic recession, technology, and social and political unrest.

Part III challenges common notions of career and career education, offering several new paradigms. The growing popularity of design-thinking, the evolving role of the career center, integrated models of career development, the pursuit of multiple, simultaneous career paths, challenges to the concept of career as job title, the use of narrative in career development, and the integration of career learning into academic curricula are explored.

Part IV focuses on the impact of experiential learning, describing current and emerging forms of work and learning integration. The value of internships, cooperative learning, service-learning, undergraduate research, learning abroad, and other forms of experiential learning are discussed. This section also highlights important structural factors for supporting student success in experiential learning. Access to STEM pathways, findings in neuroscience, the evolution of career education in the liberal arts, and the role of transdisciplinary collaboration are covered.

Naturally, as more educators, business leaders, counselors, and other professionals take on the work of career education, terms proliferate, and language evolves. In this volume, we use the following working definition of *career education*: activities within an educational context – structured and unstructured, curricular and otherwise – which support students' work and career exploration, engagement, learning, problem-solving, and preparation. This definition is intentionally broad, and includes experiential learning, career counseling, guidance, advising, instruction, coaching, and development. We draw from Kenneth Hoyt (2005), who defined career education as a policy-based movement for educational reform, and we incorporate and widen Steven Brown and Robert Lent's (2020) definition of career education, which described only those formal, early-career activities, largely in middle and high school, that focused on career exploration and preparation. Finally, we lean on the work of career development pioneers Donald Super and Sunny Hansen: "career" assumes a holistic constellation of one's paid and unpaid roles, as well as life tasks, over the course of one's lifetime (Hansen, 1997; Super, 1980).

Today's diverse undergraduate students enter institutions of higher education at different points in their lives and careers, and undergraduate learning – not to mention work itself – takes many different forms and meanings (Jaffe, 2021; Levine & Van Pelt, 2021). Our definition reflects the complication and expansion of how and for whom we provide career education. It also reinforces the idea, shared by Hoyt, Brown, and Lent, that career education is a collective, communal effort. From this perspective, we contend that *career education is everyone's business* – not solely the business of those employed in career services offices or divisions.

The undergraduate educational experience exists, at least in part, to prepare students to become critical thinkers and informed global citizens (Olds, 2012; Ostermiller, 2005). Through – and beyond – their work, our current and future students will shape our world and design solutions to address our most pressing problems. We hope this edited text supports the many individuals who have dedicated their lives and work to serving those students.

References

Abe, E. (Ed.). (2021). *Future of work, work-family satisfaction, and employee well-being in the fourth industrial revolution*. IGI Global.

Anderson, G. (2020, April 28). *Uncertain job market awaits soon-to-be graduates*. Inside Higher Education. www.insidehighered.com/news/2020/04/28/job-and-internship-market-discourages-students

Avis, J. (2020). *Vocational education in the fourth industrial revolution: Education and employment in a post-work age*. Palgrave Macmillan.

Bhargava, R., & Gupta, N. (2020). Social unrest and its impact on mental health. *Indian Journal of Social Psychiatry: Official Publication of Indian Association for Social Psychiatry*, 36(1), 3–4. www.indjsp.org/text.asp?2020/36/1/3/280832

Blass, E., & Hayward, P. (2014). Innovation in higher education: Will there be a role for "the academe/university" in 2025? *European Journal of Futures Research*, 2(41), 1–9. https://doi.org/10.1007/s40309-014-0041-x

Broadbent, E., Gougoulis, J., Lui, N., Pota, V., & Simons, J. (2017, January). *Generation Z: Global citizenship survey*. www.varkeyfoundation.org/what-we-do/research/generation-z-global-citizenship-survey

Brown, S., & Lent, R. (2020). *Career development and counseling: Putting theory and research to work* (3rd ed.). John Wiley & Sons.

Dey, F., & Cruzvergara, C. Y. (2014). Evolution of career services in higher education. *New Directions for Student Services, 2014*(148), 5–18. https://doi.org/10.1002/ss.20105

EY. (2021). *Gen Z is poised to reframe the future, but are business and education ready?* [Survey]. www.ey.com/en_gl/corporate-responsibility/how-business-and-education-can-help-gen-z-reframe-the-future

Hamilton, J. L., Nesi, J., & Choukas-Bradley, S. (2021). Reexamining social media and socioemotional well-being among adolescents through the lens of the COVID-19 pandemic: A theoretical review and directions for future research. *Perspectives on Psychological Science*. Advance online publication. https://doi.org/10.1177/17456916211014189

Hansen, L. S. (1997). *Integrative life planning: Critical tasks for career development and changing life patterns*. Jossey-Bass.

Hoyt, K. (2001). Career education and education reform: Time for a rebirth. *Phi Delta Kappa, 83*(4), 327–331. www.jstor.org/stable/20440127

Hoyt, K. (2005). *Career education: History and future*. National Career Development Association.

Jaffe, S. (2021). *Work won't love you back: How devotion to our jobs keeps us exploited, exhausted, and alone*. Bold Type Books.

Klebs, S., Nguyen, S., Fishman, R., & Hiler, T. (2021, June 29). *One year later: COVID-19s impact on current and future college students* [Memorandum]. Third Way. www.thirdway.org/memo/one-year-later-covid-19s-impact-on-current-and-future-college-students

Kretovics, M., Honaker, S., & Kraning, J. (1999). Career centers: Changing needs require changing paradigms. *Journal of Student Affairs at Colorado State University, 8*, 77–84.

Levine, A., & Van Pelt, S. J. (2021). *The great upheaval: Higher education's past, present, and uncertain future*. Johns Hopkins University Press.

McGowan, H. E., & Shipley, C. (2020). *The adaptation advantage: Let go, learn fast, and thrive in the future of work*: Wiley.

McKinney, J. (2020, August 10). *Survey: College students have big concerns about careers amid Covid-19*. Black Enterprise. www.blackenterprise.com/survey-college-students-have-big-concerns-about-careers-amid-covid-19/

McKinsey & Company. (2020, October 5). *How COVID-19 has pushed companies over the technology tipping point – and transformed business forever. Digital and Strategy and Corporate Finance Practices*. www.mckinsey.com/business-functions/strategy-and-corporate-finance/our-insights/how-covid-19-has-pushed-companies-over-the-technology-tipping-point-and-transformed-business-forever

Olds, K. (2012, March 11). *Global citizenship – What are we talking about and why does it matter?* Inside Higher Ed. www.insidehighered.com/blogs/globalhighered/global-citizenship-%E2%80%93-what-are-we-talking-about-and-why-does-it-matter

Ostermiller, J. A. (2005). Preparing world citizens through higher education: Responsibilities, choices, and implications. *The Vermont Connection, 26*(12). https://scholarworks.uvm.edu/tvc/vol26/iss1/12

Pillay, A. (2019). Foreword. In J. G. Maree (Ed.), *Handbook of Innovative Career Counselling* (pp. v–vii). Springer.

Pope, M. (2000). A brief history of career counseling in the United States. *The Career Development Quarterly, 48*(3), 194–211. https://doi.org/10.1002/j.2161-0045.2000.tb00286.x

Ruyter, A., Brown, A., & Brown, M. (2019). *The gig economy.* Agenda Publishing.

Staley, D. (2019). *Alternative universities: Speculative design for innovation in higher education.* Johns Hopkins University Press.

Super, D. E. (1980). A life-span, life-space approach to career development. *Journal of Vocational Behavior, 16*, 282–298.

Weir, K. (2020, April 1). *Grief and COVID-19: Mourning our bygone lives.* American Psychological Association. www.apa.org/news/apa/2020/grief-covid-19

Wiley Education Services & Future Workplace. (2019). *Closing the skills gap 2019.* Wiley.

Willcocks, L. (2021). Robo-apocalypse? Response and outlook on the post-COVID-19 future of work. *Journal of Information Technology, 36*(2), 188–194. https://doi.org/10.1177/0268396220978660

Part I
The Landscape of Undergraduate Career Education and the World of Work

1
Present and Future Innovation in Career Education

Melanie V. Buford

The Seeds of Innovation

The world of work continues to change, ushering in a reshaping of both the structure and nature of career (Abe, 2021; Avis, 2020; Hall & Associates, 1996; McKinsey & Company, 2020; Schwab, 2016). Along with these changes, the workforce continues to evolve and diversify (AAUW, 2020; Ciocirlan & Pettersson, 2012; Olinger, 2011; US Census, 2017), reflecting our changing world. People of different gender, racial, cultural, and generational identities, with a range of abilities and goals, infuse new priorities into both higher education and the marketplace, expanding the international conversation on the nature of meaningful work and recontextualizing our pressing social, technical, and political challenges. Generation Z, born between 1995 and 2010 (Seemiller & Grace, 2019), is only the most recent voice in this conversation. As a result of many of these developments, undergraduate career education has already begun a process of rebirth, to better reflect a new age of connection, information, technology, and diversity (Contomanolis et al., 2015; Dey & Cruzvergara, 2014).

For our purposes, I will briefly highlight four powerful innovations in the field of undergraduate career education: technology and scalability; curricular integration of career content; emphasis on experiential learning; and the implementation of design-thinking principles. These concepts will be expanded upon in later chapters, but for now, I will provide a conceptual overview of these phenomena, each of which has gained momentum over the last ten years. Though it will not appear on this list of structural innovations, equity and inclusion has received more and more focus in higher education – and in career education – over the last few decades (Alon & Tienda, 2007; Bikos et al., 2013; Brint, 2009; Burke et al., 2016; Pasque et al., 2016). In career education, both practitioners and scholars have turned their attention to equity and addressing the needs of underserved students. Part II of this book will discuss those efforts in more detail.

DOI: 10.4324/9781003213000-3

Technology and Scalability

According to a National Association of Colleges and Employers (NACE) report (2009), more than half of college career centers faced a decrease in their operating budgets in the 2009–2010 school year, many of which have never fully recovered in the intervening decade (NACE, 2020). This was consistent with impacts to higher education in general, following the 2008 recession. At the same time, new technologies offered new opportunities to provide services at scale. Career centers – forced to think more strategically about vision, reach, and brand – adopted software solutions to support recruiting, connecting with employers, and marketing and service delivery to students (New, 2016). They also needed to support their funding requests and corporate partnership proposals with data about student needs. Here, technology provided assistance. A growing emphasis on the collection of data on attendance, postgraduate employment, satisfaction, and learning outcomes drove partnerships with new software vendors. GradLeaders is one such vendor. According to the career-center-facing page of their website, they offer "all the tools you need to better prepare your students for the workforce and prove the value of services and education you provide" (GradLeaders, 2021). Social media emerged as another strategy to connect with students and market services, with the added benefit of facilitating employer connections and networking. In general, offices turned their attention to strategic planning, improving efficiency, reducing redundancies, and occasionally merging to centralize efforts (Dey & Cruzvergara, 2014).

Though the adoption of new technologies has often generated a certain amount of fear in higher education (Stoller, 2015), a number of platforms have emerged and have been integrated into the delivery of career services. Christine Cruzvergara is the Chief Education Strategy Officer at Handshake – a leading student employment connection application that now serves more than 7 million students and 1,100 college and university partners (Handshake, 2021). According to Cruzvergara, career management technology-based platforms such as Handshake, VMock, Riipen, and Quinccia are growing in usage in career services offices. They have increased the efficacy and reach of career centers, often addressing five main areas of need: supporting resume writing and interview preparation, connecting students with employment opportunities, facilitating experiential learning, supporting mentorship initiatives, and providing information about working and living abroad (C. Cruzvergara, personal communication, February 10, 2021).

In many cases, these new software solutions were adopted in order to address the decline in fiscal investment in career services. They have additional benefits, including expanding access to career services, so that students can utilize programs from a distance, at any time of day or night, in different languages, and at their own pace. This has appealed to those members of Generation Z who value accessibility and connectivity (Prensky, 2001; Seemiller & Grace, 2019). These solutions also offer possibilities for tracking and content delivery at scale, which promises to expand career education efforts, at worst, and evolve them, at best. Yet technology presents limitations, such as the need for hardware and internet access and a certain baseline technical sophistication to fully benefit from the programs available. Income, cultural barriers, access to technology, and age might all play a role in whether or not students can access these types of programs.

Elevation of Career Services Leadership. In recent years, many college and university career centers have received more resources, recognition, and elevation (Chan, 2013; Dey & Cruzvergara, 2014; Lederman, 2021). This support has only bolstered those innovative scaling efforts born in leaner times. The 2019–2020 NACE Career Services Benchmarks Survey Report for Colleges and Universities (NACE, 2020) – which collected data just before the effects of the Covid-19 pandemic – provided a snapshot of the structure of contemporary college and university career centers. It highlighted a few key trajectories. Indeed, there has been a pronounced elevation in titles of career center leadership. The percentage of career services leaders being granted elevated titles has gone from 12% in the 2017–2018 survey, to 25.3% in 2019–2020. Most offices surveyed maintained a centralized structure (68.4%), although many of them explored hybrid structures. Elevation and centralization often come with wider responsibility, necessitating varied services that can reach a large percentage of the student body. Centers today provide a range of offerings, including career fairs, experiential learning support, assessment, on-campus interviews, both virtual and in-person coaching appointments for individuals and groups, advising, and support for specific student populations. Staffing has gradually increased over the last several years, as the importance of return on investment for higher education looms large. Of course, Covid-19 impacted this trajectory, bringing new financial uncertainty and stress to career center leadership and staff (Handshake, 2020).

Role of Peer Coaching. One innovative effort aimed at addressing the scalability problem is the development of peer coaching programs. As the workplace changes, employees are called upon to learn a range of skills, develop self-direction and confidence, navigate issues of identity and culture, and manage transitions and uncertainty. Mentoring has been found to support the development of these types of skills in career (Crisp et al., 2017). This is especially true for students with marginalized identities (Crisp et al., 2017; Museus & Neville, 2012; Parker, 2008; Tovar, 2014). Peer career coaching presents a number of benefits at the college level:

> Career learning as a relational activity includes the ability to self-reflect and expand self-awareness, personally assess what is known and what needs to be known, and to adapt to the situation by altering behavior and attitudes…Support and challenge from a trusted peer, through the peer-coaching process, can provide a powerful form of this accelerated career learning.
>
> (Parker, 2008, p. 491)

A number of centers have recognized the inherent potential in peer coaching, not just for engaging students in the career development process, but for addressing staffing shortages and budget cuts. Mary T. Calhoon, Assistant Dean of Students at University of Nevada, Reno, shared her experience of scaling career services by adopting a peer coaching model. In 2013, Calhoon was hired to redesign career services after recession-driven cutbacks resulted in the closure of her university's central career center. She and one other staff member were charged with delivering career services to approximately 20,000 students. Embracing the concept of student empowerment, they hired a team of "career mentors" drawn from the student population itself to address individual questions. They verified their success using two metrics: self-reported increases in student confidence and clarity after peer coaching and an increase in career center touchpoints with students as a result of greater staff engagement in workshops and in classrooms. Meeting the need for one-to-one appointments through peer coaching allowed their professional coaching to increase student reach by creating more large-scale programming (Calhoon, 2018).

Peer coaching, technology, and other scalability solutions have allowed centers to widen their impact on students across campus and at distance. This, combined with the elevation of structural prominence for a number of centers and directors, has increased the visibility of career services in higher education. A 2020 *Forbes* opinion piece went so far as to suggest that career services may yet save higher education, counteracting declining enrollment across the industry. According to Busteed (2020):

> Career services may be the most important yet underappreciated function in higher education…it will become one of the most important drivers of enrollment growth as students and parents seek career outcomes as their top reason for attending.
>
> (Busteed, para. 1)

Busteed (2020) specifically cited the rise in demand for career services at colleges and universities, underscoring the need to offer career support more widely. This effort to equitably reach more students is consistent with Dey and Cruzvergara's championing of the rising prominence of career services and their emphasis on outcomes, statistics, enrollment, and recruitment (Lederman, 2021).

Yet a unilateral focus on reach and numbers poses its own challenges, threatening to carry the field too far down the path of breadth over depth. Champions of career counseling advocate for the importance of meaningfully addressing the emotional needs of the individual in career decision-making and planning, through counselor and coach training, and practice rooted in theoretical frameworks (Redekopp & Huston, 2019; Sampson et al., 2020; Tang, 2003). These approaches consider students' identities, motivations, and barriers, in addition to their need for career information, networks, and experiences. Career professionals in the counseling world have grappled with changes in insurance policy, which have produced a dwindling emphasis on career issues, resulting in inadequate training for career professionals (Tang, 2003). Across the sector, career practitioners are doing more with less, while working to meet rising demand for customized support.

The Future of Technology and Scalability

Given the importance of scalability, and the inevitable need for higher education to continue to operate efficiently and bring down tuition costs, there is reason to believe that innovations that support accessibility and wide service delivery, especially those which leverage new technologies, will continue to proliferate (Moran, 2020; Thompson, 1997). Technology itself supports career centers around the world in sharing information about new vendors and solutions as they arise. The next few decades, especially given the impact of Covid-19, will likely see more of the services centers offer available remotely, using new and developing technologies (Moran, 2020). Centers will be called upon to think strategically about how to leverage staff time, skills, and knowledge, to provide human-centered and customized support. It is often more efficient to deliver knowledge through technology, than to explore an individual students' goals, motivations, and fears. Yet both are essential.

Handshake's Christine Cruzvergara has called upon career centers to leverage technology, not just to support their existing workflow, but to evolve the way they imagine career preparation and serve students. In an interview conducted for this volume, she shared her insights on the future of educational technology in career services. "Career center staff have the opportunity to work from a mindset of possibility, not from a place of fear. [Technology] frees us up to rethink our roles, and to evolve alongside it…Virtual is here to stay" (C. Cruzvergara, personal communication, February 10, 2021). Cruzvergara imagines that the future of career preparation will reflect the evolution of what we are beginning to see today, especially in light of the Covid-19 pandemic. Career centers will become more and more critical to the college experience. Due to their convenience and accessibility for recruiters and students, virtual employer events will continue beyond the pandemic, and higher education leaders will recognize the value of required career education for equity and access. Perhaps most critically, career professionals will need to determine how to deliver career education at scale, using media as a tool.

Cruzvergara suggested educators look to the media as a potential model for mass education. Television shows such as the popular children's program *Sesame Street* have been found to impact social reasoning, literacy, and other outcomes across a diverse, global audience (Mares & Pan, 2013). These models might provide inspiration for career professionals who, according to Cruzvergara, should begin to think of themselves as "channel marketers" to employers and "content creators" for students. This would represent a profound shift for career services, but does have the potential to appeal to younger generations (Prensky, 2001; Seemiller & Grace, 2019). While we explore education at scale, Cruzvergara still sees a place for one-to-one engagement for high-need and marginalized students. Technology will allow us to better track student engagement and identify those students who may be disengaged or need support. Thus, we can strategically support students in the ways they require, while managing resources efficiently (C. Cruzvergara, personal communication, February 10, 2021). Cruzvergara's vision represents one path forward, which would necessarily draw on both innovative leadership and support from the larger institutions we work within. Regardless of the path we choose, career education scholars and practitioners will need to clearly define career exploration and preparation for the new world of work, so that we can intentionally address each piece of this process and meet students where they are.

Career Courses and Curricular Integration

Credit-Bearing Courses

One powerful approach that has swept through career services is the push to integrate career development more seamlessly into the academic mission of institutions. As we have seen, more and more career centers are moving out of student affairs to be housed in academic affairs, becoming their own division, reporting to the president, or joining with more centralized academic services, such as enrollment management. This reflects a stronger institutional priority for integrating career exploration and preparation into students' core academic experiences. Career exploration can be addressed through the continued implementation of career development courses that are offered in different formats across a range of academic disciplines and institutions.

Career courses hold prominent and long-standing roles in career education. In the United States, many career courses – including those that are credit-bearing – date back to the early 20th century (Maverick, 1926), and have continued to grow and diverge in structure and scope in the intervening decades. Career planning courses have demonstrated success as a powerful form of holistic career support for students, especially those with marginalized identities (Grier-Reed et al., 2009), in a financially self-sustaining way (Reardon & Fiore, 2014). These advantages, combined with the potential for less siloed career centers to collaborate with academic departments to connect to employers and provide internship opportunities (NACE, 2019), have allowed career services to increase both reach and impact. It is estimated that 30–40% of colleges and universities offer for-credit career courses (Lenz & Reardon, 2017; NACE, 2020), a percentage that has been growing since the 1970s (Reardon & Fiore, 2014) – and will likely continue to rise in the future.

There is a significant body of research to validate the positive impacts of career courses. An extensive 2014 report by Robert Reardon and Emily Fiore reviewed 88 studies of campus-based career courses with more than 25,333 participants from 1976 to 2014, most of which used control groups to reinforce their results. Reardon and Fiore found that 92% of these studies reported positive gains for participants after completing their career courses. In his 2011 dissertation, career coach and scholar Charles Austin summarized the types of outcomes common to successful for-credit career courses. Among this list are tangible gains such as increased retention rates, decreased time to graduation, improved GPAs, and stronger professional networks.

There are also more amorphous, yet no less critical gains such as addressing the needs of students of different identities, promoting career maturity, and supporting timely career decision-making. This list is consistent with the wide body of literature on career course impacts, provided by Reardon, Fiore, Lenz, and many others.

The Future of Curricular Integration

There is plenty of evidence to suggest that for-credit career courses offered at academic institutions will continue to become a ubiquitous approach to career services, in an increasingly tight and global market (Stebleton et al., 2020). A one-time, one-size-all approach to career services no longer suits a diverse student population, and courses allow for the delivery of multiple interventions over the course of multiple weeks. Assignments can be tailored to individuals and curriculum can be developed flexibly to address various student needs. Faculty members and instructors must engage in the process of career exploration, and they should partner with student affairs professionals, mainly career educators. They have the opportunity to share their expertise and partner with career centers to provide career education, contributing to the notion of collective institutional responsibility of preparing students for the future of work (Schlesinger et al., 2021).

Postsecondary students have more access and more career options than ever before, as more remote career possibilities emerge due to expanding technical access and the impacts of Covid-19. Many graduates may therefore no longer need to limit their job search to a single geographical region. Yet this new freedom might necessitate more support in the career decision-making process. Career changes and entrepreneurship are on the rise, expanding options further and necessitating a more sophisticated and adaptable professional skill set (McGowan & Shipley, 2020).

In a 2021 podcast episode from *The Key: Inside Higher Education*, titled "Putting Career Education at Higher Ed's Core," Christine Cruzvergara and Andy Chan suggested that the primary barriers to integrating career content broadly in academic programs is structural and cultural, not financial (Lederman, 2021). They recommended that senior leaders at colleges and universities ensure that employees with career expertise are included in broad conversations about institutional goals and return on investment, and that leaders make data-informed decisions. Since structural elevation of some higher education leaders has already occurred (NACE, 2020), barriers to curricular integration may diminish in the coming years. Chapter 13 of this volume will explore curricular integration in more depth.

Experiential Learning

Experiential learning, sometimes called work-integrated learning or experience-based learning (Sharp, 2018), is a broad category of pedagogical approaches designed to expand upon traditional classroom learning by intentionally incorporating opportunities to practice skills, grapple with problems of practice, and demonstrate knowledge gained through curriculum. Experiential learning takes many forms, including traditional approaches such as cooperative learning, internships, service-learning, field work, clinical placements, study abroad, undergraduate research, and others, along with more recent innovations, such as transdisciplinary collaboratives, innovation labs, and interactive simulations (Carleton University, 2018; Roberts, 2016).

Regardless of the form, experiential learning as a pedagogical mindset has gained more and more traction in higher education. Generational shifts in student attitudes toward learning exist, with younger generations embracing opportunities to learn relevant and applicable skills (Lovett, 2020). Employers, too, have largely championed experiential learning efforts in colleges and universities, calling for stronger workforce preparation in graduates (Thelin, 2019). According to a 2014 survey of 400 employers conducted on behalf of the Association of American Colleges and Universities, 60% of respondents believed that completing a significant applied project should be a requirement for all students. Eighty percent considered recent college graduates' demonstrated ability to apply learning in real-world settings as very important during the hiring process. Moreover, 88% of surveyed employers believed that colleges and universities should ensure that all students are prepared with the skills and knowledge required to complete a significant applied project (Hart Research Associates, 2015).

Among the many benefits of work- and community-integrated experiential learning is the possibility that students may expand their professional networks and seek out mentors. Uncertainty looms large in the modern professional landscape. Gone are the days when students might start out on a career path and expect to rise steadily within that field until retirement. The shifting demands and uncertain nature of the new world of work have produced the need for students to seek mentorship, advice, support, and connections (Dey & Cruzvergara, 2014; Kretovics et al., 1999). Thus, a strong network is a critical outcome of experiential learning opportunities in higher education. Armed with both relevant experience and a foundational network of professional contacts, a student has the raw ingredients with which to build a meaningful and adaptive career. Moving forward, career educators would be wise to develop and extend experiential learning opportunities to all students.

The Future of Experiential Learning

Arguably the most widespread critique of experiential learning is its accessibility. Given the many benefits of experiential learning approaches, if they are not made available to all students, it may exacerbate inequities in higher education. In their often-cited 2015 piece, "Maximizing Experiential Learning for Student Success," Jeffrey Scott Coker and Desiree Jasmine Porter grappled with the challenges of increasing access to experiential learning at Elon University. They explored the impact of multiple experiential learning experiences on participating students. Their findings revealed that the completion of five or more experiential learning opportunities increased the likelihood that students would report career development benefits, compared with completing one, two, three, or four. Moreover, completing four experiences increased students' likelihood of reporting a change to their future plans, compared with completing one, two, or three. This portion of their research reinforced the importance of access to multiple forms of experiential learning for interested students.

Another of their key findings captures the importance of inclusive institutional policies to support equitable access to experiential learning. In exploring the barriers to student participation in various experiential learning opportunities, the authors gave special consideration to financial, cultural, and social barriers. They ultimately suggest that in order to engage students from working-class and culturally underrepresented backgrounds, it is critical for institutions to prioritize supports such as targeted advising, scholarships, minority needs assessment, and, foundationally, building experiential learning into the core curricular requirements (Coker & Porter, 2015; Kuh et al., 2013).

Colleges and universities have necessarily grappled with issues of equity in experiential learning. Experiential learning facilitates the realization of the benefits of classroom learning, and must be flexible and accessible for all students. Numerous studies have documented social and financial barriers to studying abroad for first-generation students, working-class students, and students of color, for instance (Dean & Kelly, 2020; Hurst, 2019; Murray & Fry, 2010). Coker and Porter's (2015) work emphasized the importance of institutional policy support to ensure that all students can access these opportunities, regardless of identity, ability, academic program, or financial status.

Technological advancements also hold the potential to further transform experiential learning. One of the most promising horizons for the transformation of learning exists in the form of virtual and augmented reality (West, 2018). These approaches, which use computer simulation to create interactive virtual environments or to add virtual elements to existing environments, are already being implemented in medical programs and in the life sciences (Samadbeik et al., 2018; Su & Cheng, 2019; Tremeer, n.d.). As this software improves, it may offer a way to address issues of equity and access. It may also lead the way to more speculative forms of learning, ways to reimagine what is possible for research and practice in a number of fields.

Offices housing experiential learning programs in higher education have begun to explore the possibilities of breaking down traditional silos to promote more collaboration across campus and between stakeholders off campus (Sharp, 2018). Transdisciplinary research has its roots in the work of Erich Jantsch, who proposed working across disciplinary boundaries in order to bring innovation to persistent systemic problems (1972). In recent years, transdisciplinary approaches to experiential learning have proliferated, as programs seek the benefits of supporting students in learning, working, and collaborating across disciplines and industries to solve real-world problems (Pohl & Hadorn, 2008; Servantie et al., 2019). Part IV of this book will explore possibilities for future innovation in the domain of experiential learning and Chapter 15 will specifically address transdisciplinary collaboration.

Career Construction and Life Design

The final innovation we will examine here may be best described as a theoretical paradigm shift, which, as it has developed, continues to shape the practice of career counseling and development in myriad ways. In 1999, editors of the National Career Development Association's journal, *The Career Development Quarterly*, released its Annual Review examining the body of career counseling and development literature in 1998. Its authors described the seeds of what would become the career construction movement, integrated throughout the literature that year:

> The complexity with which most authors approach the subject of career is a clear asset. Career is not a simple variable. It is a complex construct that represents many dimensions of both individual lives and society. The focus on identity and meaning is one example of this complexity.
>
> (Young & Chen, 1999, p. 127)

In 2009, Mark Savickas and his collaborators elaborated on this concept, offering a model for tackling the growing complexity of careers in the 21st century. They argued that careers themselves are increasingly unstable and unpredictable. Traditional career counseling and development approaches must be reworked to acknowledge this growing reality for modern workers. The authors described the importance of what they called "life designing," a continuous iterative process of holistic interpretation of self and career, in order to chart a personally meaningful career path into the future. This process is something counselors and coaches can facilitate, ultimately supporting the individual to grapple with complex notions of identity and career (Savickas et al., 2009).

A number of practitioners in higher education have found ways to operationalize or build upon this model, perhaps most notably two professors at Stanford University. Bill Burnett and Dave Evans (2016) applied design-thinking principles to the "wicked problem" of designing a career. Using the idea of creating prototypes and testing options, their work is consistent with the principles of Savickas et al.'s life design paradigm and builds upon the work of other career development scholars who had written about the topic prior to this point.

Burnett and Evans (2021) offer life and career coach certification programs based on the original concept. Stanford's centralized career center has transformed along those same lines, providing more innovative and connected service models to meet students where they are physically and developmentally, and renaming itself BEAM

– Bridging Education, Ambition and Meaningful Work (Sullivan, 2015). This shift toward emphasizing meaning-making and supporting students in planning for a complex and unpredictable world of work represents a growing awareness in higher education.

The Future of Career Construction and Life Design

The philosophies of career construction and life design will no doubt continue to influence counselors and career development practitioners in higher education. Editors of *The Career Development Quarterly* released a Special Issue in 2016 describing seven innovative studies designed to "advance the life-design paradigm and its practices" (Hartung, 2016, p. 2). These seven authors examine the application of life-design principles in different environments, with diverse populations and using different technologies. These efforts suggest future directions for research on life design, and for increasing accessibility to these approaches for students of different identities and around the world.

Leveraging technology to scale design-based approaches presents another challenge: significant training, expertise, and time are required to successfully engage in the process of meaning-making with a student; this relationship-building requires time and energy. Yet, as career centers rise to the challenge of structuring career support into the undergraduate experience, new approaches to career and life design hold the potential to transform students' ideas about what is possible and unlock new paths. One such approach, the Career Style Interview, originally developed by Mark Savickas (2015), has been found to increase confidence, self-awareness, and career clarity (Barclay, 2019; Rehfuss et al., 2011). This narrative technique draws on personal history to examine and reframe values and interests, and to establish new goals and commitments. There is room to replicate this work in different contexts and with diverse participants, and to explore ways to integrate this method into the undergraduate experience. Chapter 8 will cover life design in more depth and Chapter 12 will address the potential of narrative models of career education.

The forms of innovation covered in this chapter only represent a part of the evolution happening in career education around the world. The next chapter will explore what we currently know about Generation Z, who comprise the majority of students in undergraduate education at the time of this writing. Career education informed by insights about both shifting student needs and the demands of our new world of work promises to better serve undergraduates now and in the future.

References

AAUW. (2020). The future workforce: More diverse than ever. *Workplace & Economic Equity.* www.aauw.org/resources/article/future-workforce-diverse/

Abe, E. (Ed.). (2021). *Future of work, work-family satisfaction, and employee well-being in the fourth industrial revolution*. IGI Global.

Alon, S., & Tienda, M. (2007). Diversity, opportunity, and the shifting meritocracy in higher education. *American Sociological Review, 72*(4), 487–511.

Austin, C. M. (2011). *A model for integrating a career development course program into a college curriculum* [Doctoral dissertation, Pepperdine University]. Pepperdine Digital Commons Theses and Dissertations. 100. https://digitalcommons.pepperdine.edu/etd/100

Avis, J. (2020). *Vocational education in the fourth industrial revolution: Education and employment in a post-work age*. Palgrave Macmillan.

Barclay, S. R. (2019). Creative use of the career construction interview. *The Career Development Quarterly, 67*(2), 126–138. https://doi.org/10.1002/cdq.12176

Bikos, L. H., Dykhouse, E. C., Boutin, S. K., Gowen, M. J., & Rodney, H. E. (2013). Practice and research in career counseling and development – 2012. *The Career Development Quarterly, 61*(4), 290–329. https://doi.org/10.1002/j.2161-0045.2013.00058.x

Brint, S. (2019). *Two cheers for higher education: Why American universities are stronger than ever – and how to meet the challenges they face*. Princeton University Press. https://doi.org/10.1515/9780691184890

Burke, P. J., Crozier, G., & Misiaszek, L. (2016). Changing pedagogical spaces in higher education: Diversity, inequalities and misrecognition (1st ed.). Routledge. https://doi.org/10.4324/9781315684000

Burnett, B., & Evans, D. (2016). *Designing your life: How to build a well-lived, joyful life*. Alfred A. Knopf.

Burnett, B., & Evans, D. J. (2021). *Designing your new work life: How to thrive and change and find happiness – and a new freedom – at work*. Vintage.

Busteed, B. (2020, December 21). Career services will define the next big boom in college enrollment. *Forbes*. www.forbes.com/sites/brandonbusteed/2020/12/21/career-services-will-define-the-next-big-boom-in-college-enrollment/?sh=41bd956a145e

Calhoon, M. (2018). The career studio: Flipping the career center. *The NACE Journal, 78*(3), 21–28.

Carleton University. (2018, August 8). *Experiential learning*. Educational Development Center Teaching Resources. https://carleton.ca/edc/teachingresources/high-impact-practices/experiential-learning/#sect1

Chan, A. (2013). *"Career services" must die* [Video]. TEDx Lawrence U. www.tedxlawrenceu.com/speakers/andy-chan/

Ciocirlan, C., & Pettersson, C. (2012). Does workforce diversity matter in the fight against climate change? An analysis of Fortune 500 companies. *Corporate Social Responsibility and Environmental Management, 19*(1), 47–62. https://doi.org/10.1002/csr.279

Coker, J. S., & Porter, D. J. (2015). Maximizing experiential learning for student success. *Change: The Magazine of Higher Learning, 47*(1), 66–72. https://doi.org/10.1080/00091383.2015.996101

Contomanolis, E., Cruzvergara, C., Dey, F., & Steinfeld, T. (2015). The future of career services is now. *NACE Journal, 76*(2), 23–28. www.naceweb.org/career-development/trends-and-predictions/the-future-of-career-services-is-now/

Crisp, G., Baker, V., Griffin, K., Lunsford, L., & Pifer, M. (2017). Mentoring undergraduate students. *ASHE Higher Education Report, 43*(1), 7–103. https://doi.org/10.1002/aehe.20117

Dean, P., & Kelly, C. (2020). Educational travel for first-generation students. *Teaching Sociology, 48*(4), 341–352. https://doi.org/10.1177/0092055X20952826

Dey, F., & Cruzvergara, C. Y. (2014). Evolution of career services in higher education. In K. K. Smith (Ed.), *New directions for student services: No. 148* (pp. 5–18). Jossey-Bass.

GradLeaders. (2021). *GradLeaders Career Center.* www.gradleaders.com/career-center

Grier-Reed, T. L., Skaar, N. R., & Conkel-Ziebell, J. L. (2009). Constructivist career development as a paradigm of empowerment for at-risk culturally diverse college students. *Journal of Career Development, 35*, 290–305. https://doi.org/10.1177/0894845308327275

Hall, D. T. (Ed.). (1996). *The career is dead – long live the career: A relation approach to careers.* Jossey-Bass.

Handshake. (2020, Fall). *Handshake career services report: Covid-19 and Fall 2020.* Handshake Blog. https://joinhandshake.com/blog/career-centers/handshake-trends-in-higher-ed-report-fall-2020/

Handshake. (2021). *About us.* www.joinhandshake.com/about/

Hart Research Associates. (2015). *Falling short? College learning and career success: Selected findings from online surveys of employers and college students conducted on behalf of the Association of American Colleges & Universities.* Association of American Colleges and Universities.

Hartung, P. J. (2016). Introduction to the special issue: Advancing career intervention for life design. *The Career Development Quarterly, 64*(1), 2–3. https://doi.org/10.1002/cdq.12036

Hurst, A. (2019). Class and gender as predictors of study abroad participation among US liberal arts college students. *Studies in Higher Education, 44*(7), 1241–1255. https://doi.org/10.1080/03075079.2018.1428948

Jantsch, E. (1972). Towards interdisciplinarity and transdisciplinarity in education and innovation. In L. Apostel, G. Berger, Briggs, A., & Michaud. G. (Eds.), *Interdisciplinarity: Problems of teaching and research in universities* (pp. 97–121). Organisation for Economic Co-operation and Development (OECD) and Center for Educational Research and Innovation (CERI).

Kretovics, M., Honaker, S., & Kraning, J. (1999). Career centers: Changing needs require changing paradigms. *Journal of Student Affairs at Colorado State University, 8*, 77–84.

Kuh, G. D., & O'Donnell, K. (2013). *Ensuring quality and taking high-impact practices to scale.* Association of American Colleges and Universities.

Lederman, D. (Host). (2021, Sept. 29). Putting career readiness at higher ed's core (No. 61) [Audio podcast episode]. In *The Key with Inside Higher Education* https://insidehighered.podbean.com/e/putting-career-readiness-at-higher-ed-s-core/

Lenz, J. G., & Reardon, R. C. (2017, June). *Strategies for developing, managing, and evaluating a successful career course for 45 years* [Paper presentation]. National Career Development Association conference, Orlando, FL, United States.

Lovett, K. (2020). *Diverse pedagogical approaches to experiential learning: Multidisciplinary case studies, reflections, and strategies.* Palgrave Macmillan.

Mares, M., & Pan, Z. (2013). Effects of Sesame Street: A meta-analysis of children's learning in 15 countries. *Journal of Applied Developmental Psychology, 34*(3), 140–151.

Maverick, L. A. (1926). *The vocational guidance of college students.* Harvard University Press.

McGowan, H. E., & Shipley, C. (2020). *The adaptation advantage: Let go, learn fast, and thrive in the future of work.* Wiley.

McKinsey & Company. (2020, October 5). *How COVID-19 has pushed companies over the technology tipping point – and transformed business forever.* www.mckinsey.com/business-functions/strategy-and-corporate-finance/our-insights/how-covid-19-has-pushed-companies-over-the-technology-tipping-point-and-transformed-business-forever

Moran, B. (2020, May 14). *How 100+ career services leaders are responding to Covid-19.* EAB. https://eab.com/insights/expert-insight/student-affairs/how-career-services-leaders-are-responding-to-covid-19/

Murray Brux, J., & Fry, B. (2010). Multicultural students in study abroad: Their interests, their issues, and their constraints. *Journal of Studies in International Education, 14*(5), 508–527. https://doi.org/ 10.1177/1028315309342486

Museus, S. D., & Neville, K. M. (2012). Delineating the ways that key institutional agents provide racial minority students with access to social capital in college. *Journal of College Student Development, 53*(3), 436–452. https://doi.org/10.1353/csd.2012.0042

National Association of Colleges and Employers. (2009). Looking ahead: Highlights from the future trends survey. *NACE Journal, 70*(1), 22–28.

National Association of Colleges and Employers. (2020). NACE 2019–2020 career services benchmarks survey report for colleges and universities.

New, J. (2016, July 5). *Career counselors or headhunters?* Inside Higher Ed. www.insidehighered.com/news/2016/07/05/corporate-partnership-programs-increasing-college-career-centers

Olinger, B. (2011). Increasing nursing workforce diversity: Strategies for success. *Nurse Educator, 36*(2), 54–55. https://doi.org/10.1097/NNE.0b013e31820b4fab

Parker, P., Hall, D., & Kram, K. (2008). Peer coaching: A relational process for accelerating career learning. *Academy of Management Learning & Education, 7*(4), 487–503. https://doi.org/10.5465/AMLE.2008.35882189

Pasque, P. A., Ortega, N., Burkhardt, J. C., & Ting, M. P. (Eds.). (2016). *Transforming understandings of diversity in higher education: Demography, democracy, and discourse.* Stylus Publishing.

Pohl, C., & Hadorn, G. H. (2008). Core terms in transdisciplinary research. *Handbook of Transdisciplinary Research,* 427–432. Springer.

Prensky, M. (2001). Digital natives, digital immigrants. *On the Horizon*, 9(5), 1–6. www.marcprensky.com/writing/Prensky%20-%20Digital%20Natives,%20Digital%20Immigrants%20-%20Part1.pdf

Reardon, R., & Fiore, E. (2014, June 5). College career courses and learner outputs and outcomes, 1976–2014 (Technical Report No. 55). https://career.fsu.edu/sites/g/files/imported/storage/original/application/1b68db078f1cf9a964208a907318c64a.pdf

Redekopp, D. E., & Huston, M. (2019). The broader aims of career development: Mental health, wellbeing and work. *British Journal of Guidance & Counselling*, 47(2), 246–257. https://doi.org/10.1080/03069885.2018.1513451

Rehfuss, M., Corso, J., Galvin, K., & Wykes, S. (2011). Impact of the career style interview on individuals with career concerns. *Journal of Career Assessment*, 19(4), 405–419.

Roberts, J. W. (2016). *Experiential education in the college context: What it is, how it works, and why it matters*. Routledge.

Samadbeik, M., Yaaghobi, D., Bastani, P., Abhari, S., Rezaee, R., & Garavand, A. (2018). The applications of virtual reality technology in medical groups teaching. *Journal of Advances in Medical Education & Professionalism*, 6(3), 123–129. https://doi.org/10.30476/JAMP.2018.41023

Sampson, J. P., Osborn, D. S., & Bullock-Yowell, E. (2020). Promoting career choices. In S. D. Brown & R. W. Lent (Eds.), *Career development and counseling: Putting theory and research to work*. John Wiley & Sons.

Savickas, M. L. (2015). *Life-design counseling manual*. http://vocopher.com/LifeDesign/LifeDesign.pdf

Savickas, M. L., Nota, L., Rossier, J., Dauwalder, J., Daurte, M. E., Guichard, J., Soresi, S., Van Esbroeck, R., & van Vianen, A. E. M. (2009). Life designing: A paradigm for career construction in the 21st century. *Journal of Vocational Behavior*, 75, 239–250. https://doi.org/10.1016/j.jvb.2009.04.004

Schlesinger, J., O'Shea, C., & Blesso, J. (2021). Undergraduate student career development and career center services: Faculty perspectives. *The Career Development Quarterly*, 69(2), 145–157. https://doi.org/10.1002/cdq.12255

Schwab, K. (2016). *The fourth industrial revolution*. World Economic Forum.

Seemiller, C., & Grace, M. (2019). *Generation Z: A century in the making*. Routledge.

Servantie, V., Van Hoof, B., & Salamanca, M. F. (2019). Transdisciplinary research and experience based learning: The case of Consultandes. *Developments in Business Simulation and Experiential Learning*, 46, 319–326.

Sharp, M. (2018). Who are we in this tent, what do we do in here, and who else needs to come in? [Letter to the editor]. *Experience Magazine*, 2–3. www.ceiainc.org/knowledge-zone/experience-magazine/experience-magazine-issues/experience-magazine-fall-2018/

Stebleton, M. J., Kaler, L. S., Diamond, K. K., & Lee, C. (2020). Examining career readiness in a liberal arts undergraduate career planning course. *Journal of Employment Counseling*, 57(1), 14–26. https://doi.org/10.1002/joec.12135

Stoller, E. (2015, May 7). *3 reasons why we fear technology*. Inside Higher Ed. www.insidehighered. com/blogs/student-affairs-and-technology/3-reasons-why-we-fear-technology

Su, C., & Cheng, T. (2019). A sustainability innovation experiential learning model for virtual reality chemistry laboratory: An empirical study with PLS-SEM and IPMA. *Sustainability, 11*(4), 1027. https://doi.org/10.3390/su11041027

Sullivan, K. J. (2015, September 8). *BEAM, Stanford Career Education, reflects new focus on connections and meaningful work*. Stanford News. https://news.stanford.edu/2015/09/08/beam-career-education-090815/

Tang, M. (2003). Career counseling in the future: Constructing, collaborating, advocating. *The Career Development Quarterly, 52*(1), 61–69. https://doi.org/10.1002/j.2161-0045.2003.tb00628.x

Thelin, J. R. (2019). *A history of American higher education* (3rd ed.). The Johns Hopkins University Press.

Thompson, A. (1997). *College students with disabilities and assistive technology: A desk reference guide*. Mississippi State University.

Tovar, E. (2014). The role of faculty, counselors, and support programs on Latino/a community college students' success and intent to persist. *Community College Review*. Advance online publication. https://doi.org/0091552114553788

Tremeer, D. (n.d.). A systematic review of the application of interactive virtual reality to sport. *Virtual Reality, 22*(3), 1–16. https://doi.org/10.1007/s10055-017-0320-5

US Census. (2017). *2017 national population projections tables: Main series*. www.census.gov/data/tables/2017/demo/popproj/2017-summary-tables.html

West, D. M. (2018). *The future of work: Robots, A.I., and automation*. Brookings Institution Press.

Young, R. A., & Chen, C. P. (1999). Annual review: Practice and research in career counseling and development – 1998. *The Career Development Quarterly, 48*(2), 98–141. https://doi.org/10.1002/j.2161-0045.1999.tb00280.x

2

Characteristics, Engagement, Learning, and Career Aspirations of Generation Z

Melanie V. Buford

Who is Generation Z?

Before reviewing findings about Generation Z, born between 1995 and 2010 (Seemiller & Grace, 2019), it is important to acknowledge a few key limitations. While generational positionality may offer something about a person's worldview (Pew Research Center, 2015), this area of inquiry does not typically lend itself to a positivist paradigm. Each generation is made up of a vast and diverse population of individual people, all of whom see the world through their own unique lenses and are continually impacted and changed by new events. There are many truths about any generation, especially as that group moves through different phases of life. The same is true of Generation Z, especially as we consider that at the time of this writing, their oldest members have only recently turned 25 and their youngest members have not yet reached the age of 11. Many members of Generation Z have not yet reached their high school years, much less participated in higher education (if that is their path). Certainly some have entered the workforce, though likely most have not had the opportunity to experience more than a few industries. This has obvious implications for their perspectives on higher education and their career aspirations. Given the impact of Covid-19, for instance, many members of Generation Z may have yet to evolve their beliefs about work and learning as they encounter new challenges and opportunities. The research presented here is primarily rooted in the context of the United States, though it does include perspectives from other national contexts. A 2015 Ford Trends Report suggests that this generation will be the first to share more commonalities with generational peers than with older generations in their own countries (Ford Motor Company & BAV Consulting, 2015). Several authors have explored this assertion, examining how national context shapes generational identity and often finding both similarities and differences among members of Generation Z in different regions (Farrell & Phungsoonthorn, 2020; Gentina, 2020).

DOI: 10.4324/9781003213000-4

With this in mind, the author will examine what has thus far been shared about the formative context, characteristics, learning and communication styles, and career aspirations of Generation Z in the hopes that we may better inform our understanding of how career education might similarly evolve to address their needs, and the needs of Generation Alpha (Pinsker, 2020) after them.

Formative Context

As a starting point, it is useful to turn our attention to the context during which Generation Z has come of age. In some ways this is an impossible question, since the last quarter century has included events as varied as the launch of app-based rider services, the completion of the Human Genome map, the birth of Craigslist, the rise of citizen reporting via smartphone, the release of the United Nations' Sustainable Development Goals (Fast Company, 2015), and, most recently, the emergence of a global pandemic and increased public attention to issues of social injustice. Yet an undeniably unique feature of this generation's context was the presence of never-before-seen technologies, and how they impacted the way we live, think, learn, work, and interact. According to Marc Prensky, an American educator credited with describing Generation Z as "digital natives" (2001), this generation does not simply prefer superficially different styles of communication, but rather, they have been fundamentally and irrevocably changed by emerging technologies, and as a result, they process information differently. Subsequently, technology is perhaps the central factor in what distinguishes the formative context of Generation Z. This does, of course, raise the question of access – that is, how might those members of Generation Z without access to some or all of these technologies locate themselves within this context (Farrell & Phungsoonthorn, 2020)? This is undoubtedly an area that warrants further study.

Another contextual factor shaping the worldviews of many members of Generation Z is the growing reality – and growing awareness – of economic instability, unemployment, and income inequality. The financial uncertainty of the Covid-19 pandemic came on the heels of a decade of global shifts and devastating recessions (Altig et al., 2020). It also highlighted disparities in wealth that had found increasing visibility through academic and media coverage (Grisold & Theine, 2017). Similarly, social media has facilitated the sharing of information about forms of social inequality, and the ability to capture abuses as they occur (Chon & Park, 2020). These same outlets have exposed many members of Generation Z to diverse experiences and contexts, and to multiple ways to live, learn, work, and see the world. For many of them, a nearly unlimited source of information and a window into the experiences of others is easily accessible at any time of the day or night in the form of a smartphone. This context has undoubtedly shaped them in ways that will continue to reveal themselves in the coming years.

General Characteristics

Much has been written about the unique characteristics of members of Generation Z around the world (Seemiller & Grace, 2019). Yet it is important to remember that these common characteristics do not capture every member of this generation, and that it is often as critical to explore the exceptions to these generalizations as the norm. Nonetheless, the characteristics and opinions of Generation Z have been assessed often enough to provide a window into their perceptions. Two leading scholars, Corey Seemiller and Meghan Grace, have conducted several large-scale studies of Generation Z and released two books (2016, 2019) combining their own research with available literature on this generation. They described Generation Z as a diverse, loyal, independent, open-minded, and driven generation, deeply concerned about their financial futures and social and environmental issues. Of course, this does not describe every individual. Generational research always presents limitations around the inherent diversity within a group. Yet Seemiller and Grace's work provides a compelling glimpse into this population.

The authors shared one intriguing finding from their 2014 study of Generation Z college students: that Generation Z participants' self-perceptions differed somewhat from their perceptions of other members of the generation. According to Seemiller and Grace (2016), "more than 70 percent [of participants] identified as loyal, thoughtful, determined, compassionate, open-minded, and responsible. However, when asked to describe their peers of the same age, they instead chose words like competitive, spontaneous, adventuresome, and curious" (p. 29). This seems to suggest a contradiction in peer perception, perhaps due to characterizations of Generation Z in the media or perhaps the fact that members of Generation Z's perception of their friends and peers is influenced by social media, a medium that typically supports depictions of adventure, success, spontaneity, and glamour. Numerous authors have described the extensive engagement with digital media that characterizes many members of Generation Z (Prensky, 2001; Rideout et al., 2010; Turner, 2015). Seemiller and Grace (2019) and others (see Gentina, 2020) have described the extent to which many members of Generation Z engage in managing multiple identities due to their presence online. They have the ability to shape and quickly change social perceptions, especially with peers and friends they may not interact with in person. This skill set has the potential to lend them an obvious advantage in planning and pursuing their career goals. Virtual networking and career exploration, not to mention the job search and interview process, increasingly involve managing a virtual presence, which serves as a strength for many members of this generation.

Much of Generation Z is ethnically diverse and well-educated (Pew Research Associates, 2018). In the United States, 48% of this generation identifies as non-White, a higher percentage than any previous generation. In terms of national origin, Generation Z has fewer members born outside the US (7%), but more members with one foreign-born parent (22%). Similarly, there is strong evidence to suggest that Generation Z is more likely to identify as multiracial, due to rising rates of interracial relationships and transracial adoptions (American Academy of Child and Adolescent Psychiatry, 2011; Jones & Bullock, 2012). Based on 2017 Pew Research data, 80% of 18- to 20-year-olds finished high school, a higher percentage than previous generations (Pew Research Center, 2018). This generation is more likely to attend at least some college (59% of high school graduates in the 18- to 20-year-old age range).

Another often discussed characteristic of Generation Z is their rising concern about the world, the environment, and their futures. In a piece on the psychological and social profile of Generation Z, author Anthony Turner (2015) described the uncertain and stressful conditions in which many members of Generation Z were raised:

> Generation Z youth have been affected by the growing income gap and shrinking middle class. Stress levels at home increased dramatically during the national recession that can be traced to the financial crisis of 2008…These stressors have the potential to affect parental responses to behaviors, thus sometimes causing harsher parenting practices…Generation Z youth have been reared during a time of war…[they] may view the world with the belief that the world is "unsafe".
>
> (pp. 104–105)

This generation has grown up through global, social, political, and financial turmoil, and while these events aren't unique in world history, technology has brought them closer than ever. Many members of Generation Z begin and end each day on the internet, with world events accessible at all times (Turner, 2015). Many feel emotionally connected to their media content. A 2012 study revealed that 90% of Generation Z participants expressed upset at the prospect of losing access to the internet as a punishment. Moreover, they indicated that they would find it more upsetting to lose cell phone privileges than to lose material possessions or allowance money (Palley, 2012).

The Covid-19 pandemic represents another globally traumatic event, with the potential to further stoke the fires of anxiety about the future (Gentina, 2020). A 2020 survey of 849 American teenagers found that 63% were concerned about the pandemic's impact on their family's financial future. This statistic was higher for Black (74%) and Hispanic/Latino (87%) teens in the survey, drawing attention to the importance of intersectionality of identities in Generation Z. These same teens expressed feelings of isolation and loneliness. Approximately 42% percent felt "more lonely than usual," with girls reporting more feelings of loneliness than boys (Common Sense Media, 2020). In general, members of Generation Z were more likely to report feeling pessimism about our global future than optimism (Broadbent et al., 2017; Gentina, 2020).

A 2017 global citizenship survey, the largest to date, assessed the attitudes of more than 20,000 members of Generation Z in 20 countries (Broadbent et al., 2017).

According to this survey, a global average of 68% of those surveyed reported feeling happy, though this differs significantly by country. Thirty percent reported emotional wellbeing overall, defined by this study as tending not to dwell on problems, and not feeling "anxious, bullied, unloved or lonely" (p. 16). Only 17% felt that they have adequate sleep, exercise, rest, and downtime for reflection.

Broadbent et al.'s study confirmed what other authors have reported about Generation Z's vulnerability to stress about financial and educational matters. Almost exactly half (51%) reported money as one of three primary sources of anxiety; 46% are feeling pressure related to school. Only 10% named the pressures of social media as a primary cause of anxiety in this particular survey, suggesting a cohort largely concerned with present and realistic challenges. Members of Generation Z with one or more marginalized identities are likely feeling heightened stress in these areas.

Finally, this study provided some insight into the social and political beliefs of Generation Z. Approximately 89% of respondents believed in equal treatment for men and women, and 74% believed that transgender people should have equal rights. Similarly, 63% believed that the law should protect same-sex marriage and 66% believed that safe and legal abortion options should exist for women who need them (this varies widely for each country, however). In compliance with local regulations, questions about abortion and same-sex marriage were not asked in Indonesia and Russia, potentially inflating these results. Their most important personal values reported were: helping family (27%), hard work and self-advancement (27%), honesty (26%), kindness (11%), tolerance (6%), and "looking after the wider world beyond my local community" (3%) (p. 47). Around the world, Generation Z expressed concern about "extremism and global terrorism" and "conflict and war," considering these two issues to be the greatest threat to our global future (p. 9). Approximately 84% of respondents put their hopes in technical advancements to pave the way toward a brighter future.

The Higher Education Research Institute (HERI), housed in the University of California, Los Angeles, conducted a national survey of 95,505 first-time, first-year, full-time undergraduate students across 148 institutions in the fall of 2019, to assess their social, political, and academic engagement (Stolzenberg et al., 2019). They found that 43.6% of students surveyed identified as, politically, "middle-of-the-road." Another 36% percent identified as liberal or far-left, while another 19.7% identified as conservative or far-right. Not surprisingly, prior to the presidential campaign season of 2020, the students who identified as middle-of-the-road were least likely to anticipate voting. The survey found that most students, regardless of political standpoint, considered helping others in difficulty to be important. Of those who considered helping others to be an essential goal, 89.3% had themselves engaged in volunteer work either occasionally or frequently. Even among those students who did not consider helping others in difficulty to be important, 65.1% had occasionally or frequently volunteered.

Learning and Postsecondary Education

Cost of Education and Covid-19

In terms of learning, Broadbent et al.'s (2017) survey found that 80% of Generation Z respondents around the world report that increases in educational attainment for many groups around the world give them hope for the future. In the United States, the cost of college is often a significant barrier. Estimates indicated that between 54 and 66% of students took out loans to fund their bachelor's degrees (Federal Reserve Board, 2019; Velez, 2019). In 2018, 20% of Americans who still owe money on their loans were behind on payments. The typical outstanding balance on education debt in 2018, among those who have debt, was between $20,000 and $24,999 (Federal Reserve Board, 2019). The burden of debt, for many, continues far beyond the time they spend in school. One study, based on a sample of bachelor's degree recipients in the 2007–2008 academic year, linked high education debt balances to lower work/life balance satisfaction, delayed marriage, and lower net worth (Velez, 2019). Many graduates may be less able to pursue purpose-driven work, and need to prioritize generating income. Given these impacts, the cost of education is a significant factor for Generation Z students in the US. A 2017 study of 54,810 American college records found that 11% of college admits did not attend their first-choice institution, and 40% of these admits made this decision due to cost (EAB, 2017).

Another 2017 survey found that 73% of American families surveyed chose to cut costs by sending their student to an in-state college. Around half of students surveyed chose to live at home for more cost savings (Sallie Mae, 2017). In spring of 2021, a survey of approximately 2,400 American high school students revealed that 34% changed their postsecondary plans, deciding to attend colleges and universities closer to home, due to uncertainty around the Covid-19 pandemic (America's Promise Alliance & Research for Action, 2021). These trends may continue, as financial pressures and uncertainty incentivize some families to rely on each other for support and stability. Cost savings is driving an effort by many Generation Z students, especially in the United States, to move through higher education faster, leaning into strategies such as taking college credit courses in high school, choosing accelerated programs, dual-enrollment, and determining best-fit majors as early as possible (Seemiller & Grace, 2019).

Modes of Learning

Generation Z is taking advantage of modes of learning outside of the classroom. Approximately 58 million students enrolled in open online courses in 2016 (Class Central, 2016), though it is still true that only 13% of Generation Z would opt for an in-person course over an online course (Bresman & Rao, 2017). A few authors have raised the issue of a diminishing attention span among members of Generation

Z and the rise of challenges related to focus and mobile device addiction, linked to technology consumption (Seemiller & Grace, 2019; Turner, 2015; Weber & Keim, 2021). One study specifically found meeting with students one-on-one, outside of the classroom, to be effective in promoting learning and supporting the development of career capacities (Weber & Keim, 2021).

One of the most relevant findings to the discussion of career education are patterns related to major selection. There is evidence that Generation Z students are gravitating more toward marketable, vocationally focused majors, such as medicine, business, the sciences, and majors related to technology (Seemiller & Grace, 2019). Moreover, Fall 2019 HERI survey results indicated that students in the health professions and those intending to pursue graduate or professional degrees are more concerned with the academic reputation of their intended major than students in other programs. Approximately 67% of students intending to major in the health professions, 65.7% of students intending to major in education, and 56.8% of students intending to major in engineering consider the academic reputation of their institution to be an important factor in their college decision, compared with 50.8% of students intending to major in art and humanities, 45.5% of students intending to major in the social sciences, 43.8% of students intending to major in English, and 24.8% of undecided students (Stolzenberg et al., 2019). A 2014 national survey, conducted on behalf of Northeastern University, found that 72% of college student respondents agreed that colleges should allow students to design their own programs of study. This not only reflects an intent to pursue multiple interests, but perhaps an interest in developing thinking and skills across domains. After graduation, this skill building has the potential to support multiple income streams or the pursuit of more than one career path.

Earlier in this chapter, the rising student and employer interest in experiential learning was introduced. Seemiller and Grace's Generation Z Stories Study (2019) found that college students in this generation have a desire to learn real-world knowledge and skills, and they consider applied learning to be the most enjoyable. The authors shared the words of one of their participants, which captures this interest: "Learning becomes especially enjoyable to me when I can connect content we learned in class to things I care about or things that are pertinent to what's happening in the world at the time" (2019, p. 204). Integrating internships, cooperative learning, service-learning, and other experiential opportunities into academic programs promises not only to better engage students, but to support career education efforts at the same time.

Video-based learning methods may also provide more traction with Generation Z. Some survey data have indicated that Generation Z high school and college students are seeking out information through YouTube and other video-based services (Barnes & Noble, 2015; Seemiller & Grace, 2016). Much has been made of the shortened attention spans of Generation Z due to increasing consumption of digital content (Seemiller & Grace, 2016; Turner, 2015; Twenge, 2017; Vidyarthi, 2011). Taken together, these insights have significant implications for how to best adapt our educational strategies to the needs of Gen Z students, especially as career educators consider the need to prepare them for future careers.

Career Aspirations

Now that some members of Generation Z are beginning to move through their first decade in the professional world, information has emerged about their aspirations, styles, and interests. The Millennial generation was found to have high expectations for career (Ng et al., 2010). Generation Z has expressed aspirations along the same lines, including the desire for social impact and a commitment to finding a career they will enjoy (Broadbent, 2017; Seemiller & Grace, 2016, 2019; The Center for Generational Kinetics, 2017). What perhaps makes Generation Z unique, then, is their profile as digital natives, who may be able to leverage technological skills, creativity, and entrepreneurship as a means to reconcile their high expectations with the market's stark realities. Indeed, we see that their interest in innovation and entrepreneurship continues to grow.

Broadbent et al.'s global study (2017) provided a sense of their motivations. Across all countries surveyed, Generation Z respondents rated opportunities to develop skills (24%), substantial pay (23%), opportunities for advancement (19%), opportunities to travel and meet new people (15%), and the ability to have a positive impact on the world (13%) as the most important factors when thinking about career. The authors noted that seeking celebrity status and fame was not a key driver for respondents, given that only 3% selected this as the most important factor. Seemiller and Grace (2019) also raised this tension of perception vs. reality when it comes to members of Generation Z seeking fame or notoriety. Though we often hear about Generation Z's active presence on social media, survey data paints a somewhat different picture of their perceived hunger for celebrity status. Certainly, some members of Generation Z may pursue social media influencing or other forms of celebrity as a career path, but there are still many members of the generation who are less interested in high-visibility careers.

One Northeastern University national innovation report found that 63% of Generation Z student respondents wanted colleges to teach entrepreneurship, and another 42% expected to work for themselves at some point (Northeastern University, 2014). This figure may be closer to 30% for members of Generation Z in Asia (ADECCO, 2014), yet still a substantial interest. Seemiller and Grace (2019) explored Generation Z's interest in entrepreneurship, suggesting that it may be the result of a combination of unique experiences, such as their observation of earlier generations' successful use of entrepreneurship as a path through educational and professional challenges, and that they may see potential for social impact. During the Covid-19 pandemic, one survey found that 65% of Generation Z respondents already in the workforce hoped to be running their own business in ten years. They ranked "generate original thought and ideas" as their primary characteristic of an ideal career. The survey summarized their findings on Generation Z's entrepreneurial interests by stating that "Gen Z will likely seek dynamic, challenging and meaningful careers that see them solving community problems by working collaboratively across borders" (EY, 2021, p. 11).

The so-called "gig" economy describes the varied, flexible work options that had begun to proliferate in the global market and expanded dramatically following the start of the Covid-19 pandemic (Parker et al., 2020; Ruyter et al., 2019). This form of work offers some of the things Generation Z may be looking for, if one ignores the financial instability of temporary employment. As with any form of work, there are some who have chosen the gig approach and others who may not be able to access full-time work. Though many have celebrated gig work as a more flexible alternative to traditional 9–5 work (Carleton, 2018), the emotional and physical risks of "gig" work have received media attention (King, 2019).

Regardless, we know that Generation Z aspires to use their creativity and familiarity with technology to design their work. Many have expressed an interest in invention and content creation, drawing on their talents for creativity and collaboration (Gentina, 2020; Seemiller & Grace, 2019). Creativity has grown in value in the global market, rising to the third most valued skill in 2020, from tenth in 2015 (World Economic Forum, 2016). Seemiller and Grace (2019) also name *creativity* as a unique strength of Generation Z, suggesting a fortuitous match as this generation moves through their careers.

Communication and collaboration in the workplace are areas of potential evolution. Some members of Generation Z are pushing back against email and other popular forms of communication and collaboration (June, 2021), citing their inefficiency and tendency to exacerbate stress and burnout. This argument is not a new one. Cal Newport (2016, 2021), who self-identifies as a Millennial, and others have argued for an evolution of work structures and tools for several years, yet an influx of Generation Z workers, and the seismic impacts of Covid-19 and the social justice movements following the murders of George Floyd and Breonna Taylor, may represent a tipping point. Common tools will likely evolve, as work itself changes and more members of this generation move into the workforce.

Reimagining Career Education for Generation Z

Based on these characteristics and values, we have the opportunity to reimagine both the content and delivery of career education. As we have seen, Generation Z calls upon us to integrate career education more seamlessly into the undergraduate experience, without adding significant time and cost to their degrees. They seek meaningful, experience-based learning that feels relevant and applicable to their futures. The potential to design their educational pathways and careers around their interests is compelling to many, and the skills and knowledge to support an entrepreneurial path to career, if not entrepreneurship itself, are valued. By and large, members of Generation Z have strong fluency with technology, managing multiple identities and branding, lending them a potential advantage in seeking new professional opportunities and building traction around ideas. Finally, many care about addressing issues relevant to the common good and supporting the global economy.

As career professionals redesign undergraduate career education, it is critical to prioritize equitable, accessible models that build upon the talents of Generation Z, leverage expanded technical toolkits, and deliver timely and relevant knowledge and skills to a generation who will inherit a changed global community, filled with both challenge and opportunity. Educational models that emphasize addressing practical problems, developing an authentic sense of professional identity, designing meaningful work, and developing diverse skills and interests hold special promise. Collectively, educators must put creative, innovative learning at the center, and most of all encourage students to lean into their own agency and adaptability, so that they – and the generations that follow – might carve out space for themselves in the new world of work, and find new solutions to the problems they identify.

Parts II–IV of this volume will contain several strategies for engaging this generation in career education programming, coursework, and services. These include interdisciplinary forms of experiential learning, strategies for equity and inclusion and addressing the needs of underserved students, narrative methods of career counseling, models for integrating career education into academic curricula, considerations for students' mental health and wellness, and paradigm shifts in the way we conceptualize careers and other approaches. These strategies promise to better serve not only members of Generation Z, but current students of all ages and those students of the future.

Chapter 3 of this part will address the future of work, and how the Covid-19 pandemic has impacted the way we engage, communicate, create, and learn as a global community. The world of work itself is the dynamic ecosystem we seek to prepare students for, and only with a sharp understanding of this context can we innovate intentionally and sustainably.

References

ADECCO. (2014). Generation Z – The next generation of workers in Asia. *An Adecco Asia Research Study & White Paper*, Quarter 2. https://adecco.co.th/uploads/Knowledge-Center/Survey-Research/Adecco-Thailand-white-paper-z-generation-of-workers-in-asia-eng.pdf

Altig, D., Baker, S., Barrero, J. M., Bloom, N., Bunn, P., Chen, S., Davis, S. J., Leather, J., Meyer, B., Mihaylov, E., Mizen, P., Parker, N., Renault, T., Smietanka, P., & Thwaites, G. (2020). Economic uncertainty before and during the COVID-19 pandemic. *Journal of Public Economics, 191*, 104274. https://doi.org/10.1016/j.jpubeco.2020.104274

American Academy of Child and Adolescent Psychiatry. (2011, March). Facts for families: Multiracial children (No. 71). www.aacap.org/App_Themes/AACAP/docs/facts_for_families/71_multiracial_children.pdf

America's Promise Alliance & Research for Action. (2021). *Where do we go next? Youth insights on the high school experience during a year of historic upheaval* [Report]. www.americaspromise.org/sites/default/files/d8/gradnation-062321.pdf

Barnes & Noble College. (2015). *Getting to know Gen Z: Exploring middle and high schoolers' expectations for higher education.* https://next.bncollege.com/wp-content/uploads/2015/10/Gen-Z-Research-Report-Final.pdf

Bresman, H., & Rao, V. D. (2017, August 25). *A survey of 19 countries shows how Generations X, Y, and Z are – and aren't – different.* Harvard Business Review. https://hbr.org/2017/08/a-survey-of-19-countries-shows-how-generations-x-y-and-z-are-and-arent-different

Broadbent, E., Gougoulis, J., Lui, N., Pota, V., & Simons, J. (2017, January). *Generation Z: Global citizenship survey.* www.varkeyfoundation.org/what-we-do/research/generation-z-global-citizenship-survey

Carleton, C. (2018, March 29). *Why are more people doing gig work? They like it.* The Conversation. https://theconversation.com/why-are-more-people-doing-gig-work-they-like-it-93037

Chon, M. G., & Park, H. (2020). Social media activism in the Digital Age: Testing an integrative model of activism on contentious issues. *Journalism & Mass Communication Quarterly,* 97(1), 72–97. https://doi.org/10.1177/1077699019835896

Class Central. (2016). *By the numbers: MOOCs in 2016.* www.class-central.com/report/mooc-stats-2016/

Common Sense Media. (2020). *Common sense media – SurveyMonkey poll: How teens are coping and connecting in the time of the coronavirus.* www.commonsensemedia.org/sites/default/files/uploads/pdfs/2020_surveymonkey-key-findings-toplines-teens-and-coronavirus.pdf

EAB. (2017). *Why do students decline their dream schools?* www.eab.com/blogs/enrollment/2017/03/why-do-students-decline-their-dream-schools

EY. (2021). *Gen Z is poised to reframe the future, but are business and education ready?* [Survey]. www.ey.com/en_gl/corporate-responsibility/how-business-and-education-can-help-gen-z-reframe-the-future

Farrell, W. C., & Phungsoonthorn, T. (2020). Generation Z in Thailand. *International Journal of Cross Cultural Management: CCM,* 20(1), 25–51.

Fast Company. (2015, November 16). *20 moments from the past 20 years that moved the whole world forward.* www.fastcompany.com/3052958/20-moments-that-matter

Federal Reserve Board. (2019). Report on the economic well-being of U.S. households in 2018 – May 2019. www.federalreserve.gov/publications/2019-economic-well-being-of-us-households-in-2018-student-loans-and-other-education-debt.htm

Ford Motor Company & BAV Consulting. (2015). *Ford 2015 trends report.* www.at.ford.com/content/dam/atford/archive/2014_NA/Dec/Ford-2015-TrendReportBook.pdf

Gentina, E. (2020). Generation Z in Asia: A research agenda. In E. Gentina & E. Parry (Eds.), *The new Generation Z in Asia: Dynamics, differences, digitalization* (pp. 3–19). Emerald.

Grisold, A., & Theine, H. (2017). How come we know? The media coverage of economic inequality. *International Journal of Communication, 11*, 4265–4284. https://ijoc.org/index. php/ijoc/article/view/6669

Jones, N. A., & Bullock, J. (2012, September). The two or more races population: 2010. *2010 Census Briefs.* www.census.gov/prod/cen2010/briefs/c2010br-13.pdf

June, S. (2021, July 10). Could Gen Z free the world from email? *The New York Times.* www. nytimes.com/2021/07/10/business/gen-z-email.html

King, E. (2019, August 29). *The mental and physical toll on gig economy laborers.* Allure. www. allure.com/story/gig-economy-mental-physical-pain-effects

Newport, C. (2016). *Deep work: Rules for focused success in a distracted world.* Grand Central Publishing.

Newport, C. (2021). *A world without email: Reimagining work in an age of communication overload.* Penguin.

Ng, E. S. W., Schweitzer, L., & Lyons, S. T. (2010). New generation, great expectations: A field study of the millennial generation. *Journal of Business and Psychology, 25*(2), 281–292. https://doi.org/10.1007/s10869-010-9159-4

Northeastern University. (2014, November 18). *"Generation Z" is entrepreneurial, wants to chart its own future.* https://news.northeastern.edu/2014/11/18/generation-z-survey/

Palley, W. (2012). *Gen Z: Digital in their DNA.* Thompson.

Parker, K., Horowitz, J. M., & Minkin, R. (2020, December 9). *How the Coronavirus outbreak has – and hasn't – changed the way Americans work.* Pew Research Center. www. pewresearch.org/social-trends/2020/12/09/how-the-coronavirus-outbreak-has-and-hasnt-changed-the-way-americans-work/

Pew Research Center. (2015, September 5). *The whys and hows of generations research.* www. pewresearch.org/politics/2015/09/03/the-whys-and-hows-of-generations-research/

Pew Research Center. (2018, November 15). *Early benchmarks show 'post-millennials' on track to be most diverse, best-educated generation yet: A demographic portrait of today's 6-to-21-year-olds.* www.pewsocialtrends.org/2018/11/15/early-benchmarks-show-post-millennials-on-track-to-be-most-diverse-best-educated-generation-yet/

Pinsker, J. (2020, February 21). *Oh no, they've come up with another generation label: How much do members of "Generation Alpha," or any generation, really have in common?* The Atlantic. www.theatlantic.com/family/archive/2020/02/generation-after-gen-z-named-alpha/606862/

Prensky, M. (2001). Digital natives, digital immigrants. *On the Horizon, 9*(5), 1–6. www. marcprensky.com/writing/Prensky%20-%20Digital%20Natives,%20Digital%20 Immigrants%20-%20Part1.pdf

Rideout, V. J., Foehr, U. G., & Roberts, D. F. (2010). *Generation M2: Media in the lives of 8–18-year-olds.* Kaiser Family Foundation.

Ruyter, A., Brown, A., & Brown, M. (2019). *The gig economy*. Agenda Publishing.

Sallie Mae. (2017). *How America pays for college*. www.salliemae.com/assets/Research/HAP/HowAmericaPaysforCollege2017.pdf

Seemiller, C., & Grace, M. (2016). *Generation Z goes to college*. Jossey-Bass.

Seemiller, C., & Grace, M. (2019). *Generation Z: A century in the making*. Routledge.

Stolzenberg, E. B., Aragon, M. C., Romo, E., Couch, V., McLenna, D., Eagan, M. K., & Kang, N. (2019, Fall). *The American freshman: National norms fall 2019*. Higher Education Research Institute. www.heri.ucla.edu/briefs/TFS-Brief-Report-2019.pdf

The Center for Generational Kinetics. (2017). *The state of Gen Z 2017: Meet the throwback generation*. http://3pur2814p18t46fuop22hvvu.wpengine.netdna-cdn.com/wp-content/uploads/2017/04/The-State-of-Gen-Z-2017-White-Paper-c-2017-The-Center-for-Generational-Kinetics.pdf

Turner, A. (2015). Generation Z: Technology and social interest. *The Journal of Individual Psychology, 71*(2), 103–113. https://doi.org/10.1353/jip.2015.0021

Twenge, J. (2017). *IGen: Why today's super-connected kids are growing up less rebellious, more tolerant, less happy – and completely unprepared for adulthood (and what this means for the rest of us)*. Atria Books.

Velez, E., Cominole, M., & Bentz, A. (2019). Debt burden after college: The effect of student loan debt on graduates' employment, additional schooling, family formation, and home ownership. *Education Economics, 27*(2), 186–206. https://doi.org/10.1080/09645292.2018.1541167

Vidyarthyi, N. (2011). *Attention spans have dropped from 12 to 5 minutes: How social media is ruining our minds*. www.adweek.com/socialtimes/attention-spans-have-dropped-from-12-minutes-to-5-seconds-how-social-media-is-ruiningour-minds-infographic/87484

Weber, K. M., & Keim, H. (2021). Meeting the needs of Generation Z college students through out-of-class interactions. *About Campus, 26*(2), 10–16. https://doi.org/10.1177/1086482220971272

World Economic Forum. (2016). *The future of jobs*. http://reports.weforum.org/future-of-jobs-2016/

3

The Future Isn't What It Used to Be! Revisiting the Changing World of Work After Covid-19

Tristram Hooley

> People ask me to predict the future, when all I want to do is prevent it. Better yet, build it. Predicting the future is much too easy, anyway. You look at the people around you, the street you stand on, the visible air you breathe, and predict more of the same. To hell with more. I want better.
>
> (Bradbury, 1982/1991, p. 155)

Predicting the future is notoriously difficult, and as Bradbury says, why would you want to? A successful prediction of the future robs individuals of their agency and accepts that the way things are is the way that they must be. If the future is fixed, my only role is to fit into it wherever I can, to go with the flow and find my place in the coming world. For career educators such a revelation is depressing, as when we support people in their career development, we are supporting them to make their world and shape the economy and society. But of course, gaining an understanding of the world and its possibilities is also a part of career learning. To misquote Marx, we might say that people make their careers, but they do not make them in the circumstances of their own choosing. If we recognise people's careers as the expression of agency in their life, learning and work, we still need to understand the circumstances within which they are doing it. Indeed, providing people with a strong understanding of the context within which they are operating and where key social and economic trends appear to be leading may be viewed as foundational knowledge for their career building and their wider social participation.

In this chapter I will look at the future of work and identify several key trends that need to be addressed in career education, but I will also argue against deterministic views of the future. As Bradbury argues, the future should be viewed as something to 'prevent' or make 'better' rather than as something to passively 'predict'.

DOI: 10.4324/9781003213000-5

The Changing World of Work

A few years ago, terrified by reading Ford's (2015) *Rise of the Robots*, I started to investigate the shadow that the imagined future throws on the way in which people develop their careers and the way in which career education responds to this (Hooley, 2017). In his influential book, Ford argued that growing levels of automation and artificial intelligence are eroding jobs and the likelihood that workers can find employment that will guarantee them the *good life*. Elsewhere, detailed research from Frey and Osborne (2017) demonstrated that many different occupations are highly susceptible to be automated and computerised.

But although there is evidence that automation is changing work, the economic, social and career implications of this development are much more contestable. Commentators variously argue that automation is nothing new and that there is no reason to believe that it will suddenly re-engineer society (Denning, 2015), that technological change typically leads to new innovations that create new jobs (David, 2015; Khan, 2016) and importantly that individuals, organisations and societies have choices about how they will respond to these changes (Srnicek & Williams, 2015). Ford's assumptions about the future are based on the somewhat improbable idea that while there will be major technological shifts, the existing power structures in society will remain stable, with robots continuing to enable the rich to get richer, whilst the rest of us passively watch our jobs, careers and livelihoods slip away.

The fact that the future is contested presents a dilemma for career educators. On one hand there is value in offering people insights about the future, perhaps encouraging them to read these accounts of automation and consider their response to them. On the other hand, the future appears to be uncertain and contested and this asks the career educator to take a different role, supporting critical enquiry and helping manage uncertainty and consider how the future can be influenced in ways that ensure that the fruits of society go to the wider populace rather than to the owners of the robots.

Yet career education has rarely taken this kind of critical stance on the future. In another article I analysed grey literature publications about the future of work and career education conferences which addressed this topic (Hooley, 2019). I concluded that career education has typically emphasised adaptive approaches to the future which encourage the individual to change and view the future as fixed and impossible to influence. I also argued that much thinking about the future makes use of a narrative that I describe as the '*changing world of work*'.

The 'changing world of work' groups together a set of commonly anticipated changes to working life and presents them as a largely inevitable future. These changes are strongly focused on technological innovations with particular attention given to automation and artificial intelligence, growing digital connectivity, big data, 3D printing and augmented reality. The changing world of work discourse also addresses several wider contextual challenges for our working lives, including demographic change, globalisation, the 'great' (post-2008) recession, environmental change and urbanisation, but these big contextual issues are often viewed as secondary to the technological transformation (the fourth industrial revolution) that is presumed to be driving the future.

The 'changing world of work' discourse recognises that many of these changes are contingent on political decisions and the decisions taken by employers, but it pushes a great deal of the responsibility for responding to change onto individuals. The world of work is presumed to be moving in an inevitable direction and individuals need to recognise this and develop their careers by increasing their human capital through education, training and retraining, becoming more entrepreneurial, comfortable with flexibility and precarity, enhancing their tech skills and learning to work alongside the robots. As such the role of career education has been viewed as that of championing *career adaptability* (Savickas, 1997) as the best strategy available to individuals to manage the coming challenges.

But of course, career adaptability is only one strategy that individuals can take in response to a challenging set of social, technological and economic shifts. An alternative approach might be to 'stand firm' (Brinkmann, 2017) and resist changes that threaten to make your life worse. Or to do as Bradbury says in the quote at the start of this chapter and build the future. These ideas underpin the social justice approach to career education which argues that, rather than trying to encourage individuals to embrace change, regardless of its content, and accommodate themselves to the world as it is, we should be trying to encourage them to analyse, question, come together and change the world in ways that make the pursuit of decent work and a positive career possible (Hooley et al., 2018).

The concept of decent work is particularly useful as it moves us away from a view of career education as being simply about helping people to find work and encourages a qualitative interrogation of what work is and what it should offer to individuals. The concept of 'decent work' has been championed by the International Labour Organization (ILO, 2021), which seeks to ensure that work offers access to social protection, respect, development opportunities and freedom from poverty and gender discrimination. In the career development field, it has been adopted by Blustein et al. (2016) as part of their psychology of working theory. The concept of decent *work* establishes an ethical floor for the level of adaptability that should be expected of human beings and suggests that the future of work needs to be organised around our needs rather than individuals being expected to fit in with a new world of work that fails to guarantee them access to the good life.

The 'changing world of work' narrative and the possibility of responding to it in a variety of different ways reminds us that career education is a fundamentally political endeavour. Helping people to imagine their future and deal with societal narratives about what is possible within that future is grounded in an ethical belief about what people deserve from life and a strategic decision about what is possible. The 'changing world of work' narrows the future and there are good reasons for career educators to resist this vision or at least to present their students with alternative visions to choose from.

Concerns about the politics of the 'changing world of work' miss a more fundamental objection. What if the world of automation, globalisation and responsibilisation described in the 'changing world of work' is just wrong? What if the future actually looks nothing like that? What if, in Bradbury's words, this narrative is 'just predicting more of the same' and that, as the present changes, perhaps under pressure from a major globally defining event or series of events, so too does the future?

Enter Covid-19

Looking back on the future described by the 'changing world of work' from the vantage point of 2021 it is difficult not to be struck by the glaring omission of pandemics. As policymakers and pundits worried about the rise of the robots and wrung their hands like a series of modern Prometheuses, the natural world struck back in a way that quickly transformed the present and future of working life.

It was not that the pandemic was impossible to predict. Indeed, Madhav et al. argued in 2017 that 'the likelihood of pandemics has increased over the past century because of increased global travel and integration, urbanization, changes in land use, and greater exploitation of the natural environment' (p. 315). We have created a world which is susceptible to pandemic due to environmental destruction, globalisation, unfettered movement of, at least some, people and the rolling back of the state and the loss of public and state capacity to rapidly manage a public health crisis (Navarro, 2020).

So, it was not that a pandemic was an unforeseeable possibility, but rather that it did not fit neatly into the future as imagined by the changing world of work. Their future was a future of digital technology, of globalisation, of enormous volumes of information and capital flowing around the world and ultimately of escape from the limitations of the natural world. The gloomy reality of Covid-19 originating in a wet market in China and making its way around the world through coughs and sneezes seemed to be part of a different story altogether.

Yet Covid-19 very quickly demonstrated that it had the power to transform work fundamentally. The pandemic both exerted a massive impact on the labour market conditions within which individuals were developing their careers and profoundly shaped individuals' psycho-social worlds, shifting what they believed was possible and what they wanted from their careers (Hooley, 2020). It quickly forced governments into making substantial reorganisations of the labour market (ILO, 2020) in ways that impacted on the working lives of individuals across the world.

Unemployment has risen sharply with many governments creating forms of employment support and subsidy that have prevented an even sharper rise (Organisation for Economic Co-operation and Development [OECD], 2020a). And unemployment is not the only change that is taking place in the labour market. Covid-19 is also impacting on the structure of the labour market, on the task composition of jobs, on the patterns and rhythms of work, and on the transitions into, within and out of the labour market (Anderton et al., 2020). And the economic impact of the pandemic is likely to be extended, with countries facing a 'long ascent' (Gopinath, 2020) out of recession as they deal with the loss of human capital and the withering of social capital and business networks during enforced lockdowns.

Nor will we just pick up from where we were, if and when the pandemic subsides. Covid-19 is likely to be a crossroads for our societies, opening the possibility for multiple different futures. Some hope that post-pandemic reconstruction will be about building a better future (OECD, 2020b), but Blakely (2020) pointed out that the crisis has seen many corporations and oligarchs enriching themselves in close collaboration with governments who have increased the power of the state and used it to shore up vested interests.

Yet the pandemic has also offered individuals a 'pedagogic moment' (Hooley et al., 2020) in which they can think about what they want from life, what they expect from their employer and their government and how they can develop strategies that will enable them to build a career in this new and challenging environment. It is this pedagogic moment that offers opportunities for career educators to engage with students' career thinking and encourage them to consider the wider implications of the pandemic on the future of work and society and their place within it. This requires a process of reframing where students are helped to view their personal crises and fears about accessing employment in a wider context and to consider how social and economic changes are intertwined with personal opportunity. Using materials that imagine various possible post-Covid-19 futures could be a useful stimulus for this process and, thankfully, there is no shortage of predictions about what the post-pandemic world will look like.

Analysing Visions of the Future

The rest of this chapter will be devoted to an account of what grey literature produced between the start of the pandemic in 2020 and May 2021 imagines the post-pandemic future will look like. I used a Google search for 'filetype:pdf "Covid-19"+"future of work"' to identify 40 papers which examine the future of work following the pandemic. These papers were saved, read, coded and analysed through thematic analysis (Clarke & Braun, 2014). This corpus of grey literature included papers produced by consultancies (15 papers), supra-national organisations (8), think tanks (4), universities (4), tech companies (3), NGOs (3), recruitment companies (2) and a professional association (1). As such it was very similar to the corpus reviewed in my previous work on the 'changing world of work' (Hooley, 2019) and included several of the same organisations.

The papers largely purported to take a global or international focus (24 papers), although this was mostly confined to a focus on the developed world, with only two papers shifting this focus to the developing world. The rest of the papers were either focused on a particular region like Asia-Pacific (2), Asia (1) or Europe (2), or they focused on a single country, with the largest proportion focused on the UK (8) due to my location, but also examples from India (1), Malaysia (1) and the USA (1).

The papers were heterodox with a variety of different styles, anticipated audiences and foci. Some concentrated on analysis of trends, others on policy solutions and others on the implications for business. Many of them contain interesting ideas and arguments, but in this analysis I am focusing on the commonalities between them. Consequently, I will not discuss issues that were only raised in one paper and will focus on issues that reoccur. This is qualitative research and so I do not make a claim for its representativeness. My initial Google search returned 197,000 responses and so it is very likely that another 40 (or more) papers could be found with different thematic foci. Nonetheless, the current analysis is offered to capture current discourse about the post-Covid-19 future.

The Post-Pandemic Future

The future imagined in these papers has changed substantially from the one described in the 'changing world of work' discourse. The feature of the post-pandemic future that is most discussed is *the shift to home and remote working* (mentioned in 25 of the 40 papers). This shift is viewed as having both positive and negative aspects as it increases work and life flexibility, but also poses a range of *mental health issues* (9) due to social isolation and the *blurring of the boundaries between work and homelife* (2). Some commentators anticipate that this is part of a *broader reduction in mobility* (8) which rolls back some of the existing and anticipated benefits of globalisation and encourages a renewed focus on *the importance of place* (6).

However, the *changing world of work* is not dead. Almost half of the papers (18) return to this technologically driven version of the future and make the argument that Covid-19 has *accelerated many of the changing world of work trends* that were seen as dominant in the pre-pandemic world. *Rapid technological change* (12), *automation* (12), *big data* (4) and the growing *dominance of digital communication* (10) continue to be seen as important features of the future. Concern about *environmental change* (2) is also apparent, albeit still as a minority concern in comparison with the perceived importance of technological change.

There is also a recognition that the future that individuals are now dealing with is likely to be a challenging one. Many papers anticipate *growing unemployment* (14), *economic and sectoral restructuring* (6), *labour shortages* (2) and a *rise in precarity* (6).

There are also predictions of *increasing inequality* (13), including a *growth in gender inequality* (12) and *worsening employment conditions for people with disabilities* (2) which are seen as reversing pre-pandemic trends towards greater equality. These negative shifts are fuelled by both the *Covid-19 recession* (12) and by pre-existing trends and may lead to a variety of *changes in the way that employees and customers behave* (3).

So, after the pandemic work is going to be remote and decentred, with people both more atomised and more tightly aligned to place. Technology continues to be a central driver of the future, with many arguing that the pandemic has entrenched and accelerated the 'changing world of work'. But the conditions within which the future worker is likely to be operating have deteriorated, leading to the decline of decent work, worsening living standards and growing inequality.

Responding to the Future

If the pandemic has darkened the vision of the future of work somewhat, it has also expanded the palette of responses that are viewed as being available. While the 'changing world of work' responsibilised individuals and put the state and organisations in a secondary position, the post-pandemic future rebalances this, viewing a much greater role for structural actors often working together in new forms of *public–private partnership* (4). There is a belief that *investing in more technology* (5) will enhance the effectiveness of other policies, but also a willingness to go beyond the technofix.

As a collection, the authors of the papers argued that the challenges of the future, particularly increased unemployment, precarity and inequality, will require a new approach from the state. At the heart of this is a need for a *revitalised welfare safety net* (11) accompanied by a range of *employment support* measures (11) including both wage subsidies and active labour market policies. Alongside this there is a need to develop human capital through *investment in education, training and retraining* (11).

There is also a desire to see the state intervening at a macro-economic level through *economic stimulus packages* (6), *support for entrepreneurship* (5), *localisation and regional regeneration* (2), *international development funding* (2), *environmental protection* (2) and *investment in technological infrastructure* (2) including enhancing broadband provision.

As well as an enthusiasm for public investment in the economy, there is also a view that the state should take a stronger regulatory role in shaping the future of work. This includes setting out *flexible working policies* (5), regulating *decent work* (3), ensuring *wellbeing at work* (3) and supporting *labour mobility* (2). There is also some enthusiasm for policies designed to support *gender equality* (3) and *families* (2).

Many of the policy pronouncements are echoed in recommendations about how businesses need to change and adapt. The argument is made repeatedly that businesses will need to *restructure and reorganise* (17) and that this will include *rethinking how productivity is measured* (8) as metrics based on inputs are likely to be less effective in a working world which is no longer based around presence at the office or workplace.

The most important specific change that businesses will have to make is the shift to *flexible working approaches* (20), including the normalisation of home and remote working, but also in some cases the increased use of a *precarious workforce* (3). Key to this is developing approaches that allow for *sociability and effective networking* (7) even when employees are physically distanced.

Managing these challenges means that organisations will need to *invest in new technologies* (17). They will also need to invest in people through *training and development* (11) to ensure that employees have the new skills that they need. Covid-19 raises the importance of a focus on *health and safety* (17). Organisations' continued viability is understood to be strongly linked to ensuring that staff can work safely. In many cases this is connected to a wider focus on *wellbeing* (14) that picks up concerns that remote working might create or increase mental health problems. There is also a commitment to ensuring the *diversity of the workforce* (4) and developing *family friendly* (2) policies to counterbalance growing inequalities.

This corpus of literature has less to say about the strategies that individuals can use in their careers. There is an expectation that individuals need to be ready to make *career changes* (5) in a dynamic situation and to take advantage of the opportunities to participate in employment programmes and access training. But, while the individual was viewed as a key actor within the changing world of work narrative, they are now dwarfed by more structural approaches and accorded relatively little importance in comparison to state and corporate actors.

The post-Covid-19 future is understood to be in flux. There is a desire to stabilise the situation around a new working paradigm, but also considerable awareness of some of the challenges and downsides in doing this. Forms of flexible working are viewed as the direction of travel, but there are big questions about how best to organise this. Furthermore, there is a pessimism about the macro-economic context for the future of work. Change is a lot easier if there is a lot of money around, yet these papers generally anticipate a recession, a fractured labour market and rising inequality.

These problems require big structural solutions of the kind that the state and to a lesser extent businesses and employers are better placed to make than individuals. So, the hope for the future is vested in investment in people and infrastructure, the active compensation for labour market failings and the willingness to mobilise the power of the state to safeguard the future. But where does the individual fit into this, what kind of career management is required and what does effective career education look like in this post-pandemic working future?

Reflections and Implications

Richard Nixon is supposed to have said 'we are all Keynesians now' when faced with a mounting crisis in the US economy in the early 1970s. In fact, the quote is probably more accurately attributed to Milton Friedman, who vociferously protested that it was taken out of context (Snider, 2016). But the mythology of the iconic bad boy of American conservatism turning to Keynesianism during troubled times proved powerful, with the story being frequently retold as policymakers argued about the correct response to the great recession of 2008 (Weibrot, 2008).

My analysis of the grey literature of the post-pandemic working future suggests that once again we are all Keynesians. The Covid-19 recession is understood to be threatening much of what we have held to be valuable and important about work. There appears to be little faith that laissez-faire economics can solve this crisis alone and so people are reaching out to the state for a wide range of forms of support and intervention.

Some may argue that this renewed belief in the state, in planning and in intervention in the economy marks the beginning of a political shift to the left. But, as Blakeley (2020, p. 59) argues, this is a misunderstanding: 'no matter how much a government spends on healthcare and education – or in this context furlough schemes and business loans – it will never become a socialist state'. What we are witnessing is more akin to 'corporate welfare' and a coming together of the political class and the corporate world. What is missing from the visions of the future set out above are the concepts of democracy, agency, self-determination and emancipation. The futures that we have explored in this chapter repeatedly ask how we can manage the crisis, but they rarely ask in whose interest we are managing it, nor envisage any kind of transfer of power and authority. These are questions that careers educators should encourage students to consider. Shifts in economic and political power shape the opportunity structure and determine career possibilities. To be effective, students' thinking about their own career needs to be built on analysis of what is, and what should be, happening in the world.

The fact that so many commentators ignore the question of what social and political interests are shaping the future leads them to fall back on the idea of technology as the key driver of change and provider of solutions. While the pandemic has reduced the importance of automation and the other technological features of the 'changing world of work', technology continues to loom over the future of work, eroding jobs and alienating workers. Yet, as Febvre (1935/1983) argued, technology should not be understood as an external force acting on society but rather as something that is enclosed within it. The nature of new technologies and the ends that they serve can be shaped, but again the question is who has the power to shape this and to what end? Once again career education has a role to play in questioning technological determinism and encouraging students to think about who owns and shapes the technologies that are shaping working futures. As Zuboff (2019) noted, big tech, aided and abetted by the state, is involved in a project of surveillance and reworking of our subjectivities. Given this, there is a strong case for careers educators to be encouraging students to reflect on the following: the technologies that they use; students' relationships to various technologies; how these might be shaping their career thinking; and what alternative ways might exist to organise and regulate the ownership of the technologies that are shaping the future.

Students finishing degree programmes are likely to look out on the pandemic economy and their future careers with trepidation. The crisis has damaged the global market for graduates and led to considerable fears that the current generation will suffer from substantial economic scarring (Institute of Student Employers, 2020). Against such a background many will enthusiastically support economic stimulus packages, employment support schemes and opportunities for retraining. Bigger questions about the organisation of society and the economy and the trajectory of the future may seem to be irrelevant to the immediate task of finding a job and making a successful start to your employment career.

As career educators, we have an opportunity to help students to see that their career development exists in a dialectic with the future. The analysis of the future of work that I have presented in this chapter suggests that students are likely to need a lot of help and support as they enter the labour market and navigate their way through it. Career educators need to be comfortable discussing the future with students as something that is contingent on political and economic uncertainty, rather than as something that is fixed and unalterable. Meanwhile, faculty members and instructors should encourage students to repurpose their academic research skills and criticality and turn it onto themselves, their careers and the wider world. Higher education should challenge and problematise the way things are and the future that is promised rather than school its students into uncritical acceptance of what might be (Rawlinson & Rooney, 2018).

An individualistic strategy for career development that emphasises the accumulation of human capital and the internalisation of career adaptability is unlikely to be sufficient. Effective careerists need to become adept readers of the political economy, analysing how decisions made in Washington, Brussels or Beijing are transforming what is expected from them in their career. The career education that we provide needs to help them to think through strategies for effective remote working and the use of digital communication and networking tools. But it also needs to help them to manage setbacks, to preserve their employability in times of recession, to access government programmes when necessary and to look after their mental and physical health.

In practice this might include encouraging students to reflect on their ideas about the future of work and analyse where these ideas come from. It should also encourage students to recognise their individual agency, and to see the possibilities that collective action opens up. This means forging a connection between career education and wider forms of civics and citizenship education. Within higher education such issues are most likely to be addressed within the curriculum where career professionals and faculty can collaborate to move away from instrumental forms of career education focused on the preparation of resumes and the moulding of the self to the requirements of the labour market. Instead, there is a need to create expansive and emancipatory career education curricula (Hooley, 2015, 2017) which encourage learners to:

- *explore themselves and the world where they live, learn and work*, e.g., by exploring their imagined future and the kind of place within the world that they hope to inhabit;
- *examine how their experience connects to broader historical political and social systems*, e.g., by reviewing predictions about the future and considering their impact on their career aspirations;
- *develop strategies that allow individuals to make the most of their current situation*, e.g., by considering what skills, knowledge and experience might be useful in various imagined futures;
- *develop strategies that allow groups to work together and make their most of their current situation*, e.g., by thinking about the institutions, associations, networks and forms of reciprocity and mutual aid that might be able to support career building in the imagined future; and
- *consider how the current situation and structures should be changed*, e.g., by considering issues of justice, fairness and ethics to evaluate possible futures and issues of power and politics to consider how the future might be influenced.

Above all, career education should empower those who receive it to have a critical engagement with the world of work and the future. It should point out that the future is not what it used to be and remind people that the political possibilities and opportunity structures of today looked different yesterday, and may look different again tomorrow. Before the pandemic commentators advocated a vision of the future dominated by robots, the gig economy and the free movement of capital, goods and labour around the globe. After the pandemic, the political economy has changed, the world looks different and the future has been rewritten to be one of homeworking, state intervention and growing inequality. The future, as ever, tells us more about what is happening now than it does about what will happen next, and it is career educators' responsibility to remind students of the contingency of the future and to help them to recognise their agency in shaping it.

Against such a constantly morphing and highly political future, career education should encourage students to engage in norm criticism (Wikstrand, 2018) by questioning received wisdom about what is desirable and what the future will hold. It should build their critical consciousness, help them to reach out and make common cause with others and recognise that the future does not have to be the same as the present and that it certainly should not be worse (Hooley et al., 2018). If career education achieves nothing else it should inspire students to look at their future, the futures of their classmates and the future of the world and say, 'to hell with more. I want *better*'.

References

Anderton, R., Botelho, V., Consolo, A., de Silva, A. D., Foroni, C., Mohr, M., & Vivian, L. (2020). The impact of the COVID-19 pandemic on the euro area labor market. *ECB Economic Bulletin.* www.ecb.europa.eu/pub/economic-bulletin/articles/2021/html/ecb.ebart202008_02~bc749d90e7.en.html

Blakely, G. (2020). *The Corona crash: How the pandemic will change capitalism*. Verso.

Blustein, D. L., Olle, C., Connors-Kellgren, A. C., & Diamonti. A. J. (2016). Decent work: A psychological perspective. *Frontiers in Psychology, 7*, 1–10. https://doi.org/10.3389/fpsyg.2016.00407

Bradbury, R. (1982/1991). Beyond 1984: The people machines. In *Yestermorrow: Obvious answers to impossible futures*. Joshua Odell Editions, Capra Press.

Brinkmann, S. (2017). *Stand firm: Resisting the self-improvement craze*. Polity Press.

Clarke, V., & Braun, V. (2014). Thematic analysis. In T. Teo (Ed.), *Encyclopedia of critical psychology* (pp. 1947–1952). Springer. https://doi.org/10.1007/978-1-4614-5583-7_311

David, H. (2015). Why are there still so many jobs? The history and future of workplace automation. *The Journal of Economic Perspectives, 29*(3), 3–30. https://doi.org/10.1257/jep.29.3.3

Denning, S. (2015, June 4). The 'jobless future' is a myth. *Forbes*. www.forbes.com/sites/stevedenning/2015/06/04/the-robots-are-not-coming/#6d10363c2e39

Febvre, L. (1935/1983). Reflections on the history of technology. *History and Technology, An International Journal, 1*(1), 13–18. https://doi.org/10.1080/07341518308581612

Ford, M. (2015). *Rise of the robots: Technology and the threat of a jobless future*. Basic Books.

Frey, C. B., & Osborne, M. A. (2017). The future of employment: How susceptible are jobs to computerisation?. *Technological Forecasting and Social Change, 114*, 254–280. https://doi.org/10.1016/j.techfore.2016.08.019

Gopinath, G. (2020, October 13). A long, uneven and uncertain ascent. *IMFblog*. https://blogs.imf.org/2020/10/13/a-long-uneven-and-uncertain-ascent/

Hooley, T. (2015). *Emancipate yourselves from mental slavery: Self-actualisation, social justice and the politics of career guidance*. International Centre for Guidance Studies, University of Derby.

Hooley, T. (2017). A war against the robots? Career guidance, automation and neo-liberalism. In T. Hooley, R. G. Sultana, & R. Thomsen (Eds.), *Career guidance for social justice: Contesting neoliberalism* (pp. 93–107). Routledge.

Hooley, T. (2019). Career guidance and the changing world of work: Contesting responsibilising notions of the future. In M. A. Peters, P. Jandrić, & A. J. Means (Eds.), *Education and technological unemployment* (pp. 175–191). Springer.

Hooley, T. (2020, November 12). *A global pandemic and its aftermath: The way forward for career guidance* [Keynote address]. Austrian Euroguidance Conference. http://hdl.handle.net/10545/625540

Hooley, T., Sultana, R. G., & Thomsen, R. (2018). Towards an emancipatory career guidance: What is to be done?. In T. Hooley, R. G. Sultana, & R. Thomsen (Eds.), *Career guidance for emancipation: Reclaiming justice for the multitude* (pp. 247–257). Routledge.

Hooley, T., Sultana, R. G., & Thomsen, R. (2020, March 23). *Why a social justice informed approach to career guidance matters in the time of coronavirus.* Career Guidance for Social Justice. https://careerguidancesocialjustice.wordpress.com/2020/03/23/why-a-social-justice-informed-approach-to-career-guidance-matters-in-the-time-of-coronavirus/

Institute of Student Employers. (2020). *Covid-19: Global impacts on graduate recruitment.* Institute of Student Employers.

International Labour Organization. (2020). ILO monitor. Covid-19 and the world of work, 6. www.ilo.org/wcmsp5/groups/public/@dgreports/@dcomm/documents/briefingnote/wcms_755910.pdf

International Labour Organization. (2021). *Decent work.* www.ilo.org/global/topics/decent-work/lang--en/index.htm

Kahn, M. (2016, May 14). Robots won't just take jobs, they'll create them. *TechCrunch.* https://techcrunch.com/2016/05/13/robots-wont-just-take-jobs-theyll-create-them/

Madhav, N., Oppenheim, B., Gallivan, M., Mulembakani, P., Rubin, E., & Wolfe, N. (2017). Pandemics: Risks, impacts, and mitigation. In D. T. Jamison, H. Gelband, S. Horton, P. Jha, R. Laxminarayan, C. N. Mock, & R. Nugent (Eds.), *Disease control priorities: Improving health and reducing poverty* (3rd ed.) (pp. 315–346). The International Bank for Reconstruction and Development/The World Bank. https://doi.org/10.1596/978-1-4648-0527-1_ch17

Navarro, V. (2020). The consequences of neoliberalism in the current pandemic. *International Journal of Health Services, 50*(3), 271–275. https://doi.org/10.1177/0020731420925449

Organisation for Economic Co-operation and Development. (2020a). *Job retention schemes during the COVID-19 lockdown and beyond.* www.oecd.org/coronavirus/policy-responses/job-retention-schemes-during-the-covid-19-lockdown-and-beyond-0853ba1d/

Organisation for Economic Co-operation and Development. (2020b). *Building back better: A sustainable, resilient recovery after COVID-19.* www.oecd.org/coronavirus/policy-responses/building-back-better-a-sustainable-resilient-recovery-after-covid-19-52b869f5/

Rawlinson, M., & Rooney, S. G. (2018). Schooled in the work ethic. In T. Hooley, R. G. Sultana, & R. Thomsen (Eds.), *Career guidance for emancipation: Reclaiming justice for the multitude* (pp. 201–215). Routledge.

Savickas, M. L. (1997). Career adaptability: An integrative construct for life-span, life-space theory. *The Career Development Quarterly, 45*(3), 247–259. https://doi.org/10.1002/j.2161-0045.1997.tb00469.x

Snider, J. (2016, July 8). We're all Keynesians now because we have no choice. *Real Clear Markets.* www.realclearmarkets.com/articles/2016/07/08/were_all_keynesians_now_because_we_have_no_choice_102254.html

Srnicek, N., & Williams, A. (2015). *Inventing the future: Postcapitalism and a world without work*. Verso.

Weisbrot, M. (2008, January 25). We're all Keynesians – again. *The Guardian*. www.theguardian.com/commentisfree/2008/jan/25/wereallkeynesiansagain

Wikstrand, F. (2018). Norm criticism: A method for social justice in career guidance. In T. Hooley, R. G. Sultana, & R. Thomsen (Eds.), *Career guidance for emancipation: Reclaiming justice for the multitude* (pp. 216–231). Routledge.

Zuboff, S. (2019). *The age of surveillance capitalism*. Profile Books.

Part II
Critical Considerations, Inclusion, and Equity in Career Education

4
Defining Equity and Inclusion in the Future of Career Education

Tierney Bates

The way of work is evolving into a new paradigm in which the digital revolution highlights historic, yet recurring issues of social mobility, equity, accessibility, and belonging (Allen, 2019; Avramo, 2016; Veldhoen, 2013). The routine jobs of just managing day-to-day responsibilities – and repeat the cycle – have given way to positions with varied responsibilities that might serve as stepping stones for career advancement (Savickas, 2010). As the world of work changes from stability to social mobility (i.e., meaning one's ability to change their status, relative to their social location), part of the new discussion has focused on building out equity in career development through innovative strategies. The emphasis on diversity, equity, and inclusion work has become heightened since the death of George Floyd in May 2020 (Maurer, 2020). There has been a call by higher education, non-profits, and corporate industries to address equity and racial reckoning, and with the passing of Juneteenth as a holiday as a symbolic moment in June 2021, there is still more work to be done. Despite the previous call to action as presented by Pope et al. (2013) in defining social justice as a principle for the development of the National Career Development Association nearly a decade ago, more opportunities exist for student affairs and career development educators to assume a role in the promotion of equity and inclusion.

Career centers play an important role in the ongoing effort to address equity issues. These career centers will continue to evolve and make meaningful impacts. The field of career practitioners and centers is the gateway for college graduates and corporate America, a relationship that is still rooted in inequality regimes (Acker, 2006). According to Acker (2006), "inequality regimes are defined as the processes, actions, and meanings that result in and maintain class, gender, and race inequalities within particular organizations" (p. 442). *It is an analytic approach to understanding the ongoing creation of inequalities in work organizations.* More recently, the field has begun to endorse the importance of "career-enabling environment for promoting equality of opportunity and social inclusion" (Wong & Tip, 2018); however, when

DOI: 10.4324/9781003213000-7

working with historically disadvantaged populations, the majority of organizations struggle. These struggles exist due to the organizational culture, unconscious bias among team members, societal segregation, and a lack of inclusive thought due to the rootedness of Whiteness across systems and existing structures. Despite efforts to increase representation through recruiting efforts, training programs, and internal career development, the organizational culture may still be homogenous.

According to Smith and Small (2021), at a time when diversity, equity, and inclusion are at the forefront of companies, recruiting efforts need to evolve. Simultaneously, higher education enrolls more first-generation, low-income, historically disadvantaged students, and economic mobility has become a critical social justice priority for institutions. Career centers are in the business of equity, by helping historically disadvantaged and underrepresented communities gain the access and social mobility that sets them up for the future (Smith & Small, 2021). Career development educators have an opportunity to build relationships with employers, students, and organizations within their industry areas of interest. They can also gain an understanding of practices of diversity, equity, and inclusion within professional workplace environments and career development. This chapter will provide suggestions on how to create meaningful equitable, employee–employer relationships in the workplace. Ideally, all employees feel a sense of belonging and feel like their contributions are validated. By doing this, career educators are truly setting up our Black/Black Indigenous People of Color (BIPOC) and Lesbian, Gay, Bisexual, Transgender, Queer/Questioning, Intersex and Asexual students, and other marginalized groups like students with disabilities, for success. Career educators are capable of preparing students for the potential realities of "corporate or organizational trauma," which is low-level psychological stress and anxiety created by many corporate cultures. This happens in particular when microaggressive environments are not addressed (Chick, 2019; Jacobsen, 2012). At the same time, career educators are leveling the playing field and building a stronger conversation around a career development movement to right-side historical wrongs. Creating a consciousness of inclusion is a goal for career practitioners, along with helping students to be successful, growing organizational footprints, and holding employers accountable for creating a sense of equity, inclusion, and belonging.

Inequality Regimes

Today, all societal structures – public and private sector organizations, institutions of higher education, charitable organizations, and others are founded upon inequality regimes (Acker, 2006). From a historical perspective, the rules are designed for the preservation of White privilege – carefully constructed over centuries – and this translates directly into corporate policies, regulations, and "rules of behavior" that we know of today (Birk, 2021). The career counseling field that currently exists grew out of efforts at the beginning of the twentieth century to help recent immigrants and others with limited resources achieve the American Dream (Flores, 2009), and efforts to find work for majority White cis-gendered men. What Flores does not mention is that, at the beginning of the twentieth century, many Black/BIPOC communities were ostracized from this American Dream. It is the reason the Committee on Urban Conditions Among Negroes was established on September 29, 1910, in New York City, which we now know as the National Urban League (Library of Congress, 2021). Over the last 100 years, opportunities to achieve this American Dream have not been available to all individuals in our country. The career choices of BIPOC are influenced by a few factors: the economic ability to gain higher education and access, the careers available to BIPOC, and the type of careers historically allowed (Milan-Tyner, 2018). Prior to the 1960s, Black/BIPOC were not allowed to even attend Predominantly White Institutions (PWIs), therefore lacked access to education, career options, and laws. This has led to contemporary gaps and shortages in many fields for BIPOC (Journal of Blacks in Higher Education, 2021). According to Rothstein (2018), the history of state-sponsored segregation stretches as far back as the 1800s and exposes racially discriminatory policies, put forward by most presidential administrations at that time, including liberal presidents such as Franklin D. Roosevelt. If America is a byproduct of local, state, and national government policies, then corporate entities, non-profits, and educational institutions (private or public) are as well, and these organizations have reproduced systems of oppression, disparity, and biased perception. Over time, this has led to inequality regimes, poor occupational attainment, and underrepresentation in careers fields. Twenty-five years ago, Blustein et al. (1995) presented what has become foundational work in the area of career behavior and attachment theory. In more contemporary work, Blustein et al. (2019) examined the inequities in access to decent work, the psychology of working, and the implications of a changing world for career development educators (Gutowski et al., 2021).

Contemporary literature supports the fact that hierarchies, hiring managers, team structure, employees, professional organizations, and privilege itself shape how career centers and educators have contributed to the legitimate visible and invisible inequalities directly affecting gender roles, race conforming or inferiority, accessibility, recruitment, and social influences. Career centers, career coaches, counselors, even recruiters and human resources managers will need to lead with a consciousness of inclusion for the future of workforce development, and no longer participate in ways of the past. Career educators must be readily engaged in developing cultural competency, language, and unconscious bias. Dawis (2005) explained the theory of work adjustment, which describes the relationship of the individual to their work environment. This theory aligns with the person–environment fit model that predicts how well individuals will adjust to their job environment, and whether their abilities match up. This model may not be adequate to address concerns of our diverse body of students today, who may be concerned with challenges such as imposter syndrome (Harper & Hurtado, 2007). Dey and Cruzvergara (2014) discussed the shifts in delivery of career guidance, where career counseling emerged around the same period as civil rights movements (1960s–1970s). The more contemporary message from Dey and Cruzvergara (2014) encompasses the values of inclusivity and social justice in career delivery services, with significant emphasis on the role of culture and language.

Culture and Language

Peter Drucker (2006) stated that culture eats strategy for breakfast. Yet, when thinking through the ability to address changes within the field of career education and development, there must be the acknowledgement of the homogeneous culture within many organizations. Even within university career centers and the field of career education itself there exists a dominant ethnic, imperialistic, heteronormative, and patriarchal structure. Organizations and career practitioners must understand that they have conditions, culture, practices, and environments rooted in White supremacy, and that they may lack the leadership to dismantle these climates and systems (Milan & Tyner, 2018). In Black/BIPOC communities, collectivism is often embraced. Many individuals from these communities grow up looking out for each other, and this is how many have survived (Healy et al., 2004). The western, United States culture orientation fosters a sense of self as independent, yet many other cultures foster a sense of self as interdependent with others (Fouad & Kantamneni, 2020). In many western workplaces, collectivism is often overshadowed by the dominant culture and stigmatized by other cultures due to microaggressions and lack of understanding. Employees in these workplaces may not be embraced for their difference, and may be pressured to assimilate (Sue et al., 2007). In White culture and many organizations, individualism is supported and praised. There is a dissonance regarding why organizations need change and how they must address the dismantling of corporate trauma, harmful language, and an idea of "fit."

Language of "Fitness"

In hiring, how often have you heard these words, "*You were a great candidate, but it came down to fit*"? In higher education and corporate culture, we have the chance to dismantle the concept of "fit." Fit especially affects Black/BIPOC people and those from historically disadvantaged groups. As organizations examine options to increase diversity, dismantling "fit" is an area they may want to review first. Within the last year, we have seen the awakening of two pandemics in America, one health related (Covid-19) and the other race related (Black Lives Matter). With race and for the sake of this chapter, "fit" ostracizes historically disadvantaged groups and impacts those groups by keeping them from bringing their excellence, creativity, experience, and authenticity to many workspaces. There is a connection between the ideologies shaping perspectives of "fit" and implicit bias in employment discrimination (Jones, 2016), and these ideologies are grounded in the implicit biases of people (Eberhardt, 2019).

"Fit" is either an adjective or a verb, describing a candidate, or defining the potential actions of the candidate. For more than 20 years, researchers have attempted to influence how organizations use "fit" in their hiring practices (Bowen et al., 1991). Research suggests that this concept is based upon Eurocentric ideation. It was never developed with historically disadvantaged groups in mind, just like higher education in America was designed for dominant identities, relationships, and elitism. Crain and Shephard (2019) described "fit" as an ambiguous criterion used by some employers to justify social barriers in the hiring practice. For many, those social barriers have been in place for generations. Over the last two years, individuals and communities have witnessed the world expand with transformational social and racial ideas. Still, many corporate organizations or educational institutions employ performative acts to hire historically disadvantaged groups. Where many organizations will fail is in neglecting internal reviews of culture and policies that impact their hiring (Dobbin et al., 2011).

The biggest mistake is lumping together the concept of fitness and actions around diversity. According to McKinsey (2021), data shows the needle has not moved at most PWIs or corporate organizations. According to the National Center for Education Statistics, 6% of postsecondary faculty in 2017 were Black, 5% were Hispanic, and less than 1% were American Indian/Alaska Native. Black and Hispanic faculty are notably underrepresented compared with Black and Hispanic students, who make up 14 and 20% of the undergraduate student population, respectively. It is theorized that PWIs and corporations have not intentionally designed what they desire with cultural variations and accountability measures (Dobbin & Kaley, 2016), therefore creating more performative acts, reactions, and lack of trust. There are the statements of diversity, committees, and hiring of staff but most organizations who may look diverse in appearance are intrinsically homogenous. Organizations will hire the same profile of people, even when that person is from a historically disadvantaged group, based on one's pedigree, background, institution, or who they know. It will take bold leadership to promote within and recruit more historically disadvantaged groups, build pipelines, and rectify wrongs by putting money, time, talent, and resources where they need to go. According to Asare (2019), Chief Diversity Officers (CDOs) are more frequently set up to fail despite their role within an organization. Without the resources to be executive thought leaders, CDOs are often dealing with an unreasonable number of problems on their plate, along with unrealistic expectations. This is tied back to career educators in developing their own metrics and development working with undergraduates, while being a part of the solution in support for CDOs and all campus outcomes on diversity, equity, and inclusion. If an organization wants to move the needle, leaders must move it by creating a new culture, a space that is brave and inclusive where "fit" is not the norm and culture and diversity are valued.

Focus on Cultural Adds

Critics will contend that human resource directors and hiring managers examine each candidate's qualifications, experience, and education, but to critics one responds that when fit has been steeped in Whiteness and speaks to some personality type and qualification, it fails to consider cultural or racial identity. Even with all the education and experience, BIPOC and other marginalized individuals are still overlooked for job roles. Research demonstrates that highly credential BIPOC candidates are still less likely to be hired over less qualified non-minority candidates (McDonald, 2021). For BIPOC people in job searches, race and racial politics is always a consideration that weighs on their mind because evidence suggests it profoundly impacts the hiring process (Niccum, 2019). Most White employees are conditioned to having their feelings and actions normalized, and often do not have to worry about being scrutinized. This is where "corporate trauma" persists. Trauma is defined as a deeply distressing or disturbing experience or emotional shock following a stressful event, shock, or physical injury. This trauma for historically disadvantaged groups has been rooted in workplace treatment and performance for years and passed down by generations, resulting in turnover, racial battle fatigue, and ongoing microaggressions (Pitcan et al., 2018; Romano, 2019). Microaggressions have become an unspoken social norm in many organizations, resulting in feelings of isolation, alienation, and imposter syndrome for BIPOC people, who expose themselves in corporate settings to normalized behavior that demonstrates hostility and negative stereotypes of historically disadvantaged groups (Harper, 2017; Harper & Hurtado, 2007). According to Harper, who was cited in an article by Megan Zahneis (2021) in the *Chronicle of Higher Education*, West and Hannah-Jones's cases send an important message to Black academics.

> It signals to every Black scholar that if this kind of disrespect and these miscarriages of justice can be done to Cornel West and Nikole Hannah-Jones, certainly you are not exempt from also experiencing similar miscarriages of justice, no matter how accomplished you are, no matter how productive and prolific you are.
> (Zahneis, 2021, para. 19)

In reality what an organization needs is an entirely new contrast or dimension to recast hiring that brings forth education, innovation, creativity, and language. Dialogue around organizational-wide language, intersectionality, and defining each of the words (diversity, equity, inclusion, and belonging) is important since they all have a unique definition. For organizations, the skills and talents of BIPOC people impact the bottom line for companies and the educational environment of colleges. If hiring managers and organizations want to truly embrace BIPOC people and historically disadvantaged groups of talent, they have to be designed intentionally; they must appreciate their identities, mind/body, and lived experiences. The sane message can be applied to other marginalized individuals in workplace settings, including LGBTQPIA+ and those individuals with disabilities. Practical applications exist that organizations and managers can apply to benefit themselves and employees.

Practical Applications

Organizations can start changing by having leaders operate with inclusivity in mind, by developing an equity-inspired design (design think) to address barriers and inequities along with an inclusive workplace model. Administrators can start by dismantling fit and move folks from being invisible to visible. Here are a few questions and suggestions to think about.

- How does the organization define *diversity*?
- How does the organization define *equity*?
- How does the organization define *inclusion*?
- All three words must be defined and designed with language, measurements, and accountability. None of this will happen just because you hire more BIPOC people.
- Examine and review the onboarding and training processes as an organization.
- Use equity-inspired design think, which is a tool for innovative practice.
- Create an organizational-wide language and designed language use document.
- Analyze and change terms or code words rooted in Whiteness like professionalism, communication skills, or fit.
- Reflect and understand words, meanings, and culture from Black, Indigenous, and People of Color in the organization.
- Contextualize the pay gap for women and directly address how it looks different for Women of Color.
- Review same-sex or domestic partner benefits and make needed changes to address any inequities.

Career Education and Employer Relations

Career educators are uniquely positioned to work both with employers and students to transform current practices and contribute to larger campus efforts to promote diversity, equity, and inclusion into meaningful institutional change. The group of young adults currently entering college and comprising Generation Z (Gen Z) is said to be the most ethnically diverse generation in US history (Williams, 2015). Career educators may have already experienced a rise in identity-related questions in their sessions and met their needs. Gen Z already has had such a huge impact on how we shape our societal structures and communities. This is not to discount the work that has been done, and is being done, throughout previous generations, but Gen Z is a highly tech-savvy, values-driven group that is highly sought after by employers right now, and holds a specific power to influence hiring and employment practices (Seemiller & Grace, 2016).

Career education is where there is a unique opportunity to shift culture and pedagogy. The role of career and student services is to create quality learning, experiences, service, and support for students, and help improve the student experience with employment and social connection (Hill et al., 2003). The function of career education varies from institution to institution, but the most important component is how we merge students' academic and emotional needs with their personal development and practical use (McInnis, 2004). The changing student demographics, plus the relative ease of making connections via today's technology, along with the current social environment, serve as a foundation for the shifting need to provide more equitable access to social mobility and experiences (Chan & Cruzvergara, 2021). Through various courses, programs, and curriculum activity, career education must adapt to the needs of industry change and student expectations. The development of *Design Your Life* (Burnett & Evans, 2016), or Life Design, depicts the opportunity for career practitioners to pivot to a model of learning one's ideation on life and designing the type of work or career mapping to one's life and work views. These are various ways of thinking that influence how individuals will pick a career, end up in a career, or get unstuck from a career. A life designer is willing to ask questions, use wayfinding, and implement prototypes (Burnett & Evans, 2018). This format can have a major impact on how we use equity design thinking to address our career education and curriculum but even impact historically disadvantaged groups in teaching, who do not fully utilize career centers resources or programs, oftentimes waiting until it is too late into their final semester.

Life design concepts can be applied to a range of work-related contexts, including major and career decision-making, workplace issues, technology advances, equity and social justice issues, and preparing for an uncertain future of work (Burnett & Evans, 2021). Another advantage of life design approaches is their application to cross-cultural work environments (Wen et al., 2020). For many historically disadvantaged groups, taking a life design course improves their ability for wayfinding and prototyping. Therefore, career education could implement, from first year to senior year, a built-out curriculum taken by all students (especially marginalized student populations) focusing on inclusion, community, exploration, transitioning from university life, and appreciation of cultural horizons for students and staff. The contribution to the quality of career education will rely on career educators to lead within every aspect of their content delivery with diversity, equity, and inclusion in mind. Current and future career educators must look at innovative ideas and programs such as the University of North Carolina Chapel Hill University Career Services (Suggestions and Implications) and apply the new National Association of Colleges and Employers eight career-ready competencies (Gray, 2021) with the recent update of diversity, equity, and inclusion as a pillar into best practices and lead with it into every aspect of career education. The objective needs to demonstrate the awareness, attitude, knowledge, and skills required to equitably engage and include people from different local and global cultures, while actively engaging in anti-racist practices that actively challenge the systems and structures (Kendi, 2019).

Dismantling Existing Systems

For employers, career readiness can be defined as a foundation from which to demonstrate requisite core competencies that broadly prepare the college educated for success in the workplace and lifelong career management. Career readiness plays an important role in sourcing talent, providing a means of identifying key skills and abilities across all job functions. Similarly, career readiness offers employers a framework for developing talent through internship and other experiential education programs. Applying the NACE (2021) career readiness competencies as a framework, a relationship exists between employer relations and the integration of educating recruiters and employers on their practices and culture of corporate trauma. A critical lens focused on diversity, equity, and inclusion is needed where one might not be aware of the process of organizational validation. That validation must address accountability of measured inclusion in organizational practices and policy. Most recently, the Employer Anti-Racism and Gender Equality Scorecard was developed at the University of North Carolina at Chapel Hill University Career Services by Director of Employer Relations Roderick Lewis. This cutting-edge guide focuses on advancing equality and equity in the workplace, community, and academia. This guide has 12 rubrics, 36 metrics, and attachments that help organizations do an interval review and then set forth accountability on change management. Employer relations within centers and practitioners is where many career practitioners and centers have the greatest responsibility to address diversity, equity, and inclusion. In fact, since racism is part of the very cultural fabric in which we live in the United States, it often goes unnoticed, ignored, or denied. Racism becomes much like the air we breathe – it becomes normalized. Most individuals have no reason to dare or even think about questioning that which is normal – that which is business as usual (Hughes, 2014). Institutional racism persists due to a powerful system of privilege and power based on race. Those powerful structures begin and are perpetuated by seemingly innocent, normal events and daily occurrences and interactions. A large body of research exists that clearly suggests that employers tend to hire and rehire individuals who tend to act and look exactly like themselves (Hughes, 2014).

This is where the opportunity for career educators and organizations to truly self-assess best practices and look intrinsically for growth and build a culture of diversity, equity, and inclusion within the work environment lies. No longer can a culture or work environment remain homogenous in an evolving workforce and innovative society. Senior leaders should look to move beyond just adding more diversity and into creating a value of inclusion. The internal review of inequity regimes, policies, practices, and unconscious bias run prevalent in many organizations, even with the best of intent to create more diverse hiring pools. There needs to be employer relations accountability on how an organization should prioritize courage to speak, curiosity, cultural intelligence, and enabling the cultures within the organization to leverage their shared and lived experiences as actionable items. This includes understanding what words, meanings, and culture have an impact on your historically marginalized students, including BIPOC and LGBTQA+ students. Leadership should be bold, genuine, and reflective with a strategy that includes professional development, financial commitment, and key performance indicators. Career educators and leaders must keep evolving their cultural landscape internally and externally to truly build an inclusive workplace. This is more prevalent than ever before, since employers must inform and differentiate their talent strategies, as they now face a work environment that has five generations in the workforce, with five different views on the workplace and ideas. Other questions to consider: how are we making proximity and access to power accessible to BIPOC people in corporate spaces? What are existing LGBTQA policies as they relate to equity? (Reneau & Love, 2021). How are workspaces being made more accessible for persons with disabilities? What are organizations doing to reduce the pay inequities? What changes are being implemented around accessibility? Are inequities still being perpetuated? Here are some concrete suggestions for career practitioners to build an inclusive workplace, and help corporations and employers implement change management.

Suggestions and Implications

A number of approaches can be applied for career educators and leaders to evolve their cultural landscape, including:

1. Start to build out an inclusive workplace model: how is that initiated? Start with independent focus groups, produce a climate survey among staff, and even town hall meetings, where staff can learn and contribute, without fear of retribution. The goal would be to learn if employees feel unsafe, unheard, and invisible, or do they have to mask themselves and assimilate; this will speak to the organizational culture.
2. Look at executive leadership, mid-level managers, and your demographics internally. They should reflect the institution, the community you live or belong to, state or national trends. If that is not the case, implement a plan to change or develop protocols and policies with true key performance indicators and accountability metrics. No workforce should have less than 30–35% of BIPOC people.
3. Celebrate and acknowledge religious and cultural practices. For example, Ramadan or Juneteenth should be adopted as a holiday and paid day off.
4. Foster a culture where every voice is heard, welcomed, and respected.
   a. How one treats the lowest-ranking staff is a reflection of the entire organization.
   b. Look at the entry-, mid-, senior-level numbers. If everyone is BIPOC at the bottom or makes up a large (or even small) percentage, a significant problem exists.
5. Build a multigenerational workforce – learn from each other for the future, and provide employees a pathway to promotion. Another option is to build a

fellowship program for BIPOC employees and other marginalized employees to interact and learn from all facets of the organization, including meeting with senior leaders.

6. Foster inclusive and diverse thinking (use equity design thinking with staff, a process to challenge assumptions, redefine problems, and prototype and test innovative solutions).

7. Reflect everyone's needs and preferences at gatherings.
   a. For example, accessibility: some people have hidden ability needs that are not always visual.
   b. Group/company potlucks: for example, many Black employees (and other groups) avoid these but often do not share their feelings with colleagues.

8. Examine, critique, and eliminate all policies that lead to superficial and discriminatory practices.

9. Workspace – is it inclusive, from gender-neutral bathrooms, to artwork, to personalizing office space.

10. Leaders, managers, and staff –focus on personalizing your 1–1 meetings and interactions; do not just be about business. People will not trust or care, unless you show them that you trust and care. You must invest in the people in your organization, who are human and critical to your success.

Example

A great opportunity is the ability to focus your career education classes and programs to target directly historically disadvantaged groups and at the same time educate those who are disadvantaged. For example, the University of North Carolina at Chapel Hill University Career Services teaches a class called "Foundation for Professional Success: Career Development for Underrepresented Students," targeted at sophomores and juniors. This class alone addresses gaps, exposure, and imposter syndrome. Each student ends the class with an internship and students expressed heightened awareness of their professional development as a result of the internship.

Strategy and Accountability

For higher education career educators, this means implementing a strategy, with marketing constructed around campaigns, relationships, and programming with constant engagement to nurture student, employer, and campus outcomes. The practice of strategy and accountability can intentionally incorporate diversity, equity, and inclusion to support every endeavor encapsulated in the concept of Inclusive Excellence. Inclusive Excellence is a comprehensive planning process that identifies a set of actions focused on diversity, equity, and inclusion, and which infuses these actions into every layer of the work done by career practitioners and career centers. Second, accountability must be measured by performance evaluations, staff input, and metrics. The metrics developed will be used in key performance indicators, data assessment, and culture shift. They will help define your students' career readiness, and whether or not you are headed in the right direction as a career center. In preparing a team to address the changes happening, consider training in unconscious bias, perception, and historical facts. In leadership and staff meetings, diversity, equity, and inclusion should be addressed at all times. The ability to keep it at the forefront and address different facets of diversity, equity, and inclusion keeps people updated, aligned with their intersectional identities, and exposed to a set of actions that will bring forth change.

Future Outlook

The outlook for career practitioners and centers will revolve around developing cultural competence throughout programing, career education, and employer relations. Career practitioners hover at the frontline of facilitating student success, the brand of the university, and critical employer connections. Advocacy for equity starts with ongoing self-reflection. The more career practitioners push internally and externally for equity, the more inclusive operations become what we do and who we are; it is that DNA (i.e., inherent qualities or characteristics that one brings to the workplace) that will lead to mitigating discriminatory practices, bias, and historical wrongs. Culture will shape career adaptability, values, perception, and strategies (Fouad & Kantamneni, 2020). That culture must be rooted in critical values, accountability, metrics, learning, and inclusive excellence. The process of understanding language, developing curriculum, and monitoring employer relations will be an expectation of decision-making and achievement. The most important piece of this work is to maintain a consciousness of inclusion, in which one leads this work daily to effect change and outcomes. If career practitioners and centers look back in three to five years and the field is still the same, there has not been a true commitment to bring about needed change.

References

Acker, J. (2006). Inequality regimes. *Gender & Society, 20*(4). https://doi.org/10.1177/0891243206289499

Allam, Z. (2019). *Cities and the digital revolution: Aligning technology and humanity.* Springer Nature.

Asare, J. (2019, April 27). Why Chief Diversity Officers often fail. *Forbes.* www.forbes.com/sites/janicegassam/2019/04/27/why-chief-diversity-officers-often-fail/?sh=3b0dce5011b6

Avramo, P. L. (2016). *The digital revolution: Individual, social and spatial effects* [Unpublished master's thesis]. University of Eastern Piedmont.

Birk, M. (2021, August 5). *Critical race theory: 'Diversity' is not the solution, dismantling white supremacy is.* The Conversation. https://theconversation.com/critical-race-theory-diversity-is-not-the-solution-dismantling-white-supremacy-is-163398

Bowen, D. E., Ledford, G. E., Jr., & Nathan, B. R. (1991). Hiring for the organization, not the job. *Academy of Management Perspectives, 5*(4), 35–51.

Burnett, B., & Evans, D. (2016). *Designing your life: How to build a well-lived joyful life.* Alfred A. Knopf.

Blustein, D. L., Kenny, M. E., Autin, K., & Duffy, R. (2019). The psychology of working in practice: A theory of change for a new era. *The Career Development Quarterly, 67*(3), 236–254. https://doi.org/https://doi.org/10.1002/cdq.12193

Blustein, D. L., Prezioso, M. S., & Schultheiss, D. P. (1995). Attachment theory and career development: Current status and future directions. *The Counseling Psychologist, 23*(3), 416–432. https://doi.org/10.1177/0011000095233002

Burnett, B., & Evans, D. J. (2021). *Designing your new work life: How to thrive and change and find happiness – and a new freedom – at work.* Vintage.

Chan, A., & Cruzvergara, C. Y. (2021). *Outcomes and metrics that matter: Embedding career services at higher education's core.* Handshake.

Chick, G. (2019, April 4). *Corporate Traumatic Stress Disorder (CTSD) is the scourge of the 21st-century workplace.* Training Industry. https://trainingindustry.com/blog/compliance/corporate-traumatic-stress-disorder-ctsd-is-the-scourge-of-the-21st-century-workplace/

Crain, L. K., & Shepard, M. J. L. (2019). Employer definitions of and reflections on fit in hiring processes. In B. J. Reece, V. T. Tran, E. N. DeVore, G. Porcaro, & S. J. Quaye (Eds.), *Debunking the myth of job fit in higher education and student affairs* (pp. 49–66). Stylus.

Dawis, R. V. (2005). The Minnesota theory of work adjustment. In S. D. Brown & R. W. Lent (Eds.), *Career development and counseling: Putting theory and research to work* (pp. 3–23). Wiley.

Dey, F., & Cruzvergara, C. Y. (2014). Evolution of career services in higher education. *New Directions for Student Services, 148*, 5–18. https://doi.org/10.1002/ss.20105

Dobbin, F., Kim, S., & Kalev, A. (2011). You can't always get what you need: Organizational determinants of diversity programs. *American Sociological Review, 76*(3). https://doi.org/10.1177/0003122411409704

Dobbin, F., & Kalev, A. (2016, July–August). Why diversity programs fail. *Harvard Business Review.* https://hbr.org/2016/07/why-diversity-programs-fail

Drucker, P. (2006). *The effective executive.* Harper Business.

Eberhardt, J. L. (2019). *Biased: Uncovering the hidden prejudice that shapes what we see, think, and do.* Viking.

Fouad, N., & Kantamneni, N. (2020). The role of race and ethnicity in career choice, development, and adjustment. In R. Lent & S. Brown (Eds.), *Career development and counseling: Putting theory and research to work* (pp. 309–340). John Wiley & Sons.

Flores, L. Y. (2009). Empowering life choices: Career counseling in the contexts of race and social class. In N. C. Gysbers, M. J. Heppner, & J. A. Johnston (Eds.), *Career counseling: Contexts, processes, and techniques* (3rd ed., pp. 49–74). American Counseling Association.

Gray, K. (2021, February 8). *New tool empowers career centers to promote anti-racism among employers*. National Association of Colleges and Employers. www.naceweb.org/diversity-equity-and-inclusion/tools/new-tool-empowers-career-centers-to-promote-anti-racism-among-employers/

Gutowski, E., Blustein, D. L., Kenny, M. E., & Erby, W. (2021). The decline of decent work in the twenty-first century: Implications for career development. In P. J. Robertson, T. Hooley, & P. McCash (Eds.), *The Oxford handbook of career development* (pp. 23–34). Oxford University Press.

Harper, S. R. (2017). Racially responsive leadership: Addressing the longstanding problem of racism in higher education. In *Challenges in Higher Education Leadership* (pp. 145–156). Routledge.

Harper, S. R., & Hurtado, S. (2007). Nine themes in campus racial climates and implications for institutional transformation. In S. R. Harper & L. D. Patton (Eds.), *New directions for student services: Responding to the realities of race on campus (120)* (pp. 7–24). Wiley.

Healy, G., Bradley, H., & Mukherjee, N. (2004). Individualism and collectivism revisited: A study of black and minority ethnic women. *Industrial Relations Journal, 35*(5), 451–466.

Hughes, R. (2014, May 29). *10 signs of institutionalized racism*. Diverse Issues in Higher Education. www.diverseeducation.com/opinion/article/15094838/10-signs-of-institutionalized-racism

Hill, Y., Lomas, L., & MacGregor, J. (2003). Students' perceptions of quality in higher education. *Quality Assurance in Education, 11*(1), 15–20.

Jacobsen, D. (2012). *Protecting employees from organizational trauma*. www.workhuman.com/resources/globoforce-blog/protecting-employees-from-organizational-trauma

Jones, A. L. (2016). Implicit bias as social framework evidence in employment discrimination. *University of Pennsylvania Law Review, 165*, 1221. https://scholarship.law.upenn.edu/penn_law_review/vol165/iss5/4

Journal of Blacks in Higher Education. (2021). JBHE chronology of major landmarks in the progress of African Americans in higher education. www.jbhe.com/chronology/

Kendi, I. X. (2019). *How to be an antiracist*. One World.

Library of Congress. (2021). *The Civil Rights Act of 1964: A long struggle for freedom: The Segregation Era (1900–1939)*. www.loc.gov/exhibits/civil-rights-act/segregation-era.html

Maurer, R. (2020, August 6). *New DE&I roles spike after racial justice protests*. SHRM. www.shrm.org/resourcesandtools/hr-topics/talent-acquisition/pages/new-dei-roles-spike-after-racial-justice-protests.aspx

McInnis, C. (2004). Studies of student life: An overview. *European Journal of Education, 39*(4), 383–394.

McDonald, A. (2021, June 1). The racism of the 'hard-to-find' qualified Black candidate trope. *Stanford Social Innovation Review*. https://ssir.org/articles/entry/the_racism_of_the_hard_to_find_qualified_black_candidate_trope

McKinsey & Company. (2021, February). *Race in the workspace: The Black experience in the US private sector*. McKinsey & Company. www.mckinsey.com/~/media/mckinsey/featured%20insights/diversity%20and%20inclusion/race%20in%20the%20workplace%20the%20black%20experience%20in%20the%20us%20private%20sector/race-in-the-workplace-the-black-experience-in-the-us-private-sector-v3.pdf?shouldIndex=false

Milan-Tyner, N. (2018). *The impact of race, gender, and class on career development: Perceptions of African American women* (No. 2533) [Doctoral dissertation, Rowan University]. Theses and Dissertations. https://rdw.rowan.edu/etd/2533

National Association of Colleges and Employers. (2021). *What is career readiness?* www.naceweb.org/career-readiness/competencies/career-readiness-defined/

Niccum, J. (2019, April 11). *Political affiliation influences hiring practices during interview process, study finds*. University of Kansas. http://news.ku.edu/2019/11/04/political-affiliation-influences-hiring-practices-during-interview-process-study-finds-1

Pitcan, M., Park-Taylor, J., & Hayslett, J. (2018). Black men and racial microaggressions at work. *The Career Development Quarterly*, 66(4). https://doi.org/10.1002/cdq.12152

Pope, M., Briddick, W. C., & Wilson, F. (2013). The historical importance of social justice in the founding of the national career development association. *Career Development Quarterly*, 61(4), 368–373. https://doi.org/10.1002/j.2161-0045.2013.00063.x

Reneau, C.-M., & Love, C. H. (2021). The walls between us have doors: Honoring transgender student stories as an entryway to just, equitable, and inclusive practice. *Change: The Magazine of Higher Learning*, 53(5), 13–20. https://doi.org/10.1080/00091383.2021.1963147

Romano, C. S. (2019). Developing managers' skills for countering racial color blindness and constructively addressing racial microaggressions in the workplace. In M. A. Jackson, A. K. Regis, & K. Bennett (Eds.), *Career development interventions for social justice: Addressing needs across the lifespan in educational, community, and employment contexts* (pp. 249–272). Rowman & Littlefield.

Rothstein, R. (2018). *The color of law: A forgotten history of how our government segregated America*. Liveright Publishing.

Savicka, M. L. (2010). Life design: A paradigm for career intervention in the 21st Century. *Journal of Counseling and Development*, 90(1), 13–19. https://doi.org/10.1111/j.1556-6676.2012.00002.x

Seemiller, C., & Grace, M. (2016). *Generation Z goes to college*. Jossey-Bass.

Smith, M., & Small, M. (2021, August 25). *Career services are a social justice issue of colleges*. Workshift. https://workshift.opencampusmedia.org/career-services-are-a-social-justice-issue-for-colleges/

Sue, D. W., Capodilupo, C. M., Torino, G. C., Bucceri, J. M., Holder, A. M. B., Nadal, K. L., & Esquilin, M. (2007). Racial microaggressions in everyday life: Implications for clinical practice. *American Psychologist*, 62(4), 271–286. https://doi.org/10.1037/0003-066X.62.4.271

Veldhoen, E. (2013). *You-topia: The impact of the digital revolution on our work, our life and our environment.* Xlibris Corporation.

Wen, Y., Chen, H., Li, K., & Gu, X. (2020). The challenges of life design counseling in the times of the coronavirus pandemic (COVID-19). *Frontiers in Psychology, 11*, 1235. https://doi.org/10.3389/fpsyg.2020.01235

Williams, G. L. (2015, December 4). *Diverse, connected and debt-averse: Move over millennials, here comes Generation Z.* Today. www.today.com/money/generation-z-eclipse-millennials-economic-force-says-goldman-sachs-t59436

Wong, V., & Yip, T. C. (2018). Promoting change: The 'expanded notion of work' as a pro-active response to the social justice issues in career development practice. In T. Hooley, R. Sultana, & R. Thomsen (Eds.), *Career guidance for emancipation* (pp. 64–80). Routledge.

Zahneis, M. (2021, July 13). Cornel West's resignation letter cites 'decline and decay' at Harvard Divinity School. *The Chronicle of Higher Education.* www.chronicle.com/article/cornel-wests-resignation-letter-cites-decline-and-decay-at-harvard-divinity-school

5
Recent Trends in Mental Health and Career Concerns Among Undergraduate Students

Andrea DePetris and Mei Tang

In 1920, at the American Student Health Association's Annual Meeting, "mental hygiene" and the establishment of undergraduate mental health programs were identified as fundamental to students' ability to maximize their potential. Promoting college retention, preventing mental health conditions, curtailing both "inadequacy" and "unhappiness," and fostering a greater intellectual capacity were psychiatrist Frankwood Williams' justifications for implementing university mental health programs (Farnsworth, 1957; Kraft, 2011). In turn, mental health services were established on college campuses, service providers expanded beyond psychiatrists to include psychologists and social workers, and both socioemotional and vocational functioning were identified as concerns of an increasingly diverse student body (inclusive of veterans, women, international students, US racial/ethnic minorities, students of lower socioeconomic status, and others) (Forest, 1989; Hodges, 2001; Kraft, 2011). Thus, college counseling centers have historically considered the importance of psychological functioning, productivity, and vocation; they have, and continue to shift in order to meet the growing needs of student body expansion and diversification.

In 1947, a survey presented by psychiatrist Clements Fry at the third National Conference on Health and Colleges indicated that 15% of undergraduate students who had access to campus mental health services used them; the survey also suggested that approximately one-third of those students utilized services for urgent concerns (Farnsworth, 1957; Kraft, 1993, 2011). Over time, mental health service utilization has steadily increased among undergraduate students. Notably, national trends spanning the past decade and beyond indicate an apparent increase in both mental health service utilization and self-reported distress among undergraduate

DOI: 10.4324/9781003213000-8

students (Lipson et al., 2019; Xiao et al., 2017). More specifically, nationally representative data collected by the Center for Collegiate Mental Health indicates a gradual increase in the number of students seeking services (at rates higher than institutional matriculation increases), the number of appointments scheduled, and the number of appointments attended (Xiao et al., 2017). In addition to increased service utilization (and with notable differences among institutions), a small but significant upward trend in self-reported generalized anxiety, social anxiety, depression, and both academic and family distress was noted (Xiao et al., 2017); even more concerning, a significant, upward trend in reported suicidal ideation, suicide attempts, and self-harm concerns was also indicated (Xiao et al., 2017). Other studies similarly reveal national trends that suggest an increase in depression and anxiety symptoms, with notable increases in non-suicidal self-injury, suicidal ideation, and suicide attempts among US college students (Duffy et al., 2019). While these patterns may reflect an increase in prevalence and severity of mental health concerns (as well as reflect institutional differences), it is also possible that newer generations of mental health service-seekers experience decreased personal stigma (Lipson et al., 2019; Xiao et al., 2017), increased responsiveness to suicide prevention campaigns which may promote higher rates of suicide-related disclosures (Xiao et al., 2017), and a higher regard of mental health services (Xiao et al., 2017) as compared with previous generations. In this chapter, we will consider some of the unique factors that may impact the mental health of Millennials (born between 1981 and 1994) (Seemiller & Grace, 2016) and Generation Z (born between 1995 and 2010) (Seemiller & Grace, 2016), as well as values related to mental health, wellbeing, and the work environment that these generations appear to hold. This exploration will inform our understanding of how future generations regard wellbeing and approach work.

Unique Factors Impacting Millennials and Generation Z

Wellbeing and the Workplace

There are many indications that both Millennials and Generation Z value and prioritize their wellbeing in the context of work. It is estimated that as many as 50% of Millennials and 75% of Generation Z have left a job, both voluntarily and involuntarily, citing mental health reasons (Mindshare Partners, 2019; Perna, 2020; Starling Minds, 2020). This data suggests that Millennials and members of Generation Z are keenly aware of the impact of work on their mental health (Mindshare Partners, 2019); furthermore, they may be less willing to jeopardize their mental health in their line of work, compared with previous generations, and may even rank work–life balance higher than income (Bristow et al., 2011; Buzza, 2017). These mental health statistics have been exacerbated by the pandemic and other sociocultural and political events over the last several years.

Priority

Not only does wellbeing seem to be a personal priority among these generational cohorts, but there also appears to be a desire to have mental health and wellbeing as integrated components of their workplace culture. For example, one report indicates that approximately 78% of Millennials and 77% of members of Generation Z share that the desire to discuss mental health openly at work is important to them (Perna, 2020; Zapier Editorial Team, 2020). Furthermore, the following mental health benefits have also been cited as important by the majority of individuals who were surveyed: a company mental health policy, benefits that include mental health treatment with low out-of-pocket costs for mental health expenditures, respite areas on the work premises, and self-care days (Perna, 2020; Zapier Editorial Team, 2020). Transparency regarding benefits that are offered and an explanation of benefits have also been cited as desired workplace features (Greenwood et al., 2019; Mindshare Partners, 2019; Rumley, 2019). It is possible that the desire for integrated mental health services and transparency regarding mental health may conflict with workplace culture created by members of previous generations (Oaklander, 2020). In order to promote retention of the newest and burgeoning workforces, employers ought to think proactively about how to demonstrate their support of mental health and wellness through benefits, incentives, expectations, workplace structure, and public conversation.

Alteration of Career Trajectories and Necessary Skills

Unlike careers of the past which were often characterized by a long-term trajectory of progress with the same employer, the current world of work is increasingly offering opportunities for short-term assignments, part-time work and side hustles (Savickas, 2011), and advancement via multiple employer transitions and self-directed pursuits via social media platforms. In a context where juggling multiple jobs, frequent job changes, career changes, and even multiple and simultaneous careers is becoming increasingly common, traits such as adaptability and conscientiousness, along with skills that are generalizable, marketable (Savickas, 2011), and also specialized are of increased importance. Also of importance is preparation that helps current and future generations psychologically prepare for how to adjust to transitions (Savickas, 2011) and the accompanying uncertainty. Self-marketability is also becoming increasingly essential, regardless of one's job platform. As social media continues to become a pervasive component of work, preparation for how to manage and preserve one's self-esteem is becoming increasingly vital.

Technology and Social Media

Reliance on technology and participation in social media are also characteristic of the world of work that Millennials, Generation Z, and future generations will inherit. With technological devices becoming increasingly portable and wearable, and with WIFI readily accessible, opportunities for connection are everywhere; it follows that timely, if not speedy, responsiveness has become an expectation. The notion that one must always be responsive and active, both in one's social and work life, likely adds a layer of stress that was completely unknown in previous generations (Oaklander, 2020). It begs the questions: When and how can one "unplug?"

Additionally, engagement with social media is fraught with implications that could enhance or detract from one's wellbeing. On the one hand, social media may provide an avenue of support for historically marginalized groups and can amplify social justice and liberation movements; for example, the Black Lives Matter movement achieved global reach and recognition through social media. One study indicated that experiences of acceptance on social media were associated with lower symptoms of depression and anxiety among individuals identifying as LGBTQIA+ (Pellicane et al., 2021); it is possible that these social media interactions marked by acceptance may help to mitigate the negative wellbeing effects associated with hostility, and that this finding may generalize to other historically marginalized or stigmatized groups (Pellicane et al., 2021). On the other hand, social media engagement, social media preoccupation, and preoccupation with appearance-based activities among adolescents and young adults has been associated with negative mental health outcomes, such as depression, social anxiety, appearance anxiety, and appearance rejection sensitivity (Hawes et al., 2020).

Furthermore, the tendency to engage in upward comparisons on social media has been associated with both lower trait and state self-esteem and self-evaluations among undergraduate students (Vogel et al., 2014). It follows that these generational cohorts and future cohorts will have to reckon with how to implement boundaries and how to utilize social media in a strategic manner. Career counseling professionals who are aware of the mental health impacts of technology and social media use are well-positioned to prepare future workforces by sharing strategic approaches to social media engagement.

Caregiving

There is some evidence to suggest that Millennials may comprise one-fourth of US family caregivers (Flinn, 2018; National Alliance for Caregiving, 2015). Moreover, Millennials spend on average about 21 hours per week on caregiving, utilize an average of 27% of their income on caregiving costs, are more likely to be employed compared with previous generations of family caregivers, are less likely to disclose their caregiving role to their employer (as compared with previous generations of family caregivers), and comprise a larger percentage of LGBTQIA+ caregivers compared with previous generations. More than half identify as African American/ Black, Hispanic/Latino, and Asian American/Pacific Islander (Flinn, 2018;

National Alliance for Caregiving, 2015). More recent data suggests that about 6% of caregivers are Generation Z (National Alliance for Caregiving, 2020), and it is anticipated that the diversity of family caregivers will continue to grow. Regarding caregiver health, there are trends of a decline in self-reported health between 2015 and 2020, with individuals between the ages of 18 and 49 being more likely to report fair or poor health versus excellent or very good health; furthermore, self-reported rates of better health were found to be associated with being White, earning more than $50,000/year, having a college degree or higher, and believing that one has a choice in adopting a caregiving role (National Alliance for Caregiving, 2020). These privileges that are associated with reported rates of better health might not be reflective of our increasingly diverse generations.

Regarding the emotional impact of caregiving, loneliness was found to be associated with decreased health among caregivers (National Alliance for Caregiving, 2020). Additionally, if we consider the financial strain, the stress associated with having multiple responsibilities, and the growing diversity within these generations of caregivers, it follows that these and future generations will likely benefit from employer policies that allow for job flexibility, family leave, accessible mental health services, and culturally tailored mental health support. Government resources that provide assistance to families with caretaking needs are crucial given the large percentage of their salary that many Millennials are currently allocating to caregiving.

Covid-19

The advent of Covid-19 brought about a widespread shift in office workplace protocol; although telecommuting, flexible work schedules, and reliance on technology had already been on the rise, the pandemic arguably hastened these changes on a broad scale. Depending on one's circumstances, working from home may have been regarded as a luxury, a hardship, or some combination of the two. Nevertheless, individuals working from home were afforded the opportunity to limit their exposure to the widely spreading virus. Simultaneously, essential workers (inclusive of healthcare workers and service workers who perform tasks deemed essential to the operations of the country's infrastructure) experienced greater exposure to the virus. Many low-wage essential workers (who are disproportionately US racial/ethnic minorities, often living in communities that are disproportionately impacted by Covid-19) faced other barriers to health equity, such as institutional and interpersonal racism, access to quality healthcare, education and income gaps, and underlying health conditions (Centers for Disease Control and Prevention, 2021; Pryor & Tomaskovic-Devy, n.d.). Thus, pre-existing health disparities have been amplified. Regardless of work setting, the need for changes in career preparation and policies that protect workers' physical and mental health is paramount.

Changing Workforce Needs and a New Type of Workforce Preparation

Career Counseling and Education Considerations

In the wake of Covid-19, both psychological and technical preparation have emerged as two important areas for skill set development among new and future employees. Regarding psychological preparation, a case has been made to integrate mental health services into career counseling, in order to help students develop a growth mindset, manage difficult emotions that might hinder resilience (Akkermans et al., 2020), identify their strengths and capacity for resilience in the context of abrupt changes in the work environment, and identify social networks for engagement (Autin et al., 2020); the latter may be especially important, in order to alleviate potential feelings of loneliness that might result from remote work done in isolation. Given that opportunities for telework are likely to become more prevalent, the delineation of work and personal boundaries (especially in the context of time-management) may be especially important to think through and discuss during one's hiring process and throughout one's tenure with an organization.

Furthermore, developing career adaptability, or the psychological resources needed to manage challenges in one's career (Savickas, 1997), may be particularly important, as career adaptability has been associated with a host of positive outcomes related to job performance, wellbeing, and resilience when faced with unforeseen outcomes (Lee et al., 2020). Learning to adopt dialectical and holistic thinking, which includes a tolerance of contraction, attention to context, and recognition of the reality that change is continuous, may give rise to reappraisal strategies and increased optimism and resilience that is commonly observed in Easterner cultures (De Vaus et al., 2018; Guan et al., 2020; Heppner, 2008; Ji et al., 2004). Regarding technical preparation, Covid-19 highlighted a reliance on technology and the need for proactivity in developing one's technological skill set (Akkermans et al., 2020); adopting a learner's mindset for skill and technological development, regardless of career choice, will likely contribute to developing flexible and sustainable career trajectories.

Institutional and Policy Considerations

There is a need for both organizational and policy protections to support workers who may have already been negatively impacted by Covid-19, or who may be more vulnerable during potential future public health crises. Given that essential workers have compromised their physical and mental health, and may have also endured traumatic circumstances, employers should consider how to integrate mental health and wellness services into their place of business; offering on-site opportunities for therapeutic sessions, telehealth options, and insurance plans with low co-pays for mental health treatment is advisable. Implementing peer support, mentorship, and working groups would also help to create a culture of community support among essential workers and would also likely increase connection and comradery among individuals engaging in telework. Undergraduates, and particularly those preparing to enter professions that are deemed essential, may benefit from having exposure to wellness and mental health services in a manner that is integrated into their residential culture, curriculum, and/or career services programs.

For example, Yale University has recently launched a mental health and wellness community care program to provide accessible, rapid services affiliated with the undergraduate residential colleges. Details about this initiative can be found on the program website (https://yalecollege.yale.edu/getting-help/yale-college-community-care). Monitoring of this program's utilization is underway. It is conceivable that with widespread exposure to mental health and wellness services, students may develop techniques to manage stress and anxiety, may benefit from early detection of mental health conditions, and may be more likely to seek mental health services if needed in the future.

For individuals who plan to engage in telework, it is worth noting that women in dual career/heterosexual partnerships may face the extra burden of increased housework and childcare responsibilities; these additional responsibilities may contribute to a gender gap in both work productivity and job satisfaction (Feng & Savani, 2020); decreases in work productivity and job satisfaction will likely have a poor mental health impact on employees. Thus, gender discrepancies should be monitored in a holistic fashion. For example, regularly soliciting information about the impact of working from home among women (and single parents) would be beneficial to this end; offering flexibility with work deadlines and assignments (Feng & Savani, 2020) to women and single parents may be necessary if gender and/or single versus parent gaps in productivity and job satisfaction emerge. Regarding policy adaptations, expanding telehealth, along with family and sick leave, at the federal and state levels (Autin et al., 2020) will be critical to protecting the overall wellbeing of the burgeoning workforce. Furthermore, advocacy efforts and policies that protect the rights and needs of economically and racially marginalized workers (Autin et al., 2020) will be vital to reducing and ultimately eradicating health disparities.

Career Services and Mental Health Integration

Origins of Career Services and Campus-Based Counseling

Campus-based counseling services originally emerged as a response to post-WWI student needs as veteran students needed to readjust and reestablish to civilian life after coming back from the battlefield (Prince, 2015). As the mission of college counseling centers is to help students adjust to college life and be prepared for work upon graduation, it is reasonable then to have mental health and career counseling included in the scope of services. Finding appropriate majors, managing stress/anxiety, and developing psychological wellness certainly would support college students as they adjust to college as well as prepare for future work and life. To achieve this goal, counseling centers need to collaborate with various units on campus for effectiveness and efficiency. Prince (2015) also asserted that increasing mental health issues experienced by college students today require collaboration between counseling services, student health services, and student affairs to offer proactive and preventive intervention to students and entire university communities.

The evolution of college career services, described in Chapter 1 of this volume, illustrates the necessity of adapting services in both scope/content and delivery methods. As the future work world becomes unpredictable for various reasons discussed earlier in this chapter, it is certain that students need to develop adaptability and resilience in order to be prepared for sustainable employment and career success. Resilience and psychological wellness are not only helpful to career success but are key components of mental health in general. Addressing mental health in career services, then, is not just supplemental but necessary for the totality of student development and success.

Necessity and Practice of Addressing Mental Health in Career Services

Many scholars have argued for the intertwined and reciprocal nature of career and mental health in student development (e.g. Blustein, 2008; Hackett, 1993; Herr, 1989). Work and its role in psychological wellbeing was extensively supported by researchers as well (Blustein, 2006; Whiston & Cinamon, 2015). College students who sought career guidance often presented with anxiety and depression (Hinkelman & Luzzo, 2007). General anxiety was found to be associated with career indecision (Pisarik et al., 2017) and negative thoughts were found to be related to depression and hopelessness (Dieringer et al., 2017). A recent report about American mental health by the American Psychology Association (2020) revealed that Generation Z had the highest level of stress among all generations and that the source for many young adults' stress is concern about the unpredictability of future work. Since this was completed during the Covid-19 pandemic, when the early outbreaks forced lockdowns and unemployment was high, it is understandable why the younger generation would worry about the future of the nation and work.

The interrelatedness of career and mental health concerns requires integrated approaches that conceptualize clients' issues (Stoltz & Hass, 2016). College students, due to their developmental stage, have multiple developmental tasks (e.g. achieving one's identity, developing career readiness) and thus need integrated career services for optimal outcomes. Implementing integrated services requires career development practitioners in college settings to dispel the myth of separating career and mental health issues in intervention (Krumboltz, 1993). If career education truly is part of the ecosystem of a college or university, as Dey and Cruzvergara (2014) suggested, career intervention should adopt an integrated approach through a collaborative process with other shareholders in the university system to help students identify their goals, become ready to enter the world of work, and develop lifelong resilience.

One integrated approach advocated by Tang et al. (2021) includes an ecological counseling model to conceptualize students' presenting issues in order to optimize resources existing in students' ecosystems to enhance outcomes. Specifically, this ecological career counseling model should have these components: helping students identify their meaning-making process and purpose in life, understanding their behavior in the context of various levels of influence from their ecosystem, and evaluating assets and barriers within their ecosystems to build on strengths and overcome challenges. This approach broadens our perspective as career practitioners and helps students to understand the intersectionality between their psychological wellness and career development; more critically, it supports students in developing adaptability and resilience for challenges in their future careers.

Recommendations for Practice

The future work will be forever changing, as discussed earlier in this chapter. Career adaptability will be necessary for college students to enter the world of work and also to pursue success in an unpredictable work environment and economy. In addition, developing career adaptability and career resilience amidst uncertainty is an integral part of psychological wellbeing. Traditional career services approaches, which focus on finding best-fit careers for students' interests and abilities, do not adequately serve the needs of today's college students. Stebleton (2019) cautioned professionals that passion-only career guidance was not sufficient, instead suggesting that college career practitioners need to consider contextual influences, purpose, and meaning in their work with students. Educators need to support students as they manage expectations of family and communities and prepare for changes in the workplace. In other words, career services need to help students develop agency for navigating their career trajectories.

- **Help students to find meaning and purpose in their work.** Stebleton and Kaler (2020) suggested that finding meaning in work can help college students prepare for unpredictability because meaningful work can give students a sense of purpose in life. Stebleton and Kaler (2020) called upon higher education professionals, such as student affairs practitioners, faculty, and administrators, to engage students in conversation about the impact of constant changes in the work environments and about their own careers and lives. They further suggested that such conversations can occur in multiple learning environments, such as in classrooms, workshops, and online platforms, with an aim toward helping students identify their values and prepare for foreseeable changes in the workplace. Meaning-making is also an important goal and strategy in the ecological career counseling model (Cook, 2012).

- **Develop strategic collaborations with other community stakeholders.** These collaborations benefit career services by making career centers more efficient through the sharing of values and resources. Hayden and Ledwith (2014) recommended that career development staff can provide guidance to faculty members on integrating career concepts and information into courses through class assignments or presentations by career center staff. School counselors in K-12 settings, community members, and parents of college students are also important stakeholders that career service staff need to collaborate with for smooth transition and sustainable outcomes for students.

- **Consider a partnership between career services and psychological counseling services.** As integrated service is a necessity for career development and mental health wellness of college students, institutional cultures and policies, as well as administrative structures, need to be reconsidered for promoting a holistic approach (Lenz et al., 2010). One possible model is to offer both services to students through a combined office. Lent et al. also raised the challenges of training, credentials, and professional identities if mental health professionals and career development practitioners merge to form one unit on campus. While these challenges are genuine and might not be easily addressed on college campuses, aiming for seamless service for students via partnership and resource sharing should be seriously explored to identify an appropriate and feasible approach for serving students better.

- **Customize career support for students of different identities and generations.** The diverse student population of the 21st century requires that career services be more individualized to better serve everyone's needs. Customized career services need not only diverse intervention strategies, but also diverse delivery platforms. The Covid-19 pandemic illustrated the centrality of technology, evident even before the pandemic. Learning and working from distance represent a new normal for future generations, and therefore career services need to incorporate technological innovation in service scope/content and delivery. Research has shown little difference in effectiveness of helping students between in-person or online career intervention (Pordelan & Hosseinian, 2015). Virtual career development centers and hybrid career services have multiple benefits, one of which is integrated services which might be more feasible due to accessibility and boundless possibility.

The career development needs of college students go beyond selecting majors, occupations, and job placements. The unpredictability of future work necessitates career services in college settings to be integrative and university systems to function as an ecosystem to provide students transformative learning experiences that will empower them to develop agency, resilience, and mental wellness for their future careers. To accomplish these goals, college students' mental health cannot be ignored, and needs to be integrated into career education and preparation.

References

Akkermans, J., Richardson, J., & Kraimer, M. L. (2020). The COVID-19 crisis as a career shock: Implications for careers and vocational behavior. *Journal of Vocational Behavior, 119*, 103434. https://doi.org/10.1016/j.jvb.2020.103434

American Psychological Association. (2020, October). *Stress in America*^{TM}*: Generation Z.* www.apa.org/news/press/releases/stress/2018/stress-gen-z.pdf

Autin, K. L., Blustein, D. L., Ali, S. R., & Garriott, P. O. (2020). Career development impacts of COVID-19: Practice and policy recommendations. *Journal of Career Development, 47*(5), 487–494. https://doi.org/10.1177/0894845320944486

Blustein, D. L. (2006). *The psychology of working: A new perspective for career development, counseling, and public policy.* Lawrence Erlbaum Associates.

Blustein, D. L. (2008). The role of work in psychological health and well-being: A conceptual, historical, and public policy perspective. *American Psychologist, 63*(4), 228–240. https://doi.org/10.1037/0003-066X.63.4.228

Bristow, D., Amyx, D., Castleberry, S. B., & Cochran, J. J. (2011). A cross-generational comparison of motivational factors in a sales career among Gen-X and Gen-Y college students. *Journal of Personal Selling and Sales Management, 31*(1), 77–85. www.jstor.org/stable/25765020

Buzza, J. S. (2017). Are you living to work or working to live? What millennials want in the workplace. *Journal of Human Resources Management and Labor Studies, 5*(2), 15–20. https://doi.org/10.15640/jhrmls.v5n2a3

Centers for Disease Control and Prevention. (2021, April 19). *Health equity considerations and racial and ethnic minority groups.* www.cdc.gov/coronavirus/2019-ncov/community/health-equity/race-ethnicity.html

Cook, E. (2012). *Understanding people in context: The ecological perspective in counseling.* American Counseling Association.

De Vaus, J., Hornsey, M. J., Kuppens, P., & Bastian, B. (2018). Exploring the East-West divide in prevalence of affective disorder: A case for cultural differences in coping with negative emotion. *Personality and Social Psychology Review, 22*(3), 285–304. https://doi.org/10.1177/1088868317736222

Dey, F., & Cruzvergara, C. Y. (2014). Evolution of career services in higher education. *New Directions for Student Services, 2014*(148), 5–18. https://doi.org/10.1002/ss.20105

Dieringer, D. D., Lenz, J. G., Hayden, S. C., & Peterson, G. W. (2017). The relation of negative thoughts to depression and hopelessness. *The Career Development Quarterly, 65*(2), 159–172. https://doi.org/10.1002/cdq.12089

Duffy, M. E., Twenge, J. M., & Joiner, T. E. (2019). Trends in mood and anxiety symptoms and suicide-related outcomes among the U.S. undergraduates, 2007–2018: Evidence from two national surveys. *Journal of Adolescent Health*, 65(5), 590–598. https://doi.org/10.1016/j.jadohealth.2019.04.033

Farnsworth, D. L. (1957). *Mental health in college and university*. Harvard University Press.

Feng, Z., & Savani, K. (2020). COVID-19 created a gender gap in perceived work productivity and job satisfaction: Implications for dual-career parents working from home. *Gender in Management*, 35(7/8), 719–736. https://doi.org/10.1108/GM-07-2020-0202

Flinn, B. (2018). Millennials: The emerging generation of family caregivers (Spotlight 33). AARP Public Policy Institute. www.aarp.org/content/dam/aarp/ppi/2018/05/millennial-family-caregivers.pdf

Forest, L. (1989). Guiding, supporting, and advising students: The counselor role. In U. Delworth & G. R Hanson (Eds.), *Student services: A handbook for the helping professions* (pp. 265–283). Jossey-Bass.

Greenwood, K., Bapat, V., & Maughan, M. (2019, October 7). Research: People want their employers to talk about mental health. *Harvard Business Review*. https://hbr.org/2019/10/research-people-want-their-employers-to-talk-about-mental-health

Guan, Y., Deng, H., & Zhou, X. (2020). Understanding the impact of the COVID-19 pandemic on career development: Insights from cultural psychology. *Journal of Vocational Behavior*, 119, 103438. https://doi.org/10.1016/j.jvb.2020.103438

Hackett, G. (1993). Career counseling and psychotherapy: False dichotomies and recommended remedies. *Journal of Career Assessment*, 1(2), 105–117. https://doi.org/10.1177/106907279300100201

Hawes, T., Zimmer-Gembeck, M. J., & Campbell, S. M. (2020). Unique associations of social media use and online appearance preoccupation with depression, anxiety, and appearance rejection sensitivity. *Body Image*, 33(2020), 66–76. https://doi.org/10.1016/j.bodyim.2020.02.010

Hayden, S. C. W., & Ledwith, K. E. (2014). Career services in university external relations. *New Directions for Student Services*, 2014(148), 81–92. https://doi.org/10.1002/ss.20110

Heppner, P. P. (2008). Expanding the conceptualization and measurement of applied problem solving and coping: From stages to dimensions to the almost forgotten cultural context. *American Psychologist*, 63(8), 805–816. https://doi.org/10.1037/0003-066X.63.8.805

Herr, E. L. (1989). Career development and mental health. *Journal of Career Development*, 16(1), 5–18. https://doi.org/10.1007/BF01354263

Hinkelman, J. M., & Luzzo, D. A. (2007). Mental health and career development of college students. *Journal of Counseling & Development*, 85(2), 143–147. https://doi.org/10.1002/j.1556-6678.2007.tb00456.x

Hodges, S. (2001). University counseling centers in the twenty-first century: Looking forward, looking back. *Journal of College Counseling*, 4(2), 161–173. https://doi.org/10.1002/j.2161-1882.2001.tb00196.x

Ji, L. J., Zhang, Z., Usborne, E., & Guan, Y. (2004). Optimism across cultures: In response to the severe acute respiratory syndrome outbreak. *Asian Journal of Social Psychology*, 7(1), 25–34. https://doi.org/10.1111/j.1467-839X.2004.00132.x

Kraft, D. P. (1993). College health: A model for our nation's health – the college health perspective. *Journal of American College Health, 42*, 77–78. https://doi.org/10.1080/07448481.1993.9940463

Kraft, D. P. (2011). One hundred years of college mental health. *Journal of American College Health, 59*(6), 477–481. https://doi.org/10.1080/07448481.2011.569964

Krumboltz, J. D. (1993). Integrating career and personal counseling. *The Career Development Quarterly, 42*, 143–147.

Lee, P. C., Xu, S., & Yang, W. (2020). Is career adaptability a double-edge sword? The impact of work social support and career adaptability on turnover intentions during the COVID-19 pandemic. *International Journal of Hospitality Management, 94*, 102875. https://doi.org/10.1016/j.ijhm.2021.102875

Lenz, J. G., Peterson, G. W., Reardon, R. C., & Saunders, D. E. (2010). Connecting career and mental health counseling: Integrating theory and practice. http://counselingoutfitters.com/vistas/vistas10/Article_01.pdf

Lipson, S. K., Lattie, E. G., & Eisenberg, D. (2019). Increased rates of mental health service utilization by U.S. college students: 10-year population-level trends (2007–2017). *Psychiatric Services, 70*(1), 60–63. https://doi.org/10.1176/appi.ps.201800332

Mindshare Partners. (2019). *Mental health at work 2019 report.* www.mindsharepartners.org/mentalhealthatworkreport

National Alliance for Caregiving and the AARP Public Policy Institute. (2015). *Caregiving in the U.S. 2015* [Report]. www.aarp.org/content/dam/aarp/ppi/2015/caregiving-in-the-united-states-2015-report-revised.pdf

National Alliance for Caregiving and the AARP Public Policy Institute. (2020). *Caregiving in the U.S. 2020* [Report]. www.caregiving.org/wp-content/uploads/2021/01/full-report-caregiving-in-the-united-states-01-21.pdf

Oaklander, M. (2020, January 16). Millennial employees are getting companies to radically rethink workers' mental health. *Time.* https://time.com/5764680/mental-health-at-work/

Pellicane, M. J., Cooks, J. A., & Ciesa, J. A. (2021). Longitudinal effects of social media experiences on depression and anxiety in LGB+ and heterosexual young adults. *Journal of Gay & Lesbian Mental Health, 25*(1), 68–93. https://doi.org/10.1080/19359705.2020.1776805

Perna, M. C. (2020, March 10). Younger workers take mental health seriously – and employers should, too. *Forbes.* www.forbes.com/sites/markcperna/2020/03/10/younger-workers-take-mental-health-seriously-and-employers-should-too/?sh=4ae7d8b14c85

Pisarik, C. T., Rowell, P. C., & Thompson, L. K. (2017). A phenomenological study of career anxiety among college students. *The Career Development Quarterly, 65*(4), 339–352. https://doi.org/10.1002/cdq.12112

Pordelan, N., & Hosseinian, S. (2021). Online career counseling success: The role of hardiness and psychological capital. *International Journal for Educational and Vocational Guidance, 21*(3), 531–549. https://doi.org/10.1007/s10775-020-09452-1

Prince, J. P. (2015). University student counseling and mental health in the United States: Trends and challenges. *Mental Health & Prevention*, 2(1–2), 5–10. https://doi.org/10.1016/j.mhp.2015.03.001

Pryor, C., & Tomaskovic-Devy, D. (n.d.). *How COVID exposes healthcare deficits for Black workers*. University of Massachusetts Amherst Center for Employment Equity. www.umass.edu/employmentequity/how-covid-exposes-healthcare-deficits-black-workers

Rumley, J. (2019, October 10). Half of millennials have quit a job for mental health reasons: Study. *Huffpost*. www.huffingtonpost.ca/entry/mental-health-workplace_ca_5d9c892ae4b099389806a65c

Savickas, M. L. (1997). Career adaptability: An integrative construct for life-span, life-space theory. *Career Development Quarterly*, 45(3) 247–259. https://doi.org/10.1002/j.2161-0045.1997.tb00469.x

Savickas, M. L. (2011). New questions for vocational psychology: Premises, paradigms, and practices. *Journal of Career Assessments*, 19(3), 251–258. https://doi.org/10.1177/1069072710395532

Seemiller, C., & Grace, M. (2016). *Generation Z goes to college* (1st ed.). Jossey-Bass.

Starling Minds. (2020, February 11). *How to address the millennial mental health crisis in the workplace*. Starling. www.starlingminds.com/how-to-address-the-millennial-mental-health-crisis-in-the-workplace/

Stebleton, M. J. (2019). Moving beyond passion: Why "do what you love" advice for college students needs reexamination. *Journal of College and Character*, 20(2), 163–171. https://doi.org/10.1080/2194587X.2019.1591289

Stebleton, M. J., & Kaler, L. S. (2020). Preparing college students for the end of work: The role of meaning. *Journal of College and Character*, 21(2), 132–139. https://doi.org/10.1080/2194587X.2020.1741396

Stoltz, K. B., & Haas, K. J. (2016). Mental health or career counseling: A forced choice? No need! *Career Planning and Adult Development Journal*, 32(1), 43.

Tang, M., Montgomery, M., Collins, B., & Jenkins, K. (2021). Integrating career and mental health counseling: Necessity and strategies. *Journal of Employment Counseling*, 58(1), 23–35. https://doi.org/10.1002/joec.12155

Vogel, E. A., Rose, J. P., Roberts, L. R., & Eckles, K. (2014). Social comparison, social media, and self-esteem. *Psychology of Popular Media Culture*, 3(4), 206–222. https://doi.org/10.1037/ppm0000047

Whiston, S. C., & Cinamon, R. G. (2015). The work–family interface: Integrating research and career counseling practice. *The Career Development Quarterly*, 63(1), 44–56. https://doi.org/10.1002/j.2161-0045.2015.00094.x

Xiao, H., Carney, D. M., Youn, S. J., Janis, R. A., Castonguay, L. G., Hayes, J. A., & Locke, B. (2017). Are we in crisis? National mental health and treatment trends in college counseling centers. *Psychological Services*, 14(4), 407–415. https://doi.org/10.1037/ser0000130

Zapier Editorial Team. (2020). *Misunderstood generations: What Millennials and Gen Z actually think about work*. Zapier. https://zapier.com/blog/digital-natives-report/

6
Global Trends in Career Education and the Needs of International Students

Elif Balin and Arame Mbodj

While there's substantial diversity and differences among international student cultural identities and career development experiences, the chapter is organized with the intention to bring critical perspectives to the understanding of underrecognized global career education trends and the underserved career development needs of international students. These critical perspectives are rooted in the following researcher/author positionality, the intersectionality framework, and a global social justice perspective.

Author Positionality

As the authors of this chapter, we first want to acknowledge that our critical perspectives primarily come from our experiences and diverse backgrounds with intersecting identities, which have helped shape our agenda in approaching opportunities and creating space for international students. Writing this chapter as two immigrants of different backgrounds, we recognize that the experience of international students and immigrants widely varies, mainly depending on the entry point. The experience of a scholar from Turkey entering the United States as an international graduate student and the lens of an immigrant from Senegal entering the primary school system in the United States provides a diverse viewpoint of experiences as the authors carry these identities through different career education settings. It is essential to recognize the identities at hand as we explore global trends in career education and the needs of international students – additionally, the contexts where these identities interplay are essential to consider.

DOI: 10.4324/9781003213000-9

Intersectionality

Intersectionality originated from the multilayered social justice movements of several Black feminist advocates, and it was introduced to the literature by the Black legal scholar, Kimberlé Crenshaw, to tackle the marginalization of Black women in anti-discrimination law. The term intersectionality has various definitions and uses across almost all disciplines (Collins & Bilge, 2016). Several studies that focused on intersectionality in higher education scholarship defined it at the micro-level or as a combination of social identities (e.g., race, gender, social class, and sexual/gender identity) without connecting them to also intersecting structures of oppression – as originally introduced by Crenshaw (Harris & Patton, 2019). While some studies explicitly applied intersectionality to their exploration of international student experiences (Herridge & Garcia, 2019; Karaman & Christian, 2020; Malcolm & Mendoza, 2014; Mwangi et al., 2019), the vast majority of literature about international students falls short of recognizing their diversity of intersecting identities and structures of oppression that they face. One context where the intersecting identities may face systemic racism and oppression is the job application and interview process. For example, a woman international student, who has a headscarf (symbolizing their Muslim faith), heavy accent, and perhaps limited internship and job experience prior to their studies due to limited work opportunities for women in their countries of origin, might get disadvantaged at multiple levels. Beyond the United States context, a transgender international student with invisible psychological disabilities may face even more severe forms of discrimination and oppression in transitioning back to and searching jobs in their country of origin.

As the Covid-19 pandemic and most recent incidents of police violence proved, international students who look or identify as Black or Asian may experience increased levels of racism, discrimination, oppression, and violence. These pervasive experiences have also been consistent in BIPOC (Black, Indigenous, and People of Color) communities, but these pandemics have shed more light on the experiences of these marginalized identities. Additionally, the information in this chapter may not apply to all *international* constituents and stakeholders that career educators may engage. These different populations can sometimes include undocumented, DACAmented (i.e., undocumented immigrant students protected under the Deferred Action for Childhood Arrivals policy), refugee students or scholars, asylum seekers, visiting scholars, study abroad students, exchange program students, and new migrants. While this is not an exhaustive list, it is crucial to acknowledge that these populations may have different and additional needs due to differences in temporary or uncertain immigration and visa status, which is beyond the scope of this chapter. Despite the limited attention to intersectionality in the literature that studied international student career development experiences, it should be considered a key factor that shapes the diversity of international student experiences in different systems of oppression. Exploring intersectionality is an essential step to designing career education models and services.

A Global Social Justice Perspective

Career education is rooted in the vocational guidance movement of the early 1900s that emerged as a social justice movement to address the consequences of unemployment and exploitation by industrial monopolies, especially among new immigrants and other disadvantaged people (Baker, 2009). While these efforts were not the first conceptualization of vocational guidance needs and interventions, they shaped the original trait and factor theory of Parsons along with several other theories that followed (Savickas, 2009). However, the dominant cultural backgrounds (e.g., middle-class, educated, white men) that they emerged from, and the cultural contexts that they apply, shifted their focus away from social justice (Blustein et al., 2019). The internationalization trajectory in higher education was similar to that of vocational psychology, career counseling, and career education.

The original mission of international education was cooperation between countries and learning from different cultural contexts, including those non-Western national and cultural contexts (Jones & De Wit, 2012). However, both scholarly and public attention to internationalization stayed limited to the Western world for the most part as a result of its accessibility to only those with economic and mobility privileges, as well as the predominant role of the English language in shaping what is considered international education (De Wit, 2017; De Wit et al., 2017). Such countries with the most developed universities and attractive resources for innovation also benefit from the international education revenue and international student contributions in the forms of talents, skills, labor, diverse perspectives, and technological innovations (Anderson, 2021). While the recent global trends in international education have started to change this situation (as discussed in later sections of this chapter), international education and resulting talent mobility contribute to global inequality and remain a threat to social justice, especially in underdeveloped and developing countries (De Wit & Altbach, 2021). With the increasingly visible impacts of global inequality and crises (e.g., climate change, wars, anti-immigrant politics, declining academic freedom, the refugee crisis), international education has become a competitive area. There is competition for international students as both financial revenue (i.e., high tuition fees) and talent hunting (i.e., scientific innovation), leading many nations to want to reverse brain drain or attract international talent to their countries (Altbach & De Wit, 2018).

In today's rapidly changing global and local contexts, supporting the career outcomes for all students, including international students, requires a global social justice perspective beyond the traditional career education discourses and practices in the United States. In this chapter, the authors utilize the Psychology of Working Theory (PWT) to incorporate intersectionality and social justice perspectives by bringing attention to the experiences of decent work (or lack thereof) among those who hold multiple marginalized identities in numerous systems of oppression (Blustein et al., 2019). Decent work, which originated from the International Labour Organization's initiatives, is a central variable for the PWT and is "composed of physically and interpersonally safe working conditions, hours allowing free time and adequate rest, organizational values that complement family and social values, adequate compensation, and access to adequate health care" (Duffy et al., 2018, p. 281). These PWT constructs may be helpful to conceptualize international students' systemic constraints and limited work volition (e.g., work authorization and visa limitations), with several implications for supporting their career adaptability.

Global Career Education and International Students

Understanding and engaging in global career education is an unavoidable necessity as globalization is a contemporary reality that we continuously face with the recent Covid-19 pandemic, multiple economic and unemployment crises, and increasing influx of immigrants and refugees worldwide. Global career education can be framed as an opportunity to address these problems that impact everyone, especially these most vulnerable communities. For example, De Wit (2020) called international educators to support internationalization at home versus global mobility through more strategic approaches to address the ongoing inequalities in who can access and benefit from international education, as well as to consider climate change impacts of physical mobility. To embrace this increasing recognition of the value of international education for global justice, there is a need to acknowledge the multiple pathways to global career education, such as:

- international education in the forms of long-term commitment (e.g., pursuing undergraduate or graduate degree abroad) and short-term commitment (e.g., language training, study abroad);
- work authorization programs (e.g., optional practical training) and longer-term work experience (e.g., H-1B work visa)
- transnational education by participating in international universities without leaving one's country of origin (Lu, 2018), or completing a part of academic degree requirements at a university abroad; and
- virtual learning opportunities (e.g., online undergraduate or graduate degree programs, online certificate programs).

Changing Global Context

With the speed and impact of technology, all college students become global citizens. For example, the Covid-19 pandemic made international and cross-cultural learning more accessible to those who did not consider it a possibility before the physical closure of borders (e.g., taking online classes). Many international students started their studies remotely without dynamic learning and social support communities, while many others had to shift their career plans. And those who were already outside of their country of origin when the pandemic began (e.g., international students in the United States) faced unprecedented challenges from complicated policies and travel restrictions. Online learning and networking opportunities have provided new perspectives on education or career preparation pathways.

The Covid-19 pandemic also exacerbated the economic disparities around the world. For example, 60% of the overall 54 million people worldwide who fell out of the middle class were in India (Kochhar, 2021), which is the second-largest contributor for international students in the United States (Open Doors, 2020). Therefore, international education may become less accessible for students among those most economically impacted. Besides deepening the inequality in access to international education, this emerging global economic context might also motivate prospective international students to seek alternatives in their own or other countries.

Furthermore, with the ongoing political tension between the United States and China, the future of international education is uncertain besides the already declined international student enrollment in 2020 (NAFSA, 2020). This decline might be an opportunity for the higher education institutions (HEIs) and the related US policies to be aligned with the global trends and shifting expectations of international students. Accordingly, career education models should also consider a transformation by moving away from the dominance of Western models. Doing so requires policymakers, HEI administrators, faculty, career educators, and other stakeholders to be more familiar with the career education trends and college student needs around the world. One fundamental trend is the growing popularity of alternative locations for international students and globally mobile talent, which is discussed in the next section.

Global Career Education Trends

More countries invest in higher education with a growing number of college students, including those that strive to recruit from other countries with greater awareness of international student value (De Wit & Deca, 2020). The graduates from these global higher education systems also pursue career paths beyond their national borders with greater flexibility and openness for mobility. Students and graduates carry their skills and innovations to various locations where they perceive the circumstances most rewarding. The international students consider more destinations as they engage in career planning (World Education Services [WES], 2020). Accordingly, their career preparation must be inclusive of not only the job market demands in the United States but other countries.

Career educators should become more familiar with the educational system and career development in other countries (e.g., support for career planning, job search, and cultural re-adjustment in the country of origin). It's particularly important to become familiar with the career education practices in China and India because about 50% of all international students in the United States come from these countries (Open Doors, 2020). At the same time, these countries demonstrated increasing success in their international student recruitment and retention of local students by investing more in their higher education systems with new national policies (Tian & Liu, 2021) and collaboration with foreign universities to establish transnational education campuses within their borders or geographical regions (Lu, 2018).

For example, China has been implementing systematic initiatives to keep their local talent and have students abroad return to China through significant developments in global economic, technology, and military fronts. However, the students in China continue to face a highly competitive college education and job market along with traditional family expectations and Confucian values that may dismiss the difficulties of some marginalized groups (e.g., the LGBTQ community), which are found to face more mental health concerns (Lim & Lim, 2013). These difficulties are important to understand as they are possible barriers to China becoming an open and democratic society. They are also reported to be a reason for international students from China to hesitate to return to their native land after their studies or work experience in other countries (Kim & Allen, 2018). Career educators in the United States should be aware of such context that international students come from and may return to as they support them in transitions.

Like China, India has created many government policies and structured strategic plans on employment. Especially in the last decade, India has focused on improving and integrating technology into employment services and launched a National Career Service portal where job seekers, job providers, skill providers, and career counselors come together and provide various career development courses, employment and career counseling services, and apprenticeship programs (Chadha et al., 2018). Despite these developments in India, insufficient capacity of high-quality Indian institutions and students' desire to pursue professional advancement keep international education popular among students in India (Bhandari, 2019).

Furthermore, about half of students from India and around one-third of students from China pursue graduate degrees in the United States. According to the most recent available data from the National Science Foundation (NSF), temporary visa holders constituted 38% of all doctoral recipients in the United States. And 79% of the temporary visa holder doctoral recipients reported definitive commitment to stay and work in the United States, especially those in STEM fields (NSF, 2019). Additionally, the analyses of immigrant entrepreneur profiles showed that a vast majority entered the US as international students from India and East Asia, boosting local economies (Amornsiripanitch et al., 2021).

Thus, career educators should consider and address the needs of international students with entrepreneurial aspirations, especially undergraduate students who are considering graduate studies and those already at the graduate level. While many international students with graduate degrees and undergraduate students in STEM fields may have higher employment prospects in the US (e.g., longer period of post-graduation work authorization), other students may face more pressing timelines and policy restrictions to employment in the United States. Given multiple barriers and forms of competition in the United States and the countries of origin, career educators should provide proactive, realistic, and comprehensive career planning for international students. Finally, career educators should also consider ways to facilitate international students' continued engagement and community building in their countries of origin or in other countries in the context of supporting their career adaptability, as well as for global justice to foster international collaboration and contributions.

International Students in the United States

This section takes a closer look at the experiences of international students, building on the definitions of intersectionality and social justice frameworks, as presented at the beginning of this chapter. By using these frameworks, three key areas are discussed in relation to the career development needs of international students: 1) exploring the diverse and intersectional narratives of international student career development, 2) tackling work authorization and visa restrictions, and 3) existing and emerging career education practices, followed by the final section on further recommendations for social justice oriented career education practices. These areas also align with both the historical and changing trajectories of the literature about international students in US higher education systems.

Narratives of International Student Career Development

The scope and experience within the international community pursuing education in the United States has shifted, especially in the past few years, due to changes in the economy, society, and governmental policies. The United States has consistently shown that many of its systems are inherently racist and non-inclusive, leaving many diverse groups without the same opportunities as US citizens.

Examples of recent discriminatory policies are the Muslim travel ban, the creation of specialized visas based on nationality (i.e., E-3 Visa for Australians and TN Visa for Canadians and Mexicans), visa pathways becoming increasingly challenging with fewer opportunities to remain in the United States for certain groups, and restrictions on students from specific countries entering the United States, which particularly affected many international students from participating in the higher education system whether starting or continuing their educational pursuits (Shepardson, 2021). Despite the recent drop in enrollment in 2019–2020, nearly 1.5 million international student graduates remain to contribute to the US economy and workforce (Open Doors, 2020), besides their contributions through benefiting domestic students. For example, they enhance cross-cultural empathy while increasing social and cultural capital (Rose-Redwood & Rose-Redwood, 2018). They also enrich the funds in their HEIs (Shih, 2017). However, such contributions do not mean that all international students come from affluent backgrounds. International students must prove their financial capacity to pay for their education out of pocket. However, it's not unusual for them to pool their extended family resources together to showcase to universities that they can pay for their education, only to return the money to their community once their visa and admission processes are completed. The students who lack the financial means work hard to find other means to fund their education and maintain their student status in the United States.

In addition to quality education and employment outcome expectations, some international students may come to the United States for an opportunity to support their families after becoming financially successful due to the limitations of decent employment in their home countries. Some international students even come to the United States to begin transitioning their families permanently, while many others move temporarily, hoping to bring their knowledge back to their communities. Understanding diverse international student narratives can help career educators to engage in effective needs assessment and mutual goal setting to support unique international student career development needs. On the other hand, the motivations and dynamics of international student career development may shift more frequently than ever following the impact of the Covid-19 pandemic and socio-political climate in the United States. Indeed, international students report decreasing interest in pursuing their education in the United States (Fischer & Aslanian, 2021; WES, 2020).

Furthermore, given the changes and uncertainty about international student enrollment, motivations to study, and post-graduation plans in the pandemic climate, the authors argue that career educators should pay more attention to the diverse experiences of international students, especially their intersecting identities. Mwangi et al. (2019) reported several negative social positioning experiences among African graduate international students. From American students' assumptions to adjustment challenges posed by the campus systems, several systems of oppression posed threats to these international students' academic experience and wellbeing, with direct implications for career development. Moreover, international students, especially those at the graduate level, face difficult working conditions during underpaid or unpaid research or teaching assistantship programs (Cantwell et al., 2018), which are essential to their career exploration and preparation as they build competencies, skills, academic connections, and even larger professional networks. Although international students' underpaid work greatly benefits HEIs and faculty career advancement, it might hinder the career preparation process of students due to time constraints, dependability on the approval of a research supervisor/professor to move to the job search process, and limited exposure to non-academic industry contexts (Balin, 2014).

International students often navigate demanding academic studies, precarious research or teaching assistantship positions, and financial stress from uncertain institutional budgets and limiting federal policies (Modica, 2021). These experiences do not align with the criteria for decent work, which can be framed according to the PWT, as defined earlier in this chapter. Contrary to a common misconception that international students come from economically privileged backgrounds, some international students struggle to attain decent work conditions for many years if their access to education depends on a graduate assistantship or other scholarship contract with inadequate protection of their rights as academic laborers. They may also face various barriers in their internship and job search processes due to their lack of knowledge or employer misperceptions about their work authorization rights (Balin et al., 2016). Additionally, some international graduates may get stuck in exploitative working conditions under an employer that they depend on due to work visa or green card rules. Therefore, developing a critical consciousness about the barriers to international student career development due to the limited work authorization and visa policies (i.e., uncertain career outcomes or economic and personal sacrifice), as well as oppressive working conditions such as long work hours in research laboratories (Cantwell et al., 2018), can tackle marginalization and prevent psychological internalization of oppression. Because, if internalized, oppression can lead to feelings of self-doubt and alienation that can harm one's connection to and motivation for school, work, and other social institutions (Kenny et al., 2018). Thus, career education with and for international students must include social justice and advocacy interventions.

Additionally, international student career development narratives, as framed by both intersectionality and global social justice perspectives, belong with the narratives of all marginalized college students. For example, the working conditions of graduate students are receiving increasing attention in the United States. In a forum by the American Association of University Professors, Surabhi Balachander and Jeremy Glover, graduate students from the Graduate Employees' Organization (GEO) of the University of Michigan, summarized their demands related to Covid-19 safety and policing with the following:

> GEO's Covid-19 demands addressed issues such as exposure to the virus at work, lack of access to testing, and loss of childcare or wages, all of which disproportionately affect communities of color, and especially Black communities – much like police violence. GEO's strike revealed some ways that both university structures and organizing can fall short of serving the most vulnerable populations on campus.
>
> (Modica et al., 2021, para. 15)

This statement is a critical reflection of recent events beyond Covid-19 that impacted the career development of graduate student workers. The social injustices faced by Black people in the US shook up the world, shedding light on the murders of George Floyd, Breonna Taylor, Ahmaud Arbery, Elijah McClain, and countless others. This was quickly followed by a significant uptick in hate crimes against the Asian, Asian-American and Pacific Islander communities. These uncovered vulnerabilities are threats to both personal and career wellbeing, which should be considered by career educators and other student support professionals. In other words, the future of career education must be inclusive of advocacy and social justice practices to support vulnerable populations, including international students, in the face of multiple contextual and systemic threats.

Work Authorization and Visa Restrictions

Despite developing critical consciousness about the systemic restrictions and access to decent work conditions, international students have limited avenues to engage in self-advocacy due to their temporary visa status as non-citizen residents. Any work external to their campus requires work authorization and must be related to their academic field, which limits the types of experience they can pursue. There are two common work authorization paths that international students are eligible for: Optional Practical Training (OPT) and Curricular Practical Training (CPT). OPT can be used during or after a student finishes their program but has a 12-month limitation of work authorization. CPT provides an opportunity for current international students to gain internships for credit; however, it must also be used under a program that meets academic department requirements such as a minimum number of prior course credits for eligibility.

The implications of travel restrictions during the Covid-19 pandemic created more challenges to apply for and use work authorization options. For example, many international students could not return from their country of origin where they attended courses online. Not being able to engage in CPT, gain experience, or meet the internship requirements of their academic program can massively hinder postgraduation career prospects for international students. Similarly, if international students attempt to use OPT to gain experience, they may face additional barriers. Meanwhile, students or graduates from STEM fields have extended work authorization under the OPT program, which may be perceived as less problematic by some employers. Still, students from specific countries can encounter more employment barriers due to limited or delayed visas granted to individuals from these countries.

As evident in the last few years, the work authorization rights and policies may change at any time and especially as the government changes leadership. The intricacies of the system can be researched through the United States Citizenship and Immigration Services, and in close consultation with international student services to help career educators to recognize how complex these programs and systems are for international students. Accordingly, career educators can educate themselves to provide proactive support and seek effective collaboration with other student services (e.g., international student advising office) and beyond (e.g., local immigration attorneys). Furthermore, current knowledge of work authorization, work visa, and immigration policies can help career educators engage in public advocacy beyond individual and institutional-level efforts. For example, when the

Trump administration attempted to create additional barriers for international students during the peak of Covid-19 (e.g., travel bans and sending international students back to their home countries), the prompt for advocacy from several HEIs addressed such implications (American Educational Research Association, 2020), and their collective power pressed the government to cancel their proposals. This achievement is a critical example of HEIs and professional associations supporting marginalized student communities and requires continued commitment to advocacy (Mbodj et al., 2021).

The State of Career Education

A WES survey about career services for international students showed that they struggle with:

- a lack of a strong network of employers willing to hire international students, often because of misunderstandings regarding the work authorization regulations and process;
- unrealistic expectations regarding their access to jobs and internships at all points during their stay in the United States as students;
- marketing themselves to employers and understanding the importance of this cultural norm in navigating the US workforce (see also DuRose & Stebleton, 2016), as is common in the US career culture; and
- deficits in English language skills (WES, 2016, p. 2).

The WES survey also showed that international students found online channels (e.g., institutional websites and social media accounts) and one-on-one appointments that consider cultural differences most useful. Furthermore, international students believe that opportunities to connect with employers (e.g., career fairs, networking events) effectively benefit them in career preparation activities.

The results from a survey by WES (2017) indicated that international students perceive work authorization and work visa policies as their greatest challenges, which are also the areas where both career development professionals and employers report a lack of understanding (Balin et al., 2016). In addition, more than 40% of international students who participated in the WES (2017) survey did not use career services at the time and half of them reported being *not yet ready for a job search* as their reason. This result is consistent with the authors' professional experiences and observations as career educators. Some international students might not perceive career exploration and planning as a process of developing career readiness.

Furthermore, the above-mentioned studies show that international students lack an understanding of cultural differences in career development and work settings in the United States. The results also imply cultural barriers between international students and career development professionals which not only include possible language barriers, but also cultural worldviews (e.g., individualistic vs. collectivistic values). Thus, international students need proactive, timely orientation to the career development process to understand that it takes a long time to develop one's cultural understanding, network, skills, and experiences to become prepared to set and pursue career goals. Together with the need for cultural understanding, career education practices that are more interculturally competent and social justice oriented are needed to help international students proactively engage in career exploration and preparation (Anderson & Balin, 2020; Li et al., 2021).

Emerging Trends and Best Practices

Throughout the years, university resources have been focused on language and peer programs (e.g., accent reduction to help second/third language international students in communicating more effectively with employers). On the other hand, emerging best practices have focused on systemic issues more directly by tackling the challenges to networking, gaining experience (e.g., internship), and work authorization processes.

In a rapidly changing and increasingly unpredictable global context, social capital is important, especially for international students' understanding and access to the hidden job market in addition to employer misperceptions about hiring international students. Therefore, developing critical consciousness about cross-cultural circumstances and systemic barriers (e.g., institutional policies; social, political, or economic factors) may help international students proactively develop self-advocacy skills. For example, the International Student Job Search Certificate Program at the University of Illinois at Urbana-Champaign and the international student career planning workshop series at the University of Washington embrace community building, networking, skills development, and proactive planning for multiple career paths (i.e., job search in the United States or other countries) through collaborative activities with international student career development experts, international alumni, and peer or small group accountability (Field, 2018). Such career education practices have the potential to offer mentorship and peer support from an experienced pool of international alumni and senior students who can shed light on their success stories, share their best practices, and provide perspective-taking. They can also facilitate the maintenance and enrichment of professional networks for international students who may lose social capital in their country of origin or struggle to build a new network during their studies in the United States.

As discussed earlier, not all international students are interested in staying in the United States long term. However, gaining an education in the United States can affect students' the ability to land opportunities back home or in third countries. Their academic experience here may create the need to learn or re-familiarize themselves with navigating different work structures in addition to refreshing their professional network to understand the job skills demanded in other countries. Thus, there is an increased demand for comprehensive and proactive career education programs.

For example, the award-winning program UBalt Career Cycle at the University of Baltimore offers a comprehensive tool for students to engage in self-reflection, new experiences, interest and skills development, networking, and continuous career planning throughout their studies in college (University of Baltimore, 2021). Students reflect, develop, and track skills, interests, and connections in alignment with their academic progress and the career readiness competencies of the National Association of Colleges and Employers (NACE). These competencies include global and intercultural fluency: 1) value, respect, and learn from diverse cultures, races, ages, genders, sexual orientations, and religions; and 2) demonstrate openness, inclusiveness, sensitivity, and the ability to interact respectfully with all people and understand individuals' differences (NACE, 2021). The vast majority of students in the United States and around the world have limited access and opportunity for international education and global experiences (as described in the earlier sections), which necessitate more internationalization at home – integrating global career education needs on every campus instead of making it a privileged experience for those who can afford it.

At the same time, such integrative and global career education models should be more inclusive of the diverse needs of the current and future international students. For example, gaining experience and new skills is a fundamental component of career education programs; however, most international students are limited to on-campus work in addition to limited off-campus work only after they accumulate sufficient academic credits or become eligible with graduation. Therefore, the higher education institutions must create more on-campus opportunities for decent work and internship programs, such as Clemson University's paid, on-campus internship program (Nunamaker & Cawthon, 2018) and the Internship Funding Program at Duke University (2021), in addition to continued social justice and advocacy to tackle the unfair work authorization policies at the public level. Accordingly, there are implications for individual, institutional, and public-level advocacy competencies for career educators and HEIs (Toporek & Daniels, 2018).

For example, the National Career Development Association (NCDA) has been recognizing career services and educators with the International Student Services Award since 2015, and all the awarded programs reflect clear understanding of the systemic barriers (e.g., limited work authorization and complicated work visa eligibility for different international student groups); the significance of proactive career planning by making international students and career educators, as well as employers, aware of work authorization options and rights; and active collaboration with various institutional (e.g., international student advising offices) and public (e.g., immigration attorneys, international alumni) stakeholders (see also National Career Development Association–International Student Services Committe, 2020 – "Resources for Partnering with International Students").

Recommendations for Practice

The studies and recommendations covered in the previous sections indicate a clear need to support international students at both institutional (e.g., career services) and public (e.g., government policy and advocacy) levels. Therefore, we present the following recommendations:

- Develop more critical consciousness and call for action to proactively meet international students' unique needs, which stem from diverse intersectional identities, temporary immigration status, and limited work authorization options, against the deeply rooted systems of racism and other oppression.
- Consider the shared responsibility of learning from diverse national and regional practices to continue to evolve the integrity of services for the international community.
- Consider international and diverse industry stakeholders' responsibilities to spend collective efforts to prepare all students for a global job market.
- Integrate academic and experiential learning curriculums that align with the emerging and demanded transferable work skills globally, and be sure students are aware of the skills they are developing.
- Create more experiential learning and other hands-on opportunities across all academic curriculums on campus to help international students explore non-work-authorization opportunities.
- Provide long-term, sustainable funding to positions dedicated to international student career development expertise.
- Utilize more culturally inclusive and responsive career education models to help students explore their strengths through narratives and cultural contexts from a global perspective.
- Advocate to eliminate threats to decent work conditions in academia.
- Collaborate with professional organizations to create competency frameworks that are inclusive of international competencies.
- Advocate for HEIs to take more responsibility to generate time and sustainable funding resources for career educators to engage in professional development for intercultural, international, and social justice competencies.

We conclude this chapter with the words of Noam Chomsky, the world-renowned and one of the most cited scholars in modern history, from his keynote speech at the 2020 conference of the Society of Transnational Academic Researchers (STAR) network, *Shaping a Humane World*: "When the global communities and threats are so critically connected, we cannot solve these shared problems without international solidarity and collaboration." We believe that career education is one of the most essential prerequisites in the form of preparing college students as future leaders, policymakers, advocates, and other stakeholders who can choose to sustain our world with more justice and equitable distribution of resources for *all* people.

References

Altbach, P., & De Wit, H. (2018). Are we facing a fundamental challenge to higher educa-tion internationalization? *International Higher Education, 93*, 2–4. https://doi.org/10.6017/ ihe.0.93.10414

American Educational Research Association. (2020, July 9). *Statement by AERA Executive Director Felice J. Levine on ICE guidance on international students and university online-only instruction.* www.aera.net/Newsroom/Statement-by-AERA-Executive-Director-Felice-J-Levine-on-ICE-Guidance-on-International-Students-and-University-Online-Only-Instruction

Amornsiripanitch, N., Gompers, P. A., Hu, G., & Vasudevan, K. (2021). *Getting schooled: The role of universities in attracting immigrant entrepreneurs* (No. w28773). National Bureau of Economic Research. www.nber.org/system/files/working_papers/w28773/w28773.pdf

Anderson, S. (2021, August 19). International students remain a primary source of U.S. tech talent. *Forbes.* www.forbes.com/sites/stuartanderson/2021/08/19/international-students-remain-a-primary-source-of-us-tech-talent/?sh=34625f58650d

Anderson, N. M., & Balin, E. (2020). Multiculturally competent and social justice oriented career counseling services: The case of an international student. In H. N. Maietta (Ed.), *Cases in career services: A working guide for practitioners.* National Association of Colleges and Employers.

Baker, D. B. (2009). Choosing a vocation at 100: Time, change, and context. *The Career Development Quarterly, 57*(3), 199–206. https://doi.org/10.1002/j.2161-0045.2009. tb00105.x

Balin, E. (2014). *A transnational feminist analysis of life-career narratives of international women students from Turkey* [Doctoral dissertation, Penn State University]. Penn State Electronic Theses and Dissertations for Graduate School. https://etda.libraries.psu.edu/catalog/ 23659

Balin, E., Anderson, N. M., Chudasama, S. Y., Kanagasingam, S. K., & Zhang, L. (2016). Working with international students in the US and beyond: A summary of survey research by NCDA International Student Services Committee. *Journal of International Students, 6*(4), 1053–1061. https://doi.org/10.32674/jis.v6i4.335

Bhandari, R. (2019). Global student and talent flows: Reexamining the brain drain equation. *International Higher Education, 99*, 6–7. https://doi.org/10.6017/ihe.2019.99.11643

Blustein, D. L., Kenny, M. E., Autin, K., & Duffy, R. (2019). The psychology of working in practice: A theory of change for a new era. *The Career Development Quarterly, 67*(3), 236–254. https://doi.org/https://doi.org/10.1002/cdq.12193

Cantwell, B., Lee, J. J., & Mlambo, Y. A. (2018). International graduate student labor as mergers and acquisitions. *Journal of International Students, 8*(4), 1483–1498. https://doi. org/10.32674/jis.v8i4.211

Chadha, N. K., Gambhir, V., & Mahavidyalya, C. (2018). The state of career services and career professionals in India. In H. J. Yoon, B. Hutchison, M. Maze, C. Pritchard, & A. Reiss (Eds.), *International practices of career services, credentials, and training* (pp.

112–127). National Career Development Association. www.researchgate.net/profile/Brian-Hutchison-2/publication/322274830_International_Practices_of_Career_Services_Credentialing_and_Training/links/5bc33dfe92851c88fd6a0aab/International-Practices-of-Career-Services-Credentialing-and-Training.pdf#pa

Chomsky, N. (2020). *Shaping a humane world. STAR scholar conference keynote speech.* https://starscholars.org/shaping-a-humane-world/

Collins, P. H., & Bilge, S. (2016). *Intersectionality (key concepts).* Polity.

De Wit, H. (2017) Global: Internationalization of higher education: Nine misconceptions. In G. Mihut, P. G. Altbach, & H. De Wit (Eds.), *Understanding higher education internationalization. Global perspectives on higher education.* Sense Publishers. https://doi.org/10.1007/978-94-6351-161-2_2

De Wit, H. (2020). *Covid 19: The end or revival of international higher education?* UC Berkeley. https://news.berkeley.edu/2020/05/07/covid-19-the-end-or-revival-of-international-higher-education/

De Wit, H., & Altbach, P. G. (2021). Internationalization in higher education: Global trends and recommendations for its future. *Policy Reviews in Higher Education, 5*(1), 28–46. https://doi.org/10.1080/23322969.2020.1820898

De Wit, H., & Deca, L. (2020). Internationalization of higher education, challenges and opportunities for the next decade. In A. Curaj, L. Deca, & R. Pricopie (Eds.), *European Higher Education Area* (pp. 3–13). Springer. https://doi.org/10.1007/978-3-030-56316-5

De Wit, H., Gacel-Ávila, J., & Jones, E. (2017). Voices and perspectives on internationalization from the emerging and developing world: Where are we heading? In H. De Wit, J. Gacel-Ávila, E. Jones, & N. Jooste (Eds.), *The globalization of internationalization: Emerging voices and perspectives* (1st ed.). Routledge. https://doi.org/10.4324/9781315657547

Duffy, R. D., Velez, B. L., England, J. W., Autin, K. L., Douglass, R. P., Allan, B. A., & Blustein, D. L. (2018). An examination of the psychology of working theory with racially and ethnically diverse employed adults. *Journal of Counseling Psychology, 65*(3), 280–293. https://doi.org/10.1037/cou0000247

DuRose, L., & Stebleton, M. J. (2016). Lost in translation: Preparing students to articulate the meaning of a college degree. *Journal of College and Character, 17*(4), 271–277. https://doi.org/10.1080/2194587X.2016.1230759

Field, A. T. (2018, November 12). How colleges are helping international students land jobs after graduation. *The Chronicle of Higher Education.* www.chronicle.com/article/how-colleges-are-helping-international-students-land-jobs-after-graduation/

Fischer, K., & Aslanian, S. (2021). Why America is losing international students. *The Chronicle of Higher Education.* www.chronicle.com/article/fading-beacon

Harris, J. C., & Patton, L. D. (2019). Un/doing intersectionality through higher education research. *The Journal of Higher Education, 90*(3), 347–372. https://doi.org/10.1080/00221546.2018.1536936

Herridge, A. S., García, H. A., & Leong, M. C. (2019). Intersectionality of lesbian, gay, and bisexual international students: Impact of perceived experiences on campus engagement.

Journal for the Study of Postsecondary and Tertiary Education, 4, 49–65. https://doi.org/10.28945/4412

Higher Education Policy Institute. (2019). *The soft-power benefits of educating the world's leaders* [Policy note]. www.hepi.ac.uk/wp-content/uploads/2019/09/Policy-Note-16-_-The-soft-power-benefits-of-educating-the-world%E2%80%99s-leaders-05_09_19-Screen.pdf

Internship Funding Program at Duke University. (2021). https://studentaffairs.duke.edu/career/programs/internship-funding-program

Jones, E., & De Wit, H. (2012). Globalization of internationalization: Thematic and regional reflections on a traditional concept. *AUDEM: The International Journal of Higher Education and Democracy, 3*(1), 35–54. www.muse.jhu.edu/article/500242

Karaman, N., & Christian, M. (2020). "My hijab is like my skin color": Muslim women students, racialization, and intersectionality. *Sociology of Race and Ethnicity, 6*(4), 517–532. https://doi.org/10.1177/2332649220903740

Kenny, M. E., Blustein, D. L., Gutowski, E., & Meerkins, T. (2018). Combatting marginalization and fostering critical consciousness for decent work. In V. Cohen-Scali, & J. Pouyad (Eds.), *Interventions in career design and education: Transformation for sustainable development and decent work*. Springer International.

Kenyon, M. A., & Rowan-Kenyon, H. T. (2014). The globalization of career services. *New Directions for Student Services, 2014*(148), 93–102. https://doi.org/https://doi.org/10.1002/ss.20111

Kim, H., & Allen, R. M. (2018). Glocalizing cures for China's brain drain ills: The Thousand talents plan in Shanghai, Tianjin, and Guangdong. *International Journal of Comparative Education and Development, 20*(1), 16–32.

Kochhar, R. (2021, March 18). *The pandemic stalls growth in the global middle class, pushes poverty up sharply*. Pew Research Center. www.pewresearch.org/global/2021/03/18/the-pandemic-stalls-growth-in-the-global-middle-class-pushes-poverty-up-sharply/

Lim, B. K., & Lim, S.-L. (2015). Counseling in China. In T. H. Hohenshil, N. E. Amundson, & S. G. Niles (Eds.), *Counseling around the world* (pp. 75–86). https://doi.org/https://doi.org/10.1002/9781119222736.ch9

Lu, X. (2018, August 14). *Transnational education: Sino-foreign cooperative universities in China*. World Education News and Reviews. https://wenr.wes.org/2018/08/sino-foreign-cooperative-universities

Malcolm, Z. T., & Mendoza, P. (2014). Afro-Caribbean international students' ethnic identity development: Fluidity, intersectionality, agency, and performativity. *Journal of College Student Development, 55*(6), 595–614. https://doi.org/10.1353/csd.2014.0053

Mbodj, A., Balin, E., Goldman, E. Z., & Park, U. Y. (2021). *Advocating for international student wellbeing and career development in the pandemic*. NCDA Career Convergence. https://ncda.org/aws/NCDA/pt/sd/news_article/354901/_PARENT/CC_layout_details/false

Modica, J. (2021). *Graduate student workers on the rise*. American Association of University Professors. www.aaup.org/article/graduate-student-workers-rise#.YPsCpy0RoWo

Mwangi, C. A., Changamire, N., & Mosselson, J. (2019). An intersectional understanding of African international graduate students' experiences in US higher education. *Journal of Diversity in Higher Education, 12*(1), 52. https://doi.org/10.1037/dhe0000076

National Association of Colleges and Employers. (2021). Career readiness: Competencies for a career-ready workforce. www.naceweb.org/uploadedfiles/files/2021/resources/nace-career-readiness-competencies-revised-apr-2021.pdf

NAFSA: Association of International Educators. (2020). *Factors influencing international student enrollment growth and decline.* www.nafsa.org/professional-resources/browse-by-interest/immigration-executive-actions-under-trump-administration

National Science Foundation. (2019). *Survey of earned doctorates, 2019.* https://ncses.nsf.gov/pubs/nsf21308/report/executive-summary

National Career Development Association–International Student Services Committee. (2020). *Resources for partnering with international students.* www.ncda.org/aws/NCDA/pt/sp/global_resources

Nunamaker, T. D., & Cawthon, T. W. (2018, November 1). *Engaging students: On-campus internship programs.* NACE Journal. www.naceweb.org/career-development/internships/engaging-students-the-on-campus-internship-program/

Open Doors. (2020). *2020 Fast facts: International students in the United States.* https://opendoorsdata.org/wp-content/uploads/2020/05/Open-Doors-2020-Fast-Facts.pdf

Rose-Redwood, C., & Rose-Redwood, R. (2018). Building bridges across the international divide: Fostering meaningful cross-cultural interactions between domestic and international students. *Journal of International Students, 8*(3), 1328–1336. https://doi.org/10.32674/jis.v8i3.56

Savickas, M. L. (2009). Pioneers of the vocational guidance movement: A centennial celebration. *The Career Development Quarterly, 57*(3), 194. https://doi.org/10.1002/j.2161-0045.2009.tb00104.x

Shepardson, D. (2021). *U.S. eases COVID-19 restrictions on Chinese students.* Reuters. www.reuters.com/world/china/exclusive-us-ease-travel-restrictions-chinese-students-sources-2021-04-27/

Shih, K. (2017). Do international students crowd-out or cross-subsidize Americans in higher education? *Journal of Public Economics, 156,* 170–184. https:doi.org/10.1016/j.jpubeco.2017.10.003

Tian, L., & Liu, N. C. (2021). Inward international students in China and their contributions to global common goods. *Higher Education, 81*(2), 197–217. https://doi.org/10.1007/s10734-020-00522-5

Toporek, R., & Daniels. (2018). *ACA advocacy competencies: A social justice framework for counselors.* American Counseling Association. www.counseling.org/docs/default-source/competencies/aca-advocacy-competencies-updated-may-2020.pdf?sfvrsn=f410212c_4

University of Baltimore. (2021). *What is the career cycle?* www.ubalt.edu/campus-life/career-center/career-services-online/career-cycle/

World Education Services. (2016). *Career services for international students: Fulfilling high expectations.* https://knowledge.wes.org/WES-Research-Report-Career-Services-for-International-Students.html

World Education Services. (2017). *Career prospects and employment outcomes of U.S.-educated international students: Improving services, bolstering success.* https://knowledge.wes.org/wes-research-report-career-outcomes

World Education Services. (2020). *How is Covid-19 impacting international higher education in the United States?* https://knowledge.wes.org/rs/317-CTM-316/images/research-report-how-is-covid-19-impacting-international-higher-education-in-the-us.pdf

7

In Support of First-Generation and Working-Class Students' Career Development: Navigating the Hidden Curriculum of the Workplace

Rashné R. Jehangir, Kimberlie Moock, and Todd B. Williams

The phrase that has caused heated debate in my head goes, "Work to live or live to work?" After many hours of talking to myself, I have come to a conclusion: If work will run its course parallel to my life, intertwining with it at times, then I want it to have more impact in my life than just financial stability.

Pa, Hmong, first-generation college student

Higher education often trumpets its role as a vehicle for creating more equitable, meaningful lives for its graduates. An instrument for the public good, the narrative of coming to college is rooted in the promise of upward mobility. Data demonstrates that college-educated folx are more likely to vote, to own a home, to send their own children to college, and to engage in work that offers both financial security and meaning (Hout, 2020; Hurst, 2010). This narrative is not untrue, but the impact of coming to and staying in college does not translate into equitable opportunities for all. For students who are first in their family to come to college, this promise narrative is powerful. As Pa's words suggest, first-generation college students are the new majority and are eager to contribute to a workforce that will allow for prosperity and purpose. But there is also evidence to suggest that first-generation college students leave with more significant debt, are more likely to be underemployed, and cannot gain entry to engines of economic prosperity and purpose as can their non-first-generation counterparts (Hurst, 2015; Walpole, 2003).

And yet first-generation students are coming to college in growing numbers. They make up over a third of the college-going population and arrive with aspirational, navigational, linguistic, and familial capital that seeks to challenge the status quo

DOI: 10.4324/9781003213000-10

(Jehangir, 2020; Skomsvold, 2015; Yosso, 2005). Career development scholars and practitioners are taking note and increasingly attending to ways in which they can intentionally partner with these students whose presence is needed in today's workforce. Employers are also eager to capitalize on the diversity of this new majority. Yet a 2017 Gallup survey revealed that only a third of current students believed they would graduate with the skills and knowledge needed to be successful in the job market and the workplace, respectively (Strada Information Network & Gallup, 2017). In particular, a *Lumina* report highlighted that a larger percentage of lower-income Americans believe colleges prepare individuals for success in the workplace (Gallup & Lumina Foundation, 2014). And herein lies the challenge: First generation students enter institutions of higher education that were not designed for them. They navigate this complex space toward graduation and often find that this pattern persists with similar transitional pains and gaps in understanding as they move from college to workplace. This chapter cannot unpack all the ways in which generational wealth, social and cultural capital, and the confluence of racism and classism constrain employment, and educational opportunities for first-generation graduates (Hurst, 2015; Jehangir & Collins, 2021). We can, however, provide a snapshot of the complexity and assets of first-generation students and offer frames from which career development practitioners, scholars, and future employers can better support this new majority.

The three authors of this piece come to this work from different positionalities and it is collaboration with each other and with students that has brought us together. Jehangir is an associate professor of higher education and director of undergraduate studies in a program that requires students (many of whom are first-generation and students of color) to engage in internships for their major. Moock is a first-generation PhD candidate in higher education and has redesigned curriculum and served as lead instructor for both pre-internship and internship courses. As a student affairs practitioner she has supervised and mentored students in campus peer leadership and paraprofessional roles with a focus on cultivating workplace competencies and transferable skills. Williams came to higher education after over two decades of experience in private industry working in sales, merchandising, and diversity, equity, and inclusion at Procter and Gamble and Target. He currently directs the University of Minnesota's Center for Sales Leadership and Education.

Our collective research and the work of other scholar practitioners (Jehangir, 2010, 2015, 2021; Miller et al., 2018; Terry & Fobia, 2019) has raised questions about how we can be more effective in translating the benefits of experiential experience into positive returns in the workforce for first-generation working-class (FGWC) students. Often their potential is not fully realized, and they experience lower returns on their college degree (Rivera & Tilcsik, 2016; Stephens et al., 2019). Student quotes inserted throughout this chapter are drawn from a larger study by Jehangir (2021) and are featured to situate the dilemmas we address in students in the students' own words.

Data from both our research and practice has also focused on what role universities have in preparing for the *headwinds* that FGWC students experience as they enter the workforce. Also, how career professionals could engage students' *tailwinds* or assets to propel them into arenas of work that are new to them and their families. Finally, employers have articulated the need and necessity for a diverse workforce, yet the ways in which they have socialized and oriented new employees to their organizations have not necessarily changed to meet the needs of the historic demographic shifts in the US. How might employers include new employees in negotiating these new spaces while also engaging their capital?

Who are FGWC Students?

Over a third of college students in the US are first in their family to go to college. This complex group cannot be easily pigeonholed and there is variance in the way academic literature and federal policy defines the term (Jehangir, 2010; Skomsvold, 2015; Toutkoushian et al., 2019). For the purposes of this chapter, we define first-generation to be students whose caregivers have not earned a college degree in the United States (Ardoin, 2021). Of importance is recognizing the multiple identities that first-generation students hold. First-generation students find commonality amongst each other through the shared experiences of navigating the college experience but are demographically heterogeneous (Jehangir, 2021; Longwell-Grice, 2021; Soria & Stebleton, 2012).

As the term first-generation has gained popularity in higher education, there has been a tendency to use it broadly without unpacking the demographic and lived experience that shape students' arrival at college. While it is problematic to conflate first-generation status with social class or race, it is equally important to recognize that first-generation students are disproportionately poor and working-class (50.3%), female (60.2%), and students of color (Nguyen & Nguyen, 2018). Many are also immigrants and/or refugees and multilingual (Staklis & Horn, 2012). This complex heterogeneity speaks to the ways in which they have become accustomed to negotiating multiple worlds where norms, procedures, mores, and language are driven by unwritten rules shaped by dominant and primarily White middle-class contexts.

The terminology of low-income is often used in association with first-generation as an indicator of social class status. This is inappropriate as social class is more than wealth and/or income; it is a culture with values, norms, beliefs, and behaviors. Social class membership greatly shapes the experiences and opportunities in society and therefore affects our identity development. Soria and Stebleton (2013) expressed the difficulties of relying solely on economic indicators to determine class status, stating: "association with working-class is attributed to a complex array of factors including workplace power dynamics, conceptual perception of position in society, family values, cultural values, history, ancestral work history, and cultural narratives"

(p. 140). In many ways, the obstacles of being working-class have similarity to the obstacles faced by first-generation students (Ardoin & martinez, 2019; Barratt, 2011; Hurst, 2012). It may be of no surprise these similarities exist as working-class individuals, just as first-generation, hold multiple identities.

It is this complex intersection of race, social class, and immigrant status in addition to being first-generation status that speaks to the experience of straddling multiple worlds without fully feeling a part of them. Many FGWC students have already regularly traversed the borderlands between home, school, and low-wage jobs without the requisite guides on etiquette and rules that privilege students whose parents have received college degrees. This active negotiation of structural inequities reflects an opportunity gap that NASPA *Center for First-Generation Student Success* refers to as a "critical cultural capital necessary for college success because their parent did not attend college" (Center for First-Generation Student Success, 2017, para. 5). And this in and of itself is reflective of the core problem – first that college and the transition into the workforce requires a certain *type* of capital that is shaped by access to networks impacted by race and wealth; and second that higher education has not been effective at helping FGWC students translate their ways of knowing and navigational capital into college and career journeys. FGWC students will also become FGWC professionals. The college experience provides critical opportunities for students to garner capital through various means – courses, research, applied experiences, co-curricular activities, civic engagement, and studying abroad. And Barratt (2011) is quick to remind us that "the accumulation of capital does count in the job search. The one with the most capital wins the best job" (p. 145).

Equity Implications of Accumulating Capital for Career Trajectories

Much of the literature on FGWC students situates the role of *capital* as a vital resource (Hurst, 2010; Soria & Stebleton, 2012) in achieving success during college and in the workplace. Many types of capital – cultural, social, economic, community cultural wealth, human, leadership, academic, career – have been operationalized to describe different assets valued in normative society and provide benefits for enhancing an individual's life circumstances. *Cultural capital* comprises personal experience and socialization, educational credentials, and knowledge of systems (Barratt, 2011). The importance of capital is as a non-monetary form of currency providing access and worth by its perceived prestige in a given environment. Building capital takes time and is predicated on the social spaces one belongs to or has access to. The common theme running through much of the literature has to do with an individual's ability to garner the necessary capital through experiences, networks, advice, and collaboration, and to show an independent disposition (Bozionelos, 2001; Inkson & Arthur, 2001; Parks-Yancy, 2018; Stephens et al., 2019).

Bozionelos (2001) stressed that relationships and networks are crucial to gaining social capital for first-time employment, and professional work transitions are boosted by even the most tenuous connections to other professionals. Arthur et al. (1999) described career competencies, "earned through education, work, and life experience" (p. 158), as accumulated *career capital* comprising three areas of individual knowing: why (values, aspirations, motivations), how (qualifications, abilities, skills), and whom (networks and reputation). Brown and Hesketh (2004) argued that knowledge and service sector employers use academic credentials as only entry criteria and the selection process requires a candidate to show evidence of capital consisting of hard and soft skills and co-curricular involvements and accomplishments.

An Engagement Paradox

An individual presents their resume as a record of the forms of capital they possess when applying for employment. The college experience provides critical opportunities for students to garner capital through various means – courses, research, applied experiences, co-curricular activities, civic engagement, and studying abroad. Many institutions embed high-impact practices (HIPs) into the curriculum, providing avenues for students to acquire both "hard" and "soft" skills contributing to career readiness (Kuh et al., 2005). Co-curricular experiences effectively promote personal learning and development, are linked to the acquisition of career competencies, and increase the likelihood of employment post-graduation (Kuh, 2008; Miller et al., 2018). Additionally, experiential learning activities such as internships, work-integrated learning, apprenticeships, and service-learning increase a student's career readiness (Hora et al., 2016; Jackson, 2015; Jackson & Wilton, 2016; Miller et al., 2018; Robles, 2012).

FGWC students are less likely to participate in co-curricular activities – whether due to time constraints, monetary resources, or not seeing involvement as a strategy to yield tangible benefits for future employment (Hurst, 2015; Stuber, 2009; Walpole, 2003). The research indicated that a student's sociocultural background plays a critical role in forming their disposition to determine out-of-class experiences' future value. In many cases, FGWC students are working during college to support their family or to contribute to college costs. This tension is the underlying principle of the *Capital Accumulation Paradigm (CAP)* (Liu et al., 2004). In a capitalist environment, the paradigm postulates that individuals accumulate assets valued by their lived experience, allowing them to remain aligned with the values and expectations of that community or environment. Dissonance arises when individuals engage in new environments, for our purposes higher education and professional work environments, that value different behaviors, expressions, and cultural values deemed necessary. CAP provides a way to understand an individual's motivations and the behaviors, relationships, and attitudes acquired that support their worldview.

While higher education institutions seek the learning and personal development results from student participation in HIPs, their value does not align with FGWC because in many cases working unpaid opportunities or giving up hours at jobs that contribute to their family income to attend career nights are not viable. The vast majority of HIPs are not embedded in the university's required curriculum, demanding extra time outside of class, and many come with an additional financial cost (directly and indirectly). Soria et al. (2013) found that working-class students are unlikely to be able to invest extra time in activities and relationship building viewed as ancillary to classroom engagement supporting knowledge development.

It is evident that FGWC students find themselves in an engagement paradox, act in congruence with their lived experience, or adapt to the expectations of involvement as they navigate the college experience. Considering how FGWC students may be perceived as career-ready by employers, this engagement paradox must be addressed as a structural and systemic barrier that impedes equitable outcomes. The result of maintaining the status quo is the perpetual sociocultural and economic stratification of society, with non-FGWC students continuing to maintain and accumulate the capital most valued in the workplace. The equity imperative facing institutions is creating environments that guarantee FGWC students are participating in these invaluable experiences that result in competencies, skills, and attributes highly desired by employers.

FGWC Students Transitioning and Navigating Professional Workspaces

Why should one consider a student's first-generation low-income identity when considering developing career education initiatives and programs? Simply put – if career educators seek to act on the social justice premise of the field (Parsons, 1909) and focus on improving individuals' lives through work (Blustein, 2006), then reexamining systematic barriers for FGWC is imperative. Over the last decade, institutions have begun to address the ways in which FGWC students need support to achieve a college degree. This attention has focused on addressing student sense of belonging and developing academic supports, with success measured by retention and graduation rates (Soria, 2015; Whitley et al., 2018). Absent in the majority of approaches to career readiness, acquisition, and transition are approaches based on social identity (i.e., first-generation, social class) rather than an individual competency and skill-building approach. Among students who graduated with a bachelor's degree in the academic year 2015–16, 48% were first-generation, and data indicated they participated in traditional career fairs and resume planning services at lower rates than their non-first-generation counterparts (NASPA Center for First-Generation Student Success & Crimsonbridge Foundation, 2021). As this identity group begins to be the majority on college campuses our practices and programs must be reimagined to serve these students best.

Barriers to Professional Workspaces

Terry and Fobia (2019) suggested three gaps or barriers to first-generation professionals' successful workplace inclusion: wealth, access to trusted adults to aid in collegiate navigation, and access to the professional components that allow for successful navigation of white-collar culture. Many FGWC students do not have access to the resources to participate in crucial development opportunities (i.e., unpaid internships, travel for education, conferences, workshops, etc.). Generational wealth gaps may manifest as a monetary or time constraint; for instance, a student may not have the money to attend a workshop or may not be able to take time off from a job to attend; financial hardship is experienced in a variety of manners.

Secondly, students may find it difficult to determine who is best equipped to aid in understanding how not just to navigate college but to reap the full rewards of a college experience. Higher education is full of terminology and structure vastly different from the secondary education system, and understanding how to navigate and seek support can be confusing. Lastly, FGWC students may face barriers connected to navigating a white-collar culture and need several different types of support: 1) individuals that can explain the nuances of the white-collar environment and provide tips for successful navigation; 2) aid in understanding the importance of networking and building a professional support network; and 3) gateways to career mentors and sponsors that can inform and support career aspirations.

Loss of Human Potential

It is too early to know if recently adopted strategies, championed by external influencers (National Association of Colleges and Employers (NACE), Association of Public Land Grant Universities, University Innovation Alliance, American Council on Education) to increase career readiness, are moving the needle for college graduates. These efforts are yielding new ways to address building career readiness during college; however, none of the solutions address the issue from the perspective of first-generation and social class disparities. The framing of the problem and solutions continue to be perceived as individual challenges versus a social-cultural identity challenge. Just as higher education has worked on access and degree completion issues aimed at FGWC students, it needs to ensure the next step for FGWC students is access not just to professional employment but equitable employment. It is essential to ensure that as students gain the cultural capital of a degree, they are not perceived as being unprepared for the professional workplace. The report *The Permanent Detour* (Burning Glass Technologies and Strada Institute for the Future of Work, 2018) found that 43% of new college graduates are underemployed in their first post-college job and are "five times more likely to remain so after five years" (p. 10). In other words, most underemployed graduates never catch up. Underemployment has lingering effects as only a third of underemployed workers secured appropriate employment after five years, and "74% were still under-employed ten years after their first job" (p. 18.) While this report does not break the data out by first-generation or social class status, it does raise questions about the effects of systemic classism and sexism.

Navigating Multiple Worlds

As humans we desire to be seen, understood, and valued for who we are and what we contribute to our communities. This is a challenge all individuals face throughout our lifetimes, but it intensifies when we engage in new and unfamiliar environments. For FGWC individuals the college and professional environments are new territory and are centered and structured for the privileged majority culture – mainly white middle-class culture. These environments foster a feeling of invisibility, being out of step with peers, and the devaluing of FGWC ways of knowing (Ardoin, 2021; Bettencourt, 2021; Hurst, 2010). The stress of navigating the unfamiliar culture of higher education can be intimidating and hostile (Hurst, 2010; Jehangir, 2010). Resolving the discord of their identity and operating in the higher education envir-onment forces many to hide or relinquish their sociocultural values to a certain extent. The invisibility of holding a marginalized social identity and status for many results in a lack of institutional recognition, support, and valuing.

Navigating these new environments for an FGWC student may require fitting in, getting by, or passing for dominant social identity (Ardoin & martinez, 2019; Barratt, 2011; Bettencourt, 2021; Hurst, 2010). Depictions of FGWC students' lived experiences in the literature illuminate the persistent uncovering and struggle to decode the environment, learn the rules of engagement, and find belonging, and how the importance of living in two worlds simultaneously deeply affected their experiences. The constant "battling of imposter syndrome involves an infinite journey with questioning belonging and whether [they] are enough" (Ardoin & martinez, 2019, p. 167). Jehangir (2010) challenged scholars and practitioners to understand belonging and place as "not only to be welcomed but also to feel that we have something to contribute. To belong is to find connection, to leave our mark, and to be understood and valued for our unique contributions" (p. 119).

The challenges of straddling multiple worlds often result in individuals code-switching, a technique to adjust one's way of being to operate successfully in social contexts and benefit from affiliating with both communities (Morton, 2014). However, code-switching has been positioned as a forced response to negative stereotypes in order to be perceived as a member of the normative culture. Elkins and Hanke (2018) challenged professionals to view code-switching as individual agency, activating the cultural wealth of an individual's navigational, linguistic, and resistance capital to achieve desired results and goals. While employers are seemingly eager to engage and diversify their workforce there is a chasm between the individ-uals they seek to employ and the receptiveness of their organizational cultures to incorporate multiple ways of being. They do not see the adaptation FGWC individuals are required to make as they center organization culture over the sociocultural identities of their diversified workforce.

Students need to understand the capital that they possess not only in the attainment of their initial roles, but also for the purposes of self-advocacy within current and future roles. The disconnect between the students' capital and that sought by employers leads to a gap in self-perception. Additionally, the gap in access to HIP experiences further erodes human potential and creates a wider gap between the competencies and experiences that employers seek and those of FGWC students. This gap widens further as the competencies that are valued by employers differ from the capital derived from FGWC students' lived experiences along with those obtained in their higher education pursuits. As these employees transition from initial career roles into early career roles they start to discover additional skills and competencies needed to find success during this next phase of their career, such as the ability to successfully navigate complex and matrixed organizations, having resilience when faced with adversity, and the ability to inspire and engage.

Re-Framing the Career Context

While the context of wealth, mentoring, and access to professional components of white-collar capital are critical to understanding FGWC success and the timing of the career trajectory, both educators and employers would do well to consider phases of career support in how they launch and onboard FGWC students into the workforce. Specifically, the needs of new employees in the entry phases are vastly different from the needs of those who are in the early career phase. The transition points that all employees, but especially FGWC students and employees, experience as they move between not only home, community, and work worlds, but also different arenas within work, require close attention. Recognizing and bridging these different phases is critical to retaining this new majority and their capital in the workforce. Hence we differentiate between the phases of entry, early career, and advancing professional development for FGWC students and employees.

It is important to look at three distinct phases of the professional workforce: the initial phase of entry, early career phase, and an advanced phase. The entry phase represents the first role that the FGWC student might have in their professional career. The entry, early career, and advanced career positions and phases are different and require different investments to achieve the outcomes that deliver the potential to reduce or eliminate wealth and economic disparities. The entry phase is when employers are most likely to rely on the lowest common denominators to measure potential for success. These include GPA and other criteria from the NACE (2017) career competencies framework. These measures allow for disparate employment pools to be easily compared to one another and for organizations to select candidates based on the standard competencies. Cultural wealth capital may not be valued as much by the employers; however, it can get showcased in the early career phase.

The early career and advanced phases are much more reliant on historical work performance skills and talents that align to the individual, and their specific experiences. The early career phase, two to three years post the entry phase, can be shaped by the extent to which all employees, but especially FGWC, are able to have guidance and mentoring that assists with understanding the political and cultural context of the organization. Often, the need for the new workforce entrant to navigate the workforce in ways that catapult them into the early career phase is reliant on the understanding of the aforementioned white-collar culture and the organization's unwritten rules and networks. It is in this phase that intentional mentoring around rules, etiquette, and mores are critical to the success of the FGWC students' long-term career success and the transition into the advancement phase, where additional responsibilities and management of others become more evident.

Recommendations for Practice

FGWC students and their allies should recognize three components that impact their career trajectories: historic and systemic barriers, headwinds, and tailwinds. Here we set the stage for each component and suggest actions institutions and professionals can take to support the career readiness, acquisition, and transition of FGWC students.

Historic and Systemic Barriers within Higher Education

We cannot say it too many times –colleges and universities were *not* built with FGWC culture and needs as a focus. It is critical that institutions acknowledge and dismantle policies and practices that create differential rewards and outcomes for historically and ongoing marginalized students. Here three recommendations are provided:

- *Be a constant advocate.* Speak up in places where you have influence to educate, build coalitions, and change policies and practice. In situations where decisions are being made, be the voice of FGWC students and advocate for the recognition of inequitable practices and the dismantling of structures that negate, discount, or harm the success and outcomes for FGWC students.
- *Address the financial barriers to key capital-building experiences.* Many of the most beneficial experiences require additional monetary resources – study abroad, conferences, social organization involvement, etc. Institutions should work to ensure these experiences are accessible without incurring additional debt for students with financial need. If institutions view these as vital to the learning

and development process it should provide a funding mechanism for all students – not just limited scholarships or waivers.

- *Create equitable networking and applied experiences.* Historically, networking can be transactional and build on existing capital, comfort with certain types of spaces, language, etiquette – but what is needed is more spaces that have applied networking to cultivate relationships of trust, respect, and support. Additionally, FGWC students face challenges in finding equitable internships (both in experience and remuneration). Institutions must partner with alumni networks, companies and non-profits, and workforce leaders to create active pipelines for paid internships, mentoring, and employment that demonstrate an understanding of the capital and the alienation that these students feel when they leave college and enter workspaces that have not been reflected in their families' histories and work experiences.

Mitigate Headwinds

Headwinds are the hidden and non-visible systems, structures, and skills that can have an impact on an individual's trajectory within their career. Headwinds are more subtle than derailers; however, they do play a role in slowing down progression towards a goal or an outcome. Consider the following recommendations to address headwinds.

- *Incorporate and utilize language that legitimizes accumulated assets and capital.* Colleges and universities need to acknowledge, value, and recognize the assets of FGWC identities. By incorporating the strengths of social identities into curriculum and supporting programs we challenge the deficit narrative that has a long history in higher education. The power of having your identity woven into the college experience and the possessed distinctive cultural capital venerated cannot be underestimated. Empower FGWC students' pride of culture and values as assets, to be honed as distinctive capital and desired attributes in the professional workplace.
- *Intentional curriculum that reveals the hidden curriculum of work.* Oldfield (2007) remarked that "I deciphered that faculty say that working class people have 'jobs' but middle- and upper-class folks have 'professions'" (p. 7). This quote hones in on the hidden curriculum of professional work that exists on our campuses. It is critical that undergraduate career educators and student affairs professionals support students to understand the expectations of professional work environments; one cannot assume that all students conceive of work in the same context. Supporting the development of career competencies is only as relevant as one's understanding of the expectations and values they hold in the workplace. Making explicit connections between workplace competencies and students' skills, attributes, and dispositions becomes critically relevant.

Additionally, it is essential that FGWC cultural wealth capital is incorporated into our career competency schemas and curriculum and seen as a desirable and sought-after ability. This understanding must be developed prior to and intentionally reflected upon during applied experiences in order for FGWC students to reap the benefits in their career outcomes post degree.

- *Unpack and share the hidden structures of the workplace.* Organizations that wish to invest in their talent should seek to activate both formal and informal mentoring support to help FGWC students to understand the nuances and navigational needs within the organization. By creating safe spaces for exploration, learning, and development for their teams for hidden capital, organizations then can focus on building empathy and understanding of FGWC students, versus performative curiosity actions. Finally, have organizations identify systems, structures, and processes that are inequitable for FGWC employees, then advocate for their removal to ensure inclusivity within the workplace.

Leverage Tailwinds

> My life is full of leaders, advisors, and friends that have already had a full impact on my life. We are normal human beings with outrageous potential and one would not guess that majority, if not all, of us came from low-income families that didn't have much.
>
> Alexis, Black FGWC student

Tailwinds, unlike the aforementioned headwinds, play a role in accelerating an individual's progress within their career. Tailwinds represent those systems, structures, and skills that can aid an individual's trajectory within their career and can have the effect of helping to achieve goals or outcomes earlier than anticipated. Recommendations include:

- *Construct ways for students to recognize, document, and translate their cultural wealth Capital.* Career professionals should create ways to assist FGWC students in understanding and inventorying the transferable skills linked to cultural wealth capital and ensure the inclusion of these skills in their application materials and interview preparation. FGWC students need mediums by which they can accurately gauge their skills and practice translating these skills into workplace assets, especially because higher education and the workforce often fail to value their cultural wealth capital. This causes individuals to discount their assets and feel the need to assimilate into the privileged organizational capital structure as they are unable to translate their cultural wealth capital in a manner recognized and valued by the workplace. If one's assets are undervalued, then an individual focuses on accumulating other assets in order to be seen and valued. This extends beyond traditional career readiness assessments and is inclusive of the ability to accurately assess the unique skills and abilities the FGWC experiences offer. For example, Allison Pohle noted in her *Wall Street Journal* article (2021) that navigating the workplace involves understanding the nature of office politics and asking questions to learn more about how things work. This ability to quickly assess and understand unfamiliar spaces is an example of navigational capital in action; a critical skill in the workplace, however, is not one of the competencies that comes top of mind to employers seeking career entry talent. Colleges and universities must educate employers on the benefits of cultural wealth capital, create ways to help employers identify these competencies and skills, and advocate for employers to incorporate these in their evaluation of potential employees. The ability for students and employers to recognize this as capital and integrate it into the workplace can accelerate career acquisition and progression for FGWC individuals.

- *Support students to incorporate their authenticity into their professional identity.* Most students are coached to develop a 30-second elevator pitch to sell themselves during networking events and interviews. We agree but challenge professionals to go beyond this traditional notion and help students craft a strong and authentic professional identity narrative. Crafting how we perceive ourselves within our occupational context is critical in communicating our attributes, beliefs, values, and motivations to others and is vital in differentiating ourselves (Jehangir et al., 2020). The act of intentionally developing a professional identity aids students in honing their desired career environment and role. Students benefit and are empowered from developing concrete and expressive language for answering the "Tell us about yourself" question that prospective employers will undoubtedly ask. One approach to this may be to coach FGWC students around how and when to incorporate their lived experiences and community cultural wealth into their professional identity narrative. Structuring opportunities in our classrooms for students to reflect on their identities and how they influence their actions and reactions at work provides an avenue for students to better understand themselves and how they are influenced or choose to project themselves in the workplace.

- *Deepen the understanding of employers on the merit FGWC students bring to the workplace; challenge their conceptions of an inclusive workplace.* Not all employers may be familiar with the intersectional identities of first-generation students. To aid them, the Department of Commerce's First Generation Professionals Initiative guidance (2021) offers the following insights: Employers can begin by raising awareness of the population of FGWC professionals and identifying the systemic barriers, in the form of policies and practices, that may impede the ability to maximize and leverage FGWC in our workforce. With this in place, there can be implementation of programs that provide critical information and resources to realize FGWC students' full potential.

Secondly, organizations can execute procedures that continue to foster inclusive work environments by recruiting FGWC students at institutions of higher education that have a higher percentage of these students. In addition, employers must be conscientious of the systems and structures that may inhibit discovery of additional social capital the FGWC students can bring into the workplace. This involves engaging in internal dialogue between HR business partners, recruiters, hiring managers, and those interviewing the candidate, towards obtaining talent versus fit, with talent serving as the sum total of skills, abilities, and perspectives that students bring into the workplace; recognizing that the additional capital FGWC students offers helps to bring valuable experiences and perspectives. One way this can occur is having FGWC representation on hiring and selection panels, resulting in additional perspectives, improving the candidates' comfort and confidence, and potentially serving as a translator for less recognizable capital.

Finally, employers will also need to continue to understand the benefits and limitations of an ever-evolving workspace. As we continue to monitor how organizational workspaces evolve following the recent disruptions initiated by the global pandemic, remote and work from home solutions offer more flexibility and should allow for a more diverse and engaged workforce. However, the complications from this evolved workspace remain, such as technological access, limitations of underdeveloped networks and relationships, and critical collaboration moments with managers and peers, as well as absence of structure, and interference between life and work roles.

We recognize that these recommendations do not exist in a vacuum; rather there is a connective tissue between them and the emerging contexts of work, workplace, and remote work that has significant implications for how employees and employers will translate these into practice. FGWC students are adroit at negotiating unknown contexts, bureaucracy, and multiple worlds. As Blanca, a Latina first-generation student, shared: "Not everyone knows what they will go through in college; there are so many things that may change for us in order to know who we are and what our path is." The work of career educators and employers is to create more fluid crossings and transitions between these worlds and help students navigate this inevitable ambiguity that is the career journey.

References

Ardoin, S. (2021). The nuances of first-generation college student class identity. In R. Longwell-Grice & H. Longwell-Grice (Eds.), *At the intersection: First generation students and the influence of identities* (pp. 89–99). Stylus Publishing.

Ardoin, S., & martinez, b. (2019). *Straddling class in the academy: 26 stories of students, administrators, and faculty from poor and working-class backgrounds and their compelling lessons for higher education policy and practice.* Stylus Publishing.

Arthur, M. B., Inkson, K., & Pringle, J. K. (1999). *The new careers: Individual action and economic change.* Sage Publications.

Barratt, W. (2011). *Social class on campus: Theories and manifestations.* Stylus.

Bettencourt, G. M. (2021). "I belong because it wasn't made for me": Understanding working-class students' sense of belonging on campus. *The Journal of Higher Education, 92*(5), 760–783. https://doi.org/10.1080/00221546.2021.1872288

Blustein, D. L. (2006). *The psychology of working: A new perspective for career development, counseling, and public policy.* Routledge.

Brown, P., & Hesketh, A. (2004). *The mismanagement of talent: Employability and jobs in the knowledge economy.* Oxford University Press.

Bozionelos, N. (2001). Social capital and careers: Indisputable evidence and note for caution. In A. De Vos & B. I. J. Van der Heijden (Eds.), *Handbook of research on sustainable careers* (pp. 67–82). Edward Elgar Publishing Limited.

Burning Glass Technologies and Strada Institute for the Future of Work. (2018). *The permanent detour: Underemployment's long-term effects on the careers of college grads.* http://hdl.voced.edu.au/10707/457195

Center for First-Generation Student Success (2017, November 20). Defining first-generation. https://firstgen.naspa.org/blog/defining-first-generation

Elkins, B., & Hanke, E. (2018). Code-switching to navigate social class in higher education and student affairs. *New Directions for Student Services, 162*, 35–47. https://doi.org/10.1002/ss.20260

Gallup, & Lumina Foundation. (2014). *What America needs to know about higher education redesign.* www.luminafoundation.org/resource/what-america-needs-to-know-about-higher-education-redesign/

Hora, M. T., Benbow, R. J., & Oleson, A. K. (2016, December). *Beyond the skills gap: How the lack of systemic supports for teaching and learning undermine employer, student, and societal interests* (WCER Working Paper No. 2016-9). https://wcer.wisc.edu/docs/working-papers/Working_Paper_No_2016_9.pdf

Hout, M. (2020). Social and economic returns to college education in the United States. *Annual Review of Sociology, 38*(2012), 379–400. https://doi.org/10.1146/annurev.soc.012

Hurst, A. L. (2010). *The burden of academic success: Managing working-class identities while in college.* Rowman & Littlefield.

Hurst, A. L. (2012). *College and the working class: What it takes to make it.* Sense Publishers.

Hurst, A. L. (2015). Great expectations: Classed outcomes of liberal arts college graduates. In A. Sitch & C. Friele (Eds.), *The working classes and higher education: Inequality of access, opportunity, and outcome* (pp. 195–214). Routledge.

Inkson, K., & Arthur, M. B. (2001). *How to be a successful career capitalist.* www.organizational-dynamics.com

Jackson, D. (2015). Employability skill development in work-integrated learning: Barriers and best practice. *Studies in Higher Education, 40*(2), 350–367.

Jackson, D., & Wilton, N. (2016). Developing career management competencies among undergraduates and the role of work-integrated learning. *Teaching in Higher Education, 21*(3), 266–286. https://doi.org/10.1080/13562517.2015.1136281

Jehangir, R. (2010). *Higher education and first-generation students: Cultivating community, voice and place for the new majority.* Palgrave Macmillan Press.

Jehangir, R. (2020). First-generation students. In M. Amey & M. David (Eds.), *SAGE Encyclopedia of Higher Education* (pp. 550–554). SAGE.

Jehangir, R., & Collins, K. (2021, April). What's in a name? Narratives and counter-narratives of the first generation moniker. In R. Longwell-Grice & H. Longwell-Grice (Eds.), *At the intersection: First generation students and the influence of identities* (pp. 301–310). Stylus.

Jehangir, R., Stebleton, M. J., & Deenanath, V. (2015, August). *An exploration of intersecting identities of first-generation, low-income college students.* Monograph Report. University of South Carolina, National Resource Center for the First-Year Experience and Students in Transition. Stylus Press.

Jehangir, R. R., Telles, A. B., & Deenanath, V. (2020). Using photovoice to bring career into a new focus for first-generation college students. *Journal of Career Development, 47*(1), 59–79. https://doi.org/10.1177/0894845318824746

Kuh, G. D. (2008). *High-impact educational practices: What they are, who has access to them, and why they matter.* Association of American Colleges and Universities.

Kuh, G. D., Kinzie, J., Schuh, J. H., Whitt, E. J., & Associates. (2005). *Student success in college: Creating conditions that matter* (1st ed.). Jossey-Bass.

Liu, W. M., Soleck, G., Hopps, J., Dunston, K., & Pickett, T. (2004). A new framework to understand social class in counseling: The social class worldview model and modern classism theory. *Journal of Multicultural Counseling and Development, 32*(2), 95–122. https://doi.org/10.1002/j.2161-1912.2004.tb00364.x

Longwell- Grice, R. (2021). A review of the data. In R. Longwell-Grice & H. Longwell-Grice (Eds.), *At the intersection: First generation students and the influence of identities* (pp. 13–24). Stylus.

Miller, A. L., Rocconi, L. M., & Dumford, A. D. (2018). Focus on the finish line: Does high-impact practice participation influence career plans and early job attainment? *Higher Education, 75*(3), 489–506. https://doi.org/10.1007/s10734-017-0151-z

Morton, J. M. (2014). Cultural code-switching: Straddling the achievement gap. *Journal of Political Philosophy, 22*(3), 259–281. https://doi.org/10.1111/jopp.12019

National Association of Colleges and Employers. (2017). *Career readiness for the new college graduate.* www.naceweb.org/career-readiness/competencies/are-college-graduates-career-ready/

NASPA Center for First-Generation Student Success & Crimsonbridge Foundation. (2021). *First-generation college graduates: Race/ethnicity, age, and use of career planning services* [Fact sheet]. https://firstgen.naspa.org/journal-and-research/national-data-fact-sheets-on-first-generation-college-graduates/98CF9470-BD56-11EB-B5A90242AC100302

Nguyen, T., & Nguyen, B. M.D. (2018). Is the "first-generation student" term useful for understanding inequality? The role of intersectionality in illuminating the implications of an accepted – yet unchallenged – term. *Review of Research in Education, 42*(1), 146–176. https://doi.org/10.3102/0091732X18759280

Oldfield, K. (2007). Humble and hopeful: Welcoming first-generation poor and working-class students to college. *About Campus, 11*(6), 2–13. https://doi.org/10.1002/abc.188

Parks-Yancy, R. (2018). The effects of social group membership and social capital resources on careers. *Journal of Black Studies, 36*(4), 515–545. https://doi.org/10.1177/0021934704273501

Parsons, F. (1909). *Choosing a vocation*. National Career Development Association.

Pohle, A. (2021, April 19). How to navigate the workplace. *Wall Street Journal*, https://www.wsj.com/articles/how-to-navigate-the-workplace-11618862113

Rivera, L. A., & Tilcsik, A. (2016). Class advantage, commitment penalty: The gendered effect of social class signals in an elite labor market. *American Sociological Review, 81*(6), 1097–1131. https://doi.org/10.1177/0003122416668154

Robles, M. M. (2012). Executive perceptions of the top 10 soft skills needed in today's workplace. *Business Communication Quarterly, 75*(4), 453–465. https://doi.org/10.1177/1080569912460400

Skomsvold, P. (2015). *Web tables – Profile of undergraduate students: 2011–12* (NCES 2015-167). U.S. Department of Education. National Center for Education Statistics.

Soria, K. M. (2015). *Welcoming blue-collar scholars into the ivory tower: Developing class-conscious strategies for student success*. National Resource Center for The First-Year Experience and Students in Transition.

Soria, K. M., & Stebleton, M. J. (2012). First-generation students' academic engagement and retention. *Teaching in Higher Education, 17*(6), 673–685. https://doi.org/10.1080/13562517.2012.666735

Soria, K. M., Stebleton, M. J., & Huesman, R. L. (2013). Class counts: Exploring differences in academic and social integration between working-class and middle/upper-class students at large, public research universities. *Journal of College Student Retention: Research, Theory & Practice, 15*(2), 215–242. https://doi.org/10.2190/CS.15.2.e

Staklis, S., & Horn, L. (2012). *New Americans in postsecondary education: A profile of immigrants and second-generation American undergraduates*. (NCES Report No. 2012-213). National Center for Education Statistics.

Stephens, N. M., Townsend, S. S., & Dittmann, A. G. (2019). Social-class disparities in higher education and professional workplaces: The role of cultural mismatch. *Current Directions in Psychological Science, 28*(1), 67–73. https://doi.org/10.1177/0963721418806506

Strada Information Network, & Gallup. (2017). *2017 college student survey: A nationally representative survey of currently enrolled students*. https://news.gallup.com/reports/225161/2017-strada-gallup-college-student-survey.aspx

Stuber, J. (2009). Class, culture, and participation in the collegiate extra-curriculum. *Sociological Forum, 24*(4), 877–900. https://doi.org/10.1111/j.1573-7861.2009.01140.x

Terry, R. L., & Fobia, A. C. (2019). Qualitative research on barriers to workplace inclusion for first generation professionals. *Research and Methodology Directorate*, Center for Behavioral Science Methods Research Report Series (Survey Methodology 2019-03). U.S. Census Bureau.

Toutkoushian, R., Stollberg, R. A., & Slaton, K. A. (2018). Talking 'bout my generation: Defining "first-generation college students" in higher education research. *Teachers College Record: The Voice of Scholarship in Education, 120*, 1–38. https:doi.org.10.1177/016146811812000407

US Department of Commerce First Generation Professionals Initiative. (2021). www.commerce.gov/cr/programs-and-services/first-generation-professionals-initiative

Walpole, M. (2003). Socioeconomic status and college: How SES affects college experiences. *The Review of Higher Education, 27*(1), 45–73. https://doi.org/10.1353/rhe.2003.0044

Whitley, S. E., Benson, G., & Wesaw, A. (2018). *First-generation student success: A landscape analysis of programs and services at four-year institutions.* Center for First-generation Student Success, NASPA – Student Affairs Administrators in Higher Education, and Entangled Solutions.

Yosso, T. J. (2005). Whose culture has capital? A critical race theory discussion of community cultural wealth. *Race Ethnicity and Education, 8*(1), 69–91. https://doi.org/10.1080/1361332052000341006

Part III
Paradigm Shifts in Career Education

8
Design Thinking and the New Career Center

Joseph M. Catrino

Higher education and innovation are not typically considered synonymous. In fact, significant criticism has been thrust upon the higher education sector in recent years. Often framed as an institution that lacks change, moves at a glacial pace, and inhibits ingenuity, higher education has drawn the ire of critics for becoming too expensive and not preparing graduates for the future of work. Blass and Hayward (2014) exclaimed, "The history and legacy of universities [that] can make them resistant to change…is now being challenged by many government funders, industry partners and future students" (p. 1). Critics are bemoaning the traditions of higher education for failing to provide students with skills needed to be career-ready in a dramatically changing future of work, but things may not be as dire as these critics would lead us to believe. Innovation in higher education is alive and well.

This chapter will explore the possibilities inherent in the application of design thinking in career education. It will discuss the origins of design thinking in career development and describe the growing popularity of life design as an approach to career preparation. It will also address the rise of social media, and how the career center of the future can evolve to meet students where they are. Amid significant global disruption, the future of work is *now*. Professionals in career education are embracing innovation in working with students and this chapter aims to shed light on those strategies and initiatives, and outline recommendations for practitioners and counselors in career education.

Design Thinking

A human-centered approach to innovation, design thinking is a tool for creative problem solving. According to IDEO, the global design firm credited with inventing the term "design thinking:"

> Design thinking is a human-centered approach to innovation – anchored in understanding customers' needs, rapid prototyping, and generating creative

DOI: 10.4324/9781003213000-12

ideas – that will transform the way you develop products, services, processes, and organizations. By using design thinking, you make decisions based on what customers really want instead of relying only on historical data or making risky bets based on instinct instead of evidence.

(IDEOU, 2021, para. 1)

The critical component of design thinking is understanding a customer's needs – leading with empathy – and digging into the important factors causing a problem. Design thinking is a creative problem-solving approach that hinges on people, and understanding them. IDEO explained:

…we've been practicing human-centered design…and took up the phrase "design thinking" to describe the elements of the practice we found most learnable and teachable – empathy, optimism, iteration, creative confidence, experimentation, and an embrace of ambiguity and failure.

(n.d., para. 1)

These elements have formed the foundation for design thinking, although, admittedly, design thinking is a young science.

Richard Buchanan, a designer and scholar, investigated how design could impact society "through the notion of 'wicked problems'…problems that are complex, open-ended, and ambiguous" (IDEO, n.d., para. 3). Buchanan drew on the ideas of John Dewey and Horst Rittel, among others. He appreciated the interdisciplinary potential of design thinking, that it did not rely on a specific field to solve problems (Szczepanska, 2017). Design thinking is a mindset commonly used in many industries, sectors, and academic disciplines to solve wicked problems or problems that seem to be insurmountable. The world is experiencing a "new normal" of volatility, uncertainty, complexity, and ambiguity. Design thinking is just the tool to help society navigate those conditions.

The human-centered design-thinking approach to problem solving requires the following of the designer: being mindful of process, bias toward action, curiosity, radical collaboration or asking for help, and reframing problems. Maintaining these mindsets through the classic flow of design thinking is critical for wicked problem solving. The iterative "flow" of design thinking is *empathize, define, ideate or brainstorm, prototype*, and *test*. Users must remain mindful that the design-thinking process is iterative. They should embrace this iteration and the potential failures that come with it. Designers learn from failure and understand that repeating or revisiting steps in the design-thinking process is important to solving problems and encouraging innovation.

Design Thinking in Career Education

Design thinking presents a unique opportunity for career educators to coach with an empathetic, human-centered technique that engages students in the career process, which can be conceived of as a wicked problem; however, there is much more to it.

Though the concept of life design already existed in the career development literature (Savickas, 2009), more practice-centered design thinking made its way into higher education career services through the creation of the life design curriculum at Stanford University. Developed by Bill Burnett and Dave Evans, two life-long designers and Stanford d.school faculty members, life design "applies design thinking to tackling the 'wicked' problems of life and vocational wayfinding" (Stanford Life Design Lab, 2018a, para. 1). The Designing Your Life course taught at Stanford and the eventual book, *Designing Your Life: How to Build a Well-Lived, Joyful Life*, is focused on training students and readers to think like a designer, navigate major decisions, and solve life's wicked problems.

> They say the practices taught in the class and the book can help you (in designing-your-life-speak) "reframe" dysfunctional beliefs that surround life and career decisions and help you "wayfind" in a chaotic world through the adoption of such design tenets as bias-for-action, prototyping, and team-building.
>
> (Kurutz, 2016)

This new, unique approach to career education creates positive change in students' lives, through a design process that would encourage students to identify what it is they truly want to change and how they can go about manifesting it. In their book, Burnett and Evans (2016) explained that

> designers imagine things that don't yet exist, and then they build them, and then the world changes. You can do this in your own life. You can imagine a career and a life that doesn't exist; you can build that future, and as a result, your life will change.
>
> (2016, p. xxi)

Supporting students in their career journeys and encouraging them to explore and design the type of life they want to create for themselves is tantamount to life design. Students are encouraged to embrace failure by trying things (early and often according to Burnett and Evans) to learn about themselves, ask for help, be curious about life's opportunities, reframe problems to get unstuck, and understand that life design (like life) is an ongoing, iterative process. True to fashion, Burnett and Evans (2016) saw an opportunity beyond only working with students at Stanford University. A groundswell moment emerged to expand the designing your life curriculum to become a national and global movement. They decided, over the next several years, to bring in professionals from higher education, train them, and send them back to their institutions.

Burnett and Evans (2016) opened their life design curriculum by creating the Life Design Studio for University Educators. Using the foundation from the book and Stanford courses, the d.school faculty and staff train university educators in life design curriculum, in order for them to implement their learning at institutions of higher education across the globe. The Life Design Studio for University Educators program, which started in June 2017, provides attendees with the following, according to its website (Stanford Life Design Lab, 2018b, para. 8):

- *Immersive training in the life design material*: how to apply life design to yourself and your own professional development and how to launch life design projects, programs, classes, and more at your university, with a specific focus on virtual tools and delivery.
- *Virtual teaching best practices*: learn how to create community and to spark engagement even in the virtual environment. Discuss virtual best practices and tips to make every class you teach more engaging.
- *Personalized coaching*: we will have experienced facilitators to help you build prototypes and give you feedback.
- *Materials*: you will have access to our courseflow builder and, thus, all lesson plans, all our slides, recommended class and workshop sequences, and handouts and activities we use, including modules rebuilt this term for online delivery.
- *Post-workshop support*: we hold virtual office hour sessions to workshop the experiments you are trying back at home and host alumni sharing their work in addition to sending a monthly newsletter full of information to help you build your life design practice.
- A *Higher Ed Life Design Community*: access to the 500 or so other university educators also working in life design.

The training, offered multiple times a year, equips university professionals with life design skills, activities, and materials to coach, support, and guide students in their journeys into, through, and beyond their undergraduate experience. Applying the design-thinking process and adopting the design mindsets, career education professionals are empowering students to navigate their higher education experience and to thrive after graduation. This innovative training has grown in popularity since its inception in 2017. The studio and the book have been the foundation for the spread of life design. Using life design activities, lectures, and materials has equipped career educators with new tools and techniques to teach, engage, and develop the next-generation workforce. More colleges and universities are embracing life design in their career education programming, coaching, and events. Design thinking and life design are deeply embedded in over 100 colleges and universities across the globe. In fact, some colleges and universities have taken things a step further by re-branding and embracing a mission of life design. Traditional naming conventions of career development or career services centers have evolved to include language such as life design, labs, or career design. Colleges and universities are expanding beyond simply implementing life design programs, courses, and services; they have become the mission and vision for some career offices. Schools such as Johns Hopkins University have focused their career centers/offices on life design (Hub Staff, 2019).

Not only are career educators innovating by incorporating life design; many are teaching it to their students as they prepare for an uncertain future of work. Innovation in the form of design is growing exponentially through higher education, delivering career education professionals with a robust skillset to support the life design of college students across the globe.

Social Media

Social media is ingrained into our everyday communication. The practice and use of social media and mobile technologies have significantly impacted our lives. Mobile phones and tablets have become our constant companions. Because of this, literacy has shifted dramatically – how we read, research, write, collaborate, and present ideas and information has changed. Through the evaluation of common social media platforms and the evolving digital media industry, I will analyze how social media has dramatically altered the nature of human communication and how it impacts career education.

Social media has played an integral role in career education since the early 2000s. Social media has quickly become the newest version of the newspaper classified section; many people have turned to social media to explore career prospects and find a job or internship. Platforms such as LinkedIn profiles, blogs and online portfolios, and Twitter and Facebook groups emerged in a short amount of time; social media took the recruiting and career development worlds by storm (Apollo Technical, 2021).

The rapid growth of social media has required career educators to adapt new practices and procedures when working with students. Career educators were forced to familiarize themselves with social media tools and discuss their presence in and impact on job and internship searches. Additionally, career educators had to adapt to how human resources professionals evaluate, review, and leverage social media technologies to impact (or not) hiring decisions on the organizational level. It became imperative to understand how social media technologies have influenced and transformed traditional job search techniques (Apollo Technical, 2021). Social media has provided students with another outlet for the career process, so career educators have worked to understand, teach, and leverage the platforms and the messaging. As the job market continues to be ultra-competitive, it is essential to incorporate different job/internship search strategies, and social media provides another channel for a successful search, which will eventually yield a career.

Career educators must adapt to the market and discover innovative ways to engage students and discover full-time employment opportunities, fellowships, graduate education, military service, among other things. Because of disruptions in technology and the job market, career educators face significant challenges (McKinsey, 2021). Adapting to the stark disruption requires innovation: new programs, engaging different alumni networks, conducting new workshops or encouraging social media use for the job search. Social media has evolved into a tremendous resource for job seekers. Recent college graduates can scour Twitter, LinkedIn, Facebook, Pinterest, etc. for jobs and connections. With guidance from a career educator, students will find ways to network or inquire about specific roles, industries, and sectors. For example, the speed and ease with which students can interact on social media with alumni working in a similar field is reflective of the convenience and access social media provides. Career educators must be competent with these resources to teach students the fundamentals and worth of engaging on social media. Sure, there are job boards and postings all over the internet, but social media provides the personal connection, which can help land that next great opportunity.

Social Media and Personal Branding

Social media technologies have provided recent college graduates with an arsenal to build their personal brand, network with employers, and effectively search for job/internship opportunities at any time from their desktop, laptop, or smartphone. Using social media in the career process is a relatively new, but effective, way for students to gain an understanding of how to develop and leverage their personal brands within the career space. Personal branding is the practice of marketing oneself and one's career as a brand. Personal branding requires a proactive decision to take ownership in the direction one's life progresses. Discovering, developing, and implementing a personal brand are essential to personal growth, and will assist in highlighting what an individual has to offer in society (Clark, 2011).

As Burnett and Evans preach, start with where you are before you can design your way forward. Culture (one's attitudes, beliefs, values, and behaviors) constructs who a person is and wants to become (Jahoda, 2012). Burnett and Evans frame these as *worldview* and *workview* to establish coherence between what you do, what you believe, and who you are (2016). It is that diverse, cultural formation that builds the foundation of who we are and who we want to be in life design. Having a strong understanding of the "self" (self-concept, self-awareness, and perception), individuals can build their personal brands. It will be extremely difficult to develop a personal brand without an understanding of oneself.

For this reason, life design and social media were exactly the type of innovation higher education needed. Those innovations have provided students the context of storytelling and have equipped career educators with a robust skillset to support students in the uncertain future of work, in which jobs and industries are evolving from pandemic and technological disruption. Petrucă writes:

> Nowadays social media is the best and easiest way to grow a personal identity, to establish a reputation and become visible in a specific industry or niche… Social media can help promote it, would open career doors and bring new opportunities for growth and development.
>
> (2016, p. 390–392)

Social media has allowed an individual's personal brand to evolve and grow. Students now have channels to generate content connected to their personal brands via social media.

Career educators were mindful not only of the growing channels of social media and how their students would leverage them, but also the burgeoning sector of social media jobs. Technological advances impacted the future of work for many people in the early 2000s. Social media jobs and social media responsibilities did not exist in the early 2000s (Rufaid, 2015). Fast-forward to 2021 and do a quick search on your favorite job portal and you will find a significant number of social media jobs and other jobs with social media responsibilities. Almost every organization has a social media professional on the payroll. Career educators pivoted and prepared students for careers in social media. How did they do so? By innovating!

Syed Rufaid explained:

> Social media exhibits unique characteristics; its speed and scope has benefited organizations and industries and hence has created a huge job market where one has multiple career options and opportunities. Five years ago, calling yourself a "social media manager" would likely have been met with a confused look and the assumption that you waste your time goofing off social media networking. But over the last few years, careers in social media have witnessed an exponential rise as companies have realized the value of reaching the youth on the medium where they spend most of their time. Social media are increasingly blurring the boundaries between work and play by making social networks as the medium to earn and make [a] career.
>
> (Rufaid, 2015, para. 2)

Career educators dug in, did research, and evaluated the necessary skills to survive and thrive in a social media career. Not only did social media create platforms for connecting individuals and sharing content, but it also generated a whole new sector of jobs. Critics of higher education would suggest that a college degree would not provide the career readiness skills necessary for a new type of job; however, colleges and universities across the globe sent students into entry-level social media jobs because they innovated. Career educators trained and taught students the important and necessary skills, personality, and career readiness for social media careers. Learning about new roles, tasks, and responsibilities was critical to a career educator's professional development. Many career educators embraced the culture of social media and how it might affect (both positively and negatively) a student's opportunities before and after graduation (Brandpoint, 2013). Social media expanded students' reach and created more opportunities to connect. Career educators upskilled, innovated, and designed a way to empower students to embrace the future of work and the ambiguity it presents.

The Future of Work

Significant conversations have emerged about the growing concerns of the future of work. Because of technological, pandemic, economical, and ecological disruption, many jobs and industries are changing. Some jobs are going away, while others are requiring the workforce to re-skill or upskill to meet the demands of their roles and responsibilities (Guan et al., 2014; World Economic Forum, 2020). Further, the second and third jobs that current college students will have after graduation may not exist.

> After years of growing income inequality, concerns about technology-driven displacement of jobs, and rising societal discord globally, the combined health and economic shocks of 2020 have put economies into freefall, disrupted labor markets and fully revealed the inadequacies of our social contracts.
> (World Economic Forum, 2020, p. 3)

Disruption has invaded the workforce and the arrival of the future of work has accelerated and created tremendous uncertainty. College students need to prepare themselves for the future of work and jobs that do not even exist in 2021.

Today, society is experiencing disruption from all angles: economic, ecological, technological, and, of course, pandemic, which has drastically changed the future of work and how career educators prepare students for successful post-graduate careers. How can students prepare themselves for jobs that do not yet exist? This is a critical issue facing career educators across the globe. Working with students to devise a strategy to identify the unique qualities that make us human will be a challenge to many career educators. Career educators will need to help students become aware of how important human or "soft" skills are in the workplace of the future where automation and artificial intelligence may begin to take over more routine tasks. Strategies for understanding how to develop effective human–machine relationships will be required in a changing workforce.

Combatting automation and other technical disruption gives higher education an opportunity to innovate. Colleges and universities are seeking innovative ways to prepare students for the future of work. According to Jahanian:

> Higher education is unique in its power to catalyse social mobility, serving to bridge social, economic, racial, and geographic divides like no other force. As job markets constantly evolve, it is clear that the future demands a system of higher education that is as dynamic and adaptable as the technologies around which our society now revolves.
> (2020, para. 8)

The future of work is presenting an opportunity for higher education and, specifically, career educators to innovate to ensure the success of the next generation. A rapid response and creativity are crucial for higher education to meet the needs of the future of work.

Lifelong learning is the voluntary and self-motivated pursuit of knowledge for personal and professional reasons throughout one's entire life. A few examples of lifelong learning include higher education through the form of a graduate or certificate program, webinar or online badge program, and professional development training. The goal of lifelong learning is to enhance a person's social inclusion, active citizenship, and individual development. Additionally, the more an individual commits to learning, the more they will encounter increases in competitiveness and employability. Digging deeper into the future of work, lifelong learning will be critical to navigating disruption and addressing skill development (up-skilling and re-skilling). Strada Institute for the Future of Work writes, "There is a profound gap in how higher education institutions and employers talk about skills" (2018, p. 14). Innovative approaches to leadership around the implementation of lifelong learning programs are important to the success of individuals in the future of work. Many organizational leaders consider lifelong learning and professional development for their staff and individuals for a variety of reasons: the retention of good people, commitment to the future of individuals, and a better performing and more knowledgeable staff.

Like in the corporate landscape, colleges and universities are creating lifelong learning programs to provide opportunities for the expansion of career readiness skills. Higher education institutions are partnering with credential services like Credly (n.d.) to offer digital badges for skills acquired through short-term projects, internships, field study, and experiential learning paving the way for students to adapt their skills to the changing landscape of work. By awarding licenses, badges, and credentials, and investing in innovation centers and labs, higher education is innovating beyond the students simply earning a degree. According to Fain, "Digital badges aren't replacing the bachelor's degree any time soon. But a growing number of colleges are working with vendors to use badges as an add-on to degrees, to help students display skills and accomplishments that transcripts fail to capture" (2016, para. 1). The realization that skills need to be further developed beyond the degree is innovative in itself. Career educators are providing access and support for the development of skills over a lifetime. People are living longer, so they are working longer, and checking back and evaluating skills over time will lead to a smoother integration into the future of work.

Finally, some institutions of higher education are shifting to a competency-based model of learning, which tends to be more student-centered. Fain writes:

> Competency-based education has spread slower than many expected, particularly given hype in recent years about its approach, which emphasizes what students know and can do, tends to be more focused on employer needs, and often features elements of personalization and self-pacing for students.
>
> (Fain, 2019, para. 1)

This learning model differs from traditional higher education learning as it considers the previously acquired knowledge of a student and allows the students, in most cases, to self-pace and reach mastery at different times. Typically, competency-based learning programs are inclusive and interactive with employer and industry needs. Accessibility and flexibility are pillars to the structure of a competency learning model. Pursuing competencies and skill mastery will be required for the future of work as the workforce is disrupted.

In her book *Long Life Learning: Preparing for Jobs that Don't Even Exist Yet*, author Michelle Weise stated, "We must therefore begin prototyping more flexible reskilling and upskilling pathways for the future. We will have to change our approach and put some teeth into the concept of lifelong learning" (2020, p. 6). This challenge opens the door to new innovative opportunities for action and research, specifically questions like: what technical and operational skills are required to adapt to a new workforce? Furthermore, how do institutions ensure students become lifelong learners? Leading change in career development centers and offices will ensure the next generation of workers will be prepared for the obstacles facing them due to technological, ecological, pandemic, and economic disruptions. "Without more innovation in the assessment space that can yield insights into the human skills of job candidates, there will be no way to harness and display the learning that occurs beyond traditional institutions of higher education" (Strada Institute for the Future of Work, 2018, p. 29).

Recommendations for Practice

Innovating for the future of work can be daunting for career educators; however, there are plenty of opportunities to strive for new programs, initiatives, and strategies in the name of supporting students:

- **Practice Career Everywhere:** The career conversation is happening across college campuses on a regular basis. Career educators do not have to engage and oversee all conversations. Build partnerships, collaborate, and communicate across campus to ensure everyone is prepared to embrace the career-readiness conversation.
- **Consider Life Design:** Encourage students to be active agents in their career process while embracing a designer's mindset. Doing so will open students up to being informed decision makers. Students will also be able to derive meaning from those decisions on a purposeful career path.
- **Embrace the Co-Curricular:** Experiential learning is not new to career education; however, many institutions of higher education are not including internships, co-op, externships, project-based internships, or shadowing as a part of the curriculum. It is time to innovate and draw direct correlations between coursework and experiential learning.
- **Fundraise for Programs:** Career education across the country is often underfunded and understaffed. Be creative in what you ask for in donations. Parents and alumni will be supportive as it derives meaning and purpose for them.
- **Align Career-Readiness with Skills:** The research has shown that colleges/universities and employers are not speaking the same language. There is a disconnect in expectations from employers and learning outcomes/competencies

from college/universities. Working through employer partners to prototype and test links between expectations can lead to a commonly spoken language that stands to benefit all parties: students/graduates, alumni, employers, and college/ employers.

• **Support Badging and Credentialing:** Career educators should empower students to add to their repertoire of skills to be prepared for the future of work. There is a litany of options for lifelong learning. LinkedIn Learning, IDEOU, General Assembly, and Coursera, to name a few, offer courses, virtual and in-person training, and professional development opportunities (some are free).

Innovation is critical for the students of Generation Z and beyond. Jobs, industries, and demands of the workforce are changing rapidly to keep up with the disruption happening around the globe. Furthermore, career educators must keep pace and embrace adaptability to encourage students to take ownership and design their college experiences, and their experiences beyond their college degree. The innovation described in this chapter has happened in a relatively short amount of time, proving that higher education can indeed be an innovative enterprise. Whether it is design thinking, social media, personal branding, or re-skilling for the future of work, career educators are embracing innovation and stepping out of the mindset of "this is what we have always done." New programs, strategies, initiatives, and collaborations are emerging in higher education, yet there is so much more to be done. Career educators will be challenged by the ambiguous future of work and how to best prepare students for it. Simply put, innovation and creativity will be the cornerstones of the future of career education.

References

Apollo Technical. (2021, March 9). Surprising social media recruiting statistics. www.apollotechnical.com/social-media-recruiting-statistics/

Blass, E., & Hayward, P. (2014). Innovation in higher education; will there be a role for the "the academe/university" in 2025? *European Journal of Futures Research, 2*(41), 1–9.

Brandpoint. (2013, June 2). *College career services go social to connect students and employers.* Mohave Daily News. https://mohavedailynews.com/news/59074/college-career-services-go-social-to-connect-students-and-employers/

Burnett, B., & Evans, D. (2016). *Designing your life: How to build a well-lived, joyful life.* Knopf.

Clark, D. (2011, March). *Reinventing your personal brand.* Harvard Business Review. https://hbr.org/2011/03/reinventing-your-personal-brand

Credly. (n.d.). *About us.* https://info.credly.com/about-us

Fain, P. (2016, August 9). *Digital, verified and less open.* Inside Higher Ed. www.insidehighered.com/news/2016/08/09/digital-badging-spreads-more-colleges-use-vendors-create-alternative-credentials

Fain, P. (2019, January 28). *Slow and steady for competency-based education*. Inside Higher Ed. www.insidehighered.com/news/2019/01/28/slow-growth-competency-based-education-survey-finds-interest-and-optimism-about-it

Guan, Y., Guo, Y., Bond, M. H., Cai, Z., Zhou, X., Xu, J., Zhu, F., Wang, Z., Fu, R., Liu, S., Wang, Y., Hu, T., & Ye, L. (2014). New job market entrants' future work self, career adaptability and job search outcomes: Examining mediating and moderating models. *Journal of Vocational Behavior*, 85(1), 136–145. https://doi.org/10.1016/j.jvb.2014.05.003

Hub Staff. (2019, June 4). *Johns Hopkins announces ambitious changes to the way it prepares students for careers*. The Hub. https://hub.jhu.edu/2019/06/04/career-life-design-changes-farouk-dey/

IDEO. (n.d.). Design thinking history. https://designthinking.ideo.com/history

IDEOU. (2021). *Design thinking*. www.ideou.com/pages/design-thinking

Jahanian, F. (2020, January 21). *How higher education can adapt to the future of work*. World Economic Forum. www.weforum.org/agenda/2020/01/how-can-higher-education-adapt-to-a-constantly-evolving-future-of-work/

Jahoda, G. (2012). Critical reflections on some recent definitions of "culture." *Culture & Psychology*, 18(3), 289–303. https://doi.org/10.1177/1354067X12446229

Kurchina, P. (2021, March 26). *Workplace disruption and the future of work: 2025 is the new 2030*. ASUG News + Views. www.asug.com/insights/workplace-disruption-and-the-future-of-work-2025-is-the-new-2030

Kurutz, S. (2016, September 17). Want to find fulfillment at last? Think like a designer. *New York Times*. www.nytimes.com/2016/09/18/fashion/design-thinking-stanford-silicon-valley.html?_r=0

McKinsey. (2021, February 18). *The future of work after Covid-19* [Report]. www.mckinsey.com/featured-insights/future-of-work/the-future-of-work-after-covid-19

Petrucă, I. (2016). Personal branding through social media. *International Journal of Communication Research*, 6(4), 389–392.

Rufaid, S. (2015, February). Emergence of social media, a growth in career opportunities. *Higher Education Review*. www.thehighereducationreview.com/magazine/emergence-of-social-media-a-growth-in-career-opportunities-DHKD816153861.html

Savickas, M. L., Nota, L., Rossier, J., Dauwalder, J., Daurte, M. E., Guichard, J., Soresi, S., Van Esbroeck, R., & van Vianen, A. E. M. (2009). Life designing: A paradigm for career construction in the 21st century. *Journal of Vocational Behavior*, 75, 239–250. www.scinapse.io/papers/2129084881#fullText

Stanford Life Design Lab. (2018a). *Home*. http://lifedesignlab.stanford.edu/

Stanford Life Design Lab. (2018b). *Studio*. http://lifedesignlab.stanford.edu/studio

Strada Institute for the Future of Work. (2018). *Robot ready: Human + skills for the future of work* [Report]. www.economicmodeling.com/robot-ready-reports/

Szczepanska, J. (2017). *Design thinking origin story plus some of the people who made it all happen*. Medium. https://szczpanks.medium.com/design-thinking-where-it-came-from-and-the-type-of-people-who-made-it-all-happen-dc3a05411e53

Weise, M. (2020). *Long-life learning: Preparing for jobs that don't even exist yet*. Wiley.

World Economic Forum. (2020). The future of jobs [Report]. www.weforum.org/reports/the-future-of-jobs-report-2020

9
Neither Online, Nor Face-to-Face, But Integrated Career Guidance: Introducing New Ways of Engaging Undergraduate Students in Career Learning and Reflective Careering

Ingrid Bårdsdatter Bakke and Tristram Hooley

Digital technology has been widely adopted in education with the emergence of a range of e-learning technologies and pedagogies (Goh et al., 2020; Mnkandla & Minnaar, 2017; Trakru & Jha, 2019). In career education and guidance, we can learn from this wider trend and make more use of digital strategies to strengthen the quality and outcomes of career learning.

The need for digital approaches to career guidance is in part informed by the new opportunities that digital tools afford educators. But an engagement with the digital also responds to a more fundamental shift. Our careers are now increasingly enacted on, and conducted through, the internet and so it is inevitable that career guidance should engage more deeply with these technologies (Hooley, 2012). The Covid-19 pandemic has exacerbated this trend, delivering a career shock to many people (Akkermans et al., 2020) and increasing the digitization of working life (Nagel, 2020).

This chapter draws on a strand of work that developed in Norway as part of a policy commitment to digitizing public services (Norwegian Ministries, 2012), and which has become central to the provision of careers services (Hooley et al., 2015; Ministry of Education and Research, 2015). As Norway explored the digitization of careers work it became clear that the country would pursue an 'integrated career guidance' approach which combined face-to-face and digital approaches (Bakke et al., 2018). This led to the funding of a new course which afforded us the space to develop the theory and practise integrated career guidance as we developed Norwegian careers practitioners' competence.

DOI: 10.4324/9781003213000-13

Integrated career guidance is an approach to delivering career support that uses digital technologies, face-to-face interactions and any other approaches, such as the provision of printed information, that are useful to learners. The key issue is not the mode of delivery but its objectives. Integrated guidance is based on career learning and entails designing career learning processes by drawing together different modes of communication and interaction, always with the learners' needs as a central concern.

The Challenge of the Pandemic

Amidst the chaos of the 2020 pandemic, career practitioners at Poppleton University[1] recognized that they were going to have to change their approach. As they tried to shift their face-to-face services online they became frustrated. What was the point of a careers fair or lecture if you couldn't see the students and if they kept their cameras off? These frustrations prompted deeper reflection. What was it all for? What were they trying to achieve? Shunting existing approaches online was not an appealing option, but what was the alternative?

At the start of the pandemic university career services saw many of the key features of their delivery model collapse. Careers fairs disappeared, work in the curriculum was more challenging as faculty faced their own challenges in moving to e-learning, one-to-one career counselling became increasingly difficult and opportunities for industry placements dried up (Binnie, 2020; Greaves, 2020; Institute of Student Employers, 2020).

The paradigm shift was not confined to career services but impacted the whole of higher education. After decades of experimenting with e-learning, universities were propelled into full adoption of e-learning during 2020 (Adnan & Anwar, 2020; Ali, 2020; Mpungose, 2020). The rapid movement of higher education online presented universities with logistical and technical challenges as well as challenges related to ensuring equality of access, a positive student experience and the maintenance of social approaches to learning during a period of 'social distancing'.

Moving to a New Paradigm

Staff at the Poppleton University careers service took a deep breath, stepped back and considered what they were trying to achieve. So much of their practice had emerged gradually in response to accidents of history, staff preferences and the insistence of university administrators or faculty. The careers service was committed and responsive to student need, but it was rarely more than the sum of its parts. Perhaps now was the time to think differently and to think bigger.

Digital technologies have been part of career education practice since at least the 1960s (Watts, 2002). Ever since then, innovation has been ongoing with new approaches emerging regularly (Brigstock, 2019a; Pordelan & Hosseinian, 2020; Turcotte & Goyer, 2018). A recent example can be seen in Farouk Dey's work at Johns Hopkins University, where a strongly digital approach has emerged alongside initiatives designed to rethink and retheorize career learning, embed it in the curriculum and enmesh students within networks of social capital (Dey, 2019; Hub, 2019). Dey's work clearly shows that innovation, the use of educational perspectives and the centrality of digital technologies are not new. What we hope to add to this is a more thorough theorization of how to respond to both these long-standing trends and the recent shifts prompted by Covid.

Some commentators have critiqued the careers field's engagement with the digital, noting that there are issues in training, quality assurance and the integration of digital approaches into careers practice. These problems are partially brought about by the fact that there is a lack of digitally relevant counselling models and career learning pedagogies (Brigstock, 2019b; Hooley & Staunton, 2021; Kettunen & Sampson, 2019; Vigurs et al., 2017). Therefore, the counterfactual story of Poppleton University that we present in this chapter was difficult for universities to realize as they responded to the pandemic.

Existing approaches have variously emphasized the ways in which digital technologies can be used to provide information, to create forms of automated interaction or to mediate interactions between people through forms of digital communication (Hooley et al., 2010). In practice, this has seen the proliferation of careers websites and apps and the provision of career education and guidance via audio or video link, email, and chat technologies (Fusco et al., 2020; Vigurs et al., 2017). Much existing work has focused on the technologies, exploring what can be done, without really focusing on the why or the how. With *integrated career guidance* we refocus the discussion on the use of new technologies towards these questions and ask how the engagement with digital tools can enhance career learning.

We use the term 'integrated career guidance' broadly to describe all forms of interventions that support 'individuals and groups to discover more about work, leisure and learning and to consider their place in the world and plan for their future' (Hooley et al., 2018, p. 20). It is delivered by careers professionals, but also by faculty and other university staff and involves employers, external stakeholders, parents and students in a myriad of career conversations and other forms of career learning. Integrated career guidance encompasses classroom-based learning, experiential learning and traditional career counselling and utilizes a range of technologies and approaches to deliver these interventions as well as to create new and innovative forms of practice. As such it can be argued that integrated career guidance increases the accessibility of career guidance services through digital modes of communication and extends their reach beyond the careers centre or employability-focused elective modules.

In this chapter we are going to set out the theoretical basis of the integrated career guidance approach. We argue that such an approach needs:

- an *ontological basis* which sets out its morals, ethics and ideology;
- a *pedagogic basis* which establishes our understanding of how integrated career guidance supports individuals to learn and make progress in their career; and
- an approach to *instructional design* which sets out a practical approach to delivering integrated career guidance.

Why Offer Integrated Guidance? Our Ontological Basis

As they packed up the careers service ready to move their programs online, the staff of Poppleton University could be forgiven for introspective and existential thinking. What was career education even for? In a fiery email chain they generated lots of ideas, shared different perspectives and gradually came to some agreement. Career education shouldn't just be about helping privileged people to become more privileged. Rather it should encourage learners to engage in a reflective consideration of their place in the world and their impact upon it. It should support marginalized students to succeed and help all students to think about what 'success' really means.

Career, they argued, could be a democratic concept which was available to all. Career guidance should be supporting learners to be active in all parts of their life, leisure, learning and work and make a positive contribution to society.

Shifting the aims of career guidance helped the staff at Poppleton to see that they should not just be supporting decision making and brokering students into the entry point of the labour market. Instead, they needed students to engage in a deep learning process, thinking about themselves and the world around them, building new skills and knowledge and increasing their capacity to act.

Supporting learners in their careers requires practitioners to have a way of seeing the world and a set of moral, ethical and ideological beliefs about what learning is and what it is for. An underlying component of this ontology is the question about career, what it is and what place or function it has in people's lives. A common distinction between ways of thinking about career is the dichotomy between career as a race and career as a journey (Law, 2009). The journey metaphor views career as a non-hierarchical lifelong endeavour that can be shared with others, while the race metaphor implies that career is a hierarchical and competitive process in which there are both winners and losers (Bakke, 2021).

In integrated career guidance we reject the idea that career should be a race and problematize the idea that career interventions are primarily about helping people to achieve money, power, reputation and the other markers of conventional success. Of course, for some learners this will be exactly what they are seeking to achieve, and participation in integrated career guidance may well help them in these aims, but it should also help them to become reflective, to critique norms and hegemonic conceptions of career (Wikstrand, 2019), and build their capacity to exercise agency in their lives and act on the world around them. Such approaches might empower people to make choices that run counter to social expectations, for example choosing lower-paid jobs that offer moral or spiritual rewards or which simply allow more time for leisure, family life and unpaid forms of work and activity. They may also engage students in critical thinking about the structures and hierarchies that exist around them and lead them to question these things and take action through their career to change them.

How Learning Happens: The Pedagogic Basis of Integrated Guidance

> *The Poppleton University team challenged themselves to start with a blank page and think big. The fact that career guidance and learning would increasingly be done in an online environment reconfigured many of the traditional tools that could be used in learning. The time of the 'sage on the sage' was over, and face-to-face career counselling seemed less central too. They recognized that they would need to learn alongside their students, participating in informal learning online as well as engaging with faculty to review and develop the curriculum.*

Thinking of career as life-wide and life-long (Inkson et al., 2015), as democratic and for all (Bakke, 2021; Watts, 2016) and as something that exists in creative tension with existing structures and power relations, has implications for the kind of career guidance that we offer. Such a *critical* approach to careering is rooted in reflexivity, curiosity and a willingness to question assumptions. It is inevitably linked to social justice as it encourages individuals to imagine the world as it could be, not just as it is, and to consider the relationship between context, social structures and individual careering. Integrated career guidance seeks to foster learning, support growth, inquiry and development and encourage an active, experiential and critical engagement with the world. In this sense, integrated career guidance builds on recognized learning and career learning theories (Kolb, 1984; Law, 1999), viewing career learning as a cyclical, iterative and interactive process through which knowledge and skills are gradually acquired, developed and utilized in a dynamic relationship with other people and the wider context.

These approaches draw on Bruner's (1977) theories which conceptualize learning as a spiral which is at once cyclical and progressive. Learners need to engage with conceptual structures and use them to organize the acquisition of knowledge and skills whilst also building a progressively more complex conceptual understanding. Framed as a career development learning spiral this means that individuals need to build their understanding of career as a concept whilst simultaneously acquiring career management skills and knowledge (Hooley, 2021). The career educator's role is then to provide the scaffolding that supports this process of career learning.

Career learning is also understood to be a social process through which individuals come together and support each other to learn and career. The building of scaffolding is not just the creation of a ladder up which the learner can ascend, but rather the construction of a climbing frame on which learners can play together.

The career educator is a facilitator and a connector as well as an instructor and a trainer. The scaffolding is carefully constructed from content, exercises, questions and assessments to foster learning, although learners may sometimes be unaware that it even exists. The visible aspects of education, the teacher standing at the front of the class, are only the tip of the iceberg, with much going on in the preparation and structuring of learning.

This means that integrated career guidance needs to analyse both *what* the learner needs to learn about career and *how* the learner can learn about career. The fact that much of this learning takes place in a digital environment means that the educator needs to think about *what* the learner needs to learn about careering in the digital world and *how* learning takes place in a digital environment. This can sometimes mean tracing back to more elementary starting points, e.g. building digital competence to allow the learner to get online to access career learning material. Such skills-based training needs to take place within a spiral framework where the learner is motivated by the idea of developing their career, whilst they engage with the technical challenges of accessing the digital environment and building their career management skills, scaffolded by the integrated career guidance programme.

Kettunen and her colleagues (Kettunen et al., 2013; Kettunen, Vuorinen, & Sampson, 2015) have explored the different ways in which career professionals can respond to changing technologies. After surveying various ways of using digital technologies for careers work, Kettunen, Sampson, & Vuorinen (2015) argue that practitioners should recognize that there has been a paradigm change and this necessitates a new approach which they describe as 'co-careering'. Co-careering moves away from a focus on the delivery of information. It is non-hierarchical and learner centred and is based around learners using digital tools in an autonomous manner drawing on a range of online resources for their career. Hooley and Staunton (2021) link Kettunen et al.'s approach to the wider theoretical perspective of 'connectivism' (Cormier, 2008; Siemens, 2005; Wheeler & Gerver, 2015), which views digital technologies as breaking down traditional hierarchies and requiring a new facilitative role from educators of the kind that Kettunen et al. described for careers practitioners.

Kettunen's concept of co-careering is a useful building block for integrated guidance as it links a broad non-hierarchical concept of career to digital technologies and sets out an ethical and pedagogical role for the careers practitioner. But we are also mindful of the critiques that are made of connectivism by Selwyn (2016) and others including Hooley and Staunton (2020) in relation to careers education, which highlight the differential capabilities that individuals have for making use of the internet in terms of access to it and being a competent user, and raise concerns about the ownership of online spaces and their capacity to inscribe ideology and power. This leads us to argue that there is a need for practitioners to adopt more critical approaches to co-careering which acknowledge both the way in which digital technologies have changed existing hierarchies of careering and recognize and critique the new forms of hierarchy that have emerged.

What Should Careers Practitioners Do? The Instructional Design Approach

> As the University of Poppleton started to return to campus in the aftermath of the pandemic, the team reviewed their delivery. Many members of the team are involved in delivering a standard two-hour lecture on 'Resume writing' which faculty often request the career service to run for final-year students. In this session students are taken through the key principles of resume writing, provided with examples of effective resumes and given an opportunity to ask questions. The session ends with students being encouraged to go away and put their learning into practice.
>
> The team developed an alternative, flipped classroom model for this session in which students are provided with access to online resources explaining how resumes should be set out and some model resumes in advance of the session. They are told to draft a resume and/or LinkedIn profile before the session starts. This means that the two hours of face-to-face time are then used for reviewing the work that the students have done and discussing how to improve it and make use of it as a part of their career transition.

Integrated career guidance draws on blended learning pedagogies (Bersin, 2004; Bonk & Graham, 2012), which argue that effective learning needs to identify the learner's need and the learning problem and then to design the instructional approach to meet these. This approach is often described as instructional design (Merrill, 2002; Wilson, 2005; Zemke, 1998), and covers a wide range of different approaches. The idea of instructional design can be illustrated through the example of the flipped classroom (Akçayır & Akçayır, 2018), where contact time is reorganized so that students begin with the self-study of, usually digital, learning materials and time together with the tutor is used for questions, debate and other social learning activities and to deepen critical engagement with the learning material.

The example above shows the importance of the design of the instruction. By flipping the classroom and ordering the components of instruction differently, students are scaffolded to move further round a career learning spiral. In integrated career guidance, we think carefully about how delivery is organized to best effect and make use of traditional methods including face-to-face counselling sessions, group sessions and the provision of career information as well as digital forms of communication and interaction (e.g. chat, video-link, email or wikis).

In choosing the right tool for the right job, we must pay attention to the affordances of the technology (what it can actually do) and consider how these can support our aims. Key decisions include whether we want students to interact with us and each other:

- face-to-face, digitally or in some blend of the two;
- in a synchronous or asynchronous way;
- through text-based chat or multi-media forms of communication;
- using video or audio;
- one-to-one; one-to-many; or many-to-many;
- in open/public spaces, such as LinkedIn or Facebook, or behind the closed doors of the virtual learning environment or classroom;

- for minutes, hours, days or weeks; and
- once, repeatedly or regularly.

These are decisions that we make in all forms of learning and ones which are often pre-decided for us by the infrastructure, budget, resources, policies, quality assurance, geography, architecture and design that shape our teaching. In conventional lecture halls, seminar rooms and counselling offices, decisions have already been made about the forms and format of interactions that can and should take place; for example, placing the teacher at the front of the lecture hall and the students facing them rather than one another is one such decision. The instruction has already been designed, just not always consciously or purposefully. This is where the use of technology becomes important because it offers new opportunities and, in some cases, gives us new choices that can transcend existing limitations.

As noted above, integrated career guidance applies the idea of co-careering and career as a democratic project, and as such the approach emphasizes the importance of a community of career learners, including the careers practitioners themselves, learning together. Sometimes individual activity is the right choice, but much potential exists in group-based career learning activity. Interacting and participating in a mutually supportive learning community can build capacity for reflexivity and critique, which is also central to developing individuals' capacity to transform the world through their career.

Integrated Guidance in Practice

Using all of the tools, ideas and approaches that they had reviewed, the Poppleton team began to build a new type of programme, one that was not just preparation for recruitment processes or career training, but which supported students to become critical, lifelong learners and careerists. The programme took place in the curriculum delivered both by faculty and by careers practitioners working in partnership with them, in the careers centre, as part of student activities and in informal online spaces, and it used a range of tools to support this, from whiteboards and classrooms, to LinkedIn and TikTok, but the technology was always in service of learning and never an end in itself.

Integrated career guidance starts with an investigation into learners' needs, often using dialogic and participatory techniques to get learners to define what they want and to inform how the learning itself is structured. This starting point supports the creation of learning aims which can be used to design learning processes that utilize a range of modes of delivery and which scaffold the career learning process.

Using Salmon's (2000, 2002) five-stage online learning model is helpful, although this is only one model that can be used and it can be critiqued for imposing an artificial and simplistic linearity onto a process that is actually recursive and complex. But its approach and philosophy align well with the ontology, pedagogy and instructional design approach that we have outlined so far. Models are inevitably reductive, but they help to provide structure to the messiness of reality and provide practitioners with insights about how to act.

The five-stage model provides a ready-made instructional design which was created for asynchronous, text-based e-learning environments but has since been adapted for a wide range of different technologies (Ruzmetova, 2018; Salmon et al., 2010). The model scaffolds learners to move around a learning spiral, gradually increasing their capacity and competence both as online learners and in the learning outcomes of the programme by structuring learning programmes through five stages (see Table 9.1).

Table 9.1 Integrated career guidance tool adapted from Salmon's five-stage model

Stage	Focus	Pedagogical considerations	Technological considerations
1	Access and motivation	Welcoming and encouraging students. Exploring what they want and expect from participating.	Ensuring that students can utilize the technologies that are going to be important for the delivery of the programme and providing support for those that cannot.
2	Socialization	Introducing students to each other and supporting them to build a relationship as a community of learners. Encouraging students to consider the benefits that can be gained from learning and careering in a community.	Giving students an opportunity to send and receive messages and try out other approaches to communication that they will use in the course.
3	Information exchange	Providing content, resources and materials to inform students' career thinking. This might include presenting students with labour market information, career theories and models and case studies.	Choosing the technologies through which information can be communicated e.g. deciding whether to provide reading or video lectures.

Table 9.1 Cont.

Stage	Focus	Pedagogical considerations	Technological considerations
4	Construction of knowledge and skills	Scaffolding students to move round the career learning spiral and begin the process of putting this into practice in their career. This will typically take the form of asking students to respond to materials, demonstrate how they would put them into practice and comment on other students' responses.	Using technology to create the spaces within which knowledge and skills can be developed.
5	Development and enactment	Building connections to content, resources and opportunities outside of the course to support career enactment. This includes providing scaffolding to help students make use of the knowledge and skills that they have developed during the programme and put them into practice in their lives.	Encouraging engagement with new technologies that support further development.

Salmon's model is a social constructivist approach which sees learning as a social process. Social constructivist approaches draw on theorists like Vygotsky (1978), who argued that learners develop skills and knowledge through social interaction with both the teacher and each other. Learning is not simply the assimilation of knowledge, but also includes the integration of learners into a community of knowledge. Drawing on this theoretical base, Salmon's work focuses on developing the *collective* of learners and their relationships with each other and views these relationships as a key resource for learners. This social learning aim has implications for the instructional design of an integrated career guidance course, requiring the selection of fora (both online and face-to-face) that support communication between learners, the formation of community and social learning to happen. It also requires the career educator to spend time building students' motivation and encouraging their inclination to share questions and knowledge with the others. The career educator needs to design a program which meets learners' needs and provides a supportive scaffold and then helps learners get access to the system and the e-learning platform, to facilitate and encourage communication, and structure and follow the learners' process. The careers educator may provide information and resources that support learning, or they may curate this information from other sources (e.g. YouTube).

Embedded within the five-stage model, Salmon provided us another pedagogic technique, called the 'e-tivity' (Salmon, 2002). The e-tivity is a framework for structuring and enabling active and participative online learning for groups. If the five-stage model provides a suggested instructional design for a career education programme, the e-tivity provides a suggested design for an individual activity. Designing an e-tivity begins with thinking about the learning aims and then identifying what new tasks and content learners need to encounter. This means considering how the learning material can be delivered and deciding how to facilitate the processing of it, typically through interaction with other students and the production of an output. Salmon described this process as providing a *spark* for learning, requiring a *response* from learners (typically involving presenting ideas to others and discussing them) and a *summary* or *critique* which is provided by the career educator to support students to identify what is important.

Using Salmon's approaches provides a model for the development of a career education programme which might include multiple e-tivities (and potentially face-to-face activities) linked together through the five-stage model.

> *The University of Poppleton team launched the Poppleton Digital Career Bootcamp aimed at students in their final year. Students are invited to join the programme on the University's Virtual Learning Environment and welcomed when they enrol with a video from one of the team, which presents the programme's structure. Students are then asked to create their own video to present themselves and say a few words about what kind of work or employers they are interested in. Learners are asked to watch all videos, and post 'likes' or encouraging comments on both this and future posts. They are also presented with a new spark encouraging them to think about their fellow students as an important part of their network and to explore ways in which they might help each other in their career.*
>
> *In the next stage, students watch promotional films from a variety of different employers. They are formed into small groups and encouraged to work together to produce a presentation on one of the employers. In the presentation they are asked to cover what the employer does, what job roles they have on offer, and what recruitment process they use. They are also asked to take a critical look at that employer and find out what the employer has been challenged and criticized for in the media. The group posts their presentation online and reviews and comments on the presentations of other groups.*
>
> *In the next stage of the programme students are encouraged to think about what the experience of transition looks like. They are presented with a new spark, which is a series of narratives from recent graduates about how they experienced transition, and are encouraged to reflect on these narratives. They are also encouraged to identify, make contact with and interview a recent graduate from the University of Poppleton. The students are introduced to LinkedIn to support them in this networking. They then have to post a short summary of their learning about transition and discuss how they will approach transitions themselves. They are asked to comment on each other's posts and the career educator draws together the learning and offers a summary of the good advice that the group has identified.*

Finally, the students are encouraged to set up a LinkedIn account for themselves. They are provided with one spark that talks about how to optimize a LinkedIn account and another that provides detail on the business model of LinkedIn and the way that the site uses your data. They share their LinkedIn account with other students and discuss how best to manage engagement with the platform safely and in a way that they are comfortable with. The career educator invites them to a final synchronous plenary session and summarizes their thoughts, wishes them luck in their careers and provides links to more resources, including highlighting other programmes and services run by the career service.

At the end of the example above, students have built their knowledge about how career transitions work, but they have also formed a supportive network of fellow students and begun the process of building a broader professional network. Through a well-designed learning process multiple career learning outcomes can be achieved by using a range of technological tools in service of learning. For career educators these kinds of programmes also offer the advantage that they can be designed once and used many times as once the resources are in place different groups of students can work with them repeatedly.

Reflections on Integrated Guidance

As students started to engage with the programme it became clear that the new integrated career guidance approach was challenging and effective in equal measures. New types of students started to access career education and the quality of conversations and depth of learning increased. But it was also strange and unexpected. Some students wanted to focus on conventional notions of success and expressed concerns that taking a learning-centred, critical approach was a distraction. Others found the use of multiple technologies challenging. But the co-careering approach, involving students, faculty and careers professionals in dialogue and review, gradually saw the programme evolve and develop, ultimately leading to a fundamental change in the place of career in the University of Poppleton's curriculum and culture.

In this chapter we have introduced you to the integrated career guidance approach. Inevitably much of this has focused on how to use digital technologies to deliver career education. But integrated career guidance is not primarily a *digital approach*; it is primarily an *educational approach* which is comfortable in using all of the technologies available to deliver career guidance through learning. Integrated guidance is about choosing the right tool and the right venue for learning, not about a drive to technological adoption. There is huge value in human connection and face-to-face meetings where this is possible and appropriate. The principles of integrated career guidance can still be applied in wholly face-to-face environments.

Practitioners seeking to take these ideas forward in their context should ask themselves the following questions:

- Why do we offer career guidance at all? What is it we are trying to achieve?
- How do we believe that students best learn about the world beyond the institution and decide what kind of career they wish to pursue in it?
- What approaches, tools and technologies should we use to support career learning?
- How can we engage, involve and listen to students and other stakeholders as we build and deliver our integrated guidance approach?

We hope that the chapter provides sufficient insights to allow readers to begin to create their own integrated career guidance approaches. We need to build up more examples of practice to find out how this approach works. Further research needs to explore how comfortable practitioners are with paradigm change, how different types of students, with different levels of career competencies and digital literacy, respond to this approach. But for now, we wish you luck and look forward to co-careering with you as you experiment with integrated career guidance.

Note

1   Poppleton University is a fictional British university invented by the columnist and academic Laurie Taylor. Like many before us we are using it to illustrate some of the typical dynamics that we find in universities across the UK (and indeed across the world) and to present a counterfactual about how integrated guidance could offer a way forward.

References

Adnan, M., & Anwar, K. (2020). Online learning amid the COVID-19 pandemic: Students' perspectives. *Journal of Educational Technology Systems, 2*(1), 45–51. https://doi.org/10.1177/0047239520934018

Akçayır, G., & Akçayır, M. (2018). The flipped classroom: A review of its advantages and challenges. *Computers & Education, 126,* 334–345. https://doi.org/10.1016/j.compedu.2018.07.021

Akkermans, J., Richardson, J., & Kraimer, M. (2020). The Covid-19 crisis as a career shock: Implications for careers and vocational behavior. *Journal of Vocational Behavior, 119,* 1–5. https://doi.org/10.1016/j.jvb.2020.103434

Ali, W. (2020). Online and remote learning in higher education institutes: A necessity in light of COVID-19 pandemic. *Higher Education Studies, 10*(3), 16–25. https://doi.org/10.5539/hes.v10n3p16

Bakke, I. B. (2021). *No culture for career?: Conceptualisations of career as a cultural phenomenon and as experienced by tenth graders and career counsellors in Norway* [Doctoral dissertation]. Inland Norway University of Applied Sciences. https://brage.inn.no/inn-xmlui/bitstream/handle/11250/2731828/PhD%20A4%20Bakke%202021.pdf?sequence=1&isAllowed=y (22)

Bakke, I. B., Hagaseth Haug, E., & Hooley, T. (2018). Moving from information provision to co-careering: Integrated guidance as a new approach to e-guidance in Norway. *Journal of* the National Institute for Career Education and Counselling, 41(1), 48–55. https://doi.org/10.20856/jnicec.4108

Bersin, J. (2004). The blended learning book: Best practices, proven methodologies, and lessons learned. Jossey-Bass/Pfeiffer.

Binnie, G. (2020). How university careers services are supporting graduates through Covid-19. Universities UK. www.universitiesuk.ac.uk/latest/insights-and-analysis/how-university-careers-services-are

Bonk, C. J., & Graham, C. R. (2012). The handbook of blended learning: Global perspectives, local designs. John Wiley & Sons.

Bridgstock, R. (2019a). Employability and career development learning through social media: Exploring the potential of LinkedIn. In J. Higgs, S. Cork, & D. Horsfall (Eds.), Challenging future practice possibilities (pp. 143–152). Brill Sense.

Bridgstock, R. (2019b). Graduate employability 2.0: Learning for life and work in a socially networked world. In J. Higgs, G. Crisp, & W. Letts (Eds.), Education for employability (Vol. 1, pp. 97–106). Leiden: Brill Sense. https://doi.org/10.1163/9789004400832_008

Bruner, J. S. (1977). The process of education. Harvard University Press.

Cormier, D. (2008). Rhizomatic education: Community as curriculum. Innovate: Journal of Online Education, 4, 5.

Dey, F. (2019). Five future directions in university career services. LinkedIn. www.linkedin.com/pulse/five-future-directions-university-career-services-farouk-dey/

Fusco, L., Parola, A., & Sica, L. S. (2020). Designing meaningful career tools: A proposal for an optimal use of technology in career guidance [Paper presentation]. Second Symposium on Psychology-Based Technologies, Naples, Italy. http://ceur-ws.org/Vol-2730/paper35.pdf

Goh, C. F., Hii, P. K., Tan, O. K., & Rasli, A. (2020). Why do university teachers use E-learning systems?. The International Review of Research in Open and Distributed Learning, 21(2), 136–155. https://doi.org/10.19173/irrodl.v21i2.3720

Greaves, L. (2020). Careers services and COVID-19: 'We have all been upskilling'. Prospects Luminate. https://luminate.prospects.ac.uk/careers-services-and-covid-19-we-have-all-been-upskilling

Hooley, T. (2012). How the internet changed career: Framing the relationship between career development and online technologies. Journal of the National Institute for Career Education and Counselling (NICEC), 29: 3–12.

Hooley, T. (2021). Redeveloping the CDI framework. Stourbridge Career Development Institute. www.thecdi.net/write/CDI_89-Framework-Redeveloping_the_CDI_Framework-web.pdf

Hooley, T., Hutchinson, J., & Watts, A. G. (2010). Careering through the web. The potential of web 2.0 and 3.0 technologies for career development and career support services. UKCES.

Hooley, T., Shepherd, C., & Dodd, V. (2015). Get yourself connected: Conceptualising the role of digital technologies in Norwegian career guidance. International Centre for Guidance Studies, University of Derby.

Hooley, T., & Staunton, T. (2021). The role of digital technology in career development. In P. J. Robertson, T. Hooley, & P. McCash (Eds.), *The Oxford handbook of career development* (pp. 297–311). Oxford University Press. https://doi.org/10.1093/oxfordhb/9780190069704.013.22

Hooley, T., Sultana, R., & Thomsen, R. (2018). The neoliberal challenge to career guidance. Mobilising research, policy and practice around social justice. In T. Hooley, R. G. Sultana, & R. Thomsen (Eds.), *Career guidance for social justice: Contesting neoliberalism* (pp.1–28). Routledge.

Hub. (2019, June 4). *Johns Hopkins announces ambitious changes to the way it prepares students for careers.* https://hub.jhu.edu/2019/06/04/career-life-design-changes-farouk-dey/

Inkson, K., Dries, N., & Arnold, J. (2015). *Understanding careers* (2nd ed.). SAGE Publications Ltd.

Institute of Student Employers. (2020). *Covid-19: Global impacts on graduate recruitment.* Institute of Student Employers.

Kettunen, J., & Sampson, J. P. (2019). Challenges in implementing ICT in career services: Perspectives from career development experts. *International Journal for Educational and Vocational Guidance, 19*(1), 1–18. https://doi.org/10.1007/s10775-018-9365-6

Kettunen, J., Sampson, J. P., & Vuorinen, R. (2015). Career practitioners' conceptions of competency for social media in career services. *British Journal of Guidance & Counselling, 43*, 43–56. https://doi.org/10.1080/03069885.2014.939945

Kettunen, J., Vuorinen, R., & Sampson, J. P. (2013). Career practitioners' conceptions of social media in career services. *British Journal of Guidance & Counselling, 41*(3), 302–317. https://doi.org/10.1080/03069885.2013.781572

Kettunen, J., Vuorinen, R., & Sampson, J. P. (2015). Practitioners' experiences of social media in career services. *The Career Development Quarterly, 63*, 268–281. https://doi.org/10.1002/cdq.12018

Kolb, D. (1984). *Experiential learning: Experience as the source of learning and development.* Prentice-Hall.

Law, B. (1999). Career-learning space: Newdots thinking for careers education. *British Journal of Guidance & Counselling, 27*(1), 35–54.

Law, B. (2009). Changing metaphors for careers-work. *The Career-learning Café.* www.hihohiho.com/magazine/features/cafmetaphor.pdf

Merrill, M. D. (2002). First principles of instruction. *Educational Technology Research and Development, 50*(3), 43–59. https://doi.org/10.1007/BF02505024

Ministry of Education and Research. (2015). *Karriereveiledning i en digital verden.* [Career guidance in a digitalized world]. First report from national expert committee. Ministry of Education and Research.

Mnkandla, E., & Minnaar, A. (2017). The use of social media in e-learning: A metasynthesis. *International Review of Research in Open and Distributed Learning: IRRODL, 18*(5), 227–248. https://doi.org/10.19173/irrodl.v18i5.3014

Mpungose, C. B. (2020). Emergent transition from face-to-face to online learning in a South African university in the context of the Coronavirus pandemic. *Humanities and Social Sciences Communications, 7*(1), 1–9. https://doi.org/10.1057/s41599-020-00603-x

Nagel, L. (2020). The influence of the COVID-19 pandemic on the digital transformation of work. *International Journal of Sociology and Social Policy, 40*(9/10), 961–875. https://doi.org/10.1108/IJSSP-07-2020-032

Norwegian Ministries. (2012). *Digitizing public sector services (Norwegian eGovernment Programme)*. Ministry of Government Administration, Reform and Church Affairs.

Pordelan, N., & Hosseinian, S. (2020). Design and development of the online career counselling: A tool for better career decision-making. *Behaviour & Information Technology*, 1–21. https://doi.org/10.1080/0144929X.2020.1795262

Ruzmetova, M. (2018). Applying Gilly Salmon's five stage model for designing blended courses. *Dil ve Edebiyat Araştırmaları, 17*(17), 271–290. https://doi.org/10.30767/diledeara.418085

Salmon, G. (2000). *E-moderating: The key to teaching and learning online*. Kogan Page.

Salmon, G. (2002). *E-tivities: The key to active online learning*. Kogan Page.

Salmon, G., Nie, M., & Edirisingha, P. (2010). Developing a five-stage model of learning in *Second Life*. *Educational Research, 52*(2), 169–182. https://doi.org/10.1080/00131881.2010.482744

Selwyn, N. (2016). *Is technology good for education?* Polity Press.

Siemens, G. (2005). *Connectivism: Learning as network creation*. www.elearnspace.org/Articles/networks.htm

Trakru, M., & Jha, T. K. (2019). E-learning effectiveness in higher education. *International Research Journal of Engineering and Technology (IRJET), 6*(5), 96–101.

Turcotte, M., & Goyer, L. (2018). The use of information and communication technologies (ICT) in the practice of Quebec career guidance counsellors?. *Canadian Journal of Career Development, 17*(2), 101–105. https://cjcd-rcdc.ceric.ca/index.php/cjcd/article/view/82

Vigurs, K., Everitt, J., & Staunton, T. (2017). *The evidence base for careers websites. What works?*. The Careers & Enterprise Company.

Vygotsky, L. (1978). *Mind in society*. Harvard University Press.

Watts, A. G. (2002). The role of information and communication technologies in integrated career information and guidance systems. *International Journal for Education and Vocational Guidance, 2*(3), 139–155. https://doi.org/10.1023/A:1020669832743

Watts, A. G. (2016). Career development: Looking back, moving forward. In T. Hooley & L. Barham (Eds.), *Career development policy & practice: The Tony Watts reader* (pp. 329–344). NICEC Ltd.

Wheeler, S., & Gerver, R. (2015). *Learning with E's: Educational theory and practice in the digital age*. Crown House Publishing.

Wikstrand. F. (2019). Norm criticism: A method for social justice in career guidance. In T. Hooley, R. G. Sultana, & R. Thomsen (Eds.), *Career guidance for emancipation: Reclaiming justice for the multitude* (pp. 216–231). Routledge.

Wilson, B. G. (2005). Foundations for instructional design: Reclaiming the conversation. In J. M. Spector, C. Ohrazda, A. Van Schaack, & D. A. Wiley (Eds.), *Innovations in instructional technology: Essays in honor of M. David Merrill* (pp. 237–252). Routledge.

Zemke, R. (1998). Wake up! (And reclaim instructional design). *Training, 35*(6), 36–42.

10

The Rise of Multipotentiality in a New Landscape of Work

Emilie Wapnick and Melanie V. Buford

Founding an Online Community

In 2010, I (Emilie) founded an organization and online community called Puttylike. The goal was to help people who have many passions, and struggle to narrow in on a single career and life focus. Instead of encouraging these folks to pick a specialty and let go of their other interests (the advice I had been given, with numerous negative emotional consequences), I wanted to help our community members find fulfilling work that allowed them to embrace and express their multiplicity. In addition to helping individuals integrate many interests into their lives, a broader goal of Puttylike was to spread awareness and normalize the idea that engaging in work that spans multiple domains can be both healthy and lucrative. Our mission statement encapsulates these ideas:

> Puttylike is a home for multipotentialites: people with many passions and creative pursuits. We believe that, instead of picking one thing and denying all of our other interests, we can integrate our many passions into our lives. Puttylike is a space to help multipotentialites build dynamic, multifaceted lives, in practical and sustainable ways.
>
> (Puttylike, n.d.)

Since its inception, Puttylike has grown into a global community of tens of thousands of self-identified multipotentialites of all ages, from diverse cultural and socioeconomic backgrounds. My work with this population has included formal interviews and surveys, as well as thousands of informal discussions. Out of these inquiries grew my 2015 TED talk, which has been viewed nearly 8 million times, and my book, *How to Be Everything* (Wapnick, 2017), which has been translated into nine languages. Clearly, the concept of the multipotentialite resonates widely. The majority of people who participate in the Puttylike community report feeling deeply relieved upon learning that there is nothing wrong with them for having multiple, diverse interests. The message that it is okay to be who you are, and that you do not need to narrow your interests to a single focus in order to be successful or – at

DOI: 10.4324/9781003213000-14

the most basic level – respected in society, is comforting to many. We provide practical resources as well, to help our community members thrive professionally while embracing their many facets.

In this chapter, we, the authors, will discuss the history of multipotentiality in both the academic literature and in popular culture. Emilie will share what she has learned from multipotentialites in the Puttylike community who report high levels of career satisfaction. These individuals tend to structure their careers using one of four work models, which she will discuss. We will also consider the role multipotentialites might play in a post-Covid economy. As global challenges become increasingly multifaceted and interconnected, people who can think across domains and adapt to changing environments have a unique strength to offer. Finally, we will provide practical recommendations that career educators can use to better support multipotentialite students as they imagine and plan their future careers.

Multipotentiality in the Literature

The concept of multipotentiality was discussed in various forms in the literature on giftedness between 1970 and the late 1990s. Although the term has been defined somewhat inconsistently, the most commonly cited definition comes from Fredrickson and Rothney (1972), who define a multipotentialed person as "any individual who, when provided with appropriate environments, can select and develop any number of competencies to a high level." This definition was based on their work with gifted students who consistently scored high on various aptitude and achievement tests across domains (Frederickson & Rothney, 1972). Multipotentiality was often considered an aspect of giftedness and discussed within the context of gifted and talented youth (Achter, Benbow, & Lubinski, 1997; Achter, Lubinski, & Benbow, 1996; Frederickson & Rothney, 1972; Rysiew et al., 1999).

The concept of multipotentiality came under some scrutiny in 1996, when researchers Achter, Benbow, and Lubinski observed a large sample of students who ranked in the top 1% of SAT scores, and found that, at this very high level, students did not display several equivalent aptitudes (known as low differentiation or high flat interest profiles), but rather, typically had one area in which they excelled more than in others. The researchers therefore concluded that multipotentiality, as a phenomenon, does not exist. However, as Rysiew et al. (1999) pointed out, these findings contradict the persistent clinical and anecdotal reports of multipotentiality in highly able youth and adults. Counselors and teachers continue to identify the trait and its associated strengths and challenges in their students.

There are problems with much of the early research. Studying multipotentiality within the context of academic ability is likely to exclude many smart, creative people from the definition and discussion. Moreover, selecting subjects through standardized testing means the population will be influenced by the same cultural, racial, and gender biases for which tests like the SATs have been criticized (Loewen et al., 1988; Rattani, 2016). Essentially, framing multipotentiality solely within the context of high achievement suggests that multipotentiality is an "affliction" that belongs only to the most demonstrably capable among us.

In my experience working with the Puttylike community, I (Emilie) have found that there is a great deal of cultural, racial, and socioeconomic diversity among self-identified multipotentialites. It is certainly the case that a privileged background and strong social and financial safety nets may provide opportunities to explore and develop one's interests with greater ease. This reality necessitates equity-based support and programs, as well as taking individual circumstances into account when offering guidance. However, it is my belief that students who do not perform at a high academic level, for whatever reason, should not be excluded from the definition of multipotentialite. Rather than defining multipotentialites by their ability to achieve academically, it would be more helpful and inclusive to point to a person's curiosity and desire to explore many domains as their defining multipotentialite features. Curiosity is certainly more difficult to quantify, but reframing multipotentiality in this way, and letting people self-identify, would allow more folks to understand themselves and build careers that are aligned with their personalities, which have the potential to be more satisfying.

Multipotentiality has also been linked to career indecision and mental health challenges (Rysiew et al., 1994; Kerr & Erb, 1991). Numerous studies have linked multipotentiality to difficulties choosing a vocational path as well as career anxiety, and "overchoice syndrome" (Rysiew et al., 1994). In one study of academically talented high school and college students, the authors concluded that "Multipotentiality can also lead to difficulty in the development of a sense of purpose; students with many talents wonder how they can possibly integrate or prioritize abilities in order to make a meaningful contribution to society" (Kerr & Erb, 1991, p. 309).

Multipotentiality in Popular Culture

Since the early 2000s, most of the discussion around this topic has happened not within the academic community, but in popular books, blogs, and on social media. The concept of the individual with many interests is discussed in these spaces using a variety of terms. In her 2007 book *Refuse to Choose*, Barbara Sher referred to someone who is curious about many unrelated subjects as a "scanner." Author Margaret Lobenstine (2013) identified this person as a "Renaissance Soul" in her book by the same name. Marci Alboher (2007) described multiple job holders as "slashes" in her book *One Person / Many Careers*. Other terms used include "multi-hyphenate," "multi-passionate," and "creative generalist," as well as language with historical connotations, such as polymath and Renaissance person.

In the last decade, the argument that being a generalist can lead to greater creativity and innovation has gained traction in popular culture (Brooks, 2021; Grant, 2016; Safian, 2012). Articles about the strengths of generalists have been featured in publications like *The New York Times*, *Fast Company*, and *The Atlantic*. My (Emilie) own TED talk about the superpowers of multipotentialites went viral (Wapnick, 2015). Newer books, like David Epstein's *Range* (2019), have become quick bestsellers.

As far as I (Emilie) am aware, I am the only writer who has returned to the terminology of multipotentiality – though my use of the word "multipotentialite" is intended to be a playful reimagining of the idea. My definition, as well as those of Sher, Lobenstine, and other contemporary authors, uses a diversity of interests, passions or curiosity as the main defining feature, rather than emphasizing aptitude or skill level. Essentially, if you identify as a multipotentialite (or scanner, Renaissance Soul, multi-passionate, etc.), you are one, and you are welcome in the community. Those of us in this space have moved past the discussion about whether or not the phenomenon is real. We have shared our lived experiences and advice, and we have featured other people who identify with this idea and found ways of integrating their many interests into their lives.

The framing of multipotentiality in popular culture is often more positive than the discussion in the early academic literature. At Puttylike, we view multipotentiality as a strength that can make someone highly adaptable and good at drawing connections between disparate subjects and conceptualizing and solving complex, multifaceted problems. There are certainly challenges associated with having multiple interests, but we consider these challenges to be a result of a widespread, cultural misunderstanding of generalists and their strengths, rather than an inherent problem with multipotentialites themselves. Nonetheless, multipotentialites need to fit into the modern (and quickly evolving) world of work. With a dearth of resources for those who require variety in their lives to be happy, as well as the widespread norm that hyper-specialization is the only path to success, it can be difficult for people to figure out how to build a life around their many diverse interests.

How Multipotentialites Build Satisfying Careers

Happy, fulfilled multipotentialites can be found in any career and industry, even in seemingly specialized fields like medicine and engineering. In fact, it can be difficult to identify a multipotentialite based on their job title alone. One determinative factor in their career satisfaction is variety (Wapnick, 2017). Happy and fulfilled multipotentialites have found different ways to get the variety they need in their lives. Sometimes that variation is built into their careers. Other times, multipotentialites pair a more specialized career with an array of meaningful hobbies or side projects. There are several career structures that allow one to build a life with plenty of variety. In my (Emilie's) interviews, surveys, and discussions over the years, I have identified four work models that are commonly used by multipotentialites, each of which offers variety in different ways. Some people blend or customize these models, but they are a good starting point to begin conceptualizing career options that allow one to do and be many things.

1. The Group Hug Approach to Work

The Group Hug approach involves having a single job or business that allows you to wear several hats and shift between different domains at work (Wapnick, 2017). The name evokes the imagery of several interests coming together in a big group hug. There are many fields in which multiple domains overlap, and which allow multipotentialites to combine different passions. Interdisciplinary fields like artificial intelligence, environmental policy, counseling, education, filmmaking, journalism, and marketing are popular choices among multipotentialites because they require an understanding of, and expertise in, multiple domains. Artificial intelligence, for example, is an integration of psychology, philosophy, technology, neuroscience, computer science, mathematics, robotics, pattern recognition, machine learning, and visual perception.

Multipotentialites sometimes find a multifaceted niche within their area of study. A specialty like science communication, for example, involves the blending of scientific knowledge with writing, storytelling, media, and art. This might be a good fit for a multipotentialite who is studying science but doesn't want to *just* focus on science. I (Emilie) spoke with a teacher (Wapnick, 2017) who was drawn to the Waldorf educational model because Waldorf teachers teach multiple subjects to one class over the course of a single day (Stehlik, 2019). This allows her to shift between different subjects regularly and draw analogies between those subjects. Specialties like science communication and Waldorf education are two examples of niches within broader areas of study that are well suited to those who want or need more variety.

Entrepreneurship is another "group hug" in which multipotentialites tend to excel, because running a business typically necessitates wearing multiple hats. Business owners need to switch between activities like product development, marketing, design, sales, customer service, team management, legal matters, bookkeeping, etc. Often, a multipotentialite business owner will start out by doing everything themselves, and later outsource the parts of their business they do not enjoy as the business grows. Multipotentialites also tend to be quick, passionate learners. Many of the business owners I spoke with began their ventures without all of the necessary skills in tow. They learned as they went – and the opportunity to learn was part of what appealed to them about starting their own business.

Both traditional employment in an interdisciplinary field and business ownership can be vehicles that allow one to combine multiple interests in a single career. The Group Hug approach is a good fit for people who enjoy working on multi-dimensional projects and desire an alignment between their professional and personal identities. In other words, it allows them to engage with one form of work that reflects their multitudes.

2. The Slash Approach to Work

The Slash approach involves having multiple part-time jobs and/or businesses that you move between on a regular basis (Wapnick, 2017). It is the teacher/programmer/ standup comedian or the playwright/engineer/yoga instructor/designer. The Slash approach gets its name from the fact that people using this work model often have a number of slashes in their professional title. Some also refer to this work model as a portfolio career (Alboher, 2007).

Slash careerists usually divide their week up between several very different forms of work. Morgan Siem spends two to three days per week working as a freelance marketing consultant, two days employed at a local non-profit, and performs as an aerial silks artist on the weekend. Similarly, Neil Hughes splits his week up between giving educational presentations in schools about anxiety, programming, freelance writing, and the occasional standup gig. The Slash approach tends to provide more flexibility than the other three work models, and can be a nice fit for people who dislike conventional work environments and/or have projects with less consistent schedules, such as artistic pursuits or freelance projects (Wapnick, 2017).

There is a misconception that Slash careerists are unhappy or that they structure their work this way because they lack options. There are certainly people (including multipotentialites) who, at times, pursue multiple income streams solely out of necessity. However, for multipotentialites who are happy in their Slash careers, the choice to pursue part-time work is intentional. In the words of author and entrepreneur, Penelope Trunk:

> A portfolio career is not the same thing as holding down three bad jobs and wishing you could figure out what to do with yourself. Rather, it's a scheme you pursue purposefully and positively, as a way to achieve a mixture of financial and personal goals.
>
> (2006, para. 3)

Many of the multipotentialites I (Emilie) interviewed report loving each of their "slashes" for different reasons. Each work project allows them to "tap into different parts of their brain" and use different skillsets. Satisfied slash careerists love the variety in their week and are adamant that, if given the chance, they would not want to pursue any one of their "slashes" full time.

3. The Einstein Approach to Work

The Einstein approach is having one job or business that fully supports you financially, leaving you with time and energy to pursue your other passions on the side (Wapnick, 2017). This model is named for Albert Einstein, who famously worked for the government as a patent officer and developed his theories, including the theory of special relativity, on the side (Isaacson, 2008). Like all of the work models, the Einstein approach is not a good fit for everyone. Yet multipotentialites who have chosen this model find that having their financial goals reliably met relieves the pressure to monetize every new interest, and allows them to pursue their hobbies and projects with less stress.

The Einstein approach is a good fit for those who desire greater financial security and do not necessarily care if their professional work reflects the entirety of who they are. Charlie Harper is an IT manager, with a traditional day job. He works in the office five days a week, eight hours a day. Outside of his work he is very involved with his local community theater and sings in an a cappella group. Harper is also a skilled carpenter, who builds furniture and boats for fun on the weekend. Though he loves performing arts and carpentry, he has chosen not to pursue either field professionally. His community theater, singing group, and building projects enrich his life and bring him great fulfillment, and he has no interest in monetizing these activities. The IT job helps to pay the bills, while the hobbies fulfill Charlie's creative side. He feels no pressure for the personal projects to earn him money, and no pressure for the IT work to be his passion in life (Wapnick, 2017).

When pursuing the Einstein work model, it is important that one's day job not be so all-consuming or exhausting that they run out of time or energy to pursue their passions. The Einstein career does not have to be a "dream job" but it should be enjoyable and there should be appropriate boundaries, such that it doesn't get in the way of personal projects and hobbies. An 80-hour-a-week job in a stressful environment, where one is expected to answer emails late into the night, probably would not qualify. When using this work model, one's day job should make it possible for them to explore their many interests without financial or emotional stress after, and around, their work hours.

4. The Phoenix Approach to Work

The Phoenix approach requires working in a single field for several years, then changing gears and starting a new career in a new field (Wapnick, 2017). It is as though the multipotentialite reinvents themselves every five to fifteen years, like a mythical phoenix rising from the ashes. One example would be someone who works as a musician for five years, then works in education for eight years, then goes back to school to study and then practice law for twelve years, then moves on to produce a documentary and work in the film industry for a decade.

It can be difficult to plan out a phoenix career at the beginning. A multipotentialite's interests tend to change over time, so it is hard to know what subjects one will want to pursue many years down the road. For this reason, many phoenix careerists only recognize their pattern of starting over in new fields when looking backwards at their career. However, it can be helpful to know that this work model is an option that many people find satisfying, and that choosing to pursue a single passion now does not mean you cannot pursue others in the future. Normalizing this work model is important, as most phoenix careerists change paths not because of any failing on their part, but due to an eventual sense that they achieved what they needed to achieve in a particular area and are ready for a change.

There can be costs associated with radical career shifts, including educational and time costs as well as possible changes in salary. However, multipotentialites who choose to undergo this kind of career reinvention – and who have the means to do so – typically find that the emotional and creative relief associated with the shift is worth the associated challenges. Moreover, most multipotentialites have transferable skills that they bring with them from one field to the next. When applying for a paralegal position, health and sexuality educator Mariah Wilberg described the relevant skills she used in her previous career in her application. These included working under pressure, meeting strict deadlines, adhering to grant requirements, and dealing with emotional clients (Wapnick, 2017). These skills were applicable in two very different fields and emphasizing them helped her establish a new career without much experience in the industry.

Finally, multipotentialites who use the Phoenix approach successfully do not typically make their career changes abruptly. They usually take their time and develop their next career on the side before making the leap. This allows them to seek out opportunities, develop their skills, and make new contacts. This often makes the transition much smoother. Some Phoenix careerists I have spoken with tell me that they try to honor their work commitments and move on from their previous careers as thoughtfully as possible.

Multipotentialites in the Post-Covid Economy

Running an online community for multipotentialites during the pandemic has been interesting, to say the least. Despite the widespread fear, loss, grief, and trauma experienced by the world at large (including within our community), I (Emilie) witnessed some remarkable resourcefulness and resilience. Many multipotentialites in the Puttyverse community found ways to pivot to digital and remote forms of work. Some started online businesses or freelance careers. Having a range of diverse skills allowed many of our community members to lean on their more profitable skills during a time of great uncertainty. If the demand for one of their skills decreased due to the pandemic, they could make use of a different skillset. In this way, their multipotentiality became a useful tool, not just for personal, creative, and professional satisfaction, but as a means of survival. The way people make a living in industrialized countries has been changing rapidly since the Great Recession (Farber, 2011; Kallenberg & Dunn, 2016), and the pandemic has only intensified these changes. Multipotentialites, with their diverse abilities and knack for creativity, are not only well-suited to navigate these changes, but are very much needed in an increasingly interconnected world.

In a 2020 paper entitled "Creative Polymathy and the COVID-19 Crisis," researchers Michael Espindola Araki and Angela Cotellessa argued that "in the context of COVID-19 crisis [sic], with its wicked and transdisciplinary nature, the disciplinary approach of specialization is ill-suited to solve our increasingly complex problems… polymathic thinking can be a crucial asset in this regard" (Abstract). The authors pointed to specific global challenges that are a direct result of a siloed, segregationist approach to thinking about them. If we, as a global society, learn to appreciate and foster polymathic thinking and polymathic individuals (multipotentialites), we may be better equipped to find solutions to complex problems that impact many different facets of life, such as poverty and health care.

Recommendations for Practice

Multipotentialites have unique needs, challenges, and strengths. It is important to take these into consideration when working with them to envision, plan, and navigate their careers. Here are six recommendations to help career practitioners better support multipotentialite students and professionals.

1. **Share resources for and about multipotentialites.** Explore role models and other examples of professionals who have integrated many different interests into their lives. It is important to normalize the idea that engaging with and exploring many domains is not only acceptable, but healthy, and that many multipotentialites have thriving careers and contribute to society in meaningful ways.
2. **Take the need for variety seriously.** Help students identify careers that can satisfy their need for exploration, learning, and novelty. Many of the people in the multipotentialite community report having negative, even traumatic, experiences working with career professionals who did not understand or appreciate their need for variety. To be happy and do their best work, multipotentialites need to find ways of expressing, and sometimes integrating, their many passions. When evaluating potential careers with a multipotentialite, encourage them to consider whether or not a particular career and lifestyle offers variety, novelty, and opportunities for learning. If a career they are considering seems particularly narrow, that should be discussed. Perhaps there are other, closely related, interdisciplinary fields or niches within the field that are more open and multifaceted. Or perhaps there are other ways in which the student can get the variety they need, such as through personal projects or hobbies (Einstein work model) or by adding additional revenue streams ("slashes") to their professional life.
3. **Help them develop a plan for managing social, emotional, and financial concerns.** It is important to consider each student's personal situation, identities, needs, and priorities. If financial stability is a primary concern, discuss how to balance or prioritize the need for stability over variety and passion. Certain career structures might be more appropriate than others in these

situations. For example, it might make sense to focus on establishing a single, well-paying "group hug" or "Einstein" job, rather than piecing together a Slash career with multiple revenue streams, which can take longer to establish. One can always shift to a different work model in the future, and it can be helpful to remind students that these choices are not set in stone. Pursuing one area of interest professionally now does not mean that they cannot explore others in the future.

4. **Help students identify themes across their divergent interests and better understand their motivations, values, and what they find meaningful.** The things we are drawn to are not always as random or disparate as they may seem. Often, there are overarching themes or motivations that draw us to different subjects and projects. To take a hypothetical example, a student is driven by the desire to make complicated ideas accessible to more people. This theme could be relevant in various fields and industries such as education, data visualization, and animation, among others. Supporting students to better understand themselves, and why the activities they enjoy appeal or feel meaningful to them, is helpful when considering potential career directions.

5. **Emphasize exploration, not just the pursuit of a single career.** The process of finding a career can be just as interesting and design-oriented as any career itself. Many multipotentialites are drawn to exploration, and this in itself can provide a motivating foundation for career. Encourage them to consider learning and exploration as continuous elements of their professional evolution, and to develop practices – such as informational interviews, job shadowing, reading, reflective writing, and taking on new projects – that intentionally integrate these activities into their lives.

6. **Take unconventional and creative projects seriously.** Online entrepreneurship, self-publishing, and creative mash-ups of revenue streams can be viable options in today's creator economy. Accept that both you and the student might be unaware of new technologies or forms of distribution that make it possible to make a living. Explore together and be open to different and novel career formats. In many ways, this is a great time to be a multipotentialite – especially with expertise in technology.

References

Achter, J. A., Benbow, C. P., & Lubinski, D. (1997). Rethinking multipotentiality among the intellectually gifted: A critical review and recommendations. *Gifted Child Quarterly*, *41*(1), 5–15. https://doi.org/10.1177/001698629704100102

Achter, J. A., Lubinski, D., & Benbow, C. P. (1996). Multipotentiality among the intellectually gifted: "It was never there and already it's vanishing." *Journal of Counseling Psychology*, *43*(1), 65–76. https://doi.org/10.1037/0022-0167.43.1.65

Alboher, M. (2007). *One person/multiple careers: A new model for work/life success.* Warner Business Books.

Araki, M. E., & Cotellessa, A. J. (2020). Creative polymathy and the COVID-19 crisis [Hypothesis and Theory]. *Frontiers in Psychology*, *11*(3580). https://doi.org/10.3389/fpsyg.2020.601508

Brooks, A. C. (2021, March 18). Here's 10,000 hours. Don't spend it all in one place. *The Atlantic*. www.theatlantic.com/family/archive/2021/03/having-dual-career-can-make-you-happier/618311/

Epstein, D. (2019). *Range: How generalists triumph in a specialized world*. Riverhead.

Farber, H. S. (2011). Job loss in the Great Recession: Historical perspective from the displaced workers survey, 1984-2010 (NBER Working Paper No. 170400). *National Bureau of Economic Research*. https://doi.org.10.3386/w17040

Fredrickson, R. H., & Rothney, J. W. M. (1972). *Recognizing and assisting multipotential youth*. Merrill.

Grant, A. (2016, January 20). How to raise a creative child. Step one: Back off. *New York Times*. www.nytimes.com/2016/01/31/opinion/sunday/how-to-raise-a-creative-child-step-one-back-off.html

Isaacson, W. (2008). *Einstein: His life and universe* (1st ed.). Simon & Schuster.

Kallenberg, A. L., & Dunn, M. (2016). Good jobs, bad jobs in the gig economy. *Perspectives on Work*, *20*, 10–75. https://michael-dunn.org/wp-content/uploads/2017/05/ALK-MD.-JQ-in-Gig-Economy.pdf

Kerr, B., & Erb, C. (1991). Career counseling with academically talented students: Effects of a value-based intervention. *Journal of Counseling Psychology*, *38*(3), 309–314. https://doi.org/10.1037/0022-0167.38.3.309

Lobenstine, M. (2013). *The renaissance soul: How to make your passions your life – a creative and practical guide*. Experiment.

Loewen, J., Rosser, P., & Katzman, J. (1988). *Gender bias in SAT items*. American Educational Research Association.

Puttylike. (n.d.). *About Puttylike*. https://puttylike.com/about/

Rattani, S. A. (2016). SAT: Does racial bias exist? *Creative Education*, *7*(15), 2151–2162. https://doi.org/10.4236/ce.2016.715213

Rysiew, K. J., Shore, B. M., & Carson, A. D. (1994). Multipotentiality and overchoice syndrome: Clarifying common usage. *Gifted and Talented International*, *9*(2), 41–46. https://doi.org/10.1080/15332276.1994.11672792

Rysiew, K. J., Shore, B. M., & Leeb, R. T. (1999). Multipotentiality, giftedness, and career choice: A review. *Journal of Counseling and Development*, *77*(4), 423–430. https://doi.org/10.1002/j.1556-6676.1999.tb02469.x

Safian, R. (2012, January 9). This is generation flux: Meet the pioneers of the new (and chaotic) frontier of business. *Fast Company*. www.fastcompany.com/1802732/generation-flux-meet-pioneers-new-and-chaotic-frontier-business

Sher, B. (2007). *Refuse to choose!: A revolutionary program for doing everything that you love*. Rodale.

Stehlik, T. (2019). *Waldorf schools and the history of Steiner education: An international view of 100 years.* Palgrave Macmillan.

Trunk, P. (2006, July 4). The portfolio career: To find fulfillment try simultaneous careers. *Penelope Trunk Blog.* https://blog.penelopetrunk.com/2006/07/04/the-portfolio-career-to-find-fulfillment-try-simultaneous-careers/

Wapnick, E. (2015, April). *Why some of us don't have one true calling* [Video]. TEDxBend. www.ted.com/talks/emilie_wapnick_why_some_of_us_don_t_have_one_true_calling?language=en

Wapnick, E. (2017). *How to be everything: A guide for those who (still) don't know what they want to be when they grow up.* HarperOne.

11

The Challenge Mindset: Empowering Students to Find Meaning and Purpose

J.P. Michel

The world of work is changing quickly. To succeed in this environment, we need to learn to adapt to these changes (McGowan & Shipley, 2020). For career educators around the globe, it is time to adapt by moving beyond job titles to help students explore challenges to work on, instead of job titles to fit into. This chapter describes a new approach called the "Challenge mindset" that is helping students overcome obstacles, broaden their horizons, and prepare for a career of meaning and purpose.

The Changing World of Work

In the past few decades, globalization, new cultural norms, and advances in technology have reshaped the world of work (Cascio, 1995, 2012; Mincer, 2003). These changes have paved the way for many new opportunities and challenges to work on. In this complex – and often confusing – reality, the field of career education is operating in different and challenging waters. There now seem to be endless problems to solve, companies to work for, tools to leverage, and skills to develop. Despite important developments in the world of work, some of our career practices are more than a hundred years old. For example, vocational guidance and the theoretical approach of matching an individual's personality, skills, and abilities to a career dates back to the early 1900s (Dey & Cruzvergara, 2014; Kazuyuki & Kuo-lin, 2006). One can therefore wonder: Are our career practices still relevant today? In order to answer this question, we need to better understand the nature and pace of change.

First, continuous advancements in technology and artificial intelligence are disrupting the world of work at a very fast pace (PwC, 2018). As per Moore's law, technological progress increases exponentially, leading to smarter machines that create new opportunities and require new skills to operate (Schaller, 1997). Novel challenges and opportunities – such as social media, big data analytics, and

DOI: 10.4324/9781003213000-15

cybersecurity – that have emerged from recent advances in technology would have been difficult to predict even 20 years ago.

Experts suggest we should expect more change, at an accelerated pace (McKinsey Global Institute, 2018). When it comes to the future, it seems the only certainty is that it will look different from today. In a *Forbes* article, Jack Kelly (2019), author and CEO of the global search firm WeCruitr, contended:

> The future job market will be radically different – almost alien – to what we have now. There are waves of forces that will significantly change the way we work and the type of jobs we hold. The rapid ascension of sophisticated technology, global connectedness, and a confluence of other factors will make the workforce of the future almost unrecognizable.
>
> (2019, p. 2)

Given the changes that are coming, how can we prepare students for the complexity of the world of work? Faced with an unpredictable future, we would be well-served to move beyond the approach of using job titles as a central component in career development.

Limitations of the Job Title Mindset

Unfortunately, the upcoming changes in the world of work threaten to outpace our systems, approaches, and mindsets to prepare students for success. Many of our practices operate under outdated assumptions, such as a predictable labor market and linear career progression (Chatzichristou & Arulmani, 2014; Parro, 2015). Because of this, many career development interventions prioritize the matching of individuals with specific job titles. I have coined the term "job title mindset" to describe this approach, which focuses on helping people choose one occupation as the goal of career development. In this section, I argue that it is contributing to negative outcomes for students and workers of all ages, and that we need a better approach if we are to unlock the true potential of career development (Arthur, 2021).

Indeed, as an approach to career exploration and development, the job title mindset has several limitations. As discussed below, students only know a handful of the available options, the ones they do know tend to focus on what they've been exposed to, and job titles themselves are changing at a pace that we often struggle to keep up with. These issues are usually triggered when youth are asked the age-old question: *What do you want to be when you grow up?* Behind this seemingly innocent question lies a slew of outdated assumptions and notions about the world of work. When young people are asked that question, it suggests they need to pick one job or occupation for the rest of their lives. However, estimates published by the Foundation for Young Australians found that today's youth may hold as many as 17 different jobs across five industries in their lifetime (The Foundation for Young Australians, 2016).

Continuous advances in technology and innovation also mean that job titles and descriptions are continuously changing, and new ones are emerging. Josh Bersin (2020), global leader in human resources and talent management, proclaimed: "In today's world of work, jobs are changing so quickly that the old-fashioned idea of building a competency model and formal job description is not keeping up" (para. 2).

Relatedly, while today's labor market features thousands of different job titles (U.S. Bureau of Labor Statistics, 2021), students usually know of only a handful of occupations. In my experience as a career practitioner, I have observed that students are aware of around 25 different jobs (with a range of approximately 10 on the low end, and 50 on the high end). In 2020, the Organisation for Economic Co-operation and Development (OECD) published results of a study that investigated the career aspirations of 500,000 youth, aged 15 years old, living in 41 countries (OECD, 2020). The report showed that around half of participants – 47% of boys and 53% of girls – expect to work in one of 10 popular jobs by the age of 30. The list included typical occupations such as teachers, doctors, police officers, and engineers. At the launch of the report (Education and Employers, 2020), Andreas Schleicher, Director of Education and Skills at the OECD, is quoted saying:

> It is a concern that more young people than before appear to be picking their dream job from a small list of the most popular, traditional occupations, like teachers, lawyers or business managers. The surveys show that too many teenagers are ignoring or are unaware of new types of jobs that are emerging, particularly as a result of digitalisation. The analysis suggests that, in many countries, young people's career aspirations increasingly bear little relation to actual labour market demand.
>
> (2020, para. 3)

This concerning trend suggests that focusing on job titles as an approach to career development may have limited value and serve to reinforce the disconnect between students' aspirations and the realities of the labor market.

A measurable consequence of practices that promote the job title mindset is that many young people are struggling to prepare for their future. More specifically, popular interest inventory assessments undertaken in schools may perpetuate the notion that students need to choose one job that they will hold for the rest of their lives (Arthur, 2021). Students are also often asked to make decisions about their future, such as which education program to pursue, through the selection of a job title. This can result in feelings of tremendous pressure to make the "right choice," despite being unaware of the full range of career options and what they entail. This pressure has been shown in the literature to manifest as stress and anxiety among students. In a study by Pisarik et al. (2017), college students reported high levels of anxiety associated with the choice of a major. Similarly, in the 2016–2017 Student Census conducted on more than 100,000 students (grades nine to 12) at the Toronto District School Board, 72% of participants reported they worry "all the time" or "often" about their future (Toronto District School Board, 2018). Likely as a result of this anxiety, 42% of students were "sometimes" or "rarely/never" hopeful about the future. As explored in the following section, the limits of the job title mindset seem to be disproportionately affecting the students that need our help the most.

Diversity and Equity

Historically, career development has served as a pathway toward upward mobility and the advancement of marginalized communities (Hartung & Blustein, 2002; Stebleton & Eggerth, 2012). Our practitioners have a key role to play if education is to be the "great equalizer," so that where you come from does not determine where you can go in life. Yet the overuse of job titles in career work may be preventing progress, especially in the areas of diversity and equity.

Studies have found that career choice is largely influenced by positionality (Harris Cornileus, 2010), defined as the social and political environment that shapes your identity in terms of race, gender, class, sexuality, and ability status (Dictionary.com, 2021). A person's career choice is also influenced by their cultural context and life experiences (Gottfredson, 2002; Leong & Hartung, 2000). This means that when we ask young people about their career aspirations or what they like, their response is often a reflection of what they already know, from their environment, family, and personal circumstances. Although the notion of traditional occupations based on sex or race may not be as prevalent as it was in past years, research demonstrates that our career guidance tools may be perpetuating these biases.

In a study conducted on more than 3,000 grade 10 students in Georgia, USA, self-reported interest scores were found to narrow young women's vision toward more traditional occupations, and away from more prestigious or high-wage careers (Engelman, 2016). Conversely, measuring aptitude did not lead to gender differences across industries (Engelman, 2016). In the fifth edition of *Career Guidance and Counseling Through the Lifespan: Systemic Approaches*, Herr and Cramer (1996) noted that "as persons explore occupational possibilities, they use stereotypes of themselves and stereotypes of occupations to guide their search" (p. 200). The impact of gender and racial stereotypes on career choice is, in fact, well documented in the literature (Clawson, 2000; Hartung et al., 2005; McMahon, 1997). Further, students in regional, rural, and remote areas may also be disadvantaged by limited exposure to different career options (Polvere, 2015).

Given these issues, if interest assessments are not used with caution, we run the risk of potential misguidance. For example, Rich Feller (2019), past president of the National Career Development Association (NCDA), stated that: "If [women] haven't been exposed to scientific and technical careers, they're less likely to self-report an interest in those job paths – after all, it's hard to be interested in something that you know nothing about" (Feller, 2019). Instead of reinforcing what students have been exposed to, the focus should be on helping them broaden their horizons. From an equity lens, this is essential when working with students from disadvantaged backgrounds, difficult family environments (e.g., lack of parental support), or oppressed groups with generational trauma. Focusing on broadening horizons can also help counter the risk of inherent bias or career stereotypes that may be perpetuated by educators (Carlana, 2019; Cross et al., 2015).

Preparing minority students – and all young people – for a different future will therefore require significant changes in the way we consider and undertake career education. At a time when we should be broadening students' horizons, we need to be careful not to prematurely limit their options. With the job title mindset contributing to these issues, one may therefore wonder about alternative approaches that could help. In the next section, we present a new way of exploring the world of work, free from the limits of job titles. The Challenge mindset – a more engaging, future-oriented approach to career exploration – holds that promise.

The Challenge Mindset: Broadening Horizons

Instead of asking students, *"What do you want to be when you grow up?"*, what if we started asking, *"What problems do you want to solve?"* This is the question posed by the Challenge mindset, a career exploration approach focused on finding challenges to tackle instead of job titles to fit into. Examples of challenges to work on include increasing sustainable energy, ending extreme poverty, redesigning the healthcare system, building better homes, and fostering understanding and respect.

Start with Challenges, Problems, and Opportunities

The traditional career exploration model typically uses a student's interest in a specific course or academic proficiency in an area as a starting point for career options. Accordingly, many educators start by asking: *"What is your favorite class?"* This can quickly lead students down a narrow or linear career path that may ultimately be unfulfilling or fail to meet their expectations. For example, a student who is good at mathematics may be encouraged to major in accounting to become an accountant. After years of study and work, they might eventually come to understand the challenge they are working on. For some accountants, that challenge is helping companies reduce the amount of taxes they pay. This challenge could spark the interest of some, but not others.

The Challenge mindset flips the model by starting with challenges first. With the support of innovative tools and exercises, students start by exploring real-world challenges, problems, and opportunities to work on. Students can then work backwards to explore the companies making an impact on these challenges, the people who work there, and their unique educational and professional paths (Figure 11.1).

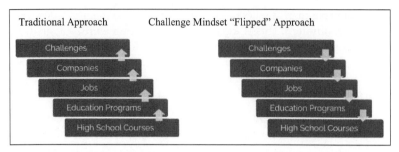

Figure 11.1 The Challenge mindset "flips" the career exploration model

With this information, students can identify what they need to learn, including the skills, experiences, knowledge, and abilities they can acquire and use.

The exploration of these five steps, starting with challenges, helps students bring the career exploration process to life. Let us walk through an example where a student has chosen "increase sustainable energy" as a challenge that speaks to them. Through some reflection prompts, the student is asked to write down why this challenge is important to them, which helps connect their choice with their values, experiences, interests, abilities, and what they find meaningful. Next, through online research, they discover that the company Tesla is working on this challenge. On the company's website, the student learns they are currently hiring for their construction team, which includes the following jobs: crane operators, carpenters, welders, and millwrights. The student can then discover the education programs available at their local community college that would help them prepare for these opportunities. Through this research process (from challenges to companies, jobs, and then education programs), young people identify real possibilities that can shape their future. This information brings the labor market to life in a way that job titles alone cannot. By exploring concrete labor market needs that align with their values, students make powerful connections between the future impact they want to have in the world and the steps they need to take to get there.

By gathering information, students are learning through action instead of being focused on a single decision (Krumboltz, 2009). Armed with this information, they are better equipped to craft their story, the importance of which has been documented (McIlveen & Patton, 2007; Savickas, 2005). Working with the Challenge mindset, students' narratives are enriched by the information uncovered through their labor market research. Instead of basing their stories strictly on their current identity, adding key details from their research helps students craft an aspirational identity informed by what inspires them (Ibarra & Barbulescu, 2010). This process is empowering because it allows students to see concrete possibilities for their future. It makes the abstract (their career, their future, etc.) tangible, and creates momentum for action.

The approach described above, which includes the Challenge mindset exploration process and the creation of a story, is a powerful combination that helps students prepare for the future world of work. Over the span of a career that might last between

40 and 60 years, or more than 100,000 hours, students may need to go through this process several times (Gratton, 2016). In fact, reinvention has been described as the most important skill of the 21st century by Yuval Noah Harari, futurist and author (Harari, 2018). This is especially true given the magnitude of anticipated disruptions to the world of work (PwC, 2018). These changes will require that workers reinvent themselves by repackaging transferable skills, learning new skills, adapting their stories, and more (Pryor & Bright, 2014). In the Happenstance Learning theory, John D. Krumboltz (2008), stated the following: "The goal of career counseling is to help clients learn to take actions to achieve more satisfying career and personal lives – not to make a single career decision" (p. 141).

Helping students explore real challenges instead of job titles, flipping the model, and advocating for reinvention are all approaches that help students integrate modern career exploration methodologies tailored to an ever-changing world of work. The process is about connecting young people to the world by asking different questions, such as: "*What does the world need and how can I help?*", "*What difference can I make?*", and "*What can I learn to help me contribute to the challenges I care about?*" The flexibility, depth, and personalization of the Challenge mindset intervention taps into several evidence-based mechanisms that can lead to positive impacts for students (Table 11.1).

Table 11.1 Examples of mechanisms and their application in the Challenge mindset

Theory/mechanism	Examples of application and impact
Autonomy (Ryan & Deci, 2000)	I choose the challenges I want to work on.
Competence (Ryan & Deci, 2000)	I can gain mastery of the skills I need to make a contribution to the challenge I care about.
Relatedness (Ryan & Deci, 2000)	Where will I work? With whom?
Hope (Niles et al., 2011)	I see possibilities and I am hopeful when I think about my future.
Adaptability/Adapt-abilities (Savickas, 1997)	I am not deciding for "the rest of my life." I am preparing to be adaptable, as I will work on several different challenges during my career.
Self-Efficacy (Bandura, 1997)	I can solve most problems if I invest the necessary effort.
Purpose (Damon, 2008)	This challenge matters to me, and I know why. I am building a plan for future action.

Below, we discuss how the Challenge mindset can lead to positive outcomes in both the short term and long term.

The Impact of the Challenge Mindset

The Challenge mindset offers several benefits to students, employees, educators, and employers. A 2020 study by Buford and Nester, which explored the impact of the Challenge mindset amongst 61 undergraduate students at the University of Cincinnati, found that: "The process of reflecting on challenges of interest and connecting these to potential careers may encourage students to find meaning in their work and increase their personal investment" (para. 7). Meaningfulness has also been found to counter negative psychological outcomes, such as depression and anxiety, and promote positive indicators, including life satisfaction, work enjoyment, and happiness (Bonebright et al., 2000; Chamberlain & Zika, 1988; Debats et al., 1993). Further studies show that work meaningfulness is associated with favorable career-related outcomes such as work engagement and job satisfaction (Duffy et al., 2011; Steger, 2016).

Given the reported impacts of meaningfulness on a range of positive outcomes, Dik et al. (2020) argue that it should be incorporated in career education and counseling:

> Minimally, there is a viable rationale for including measures of calling and meaningful work in career counseling to enable clients to reflect on the extent to which their present career paths and work experiences provide fulfillment, opportunities for self-expression, a sense of contribution, or a suitable venue for devoting one's efforts and time.
>
> (p. 258)

They also go on to write that career counseling can be deemed successful when individuals find or create work they perceive as meaningful (Dik, 2020).

In his book *Path to Purpose* (2008), psychologist William Damon stated that "purpose is a stable and generalized intention to accomplish something that is at the same time meaningful to the self and consequential for the world beyond the self" (p. 33). Finding a meaningful and purposeful career path is indeed a priority for many students. In a survey of more than 14,000 post-secondary students in Canada, 73% of respondents reported that serving a cause or the greater good is either "very important" or "extremely important" to them (Donald, 2017). In fact, this was the third most important career goal reported by the survey participants, behind work–life balance and achieving job security. A study conducted by Rutgers amongst 807 millennial full-time workers also found that 59% of participants desire a job with impact where they can "make a difference" (Zukin, 2012).

Instilling meaning in career exploration and development is important because it can translate into greater educational and career engagement. Indeed, studies have found that having a sense of purpose helps individuals organize and plan their daily and long-term activities by aligning them toward a bigger goal (Hill et al., 2010; McKnight & Kashdan, 2009). In their article, Buford and Nester (2020) go on to write that "the Challenge approach may support students in focusing on social and societal impact, thereby providing critical motivation to move through the career development process" (para. 19).

Despite the importance of career meaningfulness, some students are finding it difficult to achieve this. A Gallup and Bates College study of more than 2,200 four-year college graduates found that while 80% of participants affirmed the importance of deriving a sense of purpose from their work, less than half succeeded at doing so (Gallup, 2019). This discrepancy is believed to negatively impact young workers as well as organizations. In a statement (Bauer-Wolf, 2019), Bates College president Ava Clayton Spencer affirmed that "the purpose gap is also a challenge for employers because of a strong correlation between employees' purpose and engagement and an organization's bottom line" (para. 5).

In a study conducted by SparkPath, 105 high school students living in Ottawa, Canada, completed a questionnaire before and after participating in a 60-minute Challenge mindset workshop. Before the workshop, just over half (57%) of students agreed or strongly agreed with the statement "I feel inspired by what I can accomplish in my career" (Michel, 2021). After the workshop, that proportion increased to 90%. The workshop also increased the proportion of students who reported that they "agree" or "strongly agree" with the statement "I am prepared to have a successful career." Furthermore, there was a 29% increase in the proportion of students who reported they have ideas about what they want to do during their career, and a 20% reduction in career-related anxiety (Michel, 2021).

As the Challenge mindset gains popularity, more research is needed to measure a broader range of short-term and long-term outcomes, and investigate the specific drivers and mechanisms of action of these outcomes. What would happen if we prepared the next generation to work on challenges that are meaningful to them? The next section will showcase examples of academic institutions that are already using this approach with their students and present best practices that can be replicated by others.

Current Applications: Accessible Career Education

The Challenge mindset is currently being used in schools and colleges around the world. To facilitate the discovery of challenges and opportunities to work on, the Challenge Cards sort was created and was first presented at the NCDA conference in Orlando, Florida in 2017 (Michel, 2017). The cards are now available as a physical and digital tool. There are more than 20,000 decks of physical Challenge Cards in use and over 24,000 students have sorted the digital Challenge Cards at the time of this publication. Both the Challenge mindset and the Challenge Cards have been adopted for use with various educational and professional populations.

In higher education, the Challenge mindset is used by career services to help students move beyond the job title mindset to broaden their horizons, discover inspiring possibilities, and take action. In the face of high rates of young adult unemployment and underemployment (Certified General Accountants Association of Canada, 2012), post-secondary institutions are indeed looking for new approaches and tools to help students make a successful transition to the labor market. Starting as early as their first year of college or university, students can benefit from exploring the type of future impact they would like to have. The awareness, knowledge, skills, and motivation that can result from taking part in the Challenge mindset program may indeed help with career preparedness, planning their studies, and securing employment upon graduation.

The Challenge mindset is already being used at dozens of career services and co-op centers that cater to general or specific student populations (e.g., first-year students, first-generation students). The approach is versatile and can be used in a one-on-one setting, as part of a group workshop, or for events such as career fairs or major/minor expos. For example, the University of Florida's Major Expo leveraged the Challenge mindset to help undecided students at the high school and college levels declare a major (University of South Florida, 2019). Prior to the event, over 400 students identified their challenges of interest by undertaking the Challenge Cards sort. During the expo, students were then able to visit booths featuring different academic majors and ask tailored questions such as: *"How can this major help me contribute to the challenge I care about?"* This approach led to different and more meaningful conversations between students and faculty representatives. In a follow-up survey of 71 attendees, 92% of students indicated they enjoyed using the Challenge Cards, while 84% agreed or strongly agreed that the Challenge Cards "opened up [their] world to new possibilities." Finally, 82% of participants agreed or strongly agreed with the statement "I feel more inspired by what I can accomplish in my career," after participating in the event (Michel, 2021).

Another example of innovation in career development comes from the University of Western Ontario, which incorporated the Challenge mindset as part of an employer fair. Prior to the fair, students identified the challenges they would like to work on. Based on their choices, they were then given a list of companies they could engage with during the event. This preparatory exercise led to stronger and more effective connections between students and employers. More specifically, students were able to build on their preliminary understanding of challenges and connect that understanding with how different companies are having a real-world impact.

Though this text focuses on higher education, applying the Challenge mindset prior to students' undergraduate experience can help prepare them to maximize their post-secondary years. Studies have shown that introducing career education as early as middle school can be beneficial for students (Kerka, 2000; Martinez & Castellanos,

2017; Wigfield et al., 2018). Since this period is marked by important developments in the formation of self-identity and motivation (Wigfield et al., 2018), career education at this age should serve to present a broad range of career paths and options (Kerka, 2000). This is an ideal time to introduce the concept of challenges to work on, rather than job titles. Doing so may also help attenuate career-related stereotypes (e.g., based on sex, race, or other factors), which in turn can lead to improved outcomes as associated with student engagement and post-secondary participation rates (Kerka, 2000; Martinez & Castellanos, 2017).

Recommendations for Integrating the Challenge Mindset in Higher Education

The intersection of several social, economic, and technological factors has contributed to an accelerated pace of change in the world of work. This change has resulted in new obstacles in preparing students for meaningful careers. To overcome these obstacles, this chapter has proposed the need to look beyond job titles in the career exploration process. The following recommendations are offered for how higher education career professionals can incorporate the Challenge mindset in their work with undergraduate students.

- Help students focus the career exploration process on challenges, problems, and opportunities, instead of job titles.
- Facilitate exploration activities by providing lists of real-world challenges that students can engage with.
- Guide students in the discovery of interesting companies, people, and education paths related to the challenges they care about.
- Aim to broaden students' horizons before they commit to a specific path or job title.
- Increase awareness of exposure bias in career selection and career-related stereotypes (e.g., based on sex, race, or other factors), and use career exploration approaches that help counter these issues.
- Leverage the Challenge mindset throughout students' college journey to answer key questions at each stage.
  - For example, in the first year, reflecting on "Why am I here?" could yield the following response: "I am interested in the challenge of improving our gut microbiome to increase resistance to auto-immune diseases. To learn to contribute to this challenge, I am studying genetics and anatomy."
  - When looking for an internship, students can reflect on: "Which companies are working on the challenges I care about?"
  - To help build their network, students can explore: "Who should I connect with that is already working on the challenge I'm interested in?"
  - Finally, when applying to jobs, students can write a cover letter and resume that explain "Here is the challenge you are trying to solve, and here is how I can help."

- Be an advocate for purposeful career development on campus, driven by the notion that helping students identify meaningful career options can lead to greater academic engagement, performance, and satisfaction.
- Facilitate Challenge mindset activities with faculty, administration, and staff to help them embed this approach in their work.

Fundamentally, transitioning from the job title mindset to the Challenge mindset requires a paradigm shift in how we, as a society, think about and undertake career exploration and development. Educators and career services leaders are at the center of this shift and play a key role in bringing this message to students. Armed with accessible and impactful approaches, educators can leave a legacy by helping students find meaning and empowerment in their career preparation journey.

References

Arthur, M. B. (2021). Helping future workers be ready for the future of work. *Forbes*. www.forbes.com/sites/michaelbarthur/2021/02/07/helping-future-workers-be-ready-for-the-future-of-work/?sh=4f4afcc75014

Bandura, A. (1997). *Self-efficacy: The exercise of control*. W. H. Freeman/Times Books/Henry Holt & Co.

Bauer-Wolf, J. (2019, June 20). *Purpose as well as paycheck*. Inside Higher Ed. www.insidehighered.com/news/2019/04/11/gallup-bates-report-shows-graduates-want-sense-purpose-careers

Bersin, J. (2020). *The war of the skills clouds*. https://joshbersin.com/2020/01/the-war-of-the-skills-clouds-skillscloud/

Bonebright, C. A., Clay, D. L., & Ankenmann, R. D. (2000). The relationship of workaholism with work – life conflict, life satisfaction, and purpose in life. *Journal of Counseling Psychology, 47*(4), 469–477. https://doi.org/10.1037/0022-0167.47.4.469

Buford, M., & Nester, H. (2020). *A problem-solving approach to career exploration: Using the lens of challenge*. National Association of Colleges and Employers. www.naceweb.org/career-development/organizational-structure/a-problem-solving-approach-to-career-exploration-using-the-lens-of-challenge/

Carlana, M. (2019). Implicit stereotypes: Evidence from teachers' gender bias*. *The Quarterly Journal of Economics, 134*(3), 1163–1224. https://doi.org/10.1093/qje/qjz008

Cascio, W. F. (1995). Whither industrial and organizational psychology in a changing world of work? *American Psychologist, 50*(11), 928–939. https://doi.org/10.1037/0003-066x.50.11.928

Cascio, W. F. (2012). The changing world of work. In P. A. Linley, S. Harrington, & N. Page (Eds.), *Oxford handbook of positive psychology and work* (pp. 1–29). Oxford University Press. https://doi.org/10.1093/oxfordhb/9780195335446.013.0002

Certified General Accountants Association of Canada. (2012). *Youth unemployment in Canada: Challenging conventional thinking?* https://elcssstudentsservices.weebly.com/uploads/9/5/0/1/9501047/youthunemployment.pdf

Chamberlain, K., & Zika, S. (1988). Religiosity, life meaning and wellbeing: Some relationships in a sample of women. *Journal for the Scientific Study of Religion, 27*(3), 411. https://doi.org/10.2307/1387379

Chatzichristou, S., & Arulmani, G. (2014). Labor market and career development in the 21st century. In G. Arulmani, A. J. Bakshi, F. T. L. Leong, & A. G. Watts (Eds.), *Handbook of career development: International perspectives* (pp. 241–254). Springer. https://doi.org/10.1007/978-1-4614-9460-7_13

Clawson, R. A., & Trice, R. (2000). Poverty as we know it: Media portrayals of the poor. *The Public Opinion Quarterly, 64*(1), 53. https://doi.org/https://www.jstor.org/stable/3078840

Cross, J. C., Belich, T. J., & Rudelius, W. (2015). How marketing managers use market segmentation: An exploratory study. In B. J. Dunlap (Ed.), *Proceedings of the 1990 Academy of Marketing Science (AMS) Annual Conference* (pp. 531–536). Springer. https://doi.org/10.1007/978-3-319-13254-9_107

Damon, W. (2008). *The path to purpose: Helping our children find their calling in life.* Free Press.

Debats, D. L., van der Lubbe, P. M., & Wezeman, F. R. A. (1993). On the psychometric properties of the life regard index (LRI): A measure of meaningful life. *Personality and Individual Differences, 14*(2), 337–345. https://doi.org/10.1016/0191-8869(93)90132-m

Dey, F., & Cruzvergara, C. Y. (2014). Evolution of career services in higher education. *New Directions for Student Services, 2014*(148), 5–18. https://doi.org/10.1002/ss.20105

Dictionary.com. (2021). *Positionality.* Retrieved June 17, 2021, from www.dictionary.com/e/gender-sexuality/positionality/#:~:text=Positionality%20is%20the%20social%20and,and%20outlook%20on%20the%20world

Dik, B. J., Steger, M. F., & Austin, K. (2020). Calling, meaning, and volition: Emerging perspectives. In S. Brown & R. Lent (Eds.), *Career development and counseling: Putting theory and research to work* (3rd ed., pp. 237–270) Wiley.

Donald, G. (2017). *What students really want from their careers: Highlights from the 2017 brainstorm student career interests benchmark report.* https://semmforum.ca/wp-content/uploads/2017/12/graham.pdf

Duffy, R. D., Dik, B. J., & Steger, M. F. (2011). Calling and work-related outcomes: Career commitment as a mediator. *Journal of Vocational Behavior, 78*(2), 210–218. https://doi.org/10.1016/j.jvb.2010.09.013

Education and Employers. (2020, January 22). *Launch of dream jobs? Teenagers' career aspirations and the future of work.* www.educationandemployers.org/world-economic-forum-local-careers/

Engelman, S., McKlin, T., & Howell, C. (2016, July 24). *2016 YouScience pilot program, evaluation report.* https://gosa.georgia.gov/sites/gosa.georgia.gov/files/related_files/site_page/Summative%20Report_7.24.2016_Final.pdf

Feller, R. (2019, June 18). *Some industries are still lacking women, but female professionals can help.* YouScience. www.youscience.com/some-industries-are-still-lacking-women-but-female-professionals-can-help/

Gallup. (2019). *Forging pathways to purposeful work: The role of higher education.* www.gallup.com/education/248222/gallup-bates-purposeful-work-2019.aspx

Gottfredson, L. S. (2002). Gottfredson's theory of circumscription, compromise, and self cre-ation. In I. D. B. (Ed.), *Career choice and development* (4th ed., pp. 85–148). Jossey-Bass.

Gratton, L., & Scott, A. (2016). *The 100-year life: Living and working in an age of longevity.* Bloomsbury Information.

Harari, N. Y. (2018, June 21). Yuval Noah Harari on what the year 2050 has in store for humankind. *Wired.* www.wired.co.uk/article/yuval-noah-harari-extract-21-lessons-for-the-21st-century

Harris Cornileus, T. (2010). *A critical examination of the impact of racism on the career develop-ment of African-American professional men in corporate America.* The University of Georgia. https://getd.libs.uga.edu/pdfs/cornileus_tonya_h_201008_phd.pdf

Hartung, P. J., & Blustein, D. L. (2002). Reason, intuition, and social justice: Elaborating on Parsons's career decision-making model. *Journal of Counseling & Development, 80*(1), 41–47. https://doi.org/10.1002/j.1556-6678.2002.tb00164.x

Hartung, P. J., Porfeli, E. J., & Vondracek, F. W. (2005). Child vocational development: A review and reconsideration. *Journal of Vocational Behavior, 66*(3), 385–419. https://doi.org/10.1016/j.jvb.2004.05.006

Herr, E. L., & Cramer, S. H. (1996). *Career guidance and counseling through the lifespan: Systemic approaches* (5th ed.). Harper Collins.

Hill, P. L., Burrow, A. L., Brandenberger, J. W., Lapsley, D. K., & Quaranto, J. C. (2010). Collegiate purpose orientations and well-being in early and middle adulthood. *Journal of Applied Developmental Psychology, 31*(2), 173–179. https://doi.org/10.1016/j.appdev.2009.12.001

Ibarra, H., & Barbulescu, R. (2010). Identity as narrative: Prevalence, effectiveness, and consequences of narrative identity work in macro work role transitions. *Academy of Management Review, 35*(1), 135–154. https://doi.org/10.5465/amr.35.1.zok135

Kazuyuki, M., & Kuo-lin, W. (2006). Illusion of career development theories ~ for the departure of developing a demonstrative career development theory ~. *The Economic Journal of Takasaki City University of Economics, 49*(2), 17–30. www1.tcue.ac.jp/home1/k-gakkai/ronsyuu/ronsyuukeisai/49_2/mogioh.pdf

Kelly, J. (2019). Predictions for the uncharted job market of the future. *Forbes.* www.forbes.com/sites/jackkelly/2019/02/27/predictions-for-the-dystopian-job-market-of-the-future/?sh=3f4fbf660574

Kerka, S. (2000). *Middle school career education and development. Practice application brief no. 9.* C. o. E. a. T. f. Employment. https://files.eric.ed.gov/fulltext/ED442992.pdf

Krumboltz, J. D. (2008). The happenstance learning theory. *Journal of Career Assessment, 17*(2), 135–154. https://doi.org/10.1177/1069072708328861

Leong, F. T. L., & Hartung, P. J. (2000). Adapting to the changing multicultural context of career. In A. Collin & R. Young (Eds.), *The future of career* (pp. 212–227). Cambridge University Press. https://doi.org/10.1017/cbo9780511520853.014

Martinez, E., & Castellanos, M. (2017). Catching them early: An examination of Chicano/Latino middle school boys' early career aspirations. *The Urban Review, 50*(3), 378–401. https://doi.org/10.1007/s11256-017-0438-5

McGowan, H. E., & Shipley, C. (2020). *The adaptation advantage: Let go, learn fast, and thrive in the future of work*. Wiley.

McIlveen, P., & Patton, W. (2007). Narrative career counselling: Theory and exemplars of practice. *Australian Psychologist*, *42*(3), 226–235. https://doi.org/10.1080/00050060701405592

McKinsey Global Institute. (2018). *AI, automation, and the future of work: Ten things to solve for*. www.mckinsey.com/~/media/mckinsey/featured%20insights/future%20of%20organizations/ai%20automation%20and%20the%20future%20of%20work%20ten%20things%20to%20solve%20for/mgi-briefing-note-ai-automation-and-the-future-of-work_june2018.pdf

McKnight, P. E., & Kashdan, T. B. (2009). Purpose in life as a system that creates and sustains health and well-being: An integrative, testable theory. *Review of General Psychology*, *13*(3), 242–251. https://doi.org/10.1037/a0017152

McMahon, M., & Patton, W. (1997). Gender differences in children and adolescents' perceptions of influences on their career development. *School Counselor*, *44*(5), 368.

Michel, J. P. (2017, June 28–30). *What problems do you want to solve? – how to prepare for jobs that don't exist yet* [Conference session]. National Career Development Association 2017 Global Conference, Orlando, Florida, United States.

Michel, J. P. (2021, October 1). *Measuring impact: Students feel inspired, less anxious*. SparkPath. https://mysparkpath.com/blogs/news/measuring-impact-students-feel-inspired-less-anxious

Mincer, J. (2003). Technology and the labor market. *Review of Economics of the Household*, *1*(4), 249–272. https://doi.org/10.1023/B:REHO.0000004789.76199.f6

Niles, S. G., Amundson, N. E., & Neault, R. A. (2011). *Career flow: A hope-centered approach to career development*. Pearson.

Organisation for Economic Co-operation and Development. (2020). *Dream jobs? Teenagers' career aspirations and the future of work*. www.oecd.org/education/dream-jobs-teenagers-career-aspirations-and-the-future-of-work.htm

Parro, F. (2015). Private incentives for specialization in a changing and unpredictable labor market. *Theoretical Economics Letters*, *5*(2), 163–168. https://doi.org/10.4236/tel.2015.52020

Pisarik, C. T., Rowell, P. C., & Thompson, L. K. (2017). A phenomenological study of career anxiety among college students. *The Career Development Quarterly*, *65*(4), 339–352. https://doi.org/10.1002/cdq.12112

Polvere, R.-A., & Lim, P. (2015). *Career development supporting young Australians*. https://cica.org.au/wp-content/uploads/Career-Development-supporting-young-Australians-2015.pdf

Pryor, R. G. L., & Bright, J. E. H. (2014). The chaos theory of careers (CTC): Ten years on and only just begun. *Australian Journal of Career Development*, *23*(1), 4–12. https://doi.org/10.1177/1038416213518506

PwC. (2018). *Workforce of the future: The competing forces shaping 2030*. www.pwc.com/gx/en/services/people-organisation/workforce-of-the-future/workforce-of-the-future-the-competing-forces-shaping-2030-pwc.pdf

Ryan, R. M., & Deci, E. L. (2000). Self-determination theory and the facilitation of intrinsic motivation, social development, and well-being. *American Psychologist, 55*(1), 68–78. https://doi.org/10.1037/0003-066x.55.1.68

Savickas, M. L. (1997). Career adaptability: An integrative construct for life-span, life-space theory. *The Career Development Quarterly, 45*(3), 247–259. https://doi.org/10.1002/j.2161-0045.1997.tb00469.x

Savickas, M. L. (2005). The theory and practice of career construction. In I. S. D. Brown & R. W. Lent (Eds.). *Career development and counseling: Putting theory and research to work* (pp. 42–70). John Wiley & Sons.

Schaller, R. R. (1997). Moore's law: Past, present and future. *IEEE Spectrum, 34*(6), 52–59. https://doi.org/10.1109/6.591665

Stebleton, M. J., & Eggerth, D. E. (2012). Returning to our roots. *Journal of Career Development, 39*(1), 3–12. https://doi.org/10.1177/0894845311417131

Steger, M. F. (2016). Creating meaning and purpose at work. In L. G. Oades, M. F. Steger, A. D. Fave, & J. Passmore (Eds), *The Wiley Blackwell handbook of the psychology of positivity and strengths-based approaches at work* (pp. 60–81). Wiley-Blackwell. https://doi.org/https://doi.org/10.1002/9781118977620.ch5

The Foundation for Young Australians. (2016). *The new work mindset.* https://cica.org.au/wp-content/uploads/The-New-Work-Mindset-FYA-November-2016.pdf

Toronto District School Board. (2018). *Student census 2016-17: Grades 9-12.* www.tdsb.on.ca/portals/0/research/docs/Student_Census_-_Grades_9-12_-_System_Report.pdf

U.S. Bureau of Labor Statistics. (2021). *Employment by detailed occupation.* www.bls.gov/emp/tables/emp-by-detailed-occupation.htm

University of South Florida. (2019, October 24). *Majors expo at the University of South Florida – challenge cards* [Video]. www.youtube.com/watch?v=Ffjr-_BbPa4

Wigfield, A., Lutz, S. L., & Wagner, A. L. (2018). Early adolescents' development across the middle school years: Implications for school counselors. *Professional School Counseling, 9*(2), 2156759X0500900. https://doi.org/10.1177/2156759x0500900206

Zukin, C., & Szeltner, M. (2012). *Talent report: What workers want in 2012.* Net Impact. https://netimpact.org/sites/default/files/documents/what-workers-want-2012.pdf

12

Applying Narrative Approaches to Support Undergraduate Career Decision-Making

Michael J. Stebleton and Mark Franklin

Psychologist Miller Mair (1988) eloquently wrote: "Stories are habitations. We live in and through stories. They conjure worlds. We do not know the world other than as story world. Stories inform life. They hold us together and keep us apart" (p. 127). Like Mair, Alexander Payne (2004), film director, believed that the telling and re-telling of stories led to a greater understanding of the human experience, which is inevitably complex and uncertain in most cases. Storied or narrative approaches continue to hold prominence as a tool of understanding across a wide variety of disciplines, including medicine, psychology, higher education, student affairs, cultural studies, and antiracist education (Brookfield & Hess, 2021; Charon, 2004; Stebleton, 2021). Although there has been an emergence of story in academic disciplines, the concept or application of story is not novel. For generations, many cultures – primarily non-Western, non-White – use oral narratives and histories as ways to collectively share and document lived experiences, often marked by resilience (Merriam & Kim, 2008). We acknowledge the value of non-Western approaches to teaching and learning contexts focused on career education.

In this chapter, we aim to honor the role of narratives in diverse contexts and explore how narrative approaches can be applied to supporting undergraduate students and their career decision-making. Moreover, we will provide some practical models for application, and provide some recommendations for higher education and student affairs professionals. Finally, we will situate these strategies within the context of recent events, notably the global pandemic of 2020–2022 and the ongoing reckoning with racial injustice both nationally and globally. It is important to explore the trajectory of narrative approaches as applied specifically to career development contexts.

DOI: 10.4324/9781003213000-16

What Is a Narrative Approach? Providing Definitions

A working definition of "narrative" serves as a useful guide for this article. Narrative approaches view the episodes or phases of one's life as chapters to be examined and re-examined. Using this approach, the counselor or career educator works in collaboration with the client/student to gain a better understanding of those experiences. Young (1984) contended that vocational stories help address "how one engages oneself over time in a given context. These stories help individuals situate themselves in relationship to a given context" (p. 173). From this perspective, the emphasis focuses on finding and assigning *meaning* to experiences and/or changes relevant to career (Cardoso et al., 2021). Another assumption of narrative approaches is that the client/student assumes some autonomy and volition to change the outcomes or endings of chapters with the support of the career practitioner.

Narrative Approaches: A Historical Context and Commitment to Social Justice

Narrative and storied approaches continue to gain popularity in both career development theory and practice. The founding of the career development profession, started by Frank Parsons and the progressive reformers of the early 1900s, began with a rich history and commitment to reason and enlightenment (Hartung & Blustein, 2002; Parsons, 1909). Perhaps more importantly, Parsons and his colleagues committed early to supporting the arriving immigrants and other marginalized groups to the United States (Spokane & Glickman, 1994), identifying a clear direction toward fighting for social justice causes (Stebleton & Jehangir, 2020). Fast forward approximately 100 years, and the commitment to these justice principles persists in the practices of career educators of the 2000s (Hooley et al., 2019). Career development educators advocate for social change and policy change, encouraging counselors and practitioners to move toward "good trouble" in the spirit of late Congressman John Lewis from the state of Georgia (Higashi & Stebleton, 2020).

The use of story and related concepts (e.g., life roles, theaters, etc.) appears early in the work of Super (1953), Tiedeman and O'Hara (1963), and others. Applying some of these contributions from prior scholars, Savickas (1993) discussed how the field moved from *scores* to *stories*, shifting from objectivity to subjectivity. He stressed, "Using the 'career as story' analogy, career counseling may be conceptualized as a process of storying and restorying a client's vocational experience. Counselors can help clients to interpret life and career by viewing the person as a text" (p. 213). This paradigmatic shift took on different titles such as postmodernism, contextualism, and career construction theory (Busacca & Rehfuss, 2016; Savickas, 2020). According to Savickas (2020), "viewing careers from a constructionist perspective focuses attention on self-making" (p. 166). Career construction theory utilizes narrative elements to construct the story of a client's life including three phases:

constructing the story with micro narratives, reconstructing the story with a macro narrative, and consolidating change.

Given that most young people (i.e., traditional college students) will live and work longer in the future compared to previous generations, it will be important for employees to be able to navigate the many shifts in employment – and to understand the meaning of these individual and collective experiences. There will continue to be a call for new and innovative approaches to career development beyond the positivistic, objective approaches – and narrative approaches will likely gain more momentum, moving forward toward more qualitative and subjective perspectives. Trait and factor approaches will always occupy prominent roles in career development history (Holland, 1973). However, future paradigms will favor models that lean toward postmodernism, interpretivism, and critical approaches, especially as employees continue to prepare for uncertainty and perpetual change in the new world of work (Lent & Brown, 2020; Stebleton & Kaler, 2020).

Advantages and Disadvantages of Narrative Approaches

Numerous scholars have written about the merits of applying narrative approaches to career education and development (Franklin & Feller, 2017; Stebleton, 2010). Stebleton (2010) outlined several advantages and disadvantages of narrative approaches in a piece that appeared in the *Journal of Employment Counseling*. Acknowledging the work of foundational work in career development (see Super (1953) and others), a key benefit is that narrative approaches tend to be more holistic and inclusive in nature, taking into consideration roles beyond paid work only. Richardson (1993) argued that career development professionals often exhaust too much time fitting people into the "right" job or careers. Instead, Richardson suggested that career educators focus on how work (paid and unpaid) fit into people's lives "in which work is considered to be a central human activity that is not tied to or solely located in the occupational structure" (p. 427).

More recently, Blustein et al. (2019) extended this discussion by advocating for humane practices that promote *decent work*; this includes supporting individuals from marginalized identities. As traditionally studied, *career* is a Western (often privileged White) construct that has limited value in many cultures (Blustein, 2019; Stebleton, 2019). Narrative approaches take into consideration the examination of multiple life roles, intersections of identities, and circumstances, including the various types of work activities in one's portfolio which can be applied across cultures (Santilli et al., 2021).

A second related advantage is that narrative approaches can be especially relevant for clients/students who come from non-White and/or marginalized contexts (Maree, 2016). Given the emphasis on the role of oral narratives and storytelling in many of these cultures (e.g., many Indigenous communities), the narrative elements included and the re-telling of stories aligns well with some clients who hold these identities and lived experiences (Maree & Molepo, 2006). For example, recently a colleague shared a story from an Indigenous student in British Columbia, north of Vancouver. This student was attempting to pass a competency-based assessment to earn prior learning credit for a degree program. Rather than require a traditional written assessment, the student and instructor worked together to determine the best way to share the student's story, resulting in this student telling their story and sharing their knowledge during a sacred fire ritual in their home community (S. Forseille, personal communication, June 8, 2021). The student successfully passed the assessment and earned the credit toward the completion of their degree. This is just one such example of how narrative approaches can be more inclusive and holistic.

A third advantage is that this approach reinforces to clients that life-career planning is iterative as opposed to a one-time, winner-take-all decision. As Stebleton (2010) noted, "the narrative perspective helps to educate clients regarding the reality that life-career planning is an ongoing, cyclical process rather than a single-time event that is only engaged in during times of crisis" (p. 68). Moreover, narrative approaches focus on the role of contextual factors rather than placing emphasis on the individual; this has long been a critique of traditional career development theory (Collin & Young, 1986). Finally, narrative approaches embrace strength-based, positive approaches to career development that can be utilized in numerous applications such as employment counseling (Toporek & Cohen, 2017).

Several disadvantages of this narrative approach exist. For example, narrative approaches can be time intensive and involve a great deal of trust and rapport between educator and student. A potential second disadvantage is that the client typically needs to exert more effort and commitment in the counseling process. Often, students naively visit a career educator's office asking for a test that will tell them what to do with the rest of their lives (which, ironically, is a misperception based on the limitations of trait and factor, test-and-tell assumptions). A student wanting a quick fix in the form of an assessment or career inventory may not prove to be an ideal fit for narrative approaches. Finally, narrative approaches do involve training and expertise on behalf of the career educator. Practitioners who wish to use narrative approaches should possess a working knowledge of both narrative theory and practice. Since narrative approaches assume a collaboration between client/student and counselor, the practitioner will want to be fully committed to the process and the training involved in providing narrative-based interventions and resources. In sum, the authors of this chapter contend that when it comes to adopting narrative stances, the advantages usually outweigh the disadvantages.

Relevancy and the Future of Work

Evidence suggests that the average university student graduating today will have over 17 careers across five or six different industries (McGowan & Shipley, 2020).

This report was conducted on the futures of Australian youth, yet the findings can likely be applied to young people across countries. McGowan and Shipley (2020) contended that technology will continue to impact employees – but especially Gen Z and Millennials – in that skilling and re-skilling will be a continuous process. Whereas the old work paradigm rewarded mastery and maintaining the status quo, the new work model in the Fourth revolution will leverage life-long learning and adaptability (Hirschi, 2018; Lent, 2018). Retirement as a construct and idealized goal will be significantly altered and longevity will take its place as an important objective for aging workers. Engagement and ongoing learning will punctuate evolving career progress and development; the process will not be linear but rather cyclical in nature. This dramatic shift may come as a major surprise for educators and students. Work of the future will inevitably be marked by ongoing change and unpredictability.

Similarly, Weise (2020) argued that the 100-year life will soon be upon us, and work lives will comprise many of those adult years. Certainly, learning and "learning how to learn" will become the new commodity as workers move in and out of different contexts, perhaps even engaging in gig-like activity at some point in their lives. Reid Hoffman, CEO of LinkedIn, and his colleagues referred to this episodic employment landscape as "tours of duty," with the understanding that these will be short-term possibilities where significant contributions can be made before moving on to the next work environment (Hoffman et al., 2014). Other writers are predicting changes that are more draconian.

For example, in a *Mother Jones* article, journalist Kevin Drum (2017) proclaimed that the end of work is upon us and that by the year 2040 a robot will take your job. Although Drum's predictions were arguably hyperbolic, the spirit of the article was prescient and instructive: the way work will be done in the future will be dramatically different from one's parents (or grandparents), and preparing for these changes remains critical to one's success in the marketplace. The focus of this chapter emphasizes how career educators can prepare undergraduates for changes in the work and learning dimension.

Moving from Challenge to Opportunity: Developing Skills

A challenge for many undergraduate students exists. Students are frequently unable to articulate succinctly what they gained from their campus experience (DuRose & Stebleton, 2016). Often, students can describe their experiences (e.g., "I studied in Italy for a semester and had a great time meeting new friends"). Yet they are unable to translate the skills and transferable competencies that they gained from those valuable experiences (e.g., "As a result of my study abroad experience, I now possess the abilities to work with others from diverse cultures in a team setting"). By articulating these skills through mock interviews or simulated discussions, students can get comfort and confidence developing their narrative storytelling.

Similarly, educators can gain confidence by learning to hear and understand these student narratives. The process involves ongoing practice. Savickas (2020) shared the work of novelist Eudora Welty. Welty (1983) encouraged individuals to listen *for* a story rather than listen *to* a story. Charon (2004) and other scholars from the medicine fields also advocated for professionals to develop narrative competence, which is described as a set of skills that educators need to recognize, absorb, and be moved by the stories one hears, reads, and interprets. Furthermore, Charon outlined a set of skills that medical professionals (her focus is on new physicians) need to develop: textual skills, creative skills, and affective skills. The authors of this chapter contend that career educators, faculty, and others in higher education can learn more from our colleagues in the medical professions (Stebleton, 2021). The year 2020 offered numerous trials and tribulations, many that persist into the future and shape work-related contexts. These life-altering events, including Covid-19 inequities; White supremacy; systemic oppression and discrimination; police brutality, racism, the murders of George Floyd, Ahmaud Arbery, and Breonna Taylor; and US election strife and deception, have negatively affected certain marginalized individuals and communities more directly than others. Career educators can support students around managing the ramifications of these experiences, acknowledging that there are no easy answers to ongoing issues of social injustice. The challenge becomes putting these ideas into practice, the focus of this next section.

Transitioning to Narrative Practice: Models of Application

While career professionals need to engage with clients and their stories with empathy, genuineness, and unconditional positive regard (Rogers, 1951), higher education educators and career development practitioners can adopt new "story listening" skills. This involves supporting clients by in-the-moment gathering and organizing of insights from the narratives, and making these aggregate insights visible in a single, powerful, and holistic sketch. Working as a science-practitioner in a busy university career center with diverse undergraduates from over 80 countries, one co-author (Franklin), noticed that students' stories and narratives displayed patterns of elements that could be made visible to clients on a counseling room flipchart page, in-the-moment, as stories were being narrated. The resulting "Clarification Sketch" displayed these elements: strengths, desires, personal qualities, other people, assets, natural interests, and possibilities. As clients observed multiple stories transformed into their personalized, aggregating Clarification Sketch, they could see emerging patterns, and thus client and counselor collaboratively could generate more meaningful and context-sensitive possibilities aligned with the pattern of elements that emerged from the narratives.

In contemporary terms, the *wicked problem* of career development is how to take the highly variable input of human stories and narratives, and create an output of well-informed and inspiring career and life choices (Burnett & Evans, 2016). An evidence-based solution to that wicked problem is a narrative assessment framework that first appeared in the literature over a decade ago (Zikic & Franklin, 2010), and has subsequently been implemented to serve undergraduates in dozens of institutions and subject to two quantitative outcome studies (Franklin & Stebleton, 2020; Franklin et al., 2015) and a qualitative outcome study (Stebleton et al., 2019).

HEROIC Narrative Assessment System

Aligning with the contemporary need for undergrads to be resilient, and to navigate a lifetime of transitions, the HEROIC Narrative Assessment System delivers the benefits and mitigates the limitations of narrative approaches described earlier in this chapter (Feller & Franklin, 2020). The model is holistic, inclusive, supportive of students from marginalized contexts, and iterative – and with the structure of the Clarification Sketch, overcomes the time and trust limitations. HEROIC describes both the narrative assessment process, and a desired student mindset, enlivening the acronym of Hope, self-Efficacy, Resilience, Optimism, Intentional exploration, Curiosity and Clarity. Within the HEROIC constellation, the HERO asterism collectively forms the measure, psychological capital, a set of resources a person can use to help improve their success (Luthans et al., 2007), and the narrative processes described below have been shown to increase HERO (Franklin et al., 2015).

Further, the HEROIC Narrative Assessment System supports the development of the undergraduate into a "T-professional" (Gardner & Estry, 2017) illustrated as a large T, integrating both depth (stem of T) and breadth (cross-bar of T). According to Gardner and Maietta (2020):

> Depth is defined in terms of disciplinary knowledge. Breadth, on the other hand, is defined as possessing the professional abilities that allow someone with profound disciplinary knowledge to interact meaningfully with others with different disciplinary knowledge in order to affect an outcome that might not otherwise be possible.
>
> (2020, p. xviii)

To make sense of how students blend learning and experience, shape goals, and convey stories through reflective integration, the HEROIC Narrative Assessment System can be a cornerstone of T-model infused undergraduate career education (Feller & Franklin, 2020).

Reflective Practice Empowers Authenticity

Brown (2010) defined *authenticity* as the daily practice of letting go of who we think we are supposed to be and embracing who we are. For the undergraduate commonly influenced by parents, peers, and others, Brown's definition is poignantly relevant.

Her phrase, *embracing who we are*, resonates with Franklin's definition of career as "the full expression of who you are and how you want to be in the world. And, it keeps on expanding as it naturally goes through cycles of stability and change" (Franklin, 2015, p. 451). In this definition, "who you are" is operationalized into the six elements mentioned earlier, holistically arrayed in a single structure of the Clarification Statement. Now implemented in technology in the form of a web application called Online Storyteller, practitioners can engage clients in moment-by-moment storytelling and storylistening, capturing the content of client narratives in real time through a reflective practice that mirrors their growing self-awareness and authenticity. Reflective practice makes meaning from experience and transforms insights into practical strategies for personal growth and organizational impact. The HEROIC Narrative Assessment framework represents one such approach to evidence-based, reflective practice. Next, we provide an overview of the framework, an example, and finally we provide implications for practitioners and sample applications.

The Narrative Assessment Framework as Roadmap

Figure 12.1 represents a simplified version of the full HEROIC Narrative Assessment model that appears in earlier publications (Franklin et al., 2015). Both the full model and this simplified version can be used as a roadmap that practitioners can share with clients to support their buy-in to the process, and revisit in order to locate themselves as the process unfolds over time.

Here is how a practitioner can verbally describe the model to undergraduate clients in session either in-person or virtually via screen share:

Point to the title. Using this roadmap, the educator helps the student/client become empowered and proactive in their career and life choices. The "becoming empowered" part implies that clients typically come to us because they want to feel like they are in control of things, of their career and life choices. "Proactive" suggests doing things in the real world that go beyond the "reactive" way many people manage their careers by passively viewing postings and submitting resumes. "Career and life choices" means that we look at these questions in a holistic way. It is not just about a job, it is about the full expression of who you are and how you want to be in the world. In fact, that is our definition of the word "career."

Point to "Client Questions." Clients start with a question such as "What should I do when I graduate?" It can either be a "what" question, "what now," or it can be a "how" question, like "how can I be more effective in finding the career I want?" It can be both questions. On the other side, questions address choices you feel confident and excited about. How do you get from your questions to your choices?

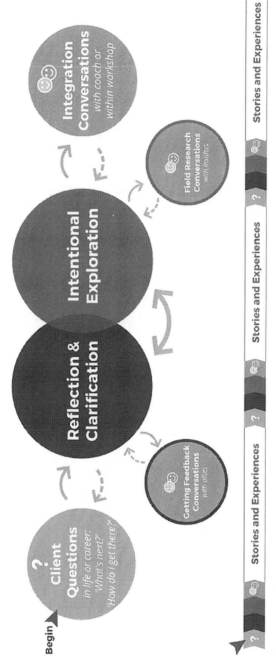

Figure 12.1 HEROIC Narrative Assessment Framework © 2021 OneLifeTools

Point to "Reflection and Clarification." The first step here is called Reflection and Clarification. The educator states: "This process looks at you, your desires, strengths, personal qualities, and assets. In addition, it includes other people, and possibilities. The way we do this is by walking through your stories and experiences, what you liked and learned in each chapter of your story." Clients seem to prefer this storytelling approach rather than a battery of assessments that they may have experienced elsewhere or even expected coming here today. Next, the educator states, "we use a one-page Clarification Sketch. It helps us gather and organize all the relevant information about your situation. While we are walking through your stories, we will also generate possibilities and curiosities. These possibilities will be linked to your stories and what we are learning about you from them."

Point to "Getting Feedback Conversations." Getting feedback from three or more allies supports clarification. Allies can pinpoint strengths and help you generate possibilities. The career educator states, "Once we have gathered all the information in Reflection and Clarification, we will distill it into a brief and empowering Clarification Statement that then guides your Intentional Exploration. Your Statement is present and future-oriented, which opens you to change, unlike a resume or LinkedIn profile, which emphasizes the past and therefore limits change."

Point to "Intentional Exploration." Most clients come to career educators already engaged in some form of exploration. How intentional has their process been? Sometimes clients say they feel "all over the map" or "lost" or "confused." With the Clarification Statement, clients find the Intentional Exploration to be fun and exciting. In this process, one watches for clues, takes inspired action, and welcomes opportunities.

Point to "Field Research Conversations." One helpful inspired action is to talk to insiders, people who have made the choice you are considering. These Field Research conversations help you decide what possibilities fit you, and align with your Clarification Statement. Out of this Intentional Exploration process come your choices.

Point to "Integration Conversations." The educator encourages, "I will be your guide through these two processes, supporting your clarification and exploration in this meeting and future meetings we may schedule."

Point to the Timeline. The career professional may say, "This is us here at the left end of the Timeline, entering this process together, resulting in your choices leading to new stories and experiences. You can re-enter this process at any time; as you can see, the Timeline shows the future characterized by life and career cycles of stability and change. Maybe your next story will be six months or six years, or 16 years. And you can learn this process to guide a lifetime of transitions." After clients receive an introduction to the roadmap, the practitioner then elicits a client story or experience and begins the guided reflection process using the Clarification Sketch (Stebleton & Franklin, 2020).

Who You Are Matters

Gamification offers a way to engage groups in narrative assessment, to scale interventions, and to offer highly engaging and interactive experience into the (often perceived as) tired career development toolkit of traditional test-and-tell assessments. Using game design innovations such as "intermixing" – combining on-topic and off-topic game content to make the focal message or theme less obvious and more accessible, and "obfuscating" – using game genres or framing devices that direct players' attention or expectations away from the game's true aims (Kaufman & Flanagan, 2015), the *Who You Are Matters!* game operationalizes the HEROIC Narrative Assessment System for groups from three to 300, and both in-person and virtually. Disguised as a fun and social game, *Who You Are Matters!* offers groups a structure to have clarification conversations that matter, linking meaningful work, personal lifestyle, and gaining a self-advocating voice. This psychologically embedded approach to game design for prosocial causes also uses the same Clarification Sketch shown above, making the group experience dovetail with one-on-one coaching or counseling, which may occur before or after the game (Kaufman & Flanagan, 2015).

Experiential Learning, Reflective Practice, and Career Development

With the growing importance of experiential learning in undergraduate programs, it is imperative that quality reflection support students to transform experience into learning, as integrated in the PEAR (Pedagogy, Experience, Assessment, Reflection) framework for experiential learning (McRae & Johnston, 2016). To enact quality reflection, the DEAL model (Describe, Examine, Articulate Learning) has emerged to support student critical reflection (Ash & Clayton, 2004). While many prompts and questions exist to support reflective practice, and operationalize DEAL, few approaches comply with theory while also exhibiting ease of use for students and offer aggregation across experiences. The HEROIC Narrative Assessment Framework offers practitioners ease of use, away from long-form reports and essays, and instead uses prompt questions that can be answered with clickable popular answers, or user-generated brief responses.

Operationalizing Framework for Educators

Practitioners may consider adding to their assessment and practice toolkit, or replacing elements from it, by embedding the HEROIC Narrative Assessment System into undergraduate curriculum, group programs, and individual service. Doing so has shown to result in increased resilience and confidence, clarity, and occupational engagement even from a first session of career counseling (Franklin & Stebleton, 2020). While institutions cannot promise undergraduates jobs upon graduation, they can increase intermediate variables such as psychological capital, favored by employers, and which correlate with employment status, career satisfaction, and person–job fit (Franklin et al., 2015).

For educators working with individual undergraduates, eliciting at least one client story or experience in the first session gets the student/client talking, and the educator can listen for skills and desires – or values – and reflect these back to the client either verbally or, better, in an organized sketch document. At Saint Mary's University, lead career counselor, Karen, opted to use the HEROIC Narrative Assessment System to gather and organize insights from client stories moving toward the resulting Clarification Statement. Karen and her team found that students appreciated the tangible takeaways and the clarification-then-exploration roadmap. Her team found it easier to get students talking, generating future possibilities, and validating their progress within the Online Storyteller platform, which situates all components of the tool.

For faculty, staff, and career practitioners leading or supporting credit-bearing courses, the HEROIC Narrative Assessment System can be embedded into curriculum in a modular format, in order to realize a learning objective such as building skills in career management related to discipline-specific knowledge. Success stories exist. At the University of Toronto, students who take a credit-bearing career management course are at first engaged in a session using the narrative tool *Who You Are Matters!* in-person game, or virtually. Students enter the Online Storyteller platform to do the systematic self-directed narrative assessment, and then use the platform to get feedback from allies, guiding field research conversations with insiders. Students read a specified career development article each week, submit a reflection, and engage in a small group "conversations café" discussion in-class – a recommended approach for career programs or curriculum. Informal pre- and post-course measures over seven offerings of the course have resulted in increases in psychological capital (+17%), clarity (+61%), organized thoughts (+61%), and occupational engagement (+19%). At Conestoga College, curriculum designer, Lisa, embedded the HEROIC Narrative Assessment System into four distinct credit-bearing career development courses, allowing over 5,000 students to identify their strengths, assets, interests, and values from stories.

While embedding career development into curriculum is ideal, staff and practitioners may find it easier to integrate narrative tools into non-credit programming. The HEROIC Narrative Assessment System has been embedded into programs targeted to experiential learning, alumni, students on probation, and research-oriented students considering non-academic careers.

Recommendations for Practice in a Post-Covid-19 World

We argue that it is the role of career educators and other student affairs professionals to challenge undergraduate students to be reflecting on their skills, values, and experiences – and how these characteristics can be channeled into narratives of growth and opportunity moving forward. Autin et al. (2020) recommended that career educators utilize the challenges presented by Covid-19 "as an opportunity for a renewed commitment to supporting worker well being" (p. 487), including less privileged workers who might not have access to decent work options. We concur with Autin et al., and this recommendation for practice and policy aligns perfectly with the social justice mission of the early roots of the career development profession. Other practical implications include the following:

- Encourage career educators and staff to become more familiar with narrative career theories and practice, using some of the newer perspectives and frameworks outlined in this chapter.
- Apply narrative approaches to one's own life. Engage in regular reflection on the chapters in one's life and use narrative tools such as journaling and writing to foster personal growth.
- Embed narrative tools and games into career workshops and career planning classes at the university and college levels, such as *Who You Are Matters!* and other qualitative assessment instruments.
- Consider the role of systems and a more holistic approach to life-career. Expand one's philosophy of helping beyond the traditional "test-and-tell" vocational theories.
- Intentionally integrate and discuss issues of DEI (diversity, equity, and inclusion) into career education. So often diversity components are integrated as special topics or add-on components; this ultimately does a disservice to students and further marginalizes BIPOC and other marginalized students.
- Encourage all students to get actively involved in creating their own stories by participating in experiential activities during their college years, and design alternative programs for non-traditional students.
- Get students out of the classroom whenever possible and challenge them to engage in new learning. Invite students to learn about others' stories through different pedagogies. These learning opportunities could include field trips, informational interviews, shadowing, and engaging in service work.
- Keep learning. Friedman (2016) encouraged students and educators to always remain in "beta" mode. In other words, individuals should individuals should consistently strive to be receptive to news ideas and be willing to change existing positions or philosophies. Similarly, Grant (2021) advised individuals to "think again" and be open to new perspectives, to think consistently like a scientist as new data becomes available.

Story as Connection and Service

Narrative approaches to career development will continue to gain attention in various disciplines, including higher education and student affairs contexts. Story and relationship serve as vital points of connection between educator and student (Felten & Lambert, 2020). Moreover, higher education and career professionals play critical roles in supporting students to better understand and assign meaning to their lived experiences and narratives. As educators, we occupy important roles in narrative approaches to career education. Mair (1988) noted, "We serve the story in many different ways. Some do so by reproducing their kind, the implicit carriers of the common themes. Some service the story by their passionate struggles to attack and change aspects of its structure" (p. 128). Moving forward, our ongoing challenge and opportunity is to serve and service the narratives of our students. The narrative frameworks provided here apply to diverse students and populations across the different contexts of higher education. Often, students will aim to shift the narrative, or re-tell their personal and collective narratives. Our task is to facilitate students in this process as they progress toward their own definitions of personal and professional success.

References

Ash, S. L., & Clayton, P. H. (2004). The articulated learning: An approach to guided reflection and assessment. *Innovative Higher Education, 29*(2), 137–154. https://doi.org/ 10.1023/ B:IHIE.0000048795.84634.4a

Autin, K. L., Blustein, D. L., Ali, S. R., & Garriott, P. O. (2020). Career development impacts of COVID-19: Practice and policy recommendations. *Journal of Career Development, 47*(5), 487–494. https://doi.org/10.1177/0894845320944486

Blustein, D. L. (2019). *The importance of work in an age of uncertainty: The eroding work experience in America.* Oxford University Press.

Blustein, D. L., Kenny, M. E., Autin, K., & Duffy, R. (2019). The psychology of working in practice: A theory of change for a new era. *The Career Development Quarterly, 67*(3), 236–254. https://doi.org/10.1002/cdq.12193

Brookfield, S. D., & Hess, M. E. (2021). *Becoming a white antiracist: A practical guide for educators, leaders, and activists.* Stylus.

Brown, B. (2010). *The gifts of imperfection: Let go of who you think you're supposed to be and embrace who you are.* Hazelden Publishing.

Burnett, W., & Evans, D. J. (2016). *Designing your life: How to build a well-lived, joyful life.* Knopf.

Busacca, L. A., & Rehfuss, M. C. (Eds.). (2016). *Postmodern career counseling: A handbook of culture, content, and cases.* John Wiley & Sons.

Cardoso, P. M., Savickas, M. L., & Gonçalves, M. M. (2021). Facilitating narrative change in career construction counseling. *Journal of Career Development, 48*(6), 863–876. https:// doi.org/10.1177/0894845319898872

Charon, R. (2004). Narrative and medicine. *New England Journal of Medicine, 350*(9), 862–864. https://doi.org/ 10.1056/NEJMp038249

Collin, A., & Young, R. A. (1986). New directions for theories of career. *Human Relations, 39*(9), 837–853. https://doi.org/10.1177/001872678603900904

Drum, K. (2017, November). You will lose your job to a robot – and sooner than you think. *Mother Jones.* www.motherjones.com/politics/2017/10/you-will-lose-your-job-to-a-robot-and-sooner-than-you-think/

DuRose, L., & Stebleton, M. J. (2016). Lost in translation: Preparing students to articulate the meaning of a college degree. *Journal of College and Character, 17*(4), 271–277. https:// doi.org/10.1080/2194587X.2016.1230759

Feller, R., & Franklin, M. (2020). The HEROIC narrative assessment system: Helping undergrads navigate transitions. In P. Gardner & H. Maietta (Eds.), *Advancing talent development: Steps toward a T-model infused undergraduate education* (pp. 125–140). Business Expert Press.

Felten, P., & Lambert, L. M. (2020). *Relationship-rich education*. Johns Hopkins University Press.

Franklin, M. (2015). CareerCycles: A holistic and narrative method of practice. In B. C. Shepard & P. S. Mani (Eds.), *Career development practice in Canada: Perspectives, principles, and professionalism* (pp. 441–463). CERIC.

Franklin, M., & Feller, R. (2017). Using the one life tools framework: From clarification to intentional exploration with an East Asian female. In L. Busacca & M. Rehfuss (Eds.), *Postmodern career counseling: A handbook of culture, context and cases* (pp. 273–284). American Counseling Association.

Franklin, M., & Stebleton, M. J. (2020). Another story to tell: Outcomes of a single session narrative approach, blended with technology. *Canadian Journal of Career Development, 19*(1), 39–45.

Franklin, M., Yanar, B., & Feller, R. (2015). Narrative method of practice increases curiosity and exploration, psychological capital, and personal growth leading to career clarity: A retrospective outcome study. *The Canadian Journal of Career Development, 14*(2), 12–23.

Friedman, T. (2016). *Thank you for being late: An optimist's guide to thriving in the age of accelerations*. Farrar, Straus, & Giroux.

Gardner, P., & Estry, D. (2017). *A primer on the T-professional*. Collegiate Employment Research Institute, Michigan State University. https://ceri.msu.edu/_assets/pdfs/t-shaped-pdfs/Primer-on-the-T-professional.pdf

Gardner, P., & Maietta, H. (2020). *Advancing talent development: Steps toward a T-Model infused undergraduate education*. Business Expert Press.

Grant, A. (2021). *Think again: The power of knowing what you don't know*. Viking.

Hartung, P. J., & Blustein, D. L. (2002). Reason, intuition, and social justice: Elaborating on Parsons's career decision-making model. *Journal of Counseling & Development, 80*(1), 41–47. https://doi.org/10.1002/j.1556-6678.2002.tb00164.x

Higashi, L., & Stebleton, M. J. (2020). Act up: Nudging career educators towards 'good trouble.' CERIC. *Career Works*. https://careerwise.ceric.ca/2020/08/21/act-up-nudging-career-practitioners-toward-good-trouble/#.YcytzWjMI2w

Hirschi, A. (2018). The fourth industrial revolution: Issues and implications for career research and practice. *Career Development Quarterly, 66*(3), 192–204. https://doi.org/10.1002/cdq.12142

Hoffman, R., Casnocha, B., & Yeh, C. (2014). The alliance: Managing talent in the networked age. *Harvard Business Review*.

Holland, J. L. (1973). *Making vocational choices: A theory of careers*. Prentice Hall.

Hooley, T., Sultana, R., & Thomsen, R. (Eds). (2019). *Career guidance for emancipation: Reclaiming justice for the multitude*. Routledge.

Kaufman, G., & Flanagan, M. (2015). A psychologically "embedded" approach to designing games for prosocial causes. *Cyberpsychology: Journal of Psychosocial Research on Cyberspace*, 9(3), Article 5. https://doi.org/10.5817/CP2015-3-5

Lent, R. W. (2018). Future of work in the digital world: Preparing for instability and opportunity. *The Career Development Quarterly*, 66(3), 205–219. https://doi.org/10.1002/cdq.12143

Lent, R. W., & Brown, S. D. (2020). Career decision making, fast and slow: Toward an integrative model of intervention for sustainable career choice. *Journal of Vocational Behavior*, 120, 1034–1048. https://doi.org/10.1016/j.jvb.2020.103448

Luthans, F., Avolio, B. J., Avey, J. B., & Norman, S. M. (2007). Positive psychological capital: Measurement and relationship with performance and satisfaction. *Personnel Psychology*, 60(3), 541–572. https://doi.org/10.1111/j.1744-6570.2007.00083.x

Mair, M. (1988). Psychology as storytelling. *International Journal of Personal Construct Psychology*, 1, 125–137.

Maree, J. G. (2016). Career construction counseling with a mid-career Black man. *Career Development Quarterly*, 64(1), 20–34. https//doi.org/10.1002/cdq.12038

Maree, K., & Molepo, M. (2006). The use of narratives in cross-cultural career counselling. In M. McMahon & W. Patton (Eds.), *Career counselling: Constructivist approaches* (pp. 69–81). Routledge.

McGowan, H. E., & Shipley, C. (2020). *The adaptation advantage: Let go, learn fast, and thrive in the future of work*. Wiley.

McRae, N., & Johnston, N. (2016). The development of a proposed global work-integrated learning framework. *Asia-Pacific Journal of Cooperative Education*, 17(4), 337–348.

Merriam, S. B., & Kim, Y. S. (2008). Non-western perspectives on learning and knowing. *New Directions for Adult and Continuing Education*, 119, 71–81. https://doi-org.ezp1.lib.umn.edu/10.1002/ace.307

Parsons, F. (1909). *Choosing a vocation*. Houghton-Mifflin.

Payne, A. (2004, October 2). Declaration of independents [Blog post]. *Xixax Film Forum*. https://xixax.com/index.php?topic=2423.15

Richardson, M. S. (1993). Work in people's lives: A location for counseling psychologists. *Journal of Counseling Psychology*, 40(4), 425–433. https://doi.org/10.1037/0022-0167.40.4.425

Rogers, C. R. (1951). *Client-centered therapy: Its current practice, implications, and theory*. Houghton Mifflin.

Santilli, S., Di Maggio, I., Ginevra, M. C., Nota, L., & Soresi, S. (2021). Stories of courage in a group of asylum seekers for an inclusive and sustainable future. *International Journal for Educational and Vocational Guidance*. Advance online publication. https://doi.org/10.1007/s10775-021-09495-y

Savickas, M. L. (1993). Career counseling in the postmodern era. *Journal of Cognitive Psychotherapy*, 7(3), 205–215. https://doi.org/ 10.1891/0889-8391.7.3.205

Savickas, M. L. (2020). Career construction and counseling model. In S. D. Brown & R. W. Lent (Eds.), *Career development and counseling: Putting theory and research to work* (3rd ed., pp. 165–199). Wiley.

Spokane, A. R., & Glickman, I. T. (1994). Light, information, inspiration, cooperation: Origins of the clinical science of career intervention. *Journal of Career Development*, 20(4), 295–304. https://doi.org/10.1177/089484539402000404

Stebleton, M. J. (2010). Narrative-based career counseling perspectives in times of change: An analysis of strengths and limitations. *Journal of Employment Counseling*, 47(2), 64–78. https://doi.org/10.1002/j.2161-1920.2010.tb00091.x

Stebleton, M. J. (2019). Moving beyond passion: Why "do what you love" advice for college students needs reexamination. *Journal of College and Character*, 20(2), 163–171. https://doi.org/ 10.1080/2194587X.2019.1591289

Stebleton, M. J. (2021). Stories to craft: Applying narrative competencies to student affairs. *Journal of College and Character*, 22(2), 171–178. https://doi.org/10.1080/ 2194587X.2021.1898985

Stebleton, M. J., & Franklin, M. (2020, March 30). *Learning how to trust our clients' stories*. CareerWise by CERIC. https://careerwise.ceric.ca/2020/03/30/learning-how-to-trust-our-clients-stories/#.YMytaWhKhEY

Stebleton, M. J., Franklin, M., Lee, C., & Kaler, L. S. (2019). Not just for undergraduates: Examining a university narrative-based career management course for engineering graduate students. *Canadian Journal of Career Development*, 18(2), 64–77.

Stebleton, M. J., & Jehangir, R. R. (2020). A call for career educators to recommit to serving first-generation and immigrant college students: Introduction to special issue. *Journal of Career Development*, 47(1), 3–10. https://doi.org/10.1177/0894845319884126

Stebleton, M. J., & Kaler, L. S. (2020). Preparing college students for the end of work: The role of meaning. *Journal of College and Character*, 21(2), 132–139. https://doi.org/ 10.1080/ 2194587X.2020.1741396

Super, D. E. (1953). A theory of vocational development. *American Psychologist*, 8(5), 185–190. https://doi.org/10.1037/h0056046

Tiedeman, D. V., & O'Hara, R. P. (1963). *Career development: Choice and adjustment*. College Entrance Examination Board.

Toporek, R. L., & Cohen, R. F. (2017). Strength-based narrative résumé counseling: Constructing positive career identities from difficult employment histories. *The Career Development Quarterly*, 65(3), 222–236. https://doi.org/10.1002/cdq.12094

Weise, M. R. (2020). *Long life learning: Preparing for jobs that don't even exist yet*. Wiley & Sons.

Welty, E. (1983). *One writer's beginnings*. Harvard University Press.

Young, R. A. (1984). Toward an ecology of career development. *Canadian Counsellor*, 18, 152–159.

Zikic, J., & Franklin, M. (2010). Enriching careers and lives: Introducing a positive, holistic, and narrative career counseling method that bridges theory and practice. *Journal of Employment Counseling*, 47(4), 180–189. https://doi.org/10.1002/j.2161-1920.2010. tb00102.x

13
Infusing Career into the Curriculum and the Problem of Indecision

Heather Nester

Exploring the Problem of Indecision

The challenge of indecision often starts long before most students step foot on campus for orientation. A study of two- and four-year public and private college programs found that "51% of students were not confident in their career path when they enrolled in college" (Robinson, 2019, para. 6). The study found nearly two-thirds of students surveyed expressed overwhelm when selecting a major. Generation Z students (Gen-Z), born between 1995 and 2010 (Seemiller & Grace, 2019), were more likely to be overwhelmed, at 68% (Robinson, 2019).

The paralysis students feel around selecting a major often ties into the fear of prolonging their graduation date, and thus incurring more debt. More than their predecessors, both "Millennials," born between 1981 and 1994, and Gen-Z seem to feel more regret about spending than their older-generation counterparts. According to one study in 2020, 83% of Millennials and Gen-Z felt regret about spending. For Generation X, born between 1961 and 1981 (Strauss & Howe, 1991), this figure was 68%, and for Baby Boomers, born between 1943 and 1960 (Strauss & Howe, 1991), it was 49% (Palmer, 2020).

The anxiety undecided students often experience around choosing a major is at best challenging, and at worst debilitating. Students who are unfamiliar with their college or university structure may feel lost as they try to figure out their options, seek resources, and grapple with the stakes of their career decisions.

Three Types of Student Indecision

The number of students struggling with indecision related to their college majors and careers is not insignificant. According to a 25-year longitudinal study of 19,813

DOI: 10.4324/9781003213000-17

students entering university, 18–20% of these new enrollees were undecided (Gordon & Steele, 2003). In addition, just because a student has declared a major does not always mean they are confident about their choice. In one 2013 study of more than 800 students, participants were asked to elaborate on their major decision-making process. The researchers found that "family and peer influence, assumptions about introductory courses, potential job characteristics, and characteristics of the major" were factors in students' decisions, leading to the conclusion that "students are choosing a major based on influence and assumption rather than through an understanding of their own personal goals and values" (Freedman, 2013, para. 2). According to the US Department of Education, about one-third of students enrolled in a bachelor's program changed majors and about 1 in 10 students changed their major more than once (National Center for Education Statistics, 2017).

This pattern of uncertainty highlights the regularity of the problem for a significant portion of students enrolling in college. Even post-graduation, we are seeing higher numbers of graduates who would change their major if they could go back and start over again. In a recent study, 61% of college graduates said they would change their major if they could do it again, with the most popular reason for that change being "I want to pursue my passion" (Johnson, 2020, para. 2–6).

To add another layer of complication, not all college students have the same level of indecision about their major and career aspirations. According to Gordon and Steele's 2003, 25-year study of undergraduate students:

> [W]hen asked how decided they were about a choice of academic major, an average of 22% indicated they were 'completely undecided.' 31% on average said they were tentatively decided' about a major, while an average of 43% indicated they had 'several ideas but were not ready to decide.
>
> (p. 23)

Based on their work, Gordon and Steele categorized undecided students into three groups (Kelly & Pullver, 2003, para. 1–3):

1. Confident Decided: Experience little career indecision and do not seek out career counseling (Wanberg & Muchinsky, 1992, p. 74)
2. Confident but Uninformed: Focal need for career information and have not begun career planning (Larson, Heppner, Ham, & Dugan, 1988, p. 442)
3. Anxious Undecided: Need career information, are highly anxious, lack decision-making confidence, perceive barriers to career decision making, and have low self-esteem and poorly developed vocational identity (Wanberg & Muchinsky, 1992, p. 76).

Each student requires a unique approach to career education, exploration, and decision-making. Part of the challenge in addressing this situation at the start of a traditional undergraduate student's education is that it is difficult to determine which group best reflects their mindset during orientation. As advisors guide students through the course registration process, they might lead students to register for professional development courses based on their major, learning community, or other programmatic requirements. Unfortunately, these courses rarely assess the level of indecision each student experiences as they enter their first semester.

Without being able to identify which form of indecision students face early enough in the process, colleges and universities cannot assign students to different sections of a career-focused course. For example, students who are "Confident Decided" might experience some exploration redundancies as instructors plan activities and reflection topics to benefit "Anxious Undecided" students. Within the same course, students who are "Anxious Undecided" might experience an increased level of anxiety in the course beside their "Confident Decided" peers, who already believe they know what major and career they want to pursue. This structural shortcoming in undergraduate programs can lead to curricular engagement challenges within their career-focused courses. The consequential lack of investment in course activities later in the semester can have an impact on their career development and retention over the long term.

Traditional Structures May Intensify the Problem of Indecision

Many career professionals acknowledge that career development is a lifelong process. One popular model of the career development process, utilized at the University of Cincinnati, includes four categories (University of Cincinnati, n.d.-a):

- Know Yourself: Values, Interests, Strengths, Traits, Ambitions
- Explore Options: Occupational Research, Industry Trends, Career Options for Degree
- Get Focused: Decision-Making, Goal Setting, Action Planning
- Take Action: Gain Experience, Job Search Tools, Connect with Employers

Based on the career development process, and what we have seen of student indecision, expecting every student to select and apply for a major before coming to campus might be short-sighted. Freedman (2013) has pointed out that "the common four-year curriculum path colleges and universities use assumes that students enter college prepared to make a decision regarding major, and ultimately career path" (para. 1). For many students, this approach does not serve them well. William Perry's theory of intellectual and ethical development implies that students may not be developmentally ready to make an informed choice about their major that early in the academic year. According to Perry, students may be in what he calls the "dualism" stage, that is, those students who "believe there is one right answer for everything, including the choice of major." To find the "right" choice these students tend to look to their adviser, parents, peers, and faculty for answers instead of conducting their own research, analyzing their own personal goals, and completing self-reflection (Freedman, 2013).

This raises the question, how are students making an informed decision about their major and career exploration, if not through exploration and self-reflection? If colleges and universities do not have career-focused classes integrated into the first semester of students' college experience, how are they ensuring that these reflective questions are being addressed? If we adhere to William Perry's developmental theory, integrated career-focused courses assist students in reaching what he has called the "multiplicity" stage where they have the "ability to recognize that various options exist" and are now "ready to narrow their major preferences" (Freedman, 2013, para. 1).

Some liberal arts colleges encourage students to declare their major at the end of their sophomore year, after they have had more time to take courses and reflect. This additional time supports some students in moving through the "Know Yourself" and "Explore Options" stages of the Career Development Wheel with more care. The structure of a traditional four-year curriculum at colleges and universities can cause students in the "Confident but Uninformed" or "Anxious Undecided" indecision categories to feel trapped if institutions do not support exploration of the early stages of the Career Development Wheel. Having a more flexible curricular structure, especially for undecided students, is beneficial as they find their place within the university (Buford & Nester, 2019). Without intentional integration of career reflection and development in first-year touchpoints, colleges could be setting their undecided and indecisive students up for long-term failure.

Social Factors and Personality Impacts

The challenge of indecision does not solely manifest within our institutions. As humans, we often struggle with indecision due to psychological factors, social factors, and factors of personality. For instance, Rogers et al. (2008) found "individuals who display confidence, or self-efficacy, in making career specific decisions were more likely to set career-related goals. In addition, individuals capable of setting goals were also more likely to create plans and explore career opportunities" (p. 141). In young adults specifically, parental attachment, peer influence, and self-efficacy are influential factors that guide them in the career exploration process (Hellmann, 2014, p. 12).

The complexity of decision-making is part of the reason so many career aptitude tests are in use, such as O*NET My Next Move, Big Five Personality, Holland's Strong Interest Inventory, Myers Briggs Type Indicator, Enneagram, etc. (Conlan, n.d.). As career professionals, we must acknowledge that students' responses to any assessment are influenced by psychological factors, social influences, and their own mental health.

Circle of Influence

From a young age, we begin to understand what career means. Through observational learning, "the process of learning by watching others, retaining the information, and then later replicating the behaviors that were observed" (Cherry, 2021, para. 1), we form opinions and conceptions of career by observing those in our lives. Early in our lives we are observing our parents, guardians, siblings, family friends, community members, etc. We form opinions about the careers of those we observe and make inferences about how those careers could impact our own lives. These people are within our circle of influence.

Many people frame their understandings of career, and what options are available to them, based on their experiences and the careers of those they know. If they are not encouraged to reflect on the subjectivity of the career stories they hear, and instead take them as fact, they might not intentionally compare them against their own values, beliefs, interests, and passions. As the writer Chimamanda Ngozi Adichie said, "The single story creates stereotypes, and the problem with stereotypes is not that they are untrue, but that they are incomplete. They make one story become the only story" (Adichie, 2009). If someone does not compare the story they hear, based on someone within their circle of influence, they might process it as the only interpretation. For some people, this could lead to prematurely committing to or closing off career options. For example, if someone has a positive relationship with a family friend who is a dentist, they might be more interested in pursuing dentistry. Without intentional reflection, this person may form positive impressions of dentistry because of their positive connection with that person. On the other hand, if a person has a negative relationship with that same family friend, they might rule out the field of dentistry as a career choice.

Another possible outcome of only being exposed to careers within your circle of influence is the "false dilemma fallacy," which occurs when individuals are compelled to choose among a limited set of options, when other options may be available but are not known (Seel, 2012). In other words, students select a career to pursue based only on what they have been exposed to. If they do not know how to research new careers, or how to get started, they are operating under a false assumption about their options. This fallacy is another reason why career exploration should intentionally be incorporated into academic curricula so that students who are "Confidently Decided," "Confident but Uninformed," and "Anxiously Undecided" can make informed career choices as their awareness of possible choices expands. Even students who have declared a major might not be familiar with all the choices available to them.

Values

Another factor that impacts career decisions is the individual values a person holds. In many career and personality assessments, a section is dedicated to career-related values. Three frequently used interest inventories, rooted in Holland's theory of vocational personalities and work environments, are the Self-Directed Search, Strong Interest Inventory, and the Campbell Interest and Skill Survey (Dobson et al., 2014). These assessments emphasize how "alignment between your career and your core values produces satisfaction, a sense of happiness and fulfillment. A misalignment can cause everything from minor problems to major disruptions" (Loffredo, 2017, para. 1).

Intentional guided reflection can be a powerful tool to help people identify their *own* values. Structural barriers within higher education may make it more difficult for students to actively reflect on their values, such as experiencing mistrust or unsafe relationships, interacting with non-reflective peers, receiving unsupportive or jarring feedback, encountering barriers due to marginalized identities, and/or interacting with unsupportive academic personnel (Davis, 2003). When people openly reflect about their values, it may place them in a position of vulnerability. This may be especially true for marginalized students.

If institutions are not prepared to intentionally support students through the reflection process, it could lead students to feel wary of reflection, negatively impacting their long-term career satisfaction. A study by IBM found that employees whose skills and talents are aligned to their employer's core values report an 80% more positive experience (IBM Smarter Workforce Institute, 2017). Equipping students with the capacity to reflect on their values helps prepare them for future success as they research and pursue employment opportunities. Through structured reflection on career values, students can feel more engaged in their personal career development and feel that their voice matters.

Personality

Personality is also a factor in career reflection and the development process. According to McAdams and Pals (2006), "Personality is an individual's unique variation on the general evolutionary design for human nature, expressed as a developing pattern of disposable traits, characteristic adaptations, and integrative life stories complex and differentially situated in culture" (p. 212). Brown et al. (2020) suggested that the acknowledgement of personality traits and the inherent perspective they provide is highly applicable to a person's vocational behavior and career development. Each person has their own career path and needs individual reflection to understand their personal values and career preferences.

For example, when considering the Myers-Briggs Type Indicator assessment (Myers, 1980), there are different preferences between what Myers called the judging-perceiving (J-P) dichotomy. Judging types like to have matters settled and decided as promptly as possible, want to be able to plan, stick to the decision they make, and are more comfortable with the choices they make. In contrast, Perceiving types like to keep their options open as long as possible before doing anything irrevocable, are more flexible with their time, enjoy considering new options and re-opening decisions, and prefer to not feel tied to one plan so they can improvise (Myers, 1980; Tieger & Barron-Tieger, 2007). If professional development and the navigation of exploration is approached in the same way for each type it may either appear overly structured to a Perceiving type or too abstract for a Judging type. Approaching each type with the same solutions, given their distinct preferences, may lead to frustration and distrust, and could potentially drive students away from career services (Nester & Buford, 2020).

Another example is the five-factor personality model, also known as the Big Five, which includes Neuroticism (as opposed to emotional stability), Extraversion, Openness to Experience, Agreeableness, and Conscientiousness (Cattell & Mead, 2008, p. 141). The results of this assessment can help guide career professionals in their conversations with students because they will have a deeper understanding of their perspective. Chartrand et al. (1993) found that Neuroticism was associated with more dependent decision-making, lower confidence, lower ability to solve problems, more indecisiveness, and more career choice anxiety. Additional cross-national research has shown that Neuroticism is also a major factor for indecision in the United States (Hacker et al., 2013) and in parts of Asia (Abrams et al., 2017).

In contrast, high Extraversion and Conscientiousness with low Neuroticism "were related to greater career-information-seeking behavior and career exploration self-efficacy" (Brown et al., 2020, p. 587). An understanding of how risk-averse, indecisive, anxious, or reflective a student is when discussing career can shape the way an advisor or instructor structures the conversation or designs an assignment.

Analysis Paralysis

One study of 19,813 new undergraduate students, surveyed over a 25-year period, found that "an average of 63% of students admitted they were 'somewhat anxious' while 21% indicated they were 'very anxious' about choosing a major" (Gordon & Steele, 2003). The anxiety students feel can lead to analysis paralysis, or "an overload of analysis options that impedes a student's [career] research progress" (Zuckerberg & Gibbs, 2008, p. 505). In this scenario, a student becomes so overwhelmed by the number of potential majors and careers that they shut down. They feel paralyzed by the number of possibilities and have a fear of ruling out an option too early.

Students who are undecided, especially at the first-year college touchpoint, are typically overloaded with a lot of new information and new experiences as they enter college. It is important to remember that these students are not typically undecided because of a lack of talent, effort, or passion; rather, "often it is a surplus of passion and career interests that leave them unwilling to foreclose on options" (Buford & Nester, 2019, para. 1). Combating this challenge requires a structured approach with multiple touchpoints throughout students' academic journey. Adequate support, and funding, at the institutional level can highlight the importance of the career process for long-term professional success and career happiness.

Curricular Integration

The challenges of indecision shared in this chapter highlight the need for intentional structures and support at the institutional level for the integration of career exploration and development into the college curriculum. Career education courses are not new to higher education. Career courses in the United States date back to the early 20th century (Maverick, 1926), with estimates of more than 35% of colleges and universities offering career courses in the late 2010s (Lenz & Reardon, 2017). The increase in the number of career education course offerings underscores the many positive gains they have produced for students (Reardon & Fiore, 2014).

These initiatives run into challenges when they are not required in academic programs and/or do not involve multiple touchpoints throughout a student's academic journey. To address this challenge for students, career education courses should be integrated into academic curricula. One study of a mandatory career course for first-year undecided students at the University of Cincinnati found that "the combination of assessments, practical skill-building, and dedicated time and space to explore career options is an effective strategy for addressing major and career indecision" (Buford & Nester, 2020, para. 4). If colleges and universities address indecision at the beginning of a student's academic journey, they can improve the overall experience.

This also allows students to identify experiential learning opportunities earlier on that match their career goals and help them create a more competitive resume upon graduation. Based on a study by the National Association of Colleges and Employers (NACE), "nearly 91% of employers responding to NACE's *Job Outlook 2017* survey prefer that their candidates have work experience, and 65% indicate that they prefer candidates to have relevant work experience" (NACE, 2017, para. 2). If a student is able to declare their major, and feel confident in their decision, during their first year or early in their second year, they have multiple semesters to find experiential learning opportunities relevant to their intended field. This may give them an advantage over students that do not declare, or fully identify, their career goals until their last year of college.

Another advantage of curricular integration is sustainability. With new financial constraints placed on higher education, especially in response to Covid-19, where a 14% average revenue decline was estimated across higher education (Friga, 2021), institutions must find the most cost-efficient way to provide services for students. A college or university with tens of thousands of students might find it difficult to offer multiple career coaching meetings to all of their students. A more sustainable approach would be the utilization of required career courses. Instead of a career coach spending one hour with one student, they could spend one hour with 40 students discussing a career-related topic in the classroom. Individual reflection and feedback could then be provided on assignments and through group reflection activities. If these courses are built into multiple career touchpoints across academic years, students will likely feel a greater sense of support.

The increased amount of time students spend with their instructor over a 15-week course, compared to sporadic career advising appointments, also allows more in-depth relationships to build. As each person learns more about each other, thus updating the information they have about the other person, the more their level of trust increases (Williams, 2001). The more students trust their instructor, the more likely they will share about their career aspirations, goals, and values. Career course integration allows students to develop a deeper relationship with their instructor, as well as increases collaborative opportunities between students and their peers. Increased cooperation and more social interaction allow students to develop deeper relationship-focused skills, gain new opportunities to network, and learn from the experiences of others.

Creating curricular career development opportunities at the first-year level, mid-collegiate level, and capstone level also ensures that student questions are being addressed at different stages of the career development process. The needs of a first-year student are different than the needs of a student getting ready to graduate. A first-year career course might focus on self-assessment and understanding, exploration of professional possibilities and goals, identification of professional habits, and an introduction to cross-cutting professional skills. A capstone-level course would focus on translating experiences and majors into professional practice, formulating a post-graduation plan, and narrating a career story during professional interviews for future careers or graduate school. With a scaffolded approach, instructors have room to grow students' understanding of core career topics over time and pose reflection questions across the academic journey that students may not think to ask themselves.

Embedded career courses address issues of inclusion. Career centers with non-mandatory advising typically rely on marketing, advertisements, and word of mouth to encourage students to schedule an appointment or attend walk-in services. If most marketing is done on campus and through word of mouth, a large segment of the student population is left out, which leads to issues of access and inequity. Distance-learning students and those who commute to campus in the evenings may not visit student unions where advertisements are shared, or access marketing at all. Students who miss career services resources and do not have the opportunity to take advantage of as many experiential learning opportunities have fewer chances to develop their professional identity and engage with the campus community. This is especially important when we acknowledge that "the impact of college is largely determined by individual effort and involvement in the academic, interpersonal, and extra-curricular offerings on a campus" (Pascarella & Terenzini, 2005, p. 602).

As educators, we must address the cultural and contextual obstacles that exist for students to engage with campus opportunities. Integrated career education courses at the first-year touchpoint allow students to better understand the experiential learning opportunities their institution offers, increases their sense of community among their instructors and peers, and ideally encourages them to persist to graduation because they feel properly supported to succeed. We know that persistence-level differences from the first to second year, including graduation rates, "continually disadvantage many Students of Color, undergraduate men, lower-income students, first-generation college-goers, undergraduates who commute to campus, and a handful of other student populations" (Harper et al., 2009, p. 5) The scaffolding support of integrated career education courses throughout the curriculum is especially important for students who face challenges to persist and engage in purposeful activities in and outside of the classroom.

Framework Example: University of Cincinnati Career Education Outcomes

One example of successfully integrated career education courses exists at the University of Cincinnati (UC). Though it founded cooperative education in 1906, UC has recently redefined experiential learning with the goal of providing every baccalaureate student the opportunity for paid experiential learning. To achieve this expanded initiative, the university implemented career education student learning outcomes for all academic programs, integrating courses at a first-year touchpoint, mid-collegiate touchpoint, and capstone/senior year touchpoint (University of Cincinnati, 2017, para. 1):

> First-Year: Self-assessment and understanding, exploration of professional possibilities and goals, identification of professional habits, and introduction to cross-cutting professional skills.
>
> Mid-Collegiate: Development of professional tools and artifacts, development of cross-cutting professional skills through experience-based learning, continued self-assessment and articulation of goals.
>
> Capstone/Senior: Connections between theory and practice, formalization of post-graduation plan.

As each academic program creates a pathway that fits their student population, some have chosen to integrate career education learning outcomes into their own courses. However, a significant number of programs have partnered with UC's centralized career education division to develop stand-alone career education courses specifically for their student populations.

Intentional Integration with Campus Partners

Part of the benefit of career education courses added as learning outcomes to students' curriculum is an opportunity to create courses tailored to major populations. Some examples of courses, and their populations, offered at UC are listed below (University of Cincinnati, n.d.-b):

- Undecided – PD1070: Exploring Professional Paths
- Liberal Arts – PD1170: Career Readiness for the Liberal Arts
- Healthcare – PD1000: Exploring Health Professions
- Biological Sciences – BIOL2061: Professionalism, Purpose, and Careers in Biology
- Information Technology: PD1010: Professional Development for BSIT
- Study Abroad – PD2010: Exploring Culture, Life, and Work Abroad
- Arts – PD2091: Applied Professional Practice – DAAP

Within some of these courses, like PD1070, sub-sections are created to address additional student populations that might require additional support, such as first-generation students and college athletes.

The impact of these courses is not lost on students either. Below are a few student feedback quotes from surveys, course evaluations, etc. from sections of these tailored courses that I have personally taught over the last few years.

- Undecided Course: *"This class really helped me to have a better understanding of the different paths I can take from this point, and it helped me to have a better understanding of my strengths and skills and how they relate to my potential career options. I feel more confident in my future after taking this course."*
- Healthcare Course: *"Of my entire freshman year of college, this class benefited me more in the outside world than any other course."*
- Biological Sciences Course: *"I'm a first-generation college student and this really opened me up to new career options that I didn't even know existed."*

Career education outcomes allow departments to respond to real-world life events and the changing world of work. With full-time faculty teaching career education courses and topics, UC has the opportunity to create transdisciplinary courses to address real-world events. One example is *MLTI2119: Unpacking COVID-19: A Multidisciplinary Approach* (Ruth Ann C., personal communication, July 28, 2020). This interactive course focused on the effects Covid-19 had on public health response, information and product design, religion and the law, mental health, and the future of work. Though an elective, it quickly reached capacity enrollment of both undergraduate and graduate students across four colleges and non-matriculating students.

Recommendations for Practice

Curricular integration of career education and experiential learning, across academic programs, ensures that students can reflect on and develop their professional personas and goals in an intentional and guided way. The following recommendations are designed to enhance career education outcomes based on the challenges we have discussed thus far:

- **Consider Intake Surveys** – On the first day of class, consider asking students to fill out an informal intake survey to learn more about who they are, their goals, what they have already ruled out, and what resources they already know about on campus. An intake survey allows educators to provide a more personalized experience for students in different indecision categories, address any specific needs causing additional anxiety, share resources students are not familiar with, and build buy-in early.
- **Change Your Language** – Students sometimes get caught up in the need to choose a major immediately. Instead, change the narrative to finding career pathways that excite or interest them. Take away some of the pressure students feel by reiterating that selecting a major is not the *only* way to move forward. Remind students that ruling out career pathways can be just as important as selecting one. After they have a better idea of what interests them, selecting a major is simply a tool to help them achieve their goals.
- **Encourage Students to Expand Their Circles of Influence** – Encourage students to expand their circle of influence to include more professionals. Instructors can invite speakers and employers to class, encourage students to join student organizations and volunteer, assign informational interview assignments, share LinkedIn Alumni resources, conduct student panels with upperclassmen, etc. This can be done for exploratory students or for students within a specific major looking to explore the options in their field.
- **Create a Safe and Engaging Environment** – Not every student will join a career education course ready to reflect and share their values. If a student does not feel safe, speaking up in class can put them in a position of vulnerability. They may not, then, fully engage in the material. Educators should spend time at the beginning of the semester building trust and engaging in activities to build buy-in.
- **Diversify Your Information** – Remember, not every student will digest information in the same way. Educators should reflect on their activities and course material to make sure they acknowledge the personalities and learning styles of all of their students. Allow students flexibility to engage with assignments in a style that matches who they are.
- **Embed Intentional Touch Points Throughout the Curriculum** – Career education courses should be integrated at multiple touchpoints throughout a student's education. This scaffolding approach reminds students that career exploration is

a continuous process, and ensures that they will continue to receive help as they grow within their majors and intended fields. Crafting multiple touchpoints has two additional advantages: 1) It allows the mid-collegiate and capstone/senior year touchpoints to explore in more depth a student's specific major and discipline, and 2) It allows flexibility in course content so that not all career education topics must be covered in a single class.

As higher education, career exploration, and experiential learning continue to evolve, educators must identify critical touchpoints to engage students. This engagement can not only shape a student's sense of the value of their degree (Busteed, 2020), but can also remind them that they are not alone in their career journey.

References

Abrams, M. D., Lee, I. H., Brown, S. D., & Carr, A. (2015). The career indecision profile: Measurement equivalence in the United States and South Korea. *Journal of Career Assessment, 23*, 225–235.

Adichie, C. N. (2009, July). *The danger of a single story* [Video]. Ted Conferences. www.ted.com/talks/chimamanda_ngozi_adichie_the_danger_of_a_single_story/transcript

Brown, S. D., Lent, R. W., Rottinghaus, P. J., Park, C. J., & Washington, D. M. (2020). Assessment of personality in career development and counseling. In R. W. Lent & S. D. Brown (Eds.), *Career development and counseling: Putting theory and research to work* (pp. 579–610). Wiley.

Buford, M., & Nester, H. (2019, May 1). *The plight of the undecided student*. NACE Journal. www.naceweb.org/career-development/special-populations/the-plight-of-the-undecided-student/

Busteed, B. (2020, December 21). Career services will define the next big boom in college enrollment. *Forbes*. www.forbes.com/sites/brandonbusteed/2020/12/21/career-services-will-define-the-next-big-boom-in-college-enrollment/?sh=611c64fd145e

Cattell, H. E. P., & Mead, A. D. (2008). The Sixteen Personality Factor Questionnaire (16PF). In G. J. Boyle, G. Matthews, & D. H. Safloske (Eds.), *The Sage handbook of personality theory and assessment* (pp. 135–159). Sage. https://people.wku.edu/richard.miller/520%2016PF%20Cattell%20and%20Mead.pdf

Chartrand, J. M., Rose, M. L., Elliott, T. R., Marmarosh C., & Caldwell, S. (1993). Peeling back the onion: Personality, problem solving, and career decision-making style correlates of career indecision. *Journal of Career Assessment. 1*(1), 66–82. https://doi.org/10.1177/106907279300100107

Cherry, K. (2021, April 28). *How observational learning affects behavior*. Verywell Mind. www.verywellmind.com/what-is-observational-learning-2795402

Conlan, C. (n.d.). *Career tests: Our top 10*. Monster Career Advice. www.monster.com/career-advice/article/best-free-career-assessment-tools

Davis, M. (2003). Barriers to reflective practice: The changing nature of higher education. *Active Learning in Higher Education, 4*(3), 243–255. https://doi.org/10.1177/14697874030043004

Dobson, L. K., Gardner, M. K., Metz, A. J., & Gore, P. A. (2014). The relationship between interests and values in career decision making: The need for an alternative method of measuring values. *Journal of Career Assessment, 22*(1), 113–122. https://doi.org/10.1177/1069072713492929

Freedman, L. (2013). The developmental disconnect in choosing a major: Why institutions should prohibit choice until second year. *The Mentor: Innovative Scholarship on Academic Advising, 15.* https://doi.org/https://doi.org/10.26209/mj1561278

Friga, P. N. (2021, February 5). *How much has covid cost colleges? $183 billion.* The Chronicle. www.chronicle.com/article/how-to-fight-covids-financial-crush?cid=gen_sign_in

Gordon, V., & Steele, G. E. (2003). Undecided first-year students: A 25-year longitudinal study. *Journal of the First-Year Experience, 15*(1), 19–38.

Hacker, J., Carr, A., Abrams, M., & Brown, S. D. (2013). Development of the career indecision profile factor structure, reliability, and validity. *Journal of Career Assessment, 21*, 32–41. https://doi-org.uc.idm.oclc.org/10.1177/1069072712453832

Harper, S. R., Quaye, S. J., & Pendakur, S. L. (Eds.). (2009). The heart of our work: Equitable engagement for students in US higher education. In *Student engagement in higher education: Theoretical perspectives and practical approaches for diverse populations* (pp. 1–16). Routledge.

Hellmann, J. N. (2014). *Social and psychological factors related to the career exploration process of young adults* [Master's thesis, University of Kentucky]. UKnowledge. https://uknowledge.uky.edu/hes_etds/19/

IBM Smarter Workforce Institute. (2017). *The employee experience index.* IBM Analytics. www.ibm.com/downloads/cas/JDMXPMBM

Johnson, R. (2020, February 27). *New survey finds most college grads would change majors.* Best Colleges. www.bestcolleges.com/blog/college-graduate-majors-survey/

Kelly, K. R., & Pulver, C. A. (2003). Refining measurement of career indecision types: A validity study. *Journal of Counseling and Development, 81*(4), 445–454. https://dx.doi.org.proxy.libraries.uc.edu/10.1002/j.1556-6678.2003.tb00271.x

Larson, L. M., Heppner, P. P., Ham, T., & Dugan, K. (1988). Investigating multiple subtypes of career indecision through cluster analysis. *Journal of Counseling Psychology, 35*(4), 439–446. https://doi.org/10.1037/0022-0167.35.4.439

Lenz, J. G., & Reardon, R. C. (2017, June 28–30). *Strategies for developing, managing, and evaluating a successful career course for 45 years* [Paper presentation]. National Career Development Association Conference, Orlando, FL, United States.

Loffredo, S. (2017, November 13). *Do your career and work values align?* Inside Higher Ed. www.insidehighered.com/advice/2017/11/13/importance-aligning-your-career-your-core-values-essay#:~:text=Your%20core%20values%20are%20principles,minor%20problems%20to%20major%20disruptions

Maverick, L. A. (1926). *The vocational guidance of college students*. Harvard University Press.

McAdams, D. P., & Pals, J. L. (2006). A new big five: Fundamental principles for an integrative science of personality. *American Psychologist, 61*, 204–217.

Myers, I. (1980). *Gifts differing*. Consulting Psychologists Press.

National Association of Colleges and Employers (Ed.). (2017, April 5). *Employers prefer candidates with work experience*. www.naceweb.org/talent-acquisition/candidate-selection/employers-prefer-candidates-with-work-experience/#:~:text=Nearly%20 91%20percent%20of%20employers,to%20have%20relevant%20work%20experience

National Center for Education Statistics. (2017, December). *Beginning college students who change their majors within 3 years of enrollment*. Data Point US Department of Education. https://nces.ed.gov/pubs2018/2018434.pdf

Nester, H., & Buford, M. (2020, February 1). Undecided or declared: Engaging distinct student populations in career education. *NACE Journal*. www.naceweb.org/career-development/special-populations/undecided-or-declared-engaging-distinct-student-populations-in-career-education/

Palmer, K. (2020, March 04). *Gen ZERS: How America's NEWEST adults are doing money*. Nerdwallet. www.nerdwallet.com/blog/generation-z-money-survey/#:~:text=Gen%20 Z%20has%20plenty%20of,self%2Dconsciousness%20(30%25)

Pascarella, E. T., & Terenzini, P. T. (2005). *How college affects students: A third decade of research*. Jossey-Bass.

Reardon, R., & Fiore, E. (2014, June 5). College career courses and learner outputs and outcomes, 1976–2014 (Technical Report No. 55). https://career.fsu.edu/sites/g/files/imported/storage/original/application/1b68db078f1cf9a964208a907318c64a.pdf

Robinson, A. (2019, October 14). *New survey: Student confusion selecting majors INCREASES higher education cost and time to earn degree*. Business Wire. www.businesswire.com/news/home/20191014005009/en/New-Survey-Student-Confusion-Selecting-Majors-Increases-Higher-Education-Cost-and-Time-to-Earn-Degree

Rogers, M. E., Creed, P. A., & Glendon, A. I. (2008). The role of personality in career planning and exploration: A social cognitive perspective. *Journal of Vocational Behavior, 73*(1), 132–142. https://doi.org/10.1016/j.jvb.2008.02.002

Seel, N. M. (Ed.). (2012). False dilemma fallacy. In *Encyclopedia of the sciences of learning*. Springer. https://doi.org/10.1007/978-1-4419-1428-6_2173

Seemiller, C., & Grace, M. (2019). *Generation Z: A century in the making*. Routledge.

Strauss, W., & Howe, N. (1991). *Generations: The history of America's future, 1584 to 2069* (1st ed.). Morrow.

Tieger, P. D., & Barron-Tieger, B. (2007). *Do what you are: Discover the perfect career for you through the secrets of personality type* (4th ed.). Little, Brown and Co.

University of Cincinnati. (n.d.-a). *Choosing a career*. www.uc.edu/campus-life/careereducation/career-studio/choose.html

University of Cincinnati. (n.d.-b). *Search class offerings.* https://onestop.uc.edu/registration/class-offerings.html

University of Cincinnati. (2017). *Career education student learning outcomes.* www.uc.edu/content/dam/uc/gened/docs/3-Career-Education-SLO-9-7-2017.pdf

Wanberg, C. R., & Muchinsky, P. M. (1992). A typology of career decision status: Validity extension of the vocational decision status model. *Journal of Counseling Psychology, 39*(1), 71–80. https://doi.org/10.1037/0022-0167.39.1.71

Williams, M. (2001). In whom we trust: Group membership as an affective context for trust development. *The Academy of Management Review, 26*(3), 377–396. https://doi.org/10.2307/259183

Zuckerberg, B., & Gibbs, J. (2008). Overcoming "analysis paralysis." *Frontiers in Ecology and the Environment, 6*(9), 505–506. www.jstor.org/stable/20440994

Part IV
Experiential Learning in Career Education

14
Get Thee to an Internship: Robot-Proofing Liberal Arts Students

Sharon Belden Castonguay

Liberal Arts College-to-Career: A New Focus

As an adult developmental psychologist by training and a career educator by trade, I have helped people of all ages and backgrounds decide how to use their talents and education in ways that are both fulfilling to them and beneficial to society. In 2013, I accepted a position running the career center at Wesleyan University, a Connecticut liberal arts college with about 3,000 undergraduates that typically accepts fewer than 20% of applicants. Part of its appeal was the physical space, a two-story, glass fronted, state-of-the-art facility, the shiny new result of a multi-million-dollar gut renovation to a building that had once housed squash courts.

My start date at Wesleyan was purposely slotted during commencement week so that I would have an opportunity to meet with the financially generous trustees who would be on campus for the festivities. On one particularly cold, rainy afternoon a few days before graduation, the head of our career advising team asked me to come with her on a walk. I picked up my umbrella while openly questioning her timing. "You need to understand," she said. "You need to *see*." We made our way from our prime campus location next to the student center, passing the library and science buildings before arriving at a dormitory complex formally known as The Butterfields, colloquially as "The Butts." "This is where our office used to be," she explained. "In the basement."

Wesleyan is hardly the only institution of its kind to experience a renaissance to its career education function. Traditionally bastions of wealth and privilege, liberal arts colleges once put little emphasis on what happened after graduation, assuming, not unreasonably, that its students would either go directly to medical, law, business, or graduate school, or else find a job through their parents' connections. When students did seek out the career office, it was either out of necessity for aid navigating the formal recruiting processes required of larger organizations or to make connections

DOI: 10.4324/9781003213000-19

with alumni. But the last several decades have seen considerable changes in the socioeconomic and cultural diversity of these campuses, and with them a need to provide support to students who must learn how to navigate not only the privileged spaces in which they are learning, but the transition to professions with which their families have little or no direct familiarity. Even those whose parents are doctors, lawyers, and the like need help navigating what has become an increasingly competitive, opaque, AI-driven hiring process. Once relegated to the sidelines, career education is gaining importance as liberal arts colleges are raising money for new spaces and expanded staff, signaling the importance of both experiential education and employment outcomes to the institution.

New Spaces, Increased Resources

I first toured Colgate University's new career center in 2018 when it was still partially under construction and I was recovering from knee surgery, gingerly navigating the uneven floors and piles of wood with my crutches. But I was determined to see this two-story tour de force, with its somehow modern yet traditional architecture, all stone and glass and wood paneling with posh event spaces, interview rooms, and staff offices. Another operation that has undergone a significant expansion in recent years is at Wellesley College, which received a $50 million gift in 2015 to launch a new College to Career Initiative (Wellesley College, 2015). The administration subsequently involved the whole campus in the rethinking and resourcing of career education, making it central to the student experience. Its Associate Provost and Executive Director of Career Education reports directly to the president of the college (Wellesley College, 2020), in recognition of the position's strategic importance (Young, 2016). The first to hold that position was Christine Cruzvergara, who left Wellesley in 2019 to join the largest early career network – Handshake – where she is currently Chief Education Strategy Officer. She told me,

> It was an incredible experience to craft a vision, organization, and team that reflected a truly integrated approach to career education across the institution. With this level of investment, our students had an opportunity to build the connections needed for their success and the institution could further its mission of a more equitable world.
>
> (C. Cruzvergara, personal communication, June 28, 2021)

Stereotypes, Tropes, and a Rise from the Ashes

The stakes are high, not only for the students but for their alma mater. Liberal arts colleges have struggled against the perception that they only produce humanities majors ill-equipped to find a job in the digital age. Google "liberal arts college memes" and you will find all sorts of clever references to humanities majors taking orders for fast food and expensive coffee. Politicians dating back to Ronald Reagan have famously joked about, bashed, and railed at college majors they see as insufficiently capitalist, with even Barack Obama noting in 2014 that people can potentially make more money with an education in "skilled manufacturing or the trades than they might with an art history degree" (Obama, 2014).

This sort of skepticism relies on two main misconceptions: that all liberal arts majors are there to study esoteric subjects like Medieval poetry, and that learning things like Medieval poetry is useless in today's society. In truth, the number of students turning away from the humanities in favor of social science and STEM majors has been growing (National Center for Education Statistics, 2020), even at institutions committed to keeping those departments alive. And yet many continue to flourish, not in spite of the career outcomes of those students, but because liberal arts colleges have become more focused on helping them see the connections between what they are studying and the potential real-world applications of that work. Longitudinal research by the Association of American Colleges and Universities and the National Center for Higher Education Management Systems (Humphreys & Kelly, 2014) suggests that liberal arts graduates may make less money on average when they first complete their bachelor's degree, but they are very likely to catch up with or even surpass other, seemingly lucrative majors by midcareer. This is partly due to the tendency of liberal arts graduates to receive advanced degrees; a contributor to the enviable career center staff-to-student ratios in many liberal arts career centers is the specialized advising offered for its graduates seeking entrance to law, medical, business, and graduate school. But some may argue that if an expensive investment in professional school is necessary to achieve these outcomes, what is the inherent value of a liberal arts education?

The Value of Humanics

By now, no one is unaware that the world of work is changing and that the growth of big data and artificial intelligence is catapulting modern society into the Fourth Industrial Revolution (World Economic Forum, 2020). Such trends convince many college-bound young people to respond to public calls to major in STEM fields (Mason, 2016). But in a 2018 cross-industry survey of hiring managers and executives, the Association of American Colleges and Universities, together with Hanover Research, found that "at least half of employers view the skills of a liberal education as 'very important' for college graduates," especially the availability to work effectively in teams, critical-thinking skills, and the ability to analyze and interpret data (Finley, 2021, p. 6). Similarly, the World Economic Forum reported in 2020 that "Critical thinking and problem-solving top the list of skills that employers believe will grow in prominence in the next five years" (Whiting, 2020, bullet 2). They also note that while 85 million jobs are likely to be displaced by 2025, "even more jobs – 97 million – may emerge that are more adapted to the new division of labor between humans, machines and algorithms" (Whiting, 2020, para. 7).

Northeastern University president Joseph E. Aoun (2017) argued that what modern workers need is *humanics*, which he defines as

> a new model of learning that enables learners to understand the highly technological world around them and that simultaneously allows them to transcend it by nurturing the mental and intellectual qualities that are unique to humans – namely, their capacity for creativity and mental flexibility.
>
> (Aoun, 2017, p. 53)

The foundations of humanics are three literacies – technological, data, and human – that expand our traditional study of the written word, numeracy, and scientific literacy to allow us to "network with both people and machines" (Aoun, 2017, p. 55). As such, a full education should include study of math, coding, and basic engineering; the interpretation and contextualization of data, and in particular large data sets; and subjects that help us learn to communicate and engage with one another, including through art and design.

A well-rounded liberal arts curriculum should, and often does, include these elements. But Aoun (2017) expanded on these competencies to include four cognitive capacities that he feels are necessary to survive and thrive in a digital economy. These include critical thinking, systems thinking, entrepreneurship, and cultural agility. Modern workers need to be able to analyze and apply what they learn, see the connections between different elements of complex systems, create new ways of doing things, and be able to work well as a member of a multicultural team and serve a multicultural society. Liberal arts students undoubtedly develop these competencies throughout their courses of study. So why do some so easily dismiss this as being impractical? Aoun mused, "Perhaps the reason that applied studies and hard science often possess a reputation for greater utility is that they feature a strong laboratory or workplace component while liberal arts classes are often framed as self-expression" (Aoun, 2017, pp. 104–105). Such beliefs are hard to counteract, even by those who have embraced and are dedicated to the continuation of this type of higher education. It is not uncommon on my own campus for students to choose one major out of pure interest – like dance – and another out of a sense of anticipated utility, like economics, or biology.

The importance of career education in a liberal arts context reveals itself in the midst of this tension, as a way to help students see the value of everything they are learning, make connections between what they are learning, both inside and outside the classroom, and help them not just determine the economic utility of various career paths open to them, but identify where they will find purpose and satisfaction in putting their skills to work. The main ways that liberal arts career centers are facilitating those connections are through experiential education; relationships with alumni through mentorship, recruiting efforts, and career communities; structured curricular and extracurricular content around career discernment and exploration; finding meaning and purpose in work; and understanding the effect of personal identities on their decision making.

Experiential Liberal Arts

When meeting with prospective families visiting my campus, I find that they are just as, if not more, concerned with internships than with full-time jobs after graduation. And no wonder: research conducted by Mount Holyoke College (Townsley et al., 2017) found that GPA and internship completion had a positive effect on career outcomes six months after graduation, with those having completed two or more internships twice as likely to be employed six months out as those who had never held them. They were also more likely to be enrolled in graduate school. While prior research (Crain, 2016) suggested that unpaid internships did not have the same effect, the Mount Holyoke study found that the total number of internships and GPA were more salient factors than whether an internship was paid. It showed that funding from their institutions to complete internships – as Mount Holyoke provides – was an important on-ramp for students who might not otherwise pursue such opportunities. The researchers concluded:

> How we enable all our students to succeed academically, participate in internships, take advantage of multiple internship opportunities over the course of a college career, engage in career development activities, and understand and respond to the labor market realities are all critical institutional questions to consider as we strive to maximize post-graduate outcomes for our students.
>
> (Townsley et al., 2017, p. 29)

Equitable Access to Internships

One of the most frequent conversations I find myself having with other liberal arts college career center directors concerns raising funding for students to pursue internships, particularly for lower-income students who might not be able to pursue opportunities in industries that either do not pay interns well (or at all) or which are concentrated in metro areas with a high cost of living like New York or San Francisco. Some schools, like Mount Holyoke, Smith, and Connecticut Colleges, even offer one summer of funding to all students. While such guarantees remain rare, the Liberal Arts Career NetWORK (LACN), a consortium of about 40 such colleges across the country dedicated to the career education of their students, found in a 2020 survey that their combined membership had awarded more than $9 million in the summer of 2019 (Liberal Arts Career NetWORK, 2020).

Smith College's Praxis program was put into place more than 20 years ago, resulting in alumnae data demonstrating the effect of internships and research opportunities on outcomes. Stacie Hagenbaugh (personal communication, June 18, 2021), a longtime director of Smith's Lazarus Center for Career Development, reports that such experiential education opportunities resulted in better outcomes in six key areas:

- Enrolled in graduate school at higher rates
- Felt that Smith better prepared them for graduate school

- Felt Smith better prepared them for their current career
- Felt more satisfied with their careers
- Felt more connected to Smith
- Felt the benefits they received from Smith outweighed the financial costs to them and their families

Students do not necessarily have to leave campus to find robust ways to put their education to work. One of the great selling points of liberal arts colleges is the ability for students to develop close relationships with their professors (Crabtree, 2019). I have seen these connections lead to students working in science labs, campus museums, and greenhouses; assisting faculty with research for journal articles and book projects; and even working with a campus's physical plant on facilities management or its investment office to grow the institution's endowment.

Curricular Pathways

The blessing of a liberal arts environment for students is having the room to learn who they are through the exploration of a broad curriculum. However, I quickly observed there was a downside to the freedom a liberal arts education offered. The lack of emphasis on not just career planning, but even thinking about how one's course of study will affect one's future can easily lead to a lack of attention to life after graduation; compounded with the ambiguity inherent in the modern job market and the abundance of options available to broadly educated students, you have a recipe for choice paralysis and inaction.

Some campuses have found ways for students to earn course credit for their career exploration activities. The College of Wooster's Pathways program, for example, allows students to connect interdisciplinary interests both within and outside their majors to test possible career paths (College of Wooster, n.d.). Students complete three to four interdisciplinary courses, at least one internship or other experiential education opportunity, and reflection exercises designed to help students make connections between everything they are learning inside and outside the classroom. With about 60 participating faculty and staff, Pathways tracks include, among others, public health, digital and visual storytelling, and data exploration and communication (L. Kastor, personal communication, June 16, 2021).

Women's colleges have a long history of fulfilling their mission by providing career development support to students and alumnae. In addition to the Praxis program to support internships, Smith College has career pathways built into their curriculum, offering not only traditional majors and minors but professional concentrations like Global Financial Institutions, Museums and Community Engagement, and Social Change. These offerings play into the college's existing strengths, like its renowned Museum of Art and the Jandon Center for Community Engagement (Smith College, n.d.). Nearby Mount Holyoke College's Nexus program offers students pre-professional tracks like development studies, data science, and journalism, media, and public discourse. Their aforementioned internship grant program is part of an integrated learning initiative that spans academic departments and advising offices (Mount Holyoke, n.d.).

Connecticut College's Connections curriculum allows students to develop their own educational pathway, guided by interdisciplinary study through their major or minor, research, global and local engagement, study away, and internships, ultimately leading to a capstone presentation to the campus community in their senior year (Connecticut College, n.d.). Integrated into this academic journey is a four-year curriculum, the Career Action Program (CAP), developed by the Hale Center for Career Development. CAP involves working with a career advisor during a first-year seminar and then following up with a seven-week credit-bearing course that covers career exploration, networking, storytelling, and professionalism. From there, students gain access to opportunities with alumni, employers, and community partners, as well as flexible funding that may be used for internships or to offset costs associated with job shadowing and skill development. Persephone L. Hall, the Hale Family Executive Director of the career center since 2016, presented on Connecticut College's efforts at the 2021 annual conference of the National Association of Colleges and Employers (NACE), noting that their students "build increasingly sophisticated career skills through accumulated knowledge and experience in conjunction with their academic development. At each juncture of CAP, students are expected to reflect on their career learning and its relationship to their academic study" (Hall et al., 2021).

Building Career Communities

If you are looking for the kind of one-on-one attention characteristic of small liberal arts colleges, look no further than Grinnell College in Iowa. Planning for post-college life is an integral part of the Grinnell experience. Their First Year Advising Program connects students with career support from the moment they arrive on campus, assigning each entering first-year or transfer student with an exploratory advisor to encourage intentional career exploration from day one (Grinnell College, n.d.). As their interests begin to crystallize, they can then obtain access to one of Grinnell's career communities, allowing them to access support, mentoring, and connection with advisors who specialize and have professional backgrounds in areas like business, law, and health professions, as well as alumni in those fields. The whole program is designed to address the fact that the sort of non-linear pathways that stem from a liberal arts education punctuate the need for early engagement (M. Peltz, personal communication, June 16, 2021).

In Massachusetts, both Amherst and Williams Colleges leverage the career communities model as well to ensure that the close relationships with alumni such schools rely on and are known for continue to flourish and provide a path to career success for their students. Amherst has made substantial investment into hiring a highly seasoned career advising team with significant prior work experience and expertise in fields like Science & Technology, Business & Finance, and Arts & Communication (Amherst College, n.d.). These advisors also connect with alumni to build community within their target industries (E. Griffen, personal communication, June 17, 2021). At Williams, 95% of students and over 3,000 alumni have accounts in their alumni mentor platform, EphLink. The site is home to a number of special interest communities, including those with a career focus, like Science & Health Professions, Business, and Careers with Social Impact, as well as identity-focused options, including one for military veterans (D. Kjelleren, personal communication, June 28, 2021; Williams College, n.d.).

The Role of Meaning, Purpose, and Identity

All this exposure helps students see not only what they could do with a liberal arts background, but also what they do not want to do. In his book *The Purposeful Graduate: Why Colleges Must Talk to Students about Vocation*, Tim Clydesdale (2015) looked at 88 colleges that received a total of $225M over eight years from the Lilly Endowment to undertake vocational discernment programming. He found that, overall, program participants had significantly higher satisfaction with life after college, even years afterward, than those who did not participate. This finding held true across age, gender, race, parent educational achievement, and parent occupational status. The institutions involved included a number of liberal arts colleges, among them Grinnell, as well as Davidson and Macalester Colleges and Denison University.

In 2013, Bates College's new president, Clayton Spencer, convened a working group to "develop a conceptual case for 'purposeful work' as a core concern for the liberal arts, and to create a plan for a specific set of steps we will take as a college to translate that commitment into action" (Bates College, 2014). Bates partnered with Gallup to conduct related research, and among the findings was that while four out of five college graduates said it was important to find meaning in one's work, fewer than half had achieved it (Gallup & Bates College, 2019, p. 5). They reported that four specific types of undergraduate experiences aligned with graduates finding purpose in their work later:

- Having an applied job or internship
- Having someone who encourages students' goals and dreams
- Being given realistic expectations for post-graduation employment prospects
- Participating in a class/program that helps students think about pursuing meaning in their work

Bates subsequently launched their Center for Purposeful Work and began a number of related initiatives under their Purposeful Work program, including funded internships, job shadowing opportunities, and practitioner-taught courses (Bates College, n.d.-a). They also offer *Life Architecture*, a five-week course taught by a psychology instructor with assistance from staff from the Center for Purposeful Work (Bates College, n.d.-b). Through their Project Work Infusion Project, Bates also encourages faculty to include in their existing curricula at least one class dedicated to discussion of work and purpose, as well as at least one related reading and one writing assignment (Bates College, n.d.-c). As a result of these efforts, more than 90% of the Class of 2019 engaged with at least one aspect of the program prior to graduation – despite the fact that participation was not required (A. DeLong, personal communication, November 26, 2019).

Identity

Finding meaning and purpose is inextricably connected to identity. As liberal arts colleges have doubled down in recent years on diversifying their student bodies, career education is not just about helping them define goals for their futures, but understanding how their past, present, and emerging identities influence their decision making. I began teaching *Career Decisions: From Insight to Impact* on Coursera in 2018 (Coursera, 2021) to help learners all over the world consider these themes and have been gratified to hear from people of myriad ages, educational backgrounds, and cultural identities who were grateful for the opportunity to consider how the messages they have been receiving from their families, cultures, and other aspects of their social surround have affected their decision making. Wesleyan University students are encouraged to complete the course before their arrival in their first year.

All students graduating from college in the 21st century will need to learn to work with those of different backgrounds than themselves and navigate a world of work that is very different from what their parents or grandparents faced – regardless of socioeconomic status. Preparing students for cultural agility means helping them actively reflect on their own identities and how cultural messages they might be internalizing affect how they make sense of the opportunities that are open or closed to them. In 2020, Wesleyan received a grant from the Davis Educational Foundation to pilot Ideals into Practice, a program that allows students the opportunity to prepare for meaningful work after graduation (Davis Educational Foundation, 2020) by using an electronic portfolio as a base of operations to document for themselves how their interests and transferable skills are developing based on their experiences both inside and outside the classroom (Wesleyan University, 2021). While not meant for public consumption, participants are encouraged to give portfolio access to their faculty and career advisors, as well as other professors, staff, internship or student employment supervisors, sports coaches, alumni mentors, or any other adults they would like to include in their "personal board of advisors" for the purpose of having conversations about what they are learning about themselves and how their goals are developing during their four years of college.

Recommendations for Practice

A liberal arts education is not only a viable way to prepare for the future world of work, but likely the best way. Career educators must help guide students through the complicated process of translating a seemingly disparate mismash of humanities, social science, and STEM courses into a humanics curriculum, ensuring that students have the literacies and competencies necessary to compete in an ever-changing marketplace.

- The biggest value career educators can add is the one-on-one attention that students in such colleges expect and deserve. Transactional advising with a focus on things like resume writing or major-to-career guidance will not be enough. Students need help sorting out how their identities and cultural messages might be curtailing options.
- Career education can reveal to students the connections between everything they are learning, both inside and outside the classroom, and help them develop their narrative to explain what they can offer to employers.
- Liberal arts students should, and often do, have access to robust opportunities for experiential learning, including direct ways to make connections with alumni and recruiters.
- Helping students develop habits of mind that will allow them to seek meaning and purpose in their work, while also being mindful of the realities of an ever-changing employment landscape, will equip them to succeed in the 21st century.

References

Amherst College. (n.d.). *Loeb Center staff.* www.amherst.edu/campuslife/careers/drop-in-hours/staff

Aoun, J. E. (2017). *Robot-proof: Higher education in the age of artificial intelligence.* The MIT Press.

Bates College. (n.d.-a). *Center for purposeful work.* www.bates.edu/purposeful-work/

Bates College. (n.d.-b). *Life architecture short term course.* www.bates.edu/purposeful-work/life-architecture-short-term-course/

Bates College. (n.d.-c). *Purposeful work infusion project.* www.bates.edu/purposeful-work/infusion-2/

Bates College. (2014, September). *Final report of the Purposeful Work Working Group.* www.bates.edu/about/files/2014/09/Purposeful-Work-Faculty-Report.pdf

Clydesdale, T. (2015). *The purposeful graduate: Why colleges must talk to students about vocation.* University of Chicago.

College of Wooster. (n.d.). *Pathways.* https://wooster.edu/academics/pathways/

Connecticut College. (n.d.). *Integrative pathways and centers.* www.conncoll.edu/connections/integrative-pathways/

Coursera. (2021). *Career decisions: From insight to impact.* www.coursera.org/learn/career-decisions?

Crabtree, S. (2019, January 24). *Student support from faculty, mentors varies by major.* Gallup. https://news.gallup.com/poll/246017/student-support-faculty-mentors-varies-major.aspx

Crain, A. (2016). *Understanding the impact of unpaid internships on college student career development and employment outcomes.* NACE Foundation. www.naceweb.org/uploadedfiles/files/2016/guide/the-impact-of-unpaid-internships-on-career-development.pdf

Davis Educational Foundation. (2020). *Grant history.* www.davisfoundations.org/def/grant-history

Finley, A. (2021). *How college contributes to workforce success.* Association of American Colleges and Universities & Hanover Research. www.aacu.org/research/how-college-contributes-to-workforce-success

Gallup & Bates College. (2019). *Forging pathway to purposeful work: The role of higher education.* www.bates.edu/purpose/files/2019/05/Bates_PurposefulWork_FINAL_REPORT.pdf

Grinnell College. (n.d.). *Exploratory advising program.* www.grinnell.edu/after-grinnell/cls/students/career-exploration/assessments

Hall, P., & Singer, J. (2021, June 7–11). *An innovative approach to integrating career education into the academic curriculum* [Conference session]. National Association for Colleges and Employers. www.naceweb.org/conferenceexpo/sessiondetails.aspx?ID=678

Humphreys, D., & Kelly, P. (2014). *How liberal arts and sciences majors fare in employment: A report on earnings and long-term career paths.* Association of American Colleges and Universities.

Liberal Arts Career NetWORK. (2020). *2020 internship survey* [Unpublished survey data].

Mason, L. (2016, March 20). *STEM majors are accelerating in every state.* Emsi. www.economicmodeling.com/2016/03/20/stem-programs-humanities-in-each-state/

Mount Holyoke College. (n.d.). *Nexus: Curriculum to career.* www.mtholyoke.edu/acad/nexus

National Center for Education Statistics. (2020). *Bachelor's degrees conferred by postsecondary institutions, by field of study: Selected years, 1970-71 through 2018-19* (Table 322.10) [Data set]. https://nces.ed.gov/programs/digest/d20/tables/dt20_322.10.asp

Obama, B. (2014, January 30). *Remarks by the president on opportunity for all and skills for America's workers.* The White House. https://obamawhitehouse.archives.gov/the-press-office/2014/01/30/remarks-president-opportunity-all-and-skills-americas-workers

Smith College. (n.d.). *Courses of Study.* www.smith.edu/academics/courses-of-study

Townsley, E., Lierman, L., Watermill, J., & Rousseau, D. (2017). *The impact of undergraduate internships on post-graduate outcomes for the liberal arts.* NACE Center for Career Development and Talent Acquisition. www.naceweb.org/uploadedfiles/files/2017/publication/report/2017-nace-impact-of-internships-on-liberal-arts-report.pdf

Wellesley College. (2015, October 26). *Wellesley announces largest donation in college history.* www.wellesley.edu/news/2015/october/node/75326

Wellesley College. (2019, July 11). *Administrative organization.* www.wellesley.edu/sites/default/files/assets/departments/humanresources/files/current/org_chart_08042020.pdf

Wesleyan University. (2021). *Ideals into practice.* http://idealsintopractice.site.wesleyan.edu/

Whiting, K. (2020, October 21). *These are the top 10 job skills of tomorrow – and how long it takes to learn them.* World Economic Forum. www.weforum.org/agenda/2020/10/top-10-work-skills-of-tomorrow-how-long-it-takes-to-learn-them/

Williams College. (n.d.). *'68 Center for Career Exploration.* https://careers.williams.edu/

World Economic Forum. (2020, October). *The Future of Jobs Report 2020.* www3.weforum.org/docs/WEF_Future_of_Jobs_2020.pdf

Young, J. R. (2016, October 23). *Reinventing the career center.* The Chronicle of Higher Education. www.chronicle.com/article/reinventing-the-career-center/?cid2=gen_login_refresh&cid=gen_sign_in

15
The Service-Learning Collaboratory: Career Education Beyond Co-op

Michael J. Sharp and Erik Alanson

The world was changing rapidly before the global pandemic of 2020, and the sectors of experiential learning and career education were changing along with it. Most often, these changes proceeded with gradual, almost unnoticeable adjustments and readjustments. At times, however, rapid changes were experienced as a repeated series of fits and starts. The pandemic punctuated change and, in some ways, even sharpened it. While the pandemic era has been extraordinarily challenging, we can all point to examples of "Covid-19 silver linings" that have potentially improved the field of career education. Field practitioners were all required to rethink their practice, interrogate why we do it, and explore new ways to conduct business as (un) usual, and many of these most innovative changes will persist post-pandemic.

It could be said that the global pandemic provided much needed and even overdue opportunities to learn new things and ways of operating in higher education, particularly in the spaces of experiential learning and career education. In particular, the pandemic ushered in many facets of what could be considered an unexpectedly improved future for the field, and many colleges and universities have been leading that charge in new, interesting, intersectional, and forward-leaning ways. This chapter will highlight one way that the University of Cincinnati (hereafter, "UC") has grown a novel approach to experiential learning and career education through an academic, course-based program that focuses on *experimenting with collaboration*.

To best lay the groundwork for the iterative growth and current evolution of this experimental and collaborative academic program, we will first discuss the experiential learning and career education "umbrella" at UC. This collection of programs is charged with supporting the university's efforts to connect the entire campus to both the for-profit and not-for-profit community. After covering this breadth of experiential learning and career education umbrella housed in UC's Division of Experience-Based Learning and Career Education (hereafter, "ELCE"), we will discuss service-learning, particularly UC's approach to that work. We will then turn

DOI: 10.4324/9781003213000-20

to the ways that service-learning at UC (hereafter, "SL@UC") has been effectively leading and iteratively growing what has become one of the most innovative,
adaptive, and unique learning and career education courses on campus – the *Service-
Learning Collaboratory.*

Historical Co-op and the Experiential Learning Umbrella at UC

UC is widely credited with the founding of the first cooperative education program
in the world, dating back to 1906 (Reilly, 2006). Dean Herman Schneider of UC's
College of Engineering pioneered the idea when he decided to pilot a radical
learn and work model of education. At the time, the model was widely criticized,
as it was thought that higher education should focus solely on scholarship and
academic endeavors. Yet, despite the criticism, Schneider forged ahead with
the cooperative education model, combining traditional academics with on-site
employment.

The model proved to be more than successful. Word of the learn and work model
began spreading across the United States and eventually across the globe. Other
higher education institutions began recreating what was, at the time, called the
"Cincinnati Plan." Students began flocking to UC's engineering programs due to
the value they saw in the combination of traditional classroom learning experiences
with on-site job training (Reilly, 2006).

Since the time of Herman Schneider's "co-op experiment," UC has been
leading the world in experiential learning and career education. The unit that
supports that global leadership, ELCE, has evolved and expanded their experiential learning and career education portfolio to include many eclectic types of
programs, courses, experiences, and development opportunities for the entire
university community. At the core of ELCE's mission is maintaining exemplary
environments for faculty and students to learn while doing, and the cornerstone
of the collective work is demonstrating excellence in both undergraduate and
graduate student education.

The Pandemic Sophisticates Co-op

When the Covid-19 pandemic hit the mainland United States during the early
spring of 2020, higher education was drastically disrupted. Experiential education
was flipped upside down. Students were no longer permitted to work on-site within
many organizations; massive layoffs and furloughs occurred, thereby limiting student
options for gaining employment experience; and many long-standing employer-part-
ners went out of business. The impact of this pandemic was the single greatest hurdle
to the long-standing co-op program since the Great Depression.

During the Covid-19 pandemic in 2020, UC's cooperative education program began the process of reevaluating primary modes of co-op to consider other alternative models, such as remote employment, "gig" work, and digital upskilling experiences. Through this re-evaluation process, it was discovered that the greater flexibility in cooperative education options could serve to better optimize student learning to meet student-driven learning outcomes. This paradigmatic shift was in direct opposition to the previous conception of institution-driven learning outcomes exclusively. When the institution began embracing new models of experiential learning, it began empowering students to become significant drivers in their education. This mode of student empowerment in the determination of significant learning outcomes is consistent with constructivist perspectives relating to transformational experiential education (Ruggiero & Boehm, 2016; Briant & Crowther, 2020). Students were able to choose from a menu of experiential learning opportunities that best met professional ambitions and goals.

The rapid shift to digital learning during the pandemic forced experiential education programs to re-envision how they deliver traditional work-based learning opportunities to students (Alanson et al., 2020). Up until 2020, digital work-based learning was a nonexistent model in UC's co-op portfolio. The idea that students would be employees of an organization from a remote location was considered a quality control liability. However, when the world was forced to pivot entirely to remote work, UC was left with the choice to maintain the traditional in-person work requirement or reinvent what it meant to be a co-op student by considering positional opportunities in fully remote environments.

Fortunately, UC chose the latter and opted to create professional pathways for students in fully remote spaces. Those co-op positions in the computing and technology industry sectors were most receptive to the remote work shift. Students began learning how to meet positional responsibilities from remote locations by leveraging tools such as virtual communication platforms, social media, virtual machines, and cloud-hosted content management systems. Once the computing and technology industry embraced digital co-op experiences, other industries followed suit by discovering new ways for students to contribute value to organizations without the physical on-site requirement.

Fast forward 16 months and students have worked in fully remote capacities in every mandatory co-op major offered at the university. Further, new experiential learning programs such as virtual apprenticeships, upskilling and reskilling opportunities, and gig work experiences became prevalent. In fact, UC has amassed over 100 engineering and IT students working in non-traditional cooperative education experiences each semester since the pandemic's inception (University of Cincinnati, 2021). The world of work changed drastically, and UC leaned into its culture of innovation to embrace new forms of experiential learning formerly not readily available to students and industry.

Co-op 2.0

Despite the historical success of UC being recognized globally as the *Co-op University*, the traditional mandatory co-op programs have historically represented only a few university colleges. In fact, most of our colleges do not provide required co-op experiences, which leaves many of our students thirsty for paid, on-site opportunities. This is particularly true for those students who have been historically underserved. As an answer to this issue, UC's senior leadership launched Co-op 2.0 in 2019:

> Co-op 2.0 builds on UC's historic co-op experience in DAAP, Engineering, IT, and Business to include on-campus and part-time co-op experiences. Now, all UC students can receive supervised, major-related, compensated work experiences including those who must maintain part-time jobs, those who take courses while working to stay on track academically, and those who have had little to no professional preparation or work experience prior to starting at UC.
> (www.uc.edu/about/strategic-direction/innovation-agenda/co-op-2.html)

This approach – providing paid experiential learning and career preparation to all UC students – very much fits the culture of the university as well as the history of the city. UC is an urban-serving institution of higher education in Ohio, and we recognize that learning from experience is a mechanism by which humans construct knowledge from everyday experience. Further, we believe that experiential learning is an intentional and complex learning and pedagogical framework (Kolb, 2014) that is well suited to the character, structure, and philosophy of our institution. We work hard to support our faculty and staff to meet the educational and developmental needs of our students, which consequently provides much-needed labor market development efforts within our community's workforce.

Since its inception, Co-op 2.0 has taken on many different models, often flexing to meet the demands of changing industries and student populations. Where Schneider's first model involved alternating weeks of full-time employment and full-time classes, more current Co-op 2.0 models typically provide much more flexibility. While the traditional model of co-op utilized by UC focused on a full-time employment experience over the course of a 15-to-16-week academic semester, the changing landscape of industry, and the evolving campus response to the changing industry, has been answered by UC through the Co-op 2.0 approach.

It should be noted that students in mandatory co-op programs still complete alternating term cycles of classes followed by co-op for up to five years in bachelor's-level programs. Although the full-time model is the university's standard, newer models have been adopted by academic programs desiring to support different student needs. For instance, UC's School of Information Technology embraced a part-time co-op model (i.e., parallel co-op) to create flexible co-op pathways for nontraditional and underrepresented student populations. This parallel co-op model permits some students to engage in part-time employment while taking up to a full-time academic course load. Participating students are provided with consistent work-integrated learning on an ongoing basis and can potentially graduate up to a year earlier than students in the traditional full-time co-op model. Now that we have shared a short history of UC's evolving approach to Co-op, it is time to focus on one of UC's sister experiential learning programs – Service-Learning.

Service-Learning

Some trace the connection of *service* and *learning* to Dewey (1902), whose work for both education and democracy laid the foundation for rebuilding the connections between school and community. Dewey's classic works (1916, 1938) provide the intellectual underpinnings critical to service-learning, shifting responsibility to the educator to provide experiences that prompt meaningful learning. Ehrlich and Jacoby (1996) point to Dewey in writing that service-learning is the various pedagogies that link *community service* and *academic study* such that each strengthens the other. Ehrlich writes:

> The basic theory of service-learning is ... the interaction of knowledge and skills with experience as the key to learning. Students learn best not by reading the Great Books in a closed room but by opening the doors and windows of experience. Learning starts with a problem and continues with the application of increasingly complex ideas and increasingly sophisticated skills to increasingly complicated problems.
>
> (Ehrlich & Jacoby, 1996, p. xi)

In 1969, the Southern Regional Education Board (1973) coined the term service-learning to describe "programs [that] emphasize the accomplishment of tasks which meet human needs in combination with conscious educational growth" (p. 4). Since that time, the term has taken on many new and expanded meanings. Yet most agree that service-learning is a form of experiential education in which students are immersed in a course-related service activity and then required to reflect on that experience.

Sigmon (1994) writes that students and community partners should be considered both *teachers* and *learners* when entering the service-learning *relationship*, with the goal of leveraging the dynamism between the campus and the community. Driscoll et al. (1996) add that students and community should both be made to understand the connection between the student learning objectives for the course and the service being provided to the community. Jacoby (1996) goes further, arguing that reflection and reciprocity must take place for authentic service-learning to occur.

The literature informs us that applying course concepts to serve the needs of the community works to enhance classroom teaching and learning. Service-learning opportunities allow students to help solve local, national, and global problems by reflectively applying what they are learning in the classroom to their lived, service-oriented experiences. Service-learning expands learning opportunities for students by expanding the place where learning happens. Through coordinated reflective activities, students reflect on issues in ways that allow them to apply their skills to the community, transforming them from passive absorbers of information into active learners.

Service-Learning Impact for Students

Much research has shown that service-learning has a positive effect on students' personal development, such as their sense of personal efficacy, personal identity, spiritual growth, and moral development (Eyler & Giles, 1999). Service-learning has also been shown to have a positive effect on leadership and communication skills and to improve students' ability to work well with others (Vogelgesang & Astin, 2000). The impact of service-learning on students' cognitive moral development is mixed, yet some studies do find that service-learning contributes to a student's moral development (Boss, 1994).

In addition to research that illustrates many personal outcomes for service-learning students, there is also a large amount of research that focuses on the social outcomes for students. For example, service-learning has a positive effect on reducing stereotypes and facilitating cultural and racial understanding (Boyle-Baise & Kilbane, 2000). Additionally, service-learning may support course goals of reducing racist thinking and facilitating cultural and racial understanding (Curran, 1999), and has a positive effect on sense of social responsibility and citizenship skills (Johnson & Bozeman, 1998). Other research demonstrates that service-learning positively influences students' life-long commitment to service (Nnakwe, 1999), and the desire to participate in service-learning while in college is associated with ongoing involvement in community service and civic leadership after graduation (Sax et al., 1999).

While the research clearly supports both personal and social outcomes for service-learning students, there is also an abundance of research that demonstrates impacts on academics. Faculty report that service-learning has a positive impact on students' academic learning (Knee, 1999), while students report that service-learning improves their ability to apply what they have learned in "the real world" (Foreman, 1996). Service-learning participation has been shown to have a positive impact on academic outcomes as demonstrated complexity of understanding, problem analysis, critical thinking, and cognitive development (Osborne et al., 1998).

Most notable for this book, research indicates that service-learning contributes to career development (Tartter, 1996) as well as to students' relationship with the university. For example, it is shown that students who engage in service-learning report stronger faculty relationships than those who are not involved in service-learning (Gray et al., 1998), and that service-learning improves student satisfaction with college (Berson & Younkin, 1998) and their likelihood of graduating (Roose et al., 1997).

The above review of student impact is just the tip of the iceberg. There is a growing body of case studies that describe service-learning processes and contexts for students, exploring themes such as citizenship development (Smith, 1994), dealing with diversity (Boyle-Baise & Kilbane, 2000), institutional support and cohesion (Skilton-Silvester & Erwin, 2000), transformations in orientations toward service and community (Wade & Yarborough, 1996), self-reflection and self-instructional processes (Ikeda, 2000), and self and identity (Wang, 2000).

Service-Learning Impact for University Communities

While there is an abundance of literature pertaining to the impact of service-learning on students, there is also substantial literature discussing the impact of service-learning on universities and communities. Faculty using service-learning convey satisfaction with the quality of teaching (Sellnow & Oster, 1997). They also report commitment to research and a growing integration of real-world theory application into their courses (Driscoll et al., 1996). With that said, it has been shown that lack of faculty rewards (Euster & Weinbach, 1994) and lack of resources (Robinson & Barnett, 1996) are barriers to faculty implementing service and service-learning partnerships in their courses.

Research has also been conducted to study how service-learning impacts universities generally. A growing number of colleges and universities report institutional commitment to service-learning curriculum (Scott & Ludwig, 1995). Other research supports the trend of a growing availability of service-learning programs at colleges and universities (Calleson et al., 1996). While few colleges and universities require service-learning in the academic core, this trend is beginning to shift as more report that service-learning positively impacts student retention (Roose et al., 1997), a metric that has become increasingly important to higher education in recent years.

Service-learning has also been shown to have positive impacts on communities as well. Research demonstrates community satisfaction with service-learning student participation (Ferrari & Worrall, 2000) as service-learning provides useful service in communities (Henderson & Brookhart, 1997). In addition, communities report enhanced campus–community relations through service-learning relationships (Driscoll et al., 1996). Having provided a brief review of literature pertaining to the impacts of service-learning, we will now turn to the Cincinnati brand of the curricular approach to connecting the campus to the community.

Service-Learning at the University of Cincinnati (SL@UC)

UC's service-learning program (SL@UC) works to increase the adaptation of innovative approaches that connect student learning to the evolving needs of the workforce and community. Supporting over 340 for-credit class sections per year, representing every undergraduate college at the university, SL@UC course-work represents 47 different academic subjects that are taught by over 130 faculty members. UC boasts one of the largest service-learning programs in the world, providing over 5,000 students with curricular-based service-oriented opportunities to apply what they are learning in the classroom to the betterment of the community (www.uc.edu/content/dam/refresh/experiencebasedlearning-62/docs/annual-report/ELCE-2019-Annual-Report.pdf).

UC defines service-learning as

> a specially designed learning experience in which students combine reflection with structured participation in community-based projects to achieve specified learning outcomes as part of an academic course and/or program requirement. By participating in Campus-Community partnerships at the local, national, or international level, students gain a richer mastery of course content, enhance their sense of civic responsibility, and ultimately develop a more integrated approach to understanding the relationship between theory, practice, ideas, values, and community.
>
> (www.uc.edu/campus-life/careereducation/get-experience/service-learning.html)

Some of these underpinnings of SL@UC include student involvement in the construction of learning objectives, collaborative learning rather than learning done in isolation, connecting what is being learned with personal experience, a focus on not just intellectual development, but social development as well, and the ever-present valuing of actions directed toward the welfare of others.

Service-Learning Collaboratory

First in 2005 and later in 2017, Sharp (2005, 2017) wrote about the power of deconstructing silos, intentionally blurring the boundaries that exist between the campus and the community, between the teacher and the learner, and between the researcher and the *researched*. Several years later and having taken inspiration from Fine's (1994) writing about *working the hyphens*, the Service-Learning Collaboratory (hereafter "S-L Collaboratory") approach to teaching and learning was born. The S-L Collaboratory is the capstone-level course that intentionally works the hyphens between the campus and the community, between the teacher and the learner, and between the several types of experiential learning approaches available at UC.

The goal of S-L Collaboratory is to provide students with the opportunity to explore a community need through a transdisciplinary team charged with completing a specific project for an external educational partner. These experiences span a variety of industries/disciplines and always include a service-learning focus. This course intentionally disrupts the boundaries between teachers, learners, and communities, and attempts to dissolve the dichotomy between for-profit and not-for-profit organizing.

The "Collaboration Laboratory" was the result of not-for-profit and service-learning stakeholders (e.g., teachers, learners, and community members) experimenting with different elements of collaboration. The primary undergirding principal of the S-L Collaboratory model is that participants are actively and organically molding the class while the class is molding the participants. Like what occurs in the for-profit sectors, wherein real-time, iterative adjustments are made to an evolving project, the S-L Collaboratory facilitates the same real-time and organic adjustments to be made during the class with feedback from both the campus and community. While collaboration is the hallmark of SL@UC, the S-L Collaboratory opened up new opportunities for "trying out" experimental approaches to connecting the campus to the community.

We find that the S-L Collaboratory is teaching us as much about ourselves as it is teaching us about the work, which we consider to be a strange loop of experimenting with collaboration. We – students, faculty, and industry partners – inform the work, while the work itself in a reciprocal way informs us. The identity of the work narrates the identity of the participants (faculty, students, educational partners) as the identity of the participants narrates the work. Being comfortable in the strange loop of this interchange has been particularly useful for understanding the motivations underlying the ever-present and constantly shifting intersections of *teaching and learning, theory, and practice,* and *being and doing.*

As part of the S-L Collaboratory, teachers, learners, and community members work together to accomplish several goals, and these goals are always accomplished collaboratively. Participants demonstrate the ability to work collaboratively with a diverse, interdisciplinary team to successfully complete a project with tangible outcomes for a community organization. We gain an understanding of various processes associated with delivering high-quality deliverables to external clients within a set timeframe (such processes may include but are not limited to market research and analysis, product design, campaign management, budget utilization, brand identity development, and technology development). All participants work collectively to determine specific target demographics for special projects and demonstrate the ability to determine best practices for roll-out and implementation of deliverables to target audiences. Faculty, students, and educational partners work together to demonstrate the ability to clearly communicate ideas, designs, and plans to internal and external clients and apply discipline-specific knowledge in a diverse group setting. Stakeholders demonstrate the ability to collectively complete a multi-faceted project by effectively delegating tasks to best utilize the strengths of the team members and other resources; we demonstrate the ability to receive and respond to feedback from team members and clients; and perhaps most importantly to the course, we collaboratively learn to apply a thorough understanding of social justice and servant leadership.

Approach to Pedagogy through Theory

The S-L Collaboratory is taught through a variety of constructivist teaching methods, including group discussions/presentations, collaborative learning, experiential application, and often with methodologies of the *flipped classroom*. Very little material is delivered through didactic lecture because it is expected that most of the learning in this class occurs through interacting with peers, instructors, clients, and expert guests. Much of the class is studio-based, often with the added opportunity to learn via electronic communication and site visits.

Several theoretical models play a vital role in the structure and pedagogy informing the S-L Collaboratory. *Constructivism* sets a primary pedagogical structure for the S-L Collaboratory model. This theory posits that learners actively construct knowledge together by making meaning of content and experiences. Further, this theory emphasizes learning over performance and situates learners in environments, scaffolded by *knowledgeable others* (Vygotsky, 1978, 1980).

Popular Education is used to classify a wide array of educational endeavors and has been a strong tradition in Latin America since the end of the first half of the 20th century. Generally, one can say that popular education rejects the notion of education as transmission or banking education. Rather, it stresses a dialogical model between educator and educated. This model is explored in detail in the works of one of the foremost popular educators, Paulo Freire (Freire, 1973).

Structuration Theory is a social theory of the creation and reproduction of social systems that is based in the analysis of both structure and agents without giving primacy to either. Further, in structuration theory, neither micro nor macro-focused analysis alone are sufficient. The theory was proposed by sociologist Anthony Giddens (1984), most significantly in *The Constitution of Society*, which examines phenomenology, hermeneutics, and social practices at the inseparable intersection of structures and agents. *Collective Impact* is a framework to tackle deeply entrenched and complex social problems. It is an innovative and structured approach to making collaboration work across government, business, philanthropy, not-for-profit organizations, and citizens to achieve significant and lasting social change (Kania & Kramer, 2011).

Narrative Inquiry starts from the assumption that narrative is a basic human strategy for coming to terms with fundamental elements of our experience, such as time, process, and change, and it proceeds from this assumption to study the distinctive nature of narrative and its various structures, elements, uses, and effects (Connolly & Clandinin, 1988, 1990; Clandinin & Connolly, 2004).

Key Characteristics of S-L Collaboratory

This course is offered in the Division of Experience-Based Learning and Career Education (ELCE) and under the Service-Learning Academic Program (S-L discipline code), although it may be cross-listed in other academic units. This course is always co-facilitated by at least one ELCE faculty member or supported via consultation with an ELCE faculty member, along with at least one additional faculty member from another discipline. This course will always carry the Service-Learning "S" attribute and the UC Forward/Transformational "T" focus, although other attributes may be used, such as the International attribute ("I") and/or the Research attribute ("R"). The academic partner/client for this course will always be an organization from the not-for-profit sector and/or an organization with a cause-based mission in the for-profit sector. The academic partner/client is vetted by a committee composed of ELCE faculty members and members of UC's Service-Learning Steering Committee. This course is free for partners, meaning sponsoring this course is not a requirement for participation.

Instructional *content* in the S-L Collaboratory introduces students to research problems and community partnerships that address a significant need in the community, region, country, or the world. The course prepares students for service by studying theories and gaining academic knowledge relevant to the problem. Students are prepared for service by orienting them to the problem and the context in which they will work. Using common readings and discussion prompts to connect academic learning to service, vocation, leadership, civic responsibility, and social justice is a key part of the course content.

Service in the S-L Collaboratory provides opportunities for students to express value commitments and disciplinary knowledge in an authentic, real-life setting. The course enables students to personally connect with people involved with the issue to which the service is directed. Ideally, this will include a relationship with persons or communities directly impacted by the issue. The S-L Collaboratory establishes long-term commitments to the communities and issues that are to be addressed, which includes sufficient contact time to allow students to build relationships with people facing the issue and to develop a deep understanding of those people and their communities.

Structured *reflection* in the S-L Collaboratory includes activities completed by students, faculty, and educational partners from multiple disciplines, perspectives, and walks of life. The course works collaboratively to explore the theories, structures, and assumptions of students' academic disciplines in the context of the collaborative experience. The S-L Collaboratory helps students to link their values and academic learning to other parts of the curriculum and co-curriculum, including helping them to evaluate their personal values and commitments pre- and post-graduation. This includes helping students to develop a sense of vocation and to think about integrating service with a future occupation or career path.

The Pandemic Sophisticates the S-L Collaboratory

In March of 2020, UC was forced to move to all-remote instruction. This occurred during a semester when "Digital Innovation" was the theme of the S-L Collaboratory course, which was an irony not altogether lost on the course facilitators, students, or educational partners. In hindsight, however, we are very grateful for this disruption as we were able to rethink what we do, interrogate why we do it, and explore new ways to conduct business as (un)usual. Until this time of disruption, the S-L Collaboratory had gradually become more sophisticated over time, adding the Research ("R" attribute) to the course, for example, but being forced to move to an all-virtual space accelerated and sharpened this sophistication.

We completed the course that semester (spring of 2020), having started as a typical, face-to-face course that met three times per week, and then we had some time to rethink what we would do for the following semester. At this time, we had already established a new partnership with a new organizational partner for the class – Village Life Outreach Program – but we had to now plan for that course to be offered virtually. Of note here is the fact that Village Life is a Cincinnati organization that provides direct outreach to villagers in Tanzania. The course facilitators worked with the representatives of Village Life to create a course that would meet virtually three times per week via the Microsoft Teams platform, and the results were better than we could have imagined. Because the pandemic forced everyone in higher education to learn how to use platforms like Teams, new ways of interaction and novel ways to connect the campus to the community emerged. Specific to the S-L Collaboratory with Village Life, we were able to add several new sophistications to the course, including real-time interactions with villagers in Tanzania. Students were able to interact virtually with Village Life board members and were provided streamed (in real time) opportunities to better learn how to serve this organization and the people in Tanzania.

If not for the global pandemic, these sophistications would not have been realized. Because these new lines of communication were now open, however, new modes of collaborative experimentation were discovered. We are happy to report, in fact, that Village Life was able to support two students from Tanzania to enroll in courses at UC. These students have since moved to Cincinnati and are looking forward to attending face-to-face courses at UC. While these two students from Tanzania are on location in Cincinnati, they will serve as peer advisors to next semester's S-L Collaboratory with Village Life. Because of the pandemic, the S-L Co-op program not only took flight but grew exponentially. Several students from the online S-L Collaboratory were hired by Village Life to continue the work started in the class. Moving forward, Village Life will also be hiring S-L Co-op students to travel to Tanzania, which moves us to the final sophistication realized.

Starting the fall 2021 semester, which will be offered face-to-face, we will be adding the International "I" attribute to the course. The reason for this addition is that we plan to lead a cohort of students to travel to Tanzania at the culmination of the course. Students will be paid for their work while in-country through the S-L Co-op program, which will provide these students with real dollars ($1,000 for an 80-hour project), and which will also provide Village Life with support that was not thought possible prior to the pandemic. This value-add – for students, for faculty, and for the educational partner – was the result of experimenting with new forms of collaboration, very befitting the S-L Collaboratory model.

Recommendations for Practice

We will now conclude this chapter by sharing with the reader practical applications that could be useful for the career educators' respective work.

- Academic curricula that employ a constructivist pedagogical approach can be daunting for faculty to take on because the approach inherently requires a relinquishment of traditional classroom authority. However, if faculty can lean into dissonance experienced by this renunciation of power by developing courses that invite students and community partners to be active participants in the learning process, the collective experience can be transformational for all constituents involved.
- The world of work post-Covid-19 requires employment candidates to provide evidence of their work experiences and impacts. Service-learning courses provide a medium for students to engage in real-world experiential learning that showcases problem-solving competencies, critical thinking, communication, and teamwork. Well-structured service-learning curricula can be akin to industry experience and give students an advantage when being considered for future employment.
- Educators must be agile in practice to flex to the ever-changing expectations of the higher education ecosystem. The introduction of new student learning outcomes, new degree offerings, new modes of content delivery, and new modes of teaching are as inevitable as the rising sun. Rather than being resistant to these changes, embrace the evolution of this environment and see it as an opportunity to learn.

References

Alanson, E. R., Alanson, E. M., Arthur, B., Burdette, A., Cooper, C., & Sharp, M. (2020). Re-envisioning work-integrated learning during a pandemic: Cincinnati's Experiential Explorations Program. *International Journal of Work-Integrated Learning, 21*(5), 505–519.

Berson, J. S., & Younkin, W. F. (1998). Doing well by doing good: A study of the effects of a service-learning experience on student success. *Higher Education*. Paper 184. http://digitalcommons.unomaha.edu/slcehighered/184

Boss, J. A. (1994). The effect of community service work on the moral development of college ethics students. *Journal of Moral Education*, 23(2), 183–198.

Boyle-Baise, M., & Kilbane, J. (2000). What really happens? A look inside service-learning for multicultural teacher education. *Michigan Journal of Community Service Learning*, 7(1), 54–64.

Briant, S., & Crowther, P. (2020). Reimagining internships through online experiences: Multi-disciplinary engagement for creative industries students. *International Journal of Work-Integrated Learning*, 21(5), 617–628.

Calleson, D. C., Parker, L. G., & Serow, R. C. (1996). Service-learning in one state: Results of the North Carolina service-learning inventory. *NSEE Quarterly*, 8.

Clandinin, D. J., & Connelly, F. M. (2004). *Narrative inquiry: Experience and story in qualitative research*. John Wiley & Sons.

Connelly, F. M., & Clandinin, D. J. (1988). *Teachers as curriculum planners: Narratives of experience*. Teachers College Press.

Connelly, F. M., & Clandinin, D. J. (1990). Stories of experience and narrative inquiry. *Educational Researcher*, 19(5), 2–14. https://doi.org/10.3102/0013189X019005002

Curran, J. M. (1999). *College students' attitudes towards mental retardation: A pilot study.* Presentation at the Biennial Meeting of the Society for Research in Child Development, Albuquerque, NM, United States.

Dewey, J. (1902). The school as social center. *The Elementary School Teacher*, 3(2), 73–86.

Dewey, J. (1916). *Democracy and education*. Project Gutenberg.

Dewey, J. (1938). *Experience and education*. Macmillan.

Driscoll, A., Holland, B., Gelmon, S., & Kerrigan, S. (1996). An assessment model for service-learning: Comprehensive case studies of impact on faculty, students, community, and institutions. *Michigan Journal of Community Service Learning*, 3, 66–71.

Ehrlich, T., & Jacoby, B. (1996). *Service-learning in higher education: Concepts and practices*. Jossey-Bass.

Euster, G. L., & Weinbach, R. W. (1994). Faculty rewards for community service activities: An update. *Journal of Social Work Education*, 30(3), 317–324. https://doi.org/10.1080/10437797.1994.10672242

Eyler, J., & Giles Jr., D. E. (1999). *Where's the learning in service-learning?*. Jossey-Bass.

Ferrari, J. R., & Worrall, L. (2000). Assessments by community agencies: How "the other side" sees service-learning. *Michigan Journal of Community Service Learning*, 7, 35–40. http://hdl.handle.net/2027/spo.3239521.0007.104

Fine, M. (1994). *Working the hyphens: Reinventing self and other in qualitative research*. SAGE.

Foreman, C. W. (1996). *Service-learning in the small group communication class*. Presentation at the Speech Communication Association, San Diego, CA, United States.

Freire, P. (1973). *Education for critical consciousness*. Seabury Press.

Giddens, A. (1984). *The constitution of society*. Polity Press.

Gray, M. J., Ondaatje, E. H., Fricker, R. D., Geschwind, S., Goldman, C. A., Kaganoff, T., Robyn, A., Sundt, M., Vogelgesang, L., & Klein, S. P. (1998). *Coupling service and learning in higher education: The final report of the evaluation of the Learn and Serve America, higher education program.* The RAND Corporation.

Henderson, J. E., & Brookhart, S. M. (1997). *Service-learning for aspiring school leaders: An exploratory study.* Presentation at the Annual Meeting of the American Educational Research Association, Chicago, IL, United States.

Ikeda, E. K. (2000). *How reflection enhances learning in service-learning courses.* Presentation at the Annual Meeting of the American Educational Research Association, New Orleans, LA, United States.

Jacoby, B. (1996). Service-learning in today's higher education. In B. Jacoby & Associates (Eds.), *Service-learning in higher education: Concepts and practices* (pp. 3–25). Jossey-Bass.

Johnson, S. D., & Bozeman, M. (1998, April 2–5). *Service learning and the development of social responsibility* [Paper presentation]. 66th Annual Convention of the Central States Communication Association, Chicago, IL, United States. https://files.eric.ed.gov/fulltext/ED425483.pdf

Kania, J., & Kramer, M. (2011). Collective impact. *Stanford Social Innovation Review,* Winter 2011. https://senate.humboldt.edu/sites/default/files/senate/Chair%20Written%20Report%201-23-2018.pdf

Knee, R. T. (1999). *Service-learning in social work education: Building democracy through informed citizenship.* University of Denver.

Kolb, D. A. (2014). *Experiential learning: Experience as the source of learning and development.* FT Press.

Nnakwe, N. E. (1999). Implementation and impact of college community service and its effect on the social responsibility of undergraduate students. *Journal of Family and Consumer Sciences, 91*(2), 57–61.

Osborne, R. E., Hammerich, S., & Hensley, C. (1998). Student effects of service-learning: Tracking change across a semester. *Michigan Journal of Community Service Learning, 5,* 5–13. http://hdl.handle.net/2027/spo.3239521.0005.101

Reilly, M. B. (2006). *The ivory tower and the smokestack: 100 years of cooperative education at the University of Cincinnati.* Emmis Books.

Robinson, G., & Barnett, L. (1996). *Service learning and community colleges: Where we are.* AACC Survey Report. American Association of Community Colleges.

Roose, D., Daphne, J., Miller, A. G., Norris, W., Peacock, R., White, C., & White, G. (1997). *Black student retention study: Oberlin College.* Oberlin College.

Ruggiero, D., & Boehm, J. (2016). Design and development of a learning design virtual internship program. *International Review of Research in Open and Distributed Learning, 17*(4), 105–120.

Sax, L. J., Astin, A. W., & Avalos, J. (1999). Long-term effects of volunteerism during the undergraduate years. *The Review of Higher Education, 22*(2), 187–202.

Scott, J. A., & Ludwig, M. (1995). Community service at urban public institutions: A report on conditions and activities. *Metropolitan Universities*, 6(3), 29–44.

Sellnow, T. L., & Oster, L. K. (1997). The frequency, form, and perceived benefits of service-learning in speech communication departments. *Journal of the Association for Communication Administration*, 3, 190–197.

Sharp, M. (2005). *Sensemaking in Cincinnati: Sharing stories of racial discord* [Unpublished master's thesis]. University of Cincinnati.

Sharp, M. (2017). *Critical curriculum and just community: Making sense of service learning in Cincinnati* [Unpublished doctoral dissertation]. University of Cincinnati.

Sigmon, R. L. (1994). *Serving to learn, learning to serve. Linking service with learning* [Report]. Council of Independent Colleges.

Skilton-Silvester, E., & Erwin, E. K. (2000). Creating reciprocal learning relationships across socially constructed borders. *Michigan Journal of Community Service Learning*, 7, 65– 75. http://hdl.handle.net/2027/spo.3239521.0007.108

Smith, L. T. (1999). *Decolonizing methodologies: Research and indigenous peoples*. Zed.

Southern Regional Education Board. (1973). *Service-learning in the south: Higher education and public service 1967-1972* [Report]. ERIC Clearinghouse.

Tartter, V. C. (1996). *City College report to FIPSE*. City College Research Foundation.

University of Cincinnati. (2021, September). *Professional assessment and learning*. www.uc.edu/pal

Vogelgesang, L. J., & Astin, A. W. (2000). Comparing the effects of community service and service-learning. *Michigan Journal of Community Service Learning*, 7(1), 25–34. http://hdl.handle.net/2027/spo.3239521.0007.103

Vygotsky, L. S. (1980). *Mind in society: The development of higher psychological processes*. Harvard University Press.

Wade, R. C., & Yarborough, D. B. (1997). Community service-learning in student teaching: Toward the development of an active citizenry. *Michigan Journal of Community Service Learning*, 4, 42–55. http://hdl.handle.net/2027/spo.3239521.0004.105

Wang, W. (2000). *Service learning: Is it good for you?* Presentation at the Annual Meeting of the American Educational Research Association Conference, New Orleans, LA, United States.

16

An Integrative Pathway for Success: Undergraduate Research, Access, and Mentorship in STEM

Maya Williams, Nasitta Keita,
and Lisa Y. Flores

Advances in science, technology, engineering, and mathematics (STEM) fields touch *all* aspects of society. It is hard to imagine any facet of our daily lives that has not been improved because of STEM innovations. According to the U.S. Bureau of Labor Statistics (2021a), there are 100 occupational titles that are designated as STEM jobs, which are defined as positions that involve science or technological knowledge. The majority of STEM occupations require post-secondary education and encompass domains that are typically linked to STEM, such as life and physical sciences, computer and information technology, engineering, and mathematical occupations. However, STEM also extends to social sciences, architecture, and health domains. These occupations are categorized into five groups based on the typical job tasks: (a) research, development, design, or practitioner; (b) technologist and technician; (c) post-secondary teaching; (d) managerial; and (e) sales. Thus, STEM occupations are not limited to applied positions, but involve other positions in manufacturing, sales, and higher education that demand scientific or technical expertise.

STEM careers are vital to the economy and to a country's growth and competitiveness on the global market. Within the U.S., STEM occupations are projected to grow by 8% between 2019 and 2029 (U.S. Bureau of Labor Statistics, 2021b). STEM positions will significantly outpace the growth of all occupations (3.7%) and non-STEM occupations (3.4%) in coming years. In addition to their growth in the labor market, STEM occupations are among the highest-paying jobs, with median annual wages that are more than double the rate for non-STEM occupations (U.S. Bureau of Labor Statistics, 2021b).

DOI: 10.4324/9781003213000-21

Higher education within the U.S. serves several functions, including developing individual and intellectual capitals that are applied in work activities and that drive the U.S. economy (Ford, 2017). U.S. colleges and universities play a vital role in training the future STEM workforce in both the U.S. and globally. According to the National Science Board (2019a), the number and percentage of science and engineering associate, bachelor's, master's, and doctoral degrees awarded to students has grown since 2000. However, significant gender, racial, and gender X racial intersectional gaps exist in STEM degree attainment. Of the STEM degrees awarded in 2018, women earned about half of bachelor's degrees, 44.7% of master's degrees, and 41.2% of doctoral degrees (National Center for Science and Engineering Statistics [NCSES], 2021). The proportion of degrees awarded to women in STEM fields varies widely across specific disciplines. For example, women received the majority of bachelor's degrees awarded in 2017 in psychology (78.1%) and biological sciences (61.5%), but they were significantly underrepresented among engineering (21.5%) and computer science (19.1%) bachelor's degree recipients (National Science Board, 2019a). Racial disparities in STEM degree attainment are even more stark. Black, Latinx, and Native American students received only 24% of bachelor's degrees, 22.1% of master's degrees, and 13.6% of doctoral degrees in 2018 (NCSES, 2021). Psychology, social sciences, and biological sciences were the STEM fields with the highest representation of bachelor's degrees awarded to Latinx and Black students (18.1%, 17.3%, and 13%, respectively). According to the NCSES (2021), women of color earned a higher share of STEM associate, bachelor's, master's, and doctoral degrees than men of color, with the exception of engineering fields, where men of color outpaced women of color in receiving engineering degrees at all levels. Degrees in psychology, social sciences, and biological and agricultural sciences appear to be driving this disparity, as Black women, Latinas, and Native American women earned more degrees in these STEM fields than their male counterparts (NCSES, 2021).

These educational disparities in STEM are reflected in the STEM workforce, with women comprising 29% of the STEM labor force and, collectively, Latinx and Black individuals representing 13.1% of the STEM labor force (National Science Board, 2019b). Salaries earned by women in STEM fields are significantly lower than their male counterparts ($60,000 vs. $90,000), and between Latinx and Black STEM workers when compared to their White peers ($65,000 and $56,000 vs. $80,000; National Science Board, 2019b). University and college environments are important contexts where STEM educational and occupational interventions are needed to address the persistent gender and racial/ethnic gaps in STEM participation.

Barriers to STEM Access

Long-standing societal, systemic, and institutional barriers have resulted in disproportionate access to STEM training, education, and employment among women, indigenous individuals, people of color, individuals from poor and working-class backgrounds, and people with disabilities (American Association for University Women [AAUW], 2010, 2015). These barriers include cultural stereotypes, education, limited role models, and academic and workplace climate (AAUW, 2010, 2015; Fouad & Singh, 2011; McGillen et al., 2019). Stereotypes, particularly those related to the general academic abilities, science and math capabilities, and overall intellectual capacities of individuals from groups that are underrepresented in STEM, play a role in individual career decision-making and experiences in STEM education (e.g., McGee et al., 2017; Piatek-Jimenez et al., 2018) as well as the recruitment and selection of these individuals into STEM training and the STEM workforce (Eberhardt, 2019). Stereotypes feed into the implicit biases that inform behaviors and decisions. Early childhood, elementary, secondary, and post-secondary educational environments and experiences also contribute to limited opportunities for individuals from marginalized groups to participate in STEM occupations (Alexander & Hermann, 2016; Martin et al., 2016). This includes attending schools that are under-resourced and where advanced coursework in science and math is restricted. Cumulatively, these educational conditions create an educational gap that contributes to lower rates of high school graduation and lower academic achievement in science and math, both of which are critical filters for post-secondary educational opportunities in STEM. Environmental barriers, including the lack of role models from similar backgrounds and experiences with discrimination and harassment, also contribute to disparities in STEM participation and persistence (e.g., Byars-Winston et al., 2015; Estrada et al., 2011) as well as STEM science (e.g., Syed et al., 2018).

Limited role models and discrimination contribute to feelings of (or anticipation of) isolation and tokenism, lack of belonging, and lack of identification with the field that can dissuade individuals from underrepresented groups from pursuing or remaining in STEM occupations. Faculty advisors and research mentors from traditionally represented groups (i.e., white, men) in these environments may overlook or minimize the racialized or gendered experiences of students from underrepresented groups in STEM, which can lead to feelings of alienation and invisibility among these students (Womack et al., 2020). Academic programs and workplaces must critically assess how these environments uphold and reflect cultural values and practices that favor groups that are overrepresented in STEM fields, and implement changes in the environment that extend beyond increasing the numbers of diverse individuals in STEM fields, to transforming policies and workplace cultures that are universally welcoming and support the well-being of *all workers* (Byars-Winston, 2014; Carnes et al., 2012; Womack et al., 2020).

Overview of Chapter

Workforce development and the development of a diverse STEM workforce are key goals in the National Science Foundation's strategic plan (2018). In the remaining sections of this chapter, we highlight programs targeting access to STEM training among youth, adolescents, and young adults. We provide evidence to support the effectiveness of these programs, and summarize research on factors that influence participation, engagement, and persistence in STEM academic fields. Finally, we identify common educational and training components across STEM access programs. Given their underrepresentation in STEM fields, when available, we center research and programs that target diverse racial/ethnic students and women students. We conclude with recommendations for higher education professionals to enhance undergraduate students' research and mentorship in STEM and to broaden participation in STEM among students from underrepresented groups in STEM occupations.

STEM Career Development Programs

Technology is incorporated into virtually every domain of our lives – from social networking and the workforce, to the classroom and beyond. Given the prominence of technology in our lives today, and its role in the global economic market, initiatives aimed toward improving STEM education and strengthening the U.S.'s position as a leader in STEM fields are common (ex: National Science Foundation, 2020). Because STEM education is believed to serve as a mechanism to close inequity gaps that negatively impact women and racial/ethnic minorities, many of these programs are designed to target individuals from underrepresented groups in STEM fields (Fry et al., 2021). The following sections will detail youth, high school, pre-college summer, and college/university STEM initiatives.

Youth STEM Initiatives

Scholars have found that once children enter grade school, they begin to associate science with men. In particular, towards the end of their K-12 schooling, girls are three times more likely to draw a man rather than a woman when asked to depict a scientist (Miller et al., 2018). This reflects gender stereotypes regarding the interests and occupational aspirations girls are encouraged to have that pull them away from pursuing STEM. For racial and ethnic minority groups, particularly Black youth, believing that they can do well in STEM subjects does not always correlate with academic success in these courses (Seo et al., 2019). External factors such as low teacher expectations, receiving negative feedback, microaggressions, and other forms of discrimination in school can have a significant, negative impact on their achievement in STEM courses and future pursuit of STEM jobs (Eisenhart et al., 2015; Seo et al., 2019).

As such, STEM programming goals at the primary school level are to develop interests and increase exposure to STEM as youth begin to form their perceptions of who belongs in STEM careers (Valla & Williams, 2012). One component of youth STEM programs includes showcasing how STEM can be a part of the solution to real-world problems (Christensen et al., 2015). Since girls tend to be interested in topics and careers that center on helping others, it is especially important to integrate the positive impacts that STEM careers have on the world in STEM education and programs as a way to address gender disparities in STEM.

Bringing Up Girls in Science (BUGS) is an after-school program funded by the National Science Foundation that aims to increase girls' interest in STEM fields. BUGS is a space where elementary school girls learn about science by participating in laboratory experiments, and taking field trips where they learn what individuals who work in STEM do on a daily basis and the problems that scientists aim to solve (Tyler-Wood et al., 2011). BUGS participants also work closely with older female mentors, which provides them with a role model who may have similar identity-based experiences. Providing girls with role models who are women in STEM tends to raise girls' confidence in STEM (Albright et al., 2017; Dee, 2007). Upon completion of the BUGS program, participants had a greater awareness and confidence in their ability to succeed in STEM compared to girls who did not participate in BUGS (Tyler-Wood et al., 2011).

Similar findings have been found in STEM mentorship programs that target racial/ethnic minority youth and youth with multiple marginalized identities, as participating in STEM programs often provides youth of color with opportunities that were not previously available to them in typical academic contexts (Syed et al., 2012). For Youth of Color in particular, having STEM mentors who work within a social justice framework is important for empowering youth while increasing their social networking capital (Albright et al., 2017).

High School STEM Initiatives

While elementary school STEM education and programs focus on increasing exposure to STEM, high school initiatives are geared towards raising achievement in STEM courses, and translating an interest in STEM to a future post-secondary degree and later career in a STEM field (Valla & Williams et al., 2012). Inclusive STEM high schools (ISHS) is a new strategy that targets underrepresented groups in STEM. The mission of ISHS is to create a learning environment for underrepresented students (i.e. Students of Color, low-income, future first-generation college students) that showcases their ability to succeed in STEM when given the resources and support to do so (Lynch, 2015). There are four common components of ISHS: offering a rigorous STEM curriculum to students; supporting students; having teachers that are prepared to teach STEM courses; and a flexible administration that responds to the needs of their school community including students, students' families, and teachers alike (Lynch et al., 2018).

A rigorous STEM curriculum at an ISHS tends to be embedded into the curriculum and includes courses that are required to graduate. While traditional public schools often offer advanced STEM courses via advanced placement, students often have to receive access to enter these courses. Institutional discriminatory factors like academic tracking tend to leave students of color out of advanced placement courses; however, at ISHS, students that are traditionally tracked out of rigorous STEM classes are welcomed in (Lynch et al., 2018).

Students at ISHS often receive equitable support to ensure that they finish school and attend a post-secondary institution. This is critical as creating STEM initiatives for marginalized students without being attuned to structural barriers inhibiting their pursuit of STEM can recreate barriers. ISHS provides students support through advising, tutoring, and finding time to meet with students' parents outside of school when needed instead of pressuring families to engage with the school community during typical work/school hours (Kennedy & Odell, 2014; Lynch et al., 2018). These schools' ability to provide students with resources is connected to the relationship that the school's administration builds with the community, as these schools often are able to reach out and build connections with organizations that share a goal in supporting marginalized students.

The Texas Science, Technology, Engineering, and Mathematics initiative (T-STEM) is one example of an ISHS that took a proactive approach in supporting students who were labeled "at-risk" and their families by providing students tutoring, mentors, and career advising. The T-STEM program also includes community services, and provides the students' families with social services support in an attempt to decrease barriers that traditionally hinder students' success and interests in STEM (Kennedy & Odell, 2014). Evaluations of the T-STEM initiative found that students enrolled in the program were more likely to pass introductory mathematics and science courses compared to students who were not enrolled and that the program provided evidence of being an effective model for achievement and preparing students for college (Kennedy & Odell, 2014; Texas College and Career Readiness School Models, 2022).

The characteristics of programs like T-STEM and other ISHS highlight the importance of factors such as counseling, social engagement, parent involvement, and financial resources in helping minoritized students succeed in STEM education. Viewing these programs through a culturally relevant and systemic lens, students were able to receive *individual support* through advising, *communal support* via connecting STEM to community service, and *familial support* by providing families with resources so students were able to participate and receive support in applying to college.

Most inclusive STEM schools were not struggling prior to creating a curriculum that centers STEM and had the resources to make this change successfully (Lynch et al., 2018). However, schools that lack funding tend to be located in under-resourced neighborhoods with a majority of racial/ethnic minority students. This makes programs such as Upward Bound, which we will describe next, important as we continue to reconstruct and re-imagine STEM education at the secondary level within the U.S. education system.

Upward Bound Math and Science is a STEM initiative funded by the U.S. Department of Education that targets high school students who hold identities that are underrepresented in post-secondary institutions (U.S. Department of Education, 2020). There are three main goals of Upward Bound Math and Science: (1) to increase math and science skills; (2) to increase belief in succeeding in math and science; and (3) to increase interests in pursuing a STEM career. The program attempts to reach these goals by providing students career counseling/advising, summer programming, mentorship, tutoring, and cultural events. Students also receive college prep throughout their duration in Upward Bound Math and Science programming. A U.S. Department of Education (2007) overview of the outcomes of students enrolled in Upward Bound Math and Science programs found that Black and Latinx students had the largest increase in GPA, took more physics and chemistry courses, and were more likely to enroll in a post-secondary institution and major in math or science (for men in the group) compared to students who were not a part of the program.

Pre-College Programs

In an effort to increase recruitment and retention of students in STEM, particularly women and racial/ethnic minority groups, many colleges and universities offer pre-college STEM programs that are held over the summer to bridge the social and academic gap between high school and college. These summer "bridge" programs can be one to eight weeks long, are typically held on campus, and provide students with fundamental pre-college readiness, support services, and resources such as workshops on academic achievement, social activities, mentorship, and career planning (Ashley et al., 2017; Nostrand & Pollenz, 2017; Tomasko et al., 2016). Some programs may also include mandatory math and science courses or other supplemental necessities for success in STEM such as mock exams, mandatory office hours, and discussions with STEM faculty (Lisberg & Woods, 2018).

Research indicates that pre-college STEM programs that target engagement and degree completion among underrepresented groups also aid in increasing academic grades for STEM-related courses (Sickle et al., 2020). Among students who attend pre-college programs, underrepresented students pursuing a STEM degree traditionally have higher retention rates and higher rates of academic achievement in their courses, particularly math and science, compared to underrepresented students in STEM who do not attend these programs (Lisberg & Woods, 2018; Sickle et al., 2020). Furthermore, pre-college programs are associated with increased psychosocial mechanisms such as science identity, sense of belonging, and college readiness (Nostrand & Pollenz, 2017; Tomasko et al., 2006).

College STEM Initiatives

On the national level, there are several programs sponsored by the National Science Foundation or the National Institute of Health that provide funding to universities for the development and implementation of STEM scholarship programs. Specifically, programs that aim to increase graduation rates of historically underrepresented groups in the STEM field such as the National Science Foundation Scholarships in Science, Technology, Engineering, and Mathematics program (S-STEM) and the Louis Stokes Alliances for Minority Participation (LSAMP). Relatedly, programs such as the Alliances for Graduate Education and the Professoriate (AGEP) and the ADVANCE program provide support to institutions that encourage diversity within the STEM workforce (www.nsf.gov/funding/programs.jsp?org=HRD). There are also research experience programs such as the Ronald E. McNair Baccalaureate Program, a federal TRIO program, and Maximizing Access to Research Careers (MARC) to support underrepresented students who are interested in research and pursuing an advanced degree in STEM (www.nigms.nih.gov/training/Pages/High-School-and-Undergraduate-Programs.aspx; https://mcnairscholars.com) by linking them with faculty and engaging them in research labs during their undergraduate training.

For many women and racial/ethnic minority groups interested in STEM, the first few years of college are critical periods in predicting students' academic and career trajectory (Prescod et al., 2020). When understanding the factors that contribute to students' interest and achievement in STEM fields, it is important to consider the impact of post-secondary programs geared towards historically underrepresented minority groups in the STEM field (Ashely et al., 2017; Tomasko et al., 2016). These programs often provide support in the form of financial assistance, research opportunities, and career development guidance. Additionally, some universities offer learning communities in which STEM students not only live together in a residence hall, but also engage in social activities and have access to resources such as peer mentoring and community support (Dagley et al., 2016). The following sections will highlight the key components of post-secondary STEM programs and how they support the success of marginalized students in STEM.

Key Components in STEM College Programs

STEM programs at the college level are typically offered during the academic year and aim to support students throughout their first year and often beyond. One notable program, the Meyerhoff Scholars Program offered at the University of Maryland, Baltimore County, was originally created in 1988 to provide academic, social, and financial support to African American males interested in STEM (https://meyerhoff.umbc.edu). Presently, the program is offered to any STEM student; however, it overwhelmingly recruits and awards racial/ethnic minority students. The Meyerhoff Scholar Program provides students with support in many forms such as free tuition, academic advising, tutoring, undergraduate research opportunities, mentorship, and many others (Maton et al., 2000, 2016). Conversely, many universities have adopted an integrative and dynamic approach, commonly referred to as the Meyerhoff Model, as a way to increase diversity among students who graduate with a degree in the STEM field.

In addition to providing students with resources to support academic achievement (i.e., GPA, retention, and graduation), these programs provide psychosocial support, which is pivotal during the early stages of STEM college careers. Programs such as Meyerhoff Scholars provide necessary mentorship with peers and faculty that holds students accountable and to a higher standard than their peers who are not involved in these programs (Maton et al., 2000). This can help to decrease many of the negative stereotypes and threats to success for groups underrepresented in STEM. Specifically, these programs may decrease feelings of isolation and lack of belonging because they provide a built-in social support system. Additionally, supportive faculty and peer relations may decrease feelings of imposter syndrome and feelings of intimidation towards professors and courses as well as create a greater sense of belonging among students of color who attend historically White universities and institutions.

Learning communities are correlated with higher rates of retention for underrepresented students and higher degree completion in STEM for racial/ethnic minority students (Dagley et al., 2016). This may be due to the types of support students receive in this environment. Living with like-minded students may increase a sense of belonging and social support. Additionally, the academic support services available help students maintain grades and provide accountability. If students or faculty notice the student is falling behind, there are not only resources to help support the student but there are people to encourage those resources.

Overview of Research on Predictors of STEM Engagement

There are several factors that may impact levels of participation and engagement in STEM fields among diverse racial/ethnic students and women students. These may include internal factors such as self-efficacy and personal preferences as well as external factors such as access to STEM courses and classroom environment. This next section will highlight key academic and psychosocial factors that impact student engagement in STEM.

Academic Factors

Many first- and second-year students have to take and pass mandatory courses in mathematics and science as a requirement for their major. These classes are commonly known as "weed-out" courses as they are traditionally extremely challenging and are known for having low rates of passing. While these courses may help identify students who are seriously interested in the STEM field, they may further discourage or prevent women and racial/ethnic minority students from entering and/or persisting in the field. Relatedly, poor grades or a failure to pass a course may prevent a student from pursuing a degree in STEM due to incomplete course requirements.

There is a significant financial cost to persisting in the STEM field. Obtaining a college degree is expensive and STEM degrees are no exception. In addition to the substantial cost of college tuition and student fees, STEM students may have to pay for additional necessities such as protective wear for laboratory courses in addition to basic needs like food, clothes, etc. For many marginalized students, it may be challenging to pay for the cost of college tuition and the add-ons needed to be a STEM major. However, many pre-college and summer research programs cover the cost of room and board and provide students with a stipend for their time in the program (Lisberg & Woods, 2018). Similarly, many academic year programs provide financial assistance in the form of scholarships and stipends to help reduce the financial burden for underrepresented groups in STEM.

Another hindrance may be bias and racism in the class environment. Underrepresented students in STEM are exposed to serious racial and gender bias and discrimination, which may serve as a significant barrier (Charleston et al., 2015; Neumann et al., 2016; Robnet, 2016). Women, Black, and Latinx individuals are frequently stereotyped within the STEM field and portrayed as less competent or unintelligent (Moss-Racusin et al., 2012). STEM courses often lack diversity, which leads to classrooms with very few women and students of color. Relatedly, underrepresented students may feel alienated or ignored while trying to navigate their STEM degree (Charleston et al., 2015; Jones, 2019; Rodriguez et al., 2019). Within the classroom, they may be excluded from study groups or projects due to the stereotypical beliefs that women and people of color are less competent in topics of math and science.

In addition to peer interactions, students may find themselves in a course with a professor who has stereotyped views about women and racial/ethnic minority students in STEM course classes. For example, several studies have found that within STEM hiring practices, applicants that hold a marginalized racial and/or gender identity are seen as less competent and less hirable than applicants who are male and identify as White or Asian (Eaton et al., 2020; Moss-Racusin et al., 2012). Stereotyped views and biases are pervasive and are likely to appear throughout activities in higher education including teaching and mentoring. Consequently, STEM faculty may not provide the necessary support for women and students of color due to their prejudices or lack of awareness. Furthermore, student perceptions of stereotypes and biases as well as faculty perceptions leave underrepresented students in STEM vulnerable to experiences of discrimination including microaggressions, low sense of belonging, low self-efficacy, and imposter syndrome, which have serious negative implications for persistence and success during undergraduate STEM education and beyond (Charleston et al., 2015; Flores et al., 2014; Jones, 2019; McGee, 2020).

Psychosocial Factors

When thinking about the psychosocial factors that impact persistence in STEM, perceptions of self-efficacy, believing that one can achieve a goal, and identifying as a scientist or a member of the science community can play a significant role. For many students, success in STEM is not just achieving grades, but believing that one is capable and competent to achieve the grades and a career in STEM (Carlone & Johnson, 2007). Historically marginalized students who see themselves as scientists and identify with the science community are more likely to feel a sense of belonging and support (Nostrand & Pollenz, 2017).

Interest and engagement in a STEM field is also impacted by the role models and social support systems. Research has found that having strong familial support as well as exposure to professionals has a positive impact on persistence (Kricorian et al., 2020; Mau & Li, 2017; Piatt et al., 2019; Stipanovic & Woo, 2016; Zhang & Barnett, 2015). Relatedly, mentorship by faculty and upper-class peers is beneficial for student persistence. Formal mentorship can not only help students build relationships with faculty, but it also allows students to integrate themselves within the science community and see themselves as a scientist (Carlone & Johnson, 2007; Piatt et al., 2019). For students from underrepresented groups in STEM particularly, having a specific paired mentor (i.e., a mentor with the same or similar minoritized identities) is particularly important for persistence in the STEM field as these students may struggle to see themselves as scientists (Kricorian et al., 2020; Lawner et al., 2019; Nealy & Orgill, 2019). Online virtual mentors and popularizing scientists of color and women scientist social media accounts may also have a positive impact on science identity and interest in pursuing a STEM career (Kricorian et al., 2020; Lawner et al., 2019). This may be especially important as it will allow students to see their identities represented within the field.

Faculty as well as peers who provide mentorship often share their own experiences navigating the STEM field and provide relevant advice to new and incoming students (Lisberg & Woods, 2018). Specifically, mentors may provide support and guidance for any challenges or adversity students may face in the field including feelings of imposter syndrome and additional anxieties associated with holding a marginalized identity in the STEM field. Mentors may provide their mentees with academic and professional development through recommending courses, professional conferences, and providing suggestions to further support academic success. Mentorship is often not limited to academic support but may also serve as a supportive community network for personal and psychological concerns as well (Lisberg & Woods, 2018). As such, mentor–mentee relationships may not only persist through a student's undergraduate career but can be long lasting post-graduation and beyond.

Recommendations for STEM Career Development in Higher Education

Blustein and colleagues (in press) provide a critical analysis of the STEM career development movement by noting assumptions of STEM programs and interventions in relation to equity, self-determination, meaning, and purpose that drive interventions. Higher education personnel and career educators should carefully reflect on the explicit and implicit values and assumptions reflected in STEM programs, interventions, and advising to avoid unintended consequences. For example, are STEM programs imposing the value of financial security at the expense of pursuing occupations that reflect personal interests? Are STEM programs preparing students from underrepresented groups for the challenging occupational climates that they may encounter? Are STEM programs prioritizing labor market needs over individual determination? Blustein and colleagues recommend that STEM interventions include content on general career decision-making that addresses a variety of factors that may inform occupational decisions, such as interests, values, cultural identities, skills, occupational climate, and other important life roles. STEM programs should include exposure to personal assessments of STEM domain capabilities and interests as well as environmental factors that shape those STEM factors. These programs should also address STEM workplace climate and cultures, and career education professionals could work with industry to discuss ways that the workplace can change to accommodate a diverse group of STEM workers.

The trajectory for students interested in a career in STEM begins early in life and is impacted by a multitude of factors at the societal and structural level. Here, we provide recommendations to support and broaden the representation of women and racial/ethnic minority groups in the STEM field. It should be noted that implementing just one of these recommendations is not sufficient, but rather an integrative, collaborative, and specific method of approach is necessary.

- Utilize a social justice framework to promote an environment that supports women and racial/ethnic minorities in STEM (Byars-Winston, 2014; Owens et al., 2019).
- Understand the impact of stereotypes and biases directed at women and racial/ethnic minority groups in the STEM field regarding academic success and achievement.
- Be knowledgeable about the barriers and fears underrepresented students may have about entering the STEM field.
- Actively engage in and advocate for social justice initiatives that support underrepresented students in the STEM field.
- Get to know your students and how their cultural backgrounds and upbringing have shaped their experience as it relates to STEM.
- Collaborate with students to best understand their needs and goals to achieve academic success in a STEM field.

- Know available resources to help support students academically. This may include recommending STEM programs and organizations, faculty collaboration, scholarship programs, tutoring, summer research opportunities.
- Know available resources to help support students socially. This may include recommending STEM learning communities, identity-based student organizations, peer mentoring, paired faculty role models.
- Provide ongoing opportunities for professional development such as involvement in a research lab, attending STEM conferences as an undergraduate student, and networking with faculty from a variety of STEM-related careers.

To conclude, post-secondary education is a critical period in an individual's life and development. Students' experiences at this level may determine their career trajectory, and students in STEM fields, especially students from underrepresented groups in STEM, need academic, social, and career support to gain the required training and experiences and to understand the career opportunities in STEM fields to succeed in STEM. In this chapter, we have summarized and identified key aims of STEM education and programs at primary, secondary, and post-secondary levels. We have outlined key components of STEM programs across these levels, and provided recommendations for how college and career guidance personnel can best support college students in their STEM pursuits.

References

Albright, J. N., Hurd, N. M., & Hussain, S. B. (2017). Applying a social justice lens to youth mentoring: A review of the literature and recommendations for practice. *American Journal of Community Psychology, 59*(3–4), 363–381. https://doi.org/10.1002/ajcp.12143

Alexander, Q. R., & Hermann, M. A. (2016). African-American women's experiences in graduate science, technology, engineering, and mathematics education at a predominantly white university: A qualitative investigation. *Journal of Diversity in Higher Education, 9*(4), 307–322. https://doi.org/10.1037/a0039705

American Association for University Women. (2010). *Why so few? Women in science, technology, engineering, and mathematics.* www.aauw.org/app/uploads/2020/03/why-so-few-research.pdf

American Association for University Women. (2015). *Solving the equation: The variables for women's success in engineering and computing.* www.aauw.org/app/uploads/2020/03/Solving-the-Equation-report-nsa.pdf

Ashley, M., Cooper, K. M., Cala, J. M., & Brownell, S. E. (2017). Building better bridges into STEM: A synthesis of 25 years of literature on STEM summer bridge programs. *CBE-Life Sciences Education, 16*(4), 1–18.

Blustein, D. L., Erby, W., Meerkins, T., Soldz, I., & Ezema, G. N. (in press). A critical exploration of assumptions underlying STEM career development. *Journal of Career Development.*

Byars-Winston, A. M. (2014). Toward a framework for multicultural STEM-focused career interventions. *The Career Development Quarterly, 62*, 340–366.

Byars-Winston, A. M., Branchaw, J., Pfund, C., Leverett, P., & Newton, J. (2015). Culturally diverse undergraduate researchers' academic outcomes and perceptions of their research mentoring relationships. *International Journal of Science Education, 37*, 2533–2554. https://doi.org/10.1080/09500693.2015.1085133

Carlone, H. B., & Johnson, A. (2007). Understanding the science experiences of successful women of color: Science identity as an analytic lens. *Journal of Research in Science Teaching, 44*(8), 1187–1218. https://doi.org/10.1002/tea.20237

Carnes, M., Devine, P. G., Isaac, C., Manwell, L. B., Ford, C. E., Byars-Winston, A., Fine, E., & Sheridan, J. (2012). Promoting institutional change through bias literacy. *Journal of Diversity in Higher Education, 5*(2), 63–77. https://doi.org/10.1037/a0028128

Charleston, L. J., Adserias, R. P., Lang, N. M., & Jackson, J. F. L. (2014). Intersectionality and STEM: The role of race and gender in the academic pursuits of African American women in STEM. *Journal of Progressive Policy & Practice, 2*(3), 273–293.

Christensen, R., Knezek, G., & Tyler-Wood, T. (2015). Alignment of hands-on STEM engagement activities with positive STEM dispositions in secondary school students. *Journal of Science Education and Technology, 24*(6), 898–909.

Dagley, M., Georgiopoulos, M., Reece, A., & Young, C. (2016). Increasing retention and graduation rates through a STEM learning community. *Journal of College Student Retention: Research, Theory and Practice, 18*(2), 167–182. https://doi.org/10.1177/1521025115584746

Dee, T. S. (2007). Teachers and the gender gaps in student achievement. *Journal of Human Resources, 42*(3), 528–554.

Eaton, A. A., Saunders, J. F., Jacobson, R. K., & West, K. (2020). How gender and race stereotypes impact the advancement of scholars in STEM: Professors' biased evaluations of physics and biology post-doctoral candidates. *Sex Roles, 82*(3–4), 127–141. https://doi.org/10.1007/s11199-019-01052-w

Eberhardt, J. (2019). *Biased: Uncovering the hidden prejudice that shapes what we see, think, and do.* Viking.

Eisenhart, M., Weis, L., Allen, C. D., Cipollone, K., Stich, A., & Dominguez, R. (2015). High school opportunities for STEM: Comparing inclusive STEM-focused and comprehensive high schools in two US cities. *Journal of Research in Science Teaching, 52*(6), 763–789. https://doi.org/10.1002/tea.21213

Estrada, M., Woodcock, A., Hernandez, R. R., & Schultz, P. W. (2011). Toward a model of social influence that explains minority student integration into the scientific community. *Journal of Educational Psychology, 103*(1), 206–222. https://doi.org/10.1037/a0020743

Flores, L. Y., Navarro, R. L., Lee, H. S., Addae, D. A., Gonzalez, R., Luna, L. L., Jacquez, R., Cooper, S., & Mitchell, M. (2014). Academic satisfaction among Latino/a and white men and women engineering students. *Journal of Counseling Psychology, 61*(1), 81–92. https://doi.org/10.1037/a0034577

Ford, M. (2017). The functions of higher education. *American Journal of Economics and Sociology, 76*(3), 559–578. https://doi.org/10.1111/ajes.12187

Fouad, N. A., & Singh, R. (2011). *Stemming the tide: Why women leave engineering.* National Science Foundation. www.energy.gov/sites/prod/files/NSF_Stemming%20the%20Tide%20Why%20Women%20Leave%20Engineering.pdf

Fry, R., Kennedy, B., & Funk, C. (2021). *STEM jobs see uneven progress in increasing gender, racial and ethnic diversity.* Pew Research Center. www.pewresearch.org/science/2021/04/01/stem-jobs-see-uneven-progress-in-increasing-gender-racial-and-ethnic-diversity/

Jones, T. C. (2019). Creating a world for me: Students of color navigating STEM identity. *Journal of Negro Education, 88*(3), 358–378. https://doi.org/10.7709/jnegroeducation.88.3.0358

Kennedy, T. J., & Odell, M. R. L. (2014). Engaging students in STEM education. *Science Education International, 25*(3), 246–258.

Kricorian, K., Seu, M., Lopez, D., Ureta, E., & Equils, O. (2020). Factors influencing participation of underrepresented students in STEM fields: Matched mentors and mindsets. *International Journal of STEM Education, 7*(1). https://doi.org/10.1186/s40594-020-00219-2

Lawner, E. K., Quinn, D. M., Camacho, G., Johnson, B. T., & Pan-Weisz, B. (2019). Ingroup role models and underrepresented students' performance and interest in STEM: A meta-analysis of lab and field studies. *Social Psychology of Education, 22*(5), 1169–1195. https://doi.org/10.1007/s11218-019-09518-1

Lisberg, A., & Woods, B. (2018). Mentorship, mindset and learning strategies: An integrative approach to increasing underrepresented minority student retention in a STEM undergraduate program. *Journal of STEM Education: Innovations and Research, 19*(3), 14–20.

Lynch, S. J. (2015). Science for all: A new breed of schools is closing achievement gaps among students and may hold the key to a revitalized 21st-century workforce. *Scientific American, 3013*(2). www.scientificamerican.com/article/science-for-all/

Lynch, S. J., Burton, E. P., Behrend, T., House, A., Ford, M., Spillane, N., Matray, S., Han, E., & Means, B. (2018). Understanding inclusive STEM high schools as opportunity structures for underrepresented students: Critical components. *Journal of Research in Science Teaching, 55*(5), 712–748.

Martin, S. F., Green, A., & Dean, M. (2016). African American women in STEM education: The cycle of microaggressions from P-12 classrooms to higher education and back. In U. Thomas & J. Drake (Eds.), *Critical research on sexism and racism in STEM fields* (pp. 135–143). IGI Global.

Maton, K. I., Hrabowski, F. A., & Schmitt, C. L. (2000). African American college students excelling in the sciences: College and postcollege outcomes in the Meyerhoff Scholars Program. *Journal of Research in Science Teaching, 37*(7), 629–654.

Maton, K. I., Beason, T. S., Godsay, S., Sto. Domingo, M. R., Bailey, T. C., Sun, S., & Hrabowski, F. A. (2016). Outcomes and processes in the Meyerhoff Scholars Program: STEM PhD completion, sense of community, perceived program benefit, science identity, and research self-efficacy. *CBE Life Sciences Education, 15*(3). https://doi-org.proxy.mul.missouri.edu/10.1187/cbe.16-01-0062

Mau, W. J., & Li, J. (2018). Factors influencing STEM career aspirations of underrepresented high school students. *Career Development Quarterly*, 66(3), 246–258. https://doi.org/10.1002/cdq.12146

McGee, E. O. (2020). Interrogating structural racism in STEM higher education. *Educational Researcher*, 49(9), 633–644. https://doi.org/10.3102/0013189X20972718

McGee, E. O., Thakore, B, K., & LaBlance, S. S. (2017). The burden of being the "model:" Racialized experiences of Asian STEM college students. *Journal of Diversity in Higher Education*, 10(3), 253–270. http://dx.doi.org/10.1037/dhe0000022

McGillen, G., Flores, L. Y., & Seaton, G. (2020). Work-related barriers experienced by low-income people of color. In N. Hoffman & M. Collins (Eds.), *Teaching students about the world of work: A challenge for postsecondary educators* (pp. 113–132). Harvard Education Press.

Miller, D. I., Nolla, K. M., Eagly, A. H., & Uttal, D. H. (2018). The development of children's gender-science stereotypes: A meta-analysis of 5 decades of US draw-a-scientist studies. *Child Development*, 89(6), 1943–1955. https://doi.org/10.1111/cdev.13039

Moss-Racusin, C. A., Dovidio, J. F., Brescoll, V. L., Graham, M. J., & Handelsman, J. (2012). Science faculty's subtle gender biases favor male students. *Proceedings of the National Academy of Sciences of the United States of America*, 109(41), 16474–16479. https://doi.org/10.1073/pnas.1211286109

National Center for Science and Engineering Statistics. (2021). *Women, minorities, and persons with disabilities in science and engineering: 2021*. National Science Foundation. https://ncses.nsf.gov/pubs/nsf21321/report

National Science Board. (2019a). *Science & engineering indicators: Higher education in science and engineering*. https://ncses.nsf.gov/pubs/nsb20197/downloads

National Science Board. (2019b). *Science & engineering indicators: Science and engineering labor force*. https://ncses.nsf.gov/pubs/nsb20198/downloads

National Science Foundation. (2018). *Building the future: Investing in discovery and innovation*. www.nsf.gov/pubs/2018/nsf18045/nsf18045.pdf

National Science Foundation. (2020). *Stem education for the future: A visioning report*. www.nsf.gov/ehr/Materials/STEM%20Education%20for%20the%20Future%20-%202020%20Visioning%20Report.pdf

Nealy, S., & Orgill, M. (2019). Postsecondary underrepresented minority STEM students' perceptions of their science identity. *The Journal of Negro Education*, 88(3), 249–268.

Neumann, M. D., Lathem, S. A., & Fitzgerald-Riker, M. (2016). Resisting cultural expectations: Women remaining as civil and environment engineering majors. *Journal of Women and Minorities in Science and Engineering*, 22(2), 139–158. https://doi.org/10.1615/JWomenMinorScienEng.2016013949

Nostrand, D. F. V., & Pollenz, R. S. (2017). Evaluating psychosocial mechanisms underlying STEM persistence in undergraduates: Evidence of impact from a six-day pre-college engagement STEM academy program. *CBE Life Sciences Education*, 16(2). https://doi.org/10.1187/cbe.16-10-0294

Owens, R. L., Allan, B. A., & Flores, L. Y. (2019). The strengths-based inclusive theory of work. *The Counseling Psychologist, 47*(2), 222–265. https://doi.org/10.1177/0011000019859538

Piatek-Jimenez, K., Cribbs, J., & Gill, N. (2018). College students' perceptions of gender stereotypes: Making connections to the underrepresentation of women in STEM fields. *International Journal of Science Education, 40*(12), 1432–1454. https://doi.org.proxy.mul.missouri.edu/10.1080/09500693.2018.1482027

Piatt, E., Merolla, D., Pringle, E., & Serpe, R. T. (2020). The role of science identity salience in graduate school enrollment for first-generation, low-income, underrepresented students. *Journal of Negro Education, 88,* 269.

Prescod, D., Haynes-Thoby, L., Belser, C., & Nadermann, K. (2020). Including Gottfredson's career theory in STEM initiatives geared toward students of color. *The Journal of Negro Education, 89*(2), 158–168.

Robnett, R. D., Chemers, M. M., & Zurbriggen, E. L. (2015). Longitudinal associations among undergraduates' research experience, self-efficacy, and identity. *Journal of Research in Science Teaching, 52*(6), 847–867. https://doi.org/10.1002/tea.21221

Rodriguez, S., Cunningham, K., & Jordan, A. (2019). STEM identity development for Latinas: The role of self- and outside recognition. *Journal of Hispanic Higher Education, 18*(3), 254–272. https://doi.org/10.1177/1538192717739958

Seo, E., Shen, Y., & Alfaro, E. C. (2019). Adolescents' beliefs about math ability and their relations to STEM career attainment: Joint consideration of race/ethnicity and gender. *Journal of Youth and Adolescence, 48*(2), 306–325. https://doi.org/10.1007/s10964-018-0911-9

Sickle, J. V., Schuler, K. R., Joseph, S., Cleveland, A., Candice, O., Middle, Q., State, T., Holcomb, J. P., Carver, S. D., Resnick, A., Jackson, D. K., Duffy, S. F., & Sridhar, N. (2020). Closing the achievement gap for underrepresented minority students in STEM: A deep look at a comprehensive intervention. *Journal of STEM Education, 21*(2), 5–19.

Stipanovic, N., & Woo, H. (2017). Understanding African American students' experiences in STEM education: An ecological systems approach. *Career Development Quarterly, 65*(3), 192–206. https://doi.org/10.1002/cdq.12092

Syed, M., Goza, B. K., Chemers, M. M., & Zurbriggen, E. L. (2012). Individual differences in preferences for matched-ethnic mentors among high-achieving ethnically diverse adolescents in STEM. *Child Development, 83*(3), 896–910.

Syed, M., Santos, C., Yoo, H. C., & Juang, L. P. (2018). Invisibility of racial/ethnic minorities in developmental science: Implications for racial and institutional practices. *The American Psychologist, 73*(6), 812–826. http://dx.doi.org/10.1037/amp0000294

Texas College & Career Readiness School Models. (2022). *Benchmark 6: Student support.* www.texasccrsm.org/T-STEM/Benchmark-6-Student-Support

Tomasko, D. L., Ridgway, J. S., Waller, R. J., & Olesik, S. V. (2016). Association of summer bridge program outcomes with STEM retention of targeted demographic groups. *Journal of College Science Teaching, 45*(4), 90–99.

Tyler-Wood, T., Ellison, A., Lim, O., & Periathiruvadi, S. (2012). Bringing up girls in science (BUGS): The effectiveness of an afterschool environmental science program for increasing female students' interest in science careers. *Journal of Science Education and Technology, 21*(1), 46–55. https://doi.org/10.1007/s10956-01109279-2

U.S. Bureau of Labor Statistics. (2021a). *Occupational employment and wage statistics publications by topic, STEM.* www.bls.gov/oes/topics.htm#stem

U.S. Bureau of Labor Statistics. (2021b). *Employment in STEM occupations.* www.bls.gov/emp/tables/stem-employment.htm

U.S. Department of Education. (2007). *Upward bound math-science: Program description and interim impact estimates.* https://www2.ed.gov/rschstat/eval/highered/upward-math-science/complete-report.pdf

U.S. Department of Education. (2020). *Upward Bound Math and Science.* www2.ed.gov/programs/triomathsci/index.html

Valla, J. M., & Williams, W. (2012). Increasing achievement and higher-education representation of under-represented groups in science, technology, engineering, and mathematics fields: A review of current K-12 intervention programs. *Journal of Women and Minorities in Science and Engineering, 18*(1), 21–53.

Womack, V. Y., Wood, C. V., House, S. C., Quinn, S. C., Thomas, S. B., McGee, R., & Byars-Winston, A. (2020). Culturally aware mentorship: Lasting impacts of a novel intervention on academic administrators and faculty. *PLOS ONE, 15*(8), e0236983. https://doi.org/10.1371/journal.pone.0236983

Zhang, L., & Barnett, M. (2015). How high school students envision their STEM career pathways. *Cultural Studies of Science Education, 10*(3), 637–656. https://doi.org/10.1007/s11422-013-9557-9

17
The Role of Skill Development in Higher Education: Why It Is Brain-Smart and Encouraged by Modern Technology

James R. Stellar

In a speech at the Middle States Accreditation meeting in 2011, John Cavanaugh, then its president, gave us all a warning (Cavanaugh, 2011). He told a story about 15th-century England where the king had just made it a capital crime to have in one's possession the first-ever printed version of the holy bible. Previously, this sacred text had been held by the monks in monasteries, hand-transcribed, and passed down from antiquity. It was the source of their power in society. What Cavanaugh did next was astounding. He compared that hand-transcribed document to the modern college transcript and the monks to professors. We in higher education held the "sacred text," he said, that documented the student's progress in gaining knowledge in terms of courses taken and degrees achieved. But it was being undermined as modern technology provided other forms of documentation, notably of skills. He felt the power that the higher education industry currently held in society could be diminished, just as occurred with the monasteries, if we did not adapt. And he was the head of our accreditation organization.

At the time, I had recently transitioned from being dean of the College of Arts and Sciences at Northeastern University, a cooperative education school, to being provost at Queens College, CUNY, a classic public university serving a New York City borough with many immigrant families seeking a better life for their children through higher education. To my observation, Queens College embraced the classic mind-expanding role of higher education and the goal of a properly transcripted degree. This outcome was seen by many of our students as the ticket to a better life. I later moved to another NY public university, the University at Albany, SUNY, to be their provost, and for a year their interim president, before happily returning several years ago to the faculty to teach and pursue this kind of writing about higher education. My observation at both public universities was the same. Although they were changing with the times, it may be harder than I thought to adapt the strengths

DOI: 10.4324/9781003213000-22

of a classical higher education institution to this new demand for skills and ultimate employability.

As an administrator, one thing that I carried with me from my 22 years at Northeastern University was the power of a cooperative education school in producing high rates of employment of its graduates – typically above 95% a few months after graduation. When I was a dean, Northeastern capitalized on this work/experiential education trait without giving an inch on academic excellence, and something unusual happened. In my college of arts and sciences alone, applicants tripled from 5,000 to 15,000, and the SAT scores of entering freshmen rose about 250 points. The college just about doubled in size from 3,000 to 6,000 students. The university as a whole rose rapidly in reputation, as documented in a recent book by then President Richard Freeland (Freeland, 2019). What I also saw, particularly as dean and on a personal level, was the maturity that a six-month cooperative education period of full-time work in their chosen area brought to a young student. We used to say that, where it worked well, a student left for a six-month cooperative experience at 19 years of age and returned at age 25, or so it seemed. To me, seeing the combination of student development and institutional success stood in contrast to the warning I had heard from Cavanaugh.

There are three major universities in America that started the cooperative education program more than 100 years ago, where students alternated periods of full-time study with periods of full-time employment at a work site. They are University of Cincinnati (the founder in 1906), and Northeastern University and Drexel University, which followed shortly after. Historically, these organizations and others with cooperative education programs helped found and lead a global association, the World Association of Cooperative Education, and a national association, the Cooperative Education and Internship Association. Similar organizations exist in Canada (Cooperative Education and Work-Integrated Learning), in Australia, Thailand, South Africa, New Zealand, and many other countries around the world. The trend of incorporating experiential education or Work-Integrated Learning (WIL) in the higher education industry seems to be growing globally.

This 100-year-old history and the higher employment rates associated with cooperative education or WIL institutions does not seem to come at the expense of general university rankings. The three American cooperative education schools mentioned above are currently ranked above 140 in US News, with one ranked at 49. Given that fact, one wonders why more higher education institutions do not develop cooperative education programs. I believe that they are trying, but the cost of staff and the rearrangement of organizational structure to permit full-time experiences and deep integration with industry providers is challenging. Certainly, I felt exactly that as a senior administrator at two public universities. That gap is being partially filled by entities outside higher education, such as non-profit foundations and for-profit companies, which will be discussed later in this chapter.

Finally, there may be one other subtler reason why higher education had not earlier embraced experiential education activities. It may just be human nature to think of ourselves from the perspective of our explicit cognitive framework, and thereby tend to ignore the more implicit or emotional logic of our decision-making. In the words of 1600s philosopher and mathematician Blaise Pascale, "The heart has reasons of which reason does not know" (O'Connell, 1997). This simple quote makes the point that there is such a thing as a "heart reason," which today neuroscience would possibly ascribe to the limbic system and associated brain regions above the basic brainstem but below the crowning evolutionary achievement of the neocortex. It is the neocortex from where we operate cognitively and from where our language originates. In my mind, it is where learning of facts and theories occurs, something that higher education teaches in its class-based curriculum structure. But the second part of the quote, that "reason does not know," may be even more important today. It reflects the realization that cognitive functions tend to be ego-centric, to think of the world as what they can conceive of and no more. Perhaps that is why Antonio Damasio in 1994 received so much attention when he wrote the book *Descartes Error*, or why Daniel Kahneman won the Nobel Prize in 2002 in Economics as a psychologist with work that is well-summarized in his famous book, *Thinking Fast and Slow* (Kahneman, 2011). Finally, I think it is explicitly discussed in Michael Gazzaniga's 2011 book, *Who's in Charge: Free Will and the Science of the Brain*.

If the explicit-thinking, cognitive brain has trouble acknowledging its own implicit "heart reasons," how could we expect any organization, even in higher education, to do better? If true, it is then no wonder that colleges and universities have been slow to make skill recognition part of their operation.

Skills and Their Documentation in Higher Education – the New Transcript

The Learning and Employment Record

A good place to begin looking at the recent efforts to develop a new kind of academic transcript is with the Learning and Employment Record (LER; Torres, 2021), a digital platform for documenting employee skills and credentials, and connecting them with employment opportunities. This platform was developed in a collaborative effort led by the National Student Clearinghouse (NSC). NSC is widely recognized as America's largest provider of electronic student records, including transcript data in partnership with many colleges and universities. Connected to this initiative is an LER pilot program, led by IBM and focusing on a Learning Credential Network. This network uses a blockchain technology to secure data that addresses the skills-gap: the gap employers encounter when they seek talent, even among recent college-educated applicants, and find that applicants lack the hoped-for skills that would smooth their transition into employment (Kaplan, 2019).

This search for skills documentation is impressive and important. Among IBM's 2017 hires, 15 percent of domestic hires did not have a college degree. They were hired on skills (Kaplan, 2019). One can imagine how much more powerful a college education would be if college graduates had some documentation of these skills. Finally, the US Chamber of Commerce has endorsed the LER, which could be a game-changer going forward for an American innovation economy that is recovering its footing after the Covid-19 pandemic (Deegan, 2021).

The issue of documentation of skills in the search for employment is particularly relevant in cybersecurity. This field is so critical today that it may be no accident that we have a National Initiative for Cyber Education (NICE), working with the older National Institute for Standards and Technology (NIST) to develop a job and skill framework for educators, employers, and learners. This NICE framework lists the knowledge, skills, and abilities (KSAs) for various job roles within the cybersecurity field (NIST, 2019).

One such program in cybersecurity is led by a private company called iQ4, for which I am an advisor, and which works with the NSC more broadly. It offers project-based cybersecurity courses often in partnership with universities. They involve industry mentorship and allow students to document cybersecurity-specific and more general KSAs (iQ4, 2021). Students in these courses work in teams to solve a simulated problem with a currently practicing industry expert, just as they may someday do when employed in the industry. This project-based arrangement helps to keep relevant the KSAs learned in the fast-changing field of cybersecurity. These courses carry a certification from the Department of Labor and count as a pre-apprenticeship toward a federal program (Department of Labor, n.d.-a). This deep industry integration with NICE-based KSAs represents a kind of documentation and skill learning that deserves much more development and could properly address the skills-gap. Due to its relation to the NICE framework, it has a potential use in employment that is not found in other project-based courses (e.g., a classic college capstone course). This union of government, university, and private industry has the potential to lead to a transformation in skill learning documentation in higher education and employment that is the current manifestation of the LER.

Why Shift to a Skills-Based Transcript

Why should higher education want to change its current academic transcript to one that incorporates skill learning? First, employers in industry have long been calling for more skills from college graduates. They recognize the student's strong theoretical knowledge in their chosen discipline but note the lack of employability or professional skills in making the student less attractive to hire and requiring more onboarding training at the worksite (Bauer-Wolf, 2018; Puckett et al., 2020). It is clear that higher education serves many purposes, including developing knowledge and critical thinking in its students and building strong citizens for the nation. But it is also clear that higher education needs to better serve the employment aspirations of both students and industry to drive a strong national and local economy.

A second reason for higher education to add a focus on skills is that big data analytics has already shown which universities create more upward social mobility (Chetty et al., 2017). These statistics are expressed in terms of the basic difference between family income – when the student went to college – and the student's income a few years after graduation. This statistic is subject to the baseline income of the population the university serves and there is some debate on how strong the effect is (Cohen, 2017). Still, these upward social mobility data may yet become a new kind of college and university ranking system. That ranking may be particularly important today given that fewer children are exceeding their parents (CollegeNet, 2020). Frankly, many students have gone to college to have a better life, and that included many factors, finding meaningful work among them. The federal government's Department of Labor maintains a website called O-Net (n.d.-b) where anyone can look up professions and find the KSAs and credentials associated with thousands of professions. Companies like Burning Glass, which just merged with EMSI (Business Wire, 2021), and others maintain active databases on jobs and skills and work with the government and universities to improve training and address the skills-gap mentioned above. But this is not new. The Department of Labor compilation of jobs started a long time ago. What is new is having the data analyzed by big data analytics and easily accessible on the internet for all to use.

Now imagine a formal national registry of employability skills and an associated ranking of upward social mobility that could be constructed for each university in each field of study. While I believe there is much more to a college education than developing skills, it is easy to imagine how future universities, working through their career services offices, could attractively present themselves to prospective students with these data. It is also easy to imagine how private companies could provide competition or collaboration with higher education in getting this skill documentation in the hands of students and helping them use it to develop their interest profile and eventually get a job after their college years. Of course, some schools and cooperative training programs are already doing this work, just without a national effort at documentation. My belief is that soon we will all be documenting skills in higher education, whether our institution has a formal work-integrated learning program or not. In that world, cooperative education programs could provide important insights into how to create academic–job integration.

Why Skill Learning Is Really Brain-Natural and Therefore Important

As stated, when I was Dean of the Arts and Science College at Northeastern University, I would often notice the increased maturity of students after their period of full-time work on cooperative education. It was important that the experience was a good one and that it confirmed the student's interest in their chosen field. Yet, when it did, students had a wonderful fusion of passion and knowledge that was a result of that experience at the workplace. They resembled older alumni, who had worked for a while in the field. Why was that? The answer may lie in the brain.

Fields like neuroeconomics have grown up in recent years, predicated in part on the fact that a good deal of emotion is represented in cognitive decisions, such as making a purchase (Todd et al., 2020). Studying these decisions makes sense from a business standpoint, explaining stock market bubbles and behavioral economics (Glimcher et al., 2008; Thaler, 2015). This thinking applies to college students and to all of us because it is a built-in feature of how our brains work.

The Underlying Neuroscience

Over time, our nervous systems evolved from simpler to more complex. At the bottom of our brains exist basic circuits of reflex and instinctive action, ranging from the nursing reflex, which develops in early infancy, to the social smile and eventual development of bonding with parents in later infancy. Still later, we learn to walk, but this behavior is still basic and automatically and unconsciously learned. None of us really consciously know how we walk, and few think about keeping balance unless something goes wrong. In contrast, we use the highest levels of our brains to think, talk, observe, and decide where to go (Stellar, 2017).

This highest level of our brain is the six-layered neocortex, where brain circuits exist that support serious abstract thinking and speech. An example of a neocortex-driven cognitive abstraction might be the concept of determining the trajectory of a ball. At a certain age, children can predict the trajectory of a rolling ball and show surprise if that ball does not roll where they anticipate it will. But at a younger age, when a ball rolls out of sight, they lose track of it, unable to anticipate it based on trajectory alone. The younger child is eye-tracking the ball and does not have a concept of trajectory that the older child has with a better developed neocortex. We adult humans build cognitive models of the world that lead to sophisticated motor and sensory function and cognitive thinking, including speech (Stellar, 2017).

Let's consider an intermediate level of brain function that has to do with more complex behaviors than walking and is organized around brain circuits that mediate things like motivation. Here is where we decide to approach objects, eat when we are hungry, and take pleasure in that eating. Here is also where we withdraw and experience fear when something hurts or could hurt us. These are brain circuits with a behavioral purpose, which drive voluntary behavior and use our values to drive decision-making (Davidson, 2002; Skinner, 1938).

The neocortex and midbrain work together to combine actions and make decisions based on abstract thinking. For example, the presentation of a large or small number can unconsciously influence a later estimated decision in something called the anchoring effect (Jacowitz & Kahneman, 1995). An example I use in my teaching is seen in the following simple task: Ask someone to estimate the multiplication of the following number series, which begins with a low number (1x2x3x4x5x6x7x8). Then, compare their answer to the same question asked in the form of a series that starts with a high number, such as (8x7x6x5x4x3x2x1). Starting with a low number leads to a much lower estimate (Santos, 2015). Moreover, the subject is typically unaware of this effect (Stellar, 2017).

In terms of higher education, classroom learning is more focused on the explicit. Experiential learning adds the factor of implicit learning, such as learning from explaining technical ideas to clients or from working on projects in teams with other seasoned professionals. One simply cannot get that kind of employable skill set without actually putting knowledge to work.

My thesis here and in other writings is that when these middle-level brain circuits are integrated with neocortical circuits of abstraction, the kind of professional maturity develops that we can see in college students who have done a cooperative education experience in their field. These students know their way around their discipline in a way that can only be achieved by experiential learning. They have what Schwartz called a "practical wisdom" (Schwartz, 2011). Future research may explore how emotion, when it is broadly integrated with cognition (Todd et al., 2017), winds up manifesting itself in skills or KSAs that come from learning by doing. Direct experience does something significant to the student pursuing a classroom-based degree, and it benefits the student, the future employer, the university, and the world.

The Future of Skills in Higher Education

I remember being at a meeting at Clark University with Richard Freeland, then President of Northeastern University, when an industry leader from IBM addressed the room and told us that Northeastern students who had completed a cooperative experience were more prepared for international IBM projects than students who had not received this type of education. As competition for jobs increases, providing documentation of both academic learning and skill learning will be critical.

After 20 years in senior academic administration (ten of those years in non-coop public universities), I have to say that while this issue of developing skills is a challenge, it is also an opportunity. Meeting the challenge will be hard in terms of budget and academic structure, and it may be difficult for many schools to imitate cooperative education programs if they wish to. But it is possible to incorporate skills into the current student experience at non-cooperative education universities and to document them much more effectively than we are doing now. The LER may work to provide this KSA documentation or documentation may come from private companies such as iQ4. Some organizations already focus on skills at the high-school level and could supply colleges and universities with applicants given appropriate collaboration (Jobs for America's Graduates, 2021). Others provide supplemental project/skill-based learning or interact with the curriculum to provide digital badges (e.g., EMSI before the merger) that support employability after graduation (Verougstraete, 2020).

Recommendations for Practice

- Acknowledge the Relevance of Practical Learning
  Skills-based learning is appealing to students, who can sense authenticity. They want to learn disciplinary content from professors and appreciate their wisdom, but they also want their learning to be useful. Helping a student learn to do a presentation in a class strengthens, not weakens, the content learning. This may take more time to set up, but it is worth that investment.
- Start an Institutional Conversation About the Importance of Skills-Based Learning
  Everyone needs to have a conversation about how important it is to educate our undergraduate students vs. simply pursuing the critical research agenda for a university. Personally, I think we can do both. Being an authentic instructional institution demands we give students both the knowledge and the skills to start their careers or seek further training. Medical schools make sure their graduates have experiences in both learning and practicing medicine, and even then, still more experience is required after graduation before that person can practice with their MD degree.
- Educate the Whole Student
  Educating the whole student is more important than attending just to their cognitive capacities. Students who put the knowledge to use, even right there in the classroom and especially at the workplace, simply learn better. Cooperative education has demonstrated this, and so have scholars, such as John Dewey (1938), who long ago wrote about learning-by-doing. Ironically, some of the classical cognitive concepts, such as the famous Pythagorean theorem ($a^2+b^2=c^2$; Barry, n.d.), began as practical problems of ancient engineering. Consider my observation about cooperative education students maturing more rapidly. There is nothing like maturity to drive cognitive learning itself, not to mention provide the inspiration that can enhance a student's focus in college.
- Focus on Teaching "Practical Wisdom"
  In undergraduate learning, educators not only teach students important facts and theories, but also the context, ways to generalize that knowledge, and how to use that knowledge with other people for everyone's positive gain. In other words, how to be wiser, not just better informed. It turns out that if you want what Aristotle called "practical wisdom" (Schwartz, 2011), you must learn it by application, by argument, by discussion, even by making mistakes and fixing them. I believe you also must learn by combining the head and the heart, as in

Pascale's quote shared earlier in the chapter. Incoming data from modern brain scanners and recently developed fields of decision-making like neuroeconomics support the integration of heart and head reasoning – something cooperative education schools have known for a long time.

Now is the time to respond to the challenge of skills-based learning and continue to better integrate and document implicit learning from experience, as well as using the powerful explicit learning developed over centuries of curriculum-based classroom teaching. This fusion will allow us to truly educate the whole student.

References

Barry, A. (n.d.). *Was Pythagoras the first to discover Pythagoras's theorem?* Institute for Mathematics and its Applications. www.ima.umn.edu/press-room/mumford-and-pythagoras-theorem

Bauer-Wolf, J. (2018, February 23). Overconfident students, dubious employers. *Inside Higher Education.* www.insidehighered.com/news/2018/02/23/study-students-believe-they-are-prepared-workplace-employers-disagree

BusinessWire. (2021, June 14). *Burning glass technologies and EMSI announce merger to provide deeper labor market insights and advance workforce development.* www.businesswire.com/news/home/20210614005192/en/Burning-Glass-Technologies-and-Emsi-Announce-Merger-to-Provide-Deeper-Labor-Market-Insights-and-Advance-Workforce-Development

Cavanaugh, J. (2014, December 14). Accreditation in an era of open resources. *Inside Higher Education.* www.insidehighered.com/views/2011/12/14/cavanaugh-essay-how-accreditation-must-change-era-open-resources

Chetty, R., Friedman, J. N., Saez, E., Turner, N., & Yagen, D. (2017). Mobility report cards: The role of colleges in intergenerational mobility. *National Bureau of Economic Research* [Working papers]. www.equality-of-opportunity.org/papers/coll_mrc_paper.pdf

Cohen, R. (2017, September 26). Education isn't the key to a good income. *The Atlantic.* www.theatlantic.com/education/archive/2017/09/education-and-economic-mobility/541041/

CollegeNet. (2020). *Social mobility index.* www.socialmobilityindex.org/

Damasio, A. (1994). *Descartes' error: Emotion, reason, and the human brain.* Penguin.

Davidson, R. (2002). Anxiety and affective style: Role of prefrontal cortex and amygdala. *Biological Psychiatry, 51*(1), 68–80. https://doi.org/10.1016/s0006-3223(01)01328-2

Deegan, J. (2021, March 5). *Digital learning records make the job market more equitable and CBOs can help.* JFF. www.jff.org/points-of-view/digital-learning-records-make-job-market-more-equitable-and-cbos-can-help/

Department of Labor. (n.d.-a). *Career seekers.* www.apprenticeship.gov/career-seekers

Department of Labor. (n.d.-b). *O*Net.* www.dol.gov/agencies/eta/onet

Dewey, J. (1938). *Experience and education.* Simon and Schuster.

Freeland, R. (2019). *Transforming the urban university*. University of Pennsylvania Press.

Gazzaniga, M. (2011). *Who's in charge?: Free will and the science of the brain*. Harper Collins.

Glimcher, P., Fehr, E., Camerer, C., & Poldrack, R. A. (2008). *Neuroeconomics: Decision making and the brain*. Academic Press.

iQ4. (2021). *About us*. www.iq4.com/#about-us

Jacowitz, K. E., & Kahneman, D. (1995). Measures of anchoring in estimation tasks. *Personality and Social Psychology Bulletin, 21*, 1161–1166. https://doi.org/10.1177/01461672952111004

Jobs for America's Graduates. (2021). *About*. https://jag.org/about/

Kahneman, D. (2011). *Thinking fast and slow*. Farrar, Straus, and Giroux.

Kaplan, A. (2019, November 14). *A new learning credential blockchain to help bridge the skills gap*. IBM Supply Chain and Blockchain Blog. www.ibm.com/blogs/blockchain/2019/11/a-new-learning-credential-blockchain-to-help-bridge-the-skills-gap/

National Institute of Standards and Technology. (2019, November 8). *NICE Framework Research Center – About*. www.nist.gov/itl/applied-cybersecurity/nice/nice-framework-resource-center/about

O'Connell, M. R. (1997). *Blaise Pascale: Reasons of the heart*. William Eerdmans.

Puckett, J., Boutenko, V., Hoteit, L., Polunin, K., Perapechka, S., Stepanenko, A., Loshkareva, E., & Bikkulova, G. (2020, January 15). *Fixing the global skills mismatch*. Boston Consulting Group. www.bcg.com/publications/2020/fixing-global-skills-mismatch

Santos, L. (2015, September 16). *Critical thinking – Cognitive biases: Anchoring* [Video]. YouTube. www.youtube.com/watch?v=NFiDdbquWJY&t=1s

Schwartz, B. (2011). Practical wisdom and organizations. *Research in Organizational Behavior, 31*, 3–23. https://doi.org/10.1016/j.riob.2011.09.001

Skinner, B. F. (1938). *The behavior of organisms: An experimental analysis*. BF Skinner Foundation.

Stellar, J. R. (2017) *Education that works: The neuroscience of building a more effective higher education*. IdeaPress.

Thaler, R. (2015). *Misbehaving: The making of behavioral economics*. W. W. Norton & Co.

Todd, R. M., Miskovic, V., Chikazoe, J., & Anderson, A. K. (2017). Emotional objectivity: Neural representations of emotions and their interaction with cognition. *Annual Review of Psychology, 71*, 25–48. https://doi.org/10.1146/annurev-psych-010419-051044

Torres, R. (2021). 5 takeaways from employers, educational institutions, and the clearinghouse on advancing a skills-based workforce. *Clearinghouse Today Blog*. www.studentclearinghouse.org/nscblog/5-takeaways-from-employers-educational-institutions-and-the-clearinghouse-on-advancing-a-skills-based-workforce/

Verougstraete, R. (2020, September 8). *Badgr and Emsi partner to enable skill-based microdentials*. Economic Modeling. www.economicmodeling.com/2020/09/08/badgr-emsi-partner/

Conclusion: Looking Back, Moving Forward

Michael J. Stebleton, Melanie V. Buford, and Michael J. Sharp

The chapters included in this edited text highlight the complex and ever-shifting realities of preparing undergraduate students for an uncertain world of work. As editors of this body of work, we attempted to bring attention to some of the most urgent and pressing issues that affect students, career development educators, administrators, and other student affairs professionals. Although each chapter presented was unique to some particular issue (e.g., equity and diversity, global trends, among others), we intentionally focused our objectives around several common themes that persisted throughout the text. This brief conclusion captures five main themes that reflect the future of career education.

First, we contend that **career education is everyone's role and responsibility**. The ongoing career preparation of undergraduate students needs to involve a wider range of student affairs professionals and must be a collective effort that extends beyond career development professionals on campus. Career services staff are most qualified to take the lead in this developmental process for students, yet faculty, advisers, and administrators must be involved in the process that begins even before the student steps foot on campus. Career services has evolved over the years and will continue to do so in the future (Dey & Cruzvergara, 2014, 2019); we must all be aware of this evolution and actively participate in it on behalf of students.

Second, **the career development and career planning process should take institutional priority and result in merit documentation**. Research from UCLA's *The American Freshman* survey indicates that students and their families hold certain expectations about the purpose of college and career preparation (Stolzenberg et al., 2020). For many of these students, career or "finding a good job" is the main reason they enroll in college. Wake Forest University's Andy Chan and Christine Cruzvergara of Handshake endorsed the view that colleges and universities should be collecting and sharing data about how well they are preparing students for success in the workplace, given that is the primary reason why many students go to college. At many institutions, career services and career development positions are taking

DOI: 10.4324/9781003213000-23

on heightened roles within the university structure, gaining more prominence and visibility within university structures (Lederman, 2021). We agree with Chan and Cruzvergara and others on this important step moving forward.

Third, **social justice principles need to be embedded in the work of undergraduate career education**. Diversity, equity, and inclusion were common threads throughout the contributions in the text. Career development as a profession was founded in the early 1900s on principles of social justice, equity, and inclusion (O'Brien, 2001; Pope et al., 2013). As career educators, we need an active and deliberate return to the roots of our profession, where attention focuses on marginalized populations (Blustein et al., 2019). In terms of access to well-developed career services, all students deserve equitable inclusiveness and support. If the numerous socio-political events of 2020–2021 taught us anything, it is that massive and insidious inequities exist within our institutional structures – and that many of these oppressive systems need to be dismantled. Returning to "normal" is not a viable option (Ladson Billings, 2021). Career development educators must move towards "good trouble" and assume important roles in these transformations that will inevitably benefit all students (Higashi & Stebleton, 2020; Stebleton & Jehangir, 2020). Additionally, messages about career fulfillment must move beyond "follow your passion" and instead focus on access, equity, meaning, and purpose-finding (Cech, 2021; Horgan, 2021; Stebleton, 2019).

Fourth, **the future of work will continue to shift dramatically and students need to be ready for constant change**. Graduating students will enter workplaces that look vastly different from March 2020 – and they will likely be working much longer than workers from past generations (Weise, 2020). Many workers will continue to work remotely, while others will enter, exit, and re-enter different work roles regularly. It is vital that career educators prepare students at any post-secondary institution for perpetual uncertainty where *learning to learn* and *agility* will be vital traits, irrespective of industry or discipline (Levine & Van Pelt, 2021; McGowan & Shipley, 2020). Continual skilling and re-skilling will continue to become vital competencies, and ongoing engagement and life-long learning become the keys to success (Vanderbilt, 2021). Some writers argue that workers will need to become stronger *generalists* rather than *specialists* (Epstein, 2019) – and we see the argument of this stance given the ongoing changes ahead.

Finally, when it comes to **providing high-quality career education, relationships matter**. Felten and Lambert (2020) argued for a focus on *relationship-rich education*. In other words, the quality and quantity of interactions with undergraduate students really matters. It remains imperative that we develop and maintain meaningful connections with our students. In their book *Teaching with Compassion*, authors Kaufman and Schipper (2018) reminded readers that "teaching with compassion is a process or mind-set that we engage in as educators with the recognition that students are the endpoints of our actions" (p. 11). These high-quality connections will lead to more positive undergraduate student experiences, and in turn, prepare them for the transitions from college to the workplace.

In conclusion, we thank you – the reader – for your investment and attention to the work and issues addressed in this edited text. As noted, preparing undergraduate students for uncertain work will always be complex and somewhat ambiguous. Our hope is that the ideas presented in this collection provide both tools and strategies to support students in their journeys ahead.

References

Blustein, D. L., Kenny, M. E., Autin, K., & Duffy, R. (2019). The psychology of working in practice: A theory of change for a new era. *The Career Development Quarterly, 67*(3), 236–254. https://doi.org/10.1002/cdq.12193

Cech, E. (2021). *The trouble with passion: How searching for fulfillment at work fosters inequality.* University of California Press.

Dey, F., & Cruzvergara, C. Y. (2014). Evolution of career services in higher education. In K. K. Smith (Ed.), *New Directions for Student Services, 48* (pp. 5–18). Wiley.

Dey, F., & Cruzvergara, C. Y. (2019, November 6). *Five future directions in university career services.* LinkedIn.com

Epstein, D. (2019). *Range: Why generalists triumph in a specialized world.* Riverhead.

Felten, P., & Lambert, L. M. (2020). *Relationship-rich education.* Johns Hopkins University Press.

Higashi, L., & Stebleton, M. J. (2020). Act up: Nudging career practitioners toward "good trouble." *Career Wise.* CERIC. https://careerwise.ceric.ca/2020/08/21/act-up-nudging-career-practitioners-toward-good-trouble/#.YI01pbVKg2w

Horgan, A. (2021). *Lost in work: Escaping capitalism.* Pluto Press.

Kaufman, P., & Schipper, J. (2018). *Teaching with compassion: An educator's oath to teach from the heart.* Rowman & Littlefield.

Ladson-Billings, G. (2021). I'm here for the hard re-set: Post pandemic pedagogy to preserve our culture. *Equity & Excellence in Education, 54*(1), 68–78. https://doi.org/10.1080/10665684.2020.1863883

Lederman, D. (Host). (2021, Sept. 29). *Putting career readiness at higher ed's core (No. 61)* [Audio podcast]. The Key with Inside Higher Ed. https://insidehighered.podbean.com/e/putting-career-readiness-at-higher-ed-s-core/

Levine, A., & Van Pelt, S. J. (2021). *The great upheaval: Higher education's past, present, and uncertain future.* Johns Hopkins University Press.

McGowan, H. E., & Shipley, C. (2020). *The adaptation advantage: Let go, learn fast, and thrive in the future of work.* Wiley.

O'Brien, K. M. (2001). The legacy of Parsons: Career counselors and vocational psychologists as agents of social change. *The Career Development Quarterly, 50*(1), 66–76. https://doi.org/10.1002/j.2161-0045.2001.tb00891.x

Pope, M., Briddick, W. C., & Wilson, F. (2013). The historical importance of social justice in the founding of the national career development association. *Career Development Quarterly, 61*(4), 368–373. https://doi.org/10.1002/j.2161-0045.2013.00063.x

Stebleton, M. J. (2019). Moving beyond passion: Why "do what you love" advice for college students needs reexamination. *Journal of College and Character, 20*(2), 163–171. https://doi.org/10.1080/2194587X.2019.1591289

Stebleton, M. J., & Jehangir, R. R. (2020). A call for career educators to recommit to serving first-generation and immigrant college students: Introduction to special issue. *Journal of Career Development, 47*(1), 3–10. https://doi.org/10.1177/0894845319884126

Stolzenberg, E. B., Aragon, M. C., Romo, E., Couch, V., McLennan, D., Eagan, M. K., & Kang, N. (2020). *The American Freshman: National Norms Fall 2019*. Higher Education Research Institute, UCLA.

Vanderbilt, T. (2021). *Beginners: The joy and transformative power of lifelong learning*. Alfred A. Knopf.

Weise, M. R. (2021). *Long life learning: Preparing for jobs that don't even exist yet*. Wiley & Sons.

Index